STOCK WORK

For The
Beginner

by
S. L. Mays

Copyright 2015 by
Sherman L. Mays

Stock Work for the Beginner

All rights reserved, including right to reproduce this book or portions thereof in any form
ISBN: 978-0-578-16581-3

Text and Pictures by Sherman L. Mays

2nd Printing

4D Reamer Rentals LTD
432 E Idaho St., Suit C420
Kalispell, MT 59901

INDEX

Section	Description	Page
SECTION 1	Tools	1
SECTION 2	Stocking Side lock Shotguns	21
SECTION 3	Semi-Auto and Pump Shotguns	47
SECTION 4	Box Lock Shotguns	56
SECTION 5	Fitting Forearms	66
SECTION 6	Finishing Semi-Finished Butt Stocks and Forearms	84
SECTION 7	Installing Recoil Pads	120
SECTION 8	Adjustable Combs	131
SECTION 9	Adjustable Butt plates	163
SECTION 10	Recoil Reducers	171
SECTION 11	Stock Repairs	177
SECTION 12	Duplicating / Recutting Factory Checkering	215
SECTION 13	Custom Checkering	235
SECTION 14	Refinishing Stocks, Butt Stocks and Forearms	255
SECTION 15	Stock Fitting	276
SECTION 16	Custom Stocking	285
SECTION 17	Salvage	288
SECTION 18	Sling Swivels	300
SECTION 19	Grip Caps and Forearm Tips	316
SECTION 20	Recoil Bolts	332
SECTION 21	Glossary of Terms	342

SECTION 1
TOOLS

Block Plane

    One of the handiest tools in, around, under or over my bench is the small six-inch block plane obtained in a yard sale many years ago. I use it for a variety of tasks and am always pleased with the results and wonder at times what a skilled craftsman of the nineteenth century could do with a plane.
    The setting of the blade in a plane is still a mystery to me in many ways. After sharpening the plane blade, and re-assembling the plane, getting the blade set at just the right depth is time consuming, but once those very thin curls of wood begin collecting after an almost effortless push across the wood, you know the effort and time was worth it.
    Like any cutting instrument, cut with the grain, and watch the results of your cut. Look for a smooth surface after the cut, look for the thin curl of wood being cut, and look after your blade. Don't jam it into a cut, like it was a chisel, but ease it into a cut and cut with a smooth continuous motion. When storing the plane, lay it on the side, not on the bottom – or shoe as some call it.
    When lowering the comb, the little block plane does ninety percent of the work. The surface is level and smooth enough to sand, and if care is taken, the radius of the comb has been maintained. The secret to using the plane in this application is to cut with the grain of the wood, and not take too deep a cut. I know of no rule of thumb, but the depth of the bite is best determined by the amount of pressure required to push the plane through the wood as well as the condition of the wood after the cut. If the wood is rough, back off on the depth of the cut.
    I also use the block plane to remove the nubs of wood left on the forearm from the duplicator. After removing it, I then adjust the blade depth to shave only the thinnest of bites, and use the plane to insure the sides and bottom of the forearm are flat while removing the cutter marks left by the duplicator. I also use the plane to reduce the width of a forearm for a person with small hands. Kept sharp, never stored it on the blade – hang it or lay it on it's side – and it works well.

I am sure there are a great many bargain planes out there, but in the purchase of a good plane, I believe that you will get what you pay for. Unless a plane has been severely mis-handled, most can be returned to great shape with a little tender love and care, especially when resetting the angle and sharpening the blade.

Browsing in an Antique Store recently left me shocked. The store had most of the same planes I was using, theirs appeared to have seen hard use or mis-use and were being called antiques. I was calling mine tools and using them every day. Just goes to show a good thing can last a long time if it is cared for. Some marriages are like that. I did buy several very old wooden trim planes, not because I intend to use them, but because a master craftsman had made and used them and I could both appreciate and afford his work.

Chisels and Gouges

Carving chisels and gouges vary in use, weight and size far too much for me to begin discussing all of their many uses. Suffice to say that they are used less today than they were but a few years ago. The use of the moto tool, and the hand held high-speed grinder fitted with a carbide cutter is far more common in today's shops.

I have a variety of carving chisels around my bench - thirty-four to be exact, I just counted them - some are common use tools, others have only one specific use, and some for one specific gun. Years ago, I needed several chisels for inletting locks on a side by side shotgun, I was behind and working on Sunday, and none were available. But I did have a length of quarter inch drill rod, and I made several chisels that day, some of which I still have and use.

I have recently been presented with several chisels manufactured in Sheffield, England in the early 1800's. They are of excellent steel, a little difficult to sharpen, but once sharpened, a real pleasure to use. I intend on building a full set of these chisels as I find and can afford them.

    Please bear in mind that I needed the chisels, I do not advocate stopping work and making wood chisels. While the quality of the chisels I made was good, evidenced by their long life, I would just as soon buy them if possible. One chisel on my rack has a small "M" stamped on a flat on the shank. I made this chisel and ground it for a particular cut – the recoil lug on a Mauser bolt action rifle. The chisel is used for this purpose, and this purpose only.

    Most of my carving chisels are a straight cut of varying widths and cutting angles, I have very few angle cuts but some radius cuts because of the needs associated with sidelock shotguns. Let me make a comment here, most tasks are lessened in difficulty by having the proper tools. I base this on two experiences, one was changing a tire with only a ten-inch crescent to use on the lug nuts, and the other was inletting my first pair of sidelocks on an L.C. Smith with an Exacto knife.

    There are several excellent chisel manufacturers out there, and some starter kits that will fill most of your needs. Gunline did offer a four-chisel starter set, I purchased a set second hand and still make use of it. Brownell's offers carving chisels of several manufacturers with a wide variety of cutting edges. As you might have heard the old adage of paying for what you are getting, I can think of no more apt example that carving chisels. But I would caution the buyer to be sure of the need for the chisel before paying more than was justified. A common analogy would be of buying a Cadillac when a Chevy would do.

    The handles of the carving chisels vary almost as much as the chisels themselves. I have tried a variety of handles over the years but have found that the handle that comes on the chisel fits my need and use them. For those antique chisels I have acquired, most without handles or with handles in very bad condition, I have made a handle which fits my hand.

    The need for sharpening is most often not from use, but abuse. The carving chisel is meant to cut wood, not letting the metal of the receiver or trigger guard be the stop for your cut. Or just as bad, use the carving chisel to trim the bedding compound from around a joint.

The secret to a good carving chisel, or so I am told, is the person that sharpens it. Learning to correctly sharpen a carving chisel is an art form, it must be, so few people do it properly. At times, I would just as soon buy another chisel as spend the time sharpening a chisel, and at other times, sharpening one is quickly accomplished with excellent results. For the hobbyist, sharpening the chisels may not be a problem, for the person that uses them a lot, a piece of advice, get a fixture and a good set of stones, or find a market for dull chisels.

Blackening Agent

One of the most valuable tools a Stockmaker can have on or above his bench is his blackening agent. The blackening agent or similar product is used to identify "touch points" when fitting metal to wood. I prefer to use *Jarett's Inletting Black*, as sold by 4D Reamer Rentals. I started with it more years ago than I want to remember, have always found it satisfactory, and would change only if it became unavailable.

I keep my inletting black is a small plastic tray with a snap cover, I believe some screws or other small part came in it originally. When I need to use it, I snap the cover open and dab my sponge brush. When not being used, I try to remember to keep the lid shut as sanding dust and wood chips tend to contaminate the agent and leave false impressions.

I use a 3/4 inch-wide sponge brush with a chisel point to apply inletting black and have found it superior to all other means I have used. It lays a smooth surface and lasts several years.

About the time the inletting black dries out enough to become a little difficult to work with, something over two years, I run out and have to resupply with a new jar. I apply the agent to the sponge brush by dabbing, not dipping. This, with a little practice, appears to be the best way of laying a smooth even coat.

I have seen excellent stock makers use a variety of products to determine wood to metal contact over the years, everything from lip stick (a horrible orange shade) to spray paint as well as soot from a small kerosene lamp. I have seen a man whose ability I greatly respected, make his own inletting black from lamp black he had collected, and boiled linseed oil. In my opinion, his time could have been used more wisely, but he obviously enjoyed making the concoction. So be it. I make no judgement on what is good, bad or indifferent, I merely say that if it works…

Draw Knife

Years ago, a good friend and constant visitor to my shop informed me that a small draw knife would work better than a file when shaping pistol grips. I agreed, and asked if he had one?

He didn't, and neither did I. But several days later he presented me with a small drawknife he had made. The cutting edge was barely three inches across, slightly over an eighth of an inch thick, not over five-eighths deep, and had a beautiful bevel sharpened to a razor's edge. He had turned nylon handles and screwed them directly onto the blade a little less than a forty-five degree angle and tilted maybe twenty degrees.

I used that knife for several years, received many compliments on its design and functionality. Some time later I was given a two and a five-inch blade version, same basic design. They were great, and the variety of work on which I used them astounded me. Mr Worrell, from the bottom of my heart, Thank you.

I love yard and garage sales – Is there a difference? – and several years ago picked up several large drawknives for a dollar apiece. The handles on one were split and taped in place, the other was in better shape but the blade proved too soft to hold a good edge long.

A professional knife maker – Bob Levine of Tullahoma, TN, proved my salvation. Bob narrowed the cutting edge of the blade, reground the bevel, and put an edge on it that is fantastic.

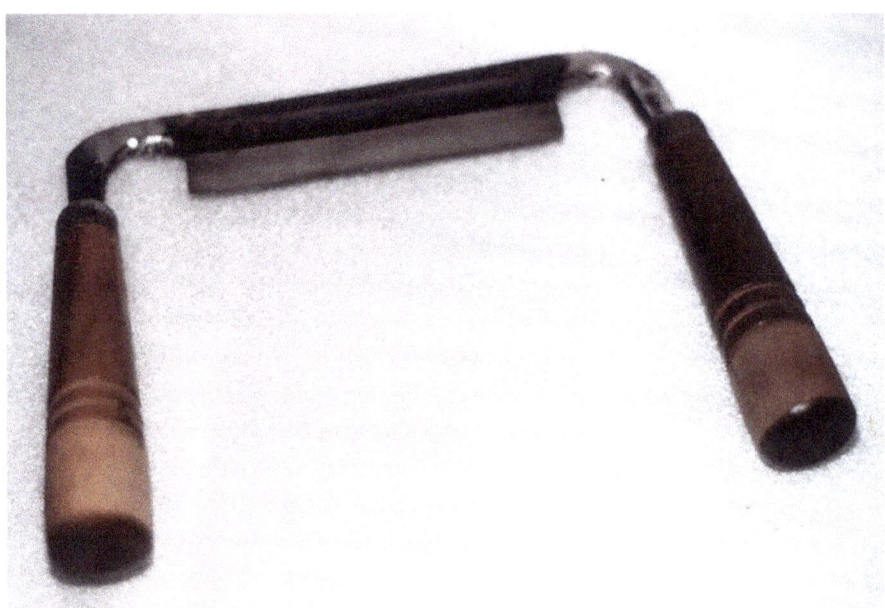

After cutting the existing shank and welding the unit together, I acra glassed on a pair of handles from checkering tools and had a very usable draw knife.

I wish someone would sell a good quality draw knife and spoke shave, there are those of us that still know how to use them and can appreciate a good quality tool. But then again, most quality tools are still being sold, we just have to find them.

Miscellaneous Tools

This is the category of tools in which I excel. In this category, I place the assorted items that I needed, sometimes only once, but for whatever reason, chose to make a tool to fit the function.

I have seen all manner of devices use to hold stocks while bring worked on. Some were quite elaborate, some functional, and others in my opinion were a danger to both e stock and the stock maker. I have always found that I work best when the material I am working on is securely held in place. For that reason, years ago, when I began refinishing and checkering wood, I developed a simple method of holding forearms when refinishing and checkering them.

I start with an eighteen-inch section of three-quarter inch black pipe, available from the local discount hardware store. This is going to be the basis of my fixture.

In cases such as Beretta or Krieghoff forearms which have threaded bushings inlet in the wood, I determine the spacing between the two bushing centers, center the forearm on the pipe and mark one of the locations. With one known location, I use my steel tape or dividers to determine the second location.

Using a three-eighths drill I drill down through one wall of the pipe and into the second layer just enough to create a spot for a smaller drill. With a clearance drill, I have found eleven-sixty-fourths to work well in most cases, I drill through the second wall.

By using a socket head allen screw of the appropriate thread, I can now drop the screw in from the top, tighten the screws and the forearm is secured to the pipe, and I have an excellent fixture for handling the forearm for stripping, sanding and even checkering.

As the basis of my checkering cradle is a very heavy six-inch jawed vise, the end of the pipe extending from either end of the forearm is held in the vise. I can elevate or rotate the work to be checkered in just a few seconds and it stays in place with no chance of damage to the forearm from over tightening the jaws of a conventional checkering cradle.

If I have completed checkering the forearm, and am going to polish or complete the refinishing, I use the same fixture.

VISE

When just starting out, I once asked a Gunsmith how big a vise I should get, telling him that what I had seen of the prices, some of the vises must be made of gold. He gave me some good advice, "Get one as big as you can afford." I started out with a small imported model with three and one half inch jaws. Over the years I have had a variety of makes, jaw sizes and configurations.

I currently have several large heavy Greatneck vises, made in China. I found them at a chain home improvement store and bought the last two on the shelf. They turn a full three-sixty, the jaws are six inches wide, and the jaws stay shut and hold whatever I have place in them.

As I use my vise to hold a variety of jigs and fixtures, I need something that is steady. The combination of the weight of the vise and the three bolts holding them to a well-built work bench does the job. But the one thing they had in common was well padded jaws.

I have a Remington Model 3200 Field grade Shotgun with Briley tubes that I used when starting out in skeet some years back. Both sides of the receiver have deep scratches. At some point in time in the gun's history, well before I came in contact with it, someone placed the receiver in an unpadded vise, or poorly padded vise, and then tilted the gun and put these deep scratches on it.

I think a lot of that gun, and hope that the person that did it has sleepless nights compounded by violent attacks by bed bugs. I've been told by several people that to buff out or surface grind the receiver sides deep enough to eliminate the scratches would also eliminate the engraving. So…

Most vises come with some form of padded jaws, some are good, some are a waste, and some aren't worth the trouble of throwing them away. I do not use any factory padded jaws but have several sets of padded vise jaws I have made hanging on a peg board over my bench, ready for use.

Half inch plywood seems to be readily available for whatever reason, and the bases for all of my padded jaws are made of it. I cut the plywood about a quarter of an inch wider that the vise jaws, then cut a piece from the bottom center to allow for the wood to slip down over the vise screw. With the piece of wood in place and resting on the screw or screw housing, I mark the wood slightly higher than the top jaw surface and cut it.

Using the wooden piece at a pattern, I cut a covering of short weave carpet sample obtained from a local carpet house. I pay a buck for a two-foot square of the stuff. Using plain old Elmer's Glue, I put the two pieces together, and place them in the vise, tighten it up, and let it dry. Makes for a very well-padded fixture for securely holding metal and wood without scarring it.

I replace the carpet when it no longer serves its purpose or becomes tainted from filings or solvents. Cheap and works well.

Surgical Tubing

Surgical tubing is one of the most versatile tools I have. The uses for this item just seem to continue on and on. First and foremost, it can be used for slingshot rubbers, and they make really great ones. Far better than the old red inner tubes I used to covet many years ago.

But the one great use is that it holds stuff in place. I use it for all manner of repairs. On the hooks in the pegboard above my bench, I have variety of different sizes of "donuts" made of of surgical tubing with the ends tied together. Straight pieces, often stained with AcraGlas or finish, hang down. But when there is a requirement of re-attach two pieces of wood, such as on a broken toe of a buttstock, surgical tubing is invaluable in keeping the pieces mated properly while the adhesive sets up. It doesn't shift or change pressures. It just holds until released.

Oh, when starting out, I make a wrap around the larger of the two pieces, letting the second wrap overlap and hold the first. On the last wrap, I simply raise up a previous wrap and insert the end of the surgical tubing, allowing the previous wrap to hold the end in place.

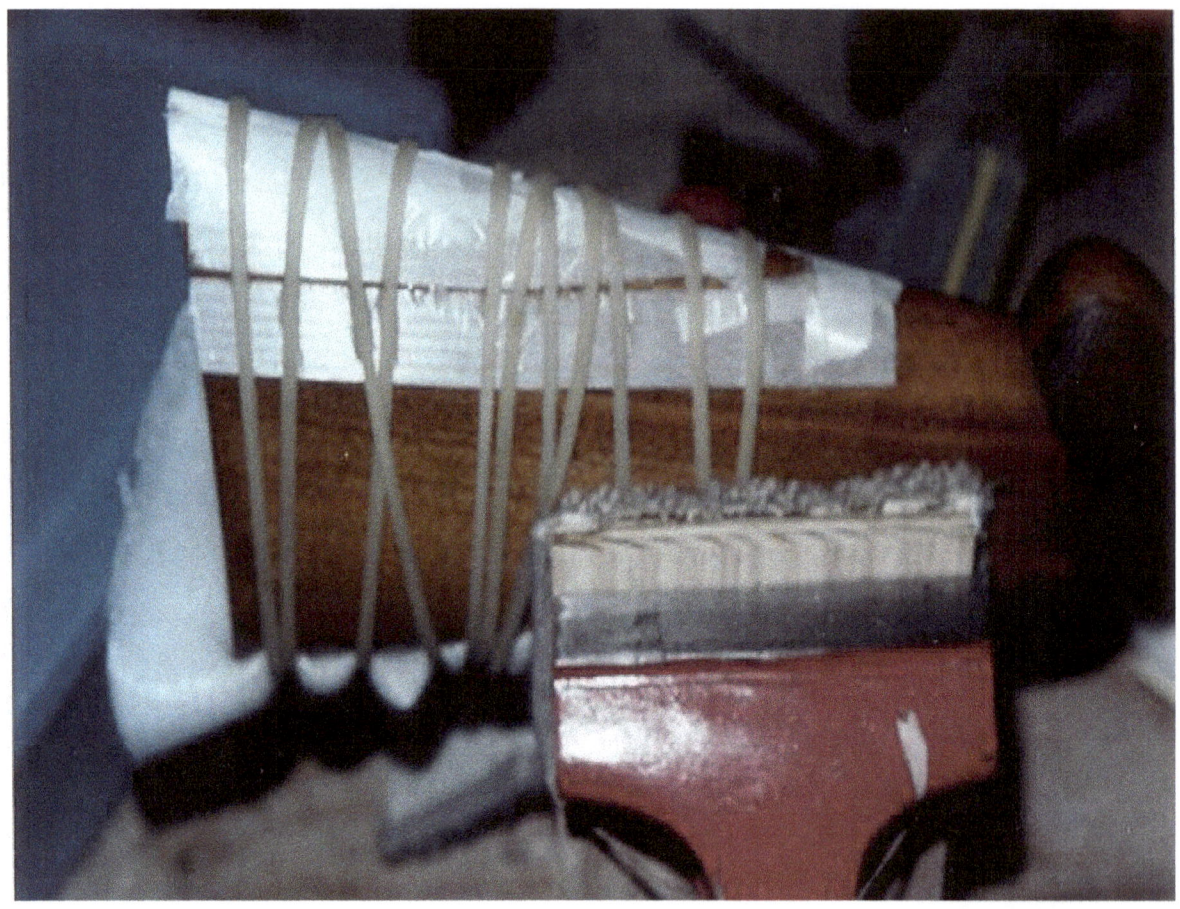

After using a number of jigs and fixtures to hold forearm iron into the forearm, I finally accepted the fact that donuts in several sizes made of surgical tubing served the purpose best. As I Glas-bed all of the forearms on competition shotguns, I use the surgical tubing to mate the pieces while the bedding cures.

I guess that a good rule of thumb would be to use surgical tubing when constant pressure in needed for long periods of time, especially the time required for adhesives or bedding to cure.

Checkering Tools

One of the first things I noticed, was the variety of tools used to checker. As I looked at the work areas of men whose work I later came to respect, I saw they actually used few tools for the job at hand but had a selection of tools in the various racks, drawers and boxes. I soon found that each person had a few tools that were used for something other than checkering jobs, but a few specialized tools for those tasks requiring something different.

Living in government housing on a military installation when I began checkering, I did not have the facilities to make the tools which I felt I needed at the time. I read of shaping tools from drill rod, of precise tooth cutting and then hardening the steel. There just wasn't any way I could do it. Even with a few friends living off base, the equipment available was limited.

A friend and fellow pistol shooter, working as a part time gunsmith, had a small work area in his garage. He confessed to having once tried checkering but swearing off of it after one attempt. After helping me make a set of three carving chisels, one of which I still have after all of these years, he gave me the two remaining checkering tools from a Gunline beginner's set: a ninety-degree edger and a twenty lines per inch spacer. He had used the handles from the other tools of the set for file handles. He emphasized that he had sworn off checkering forever… I believed him and have been tempted several times to swear off myself.

With the name of a tool manufacturer to go with, I have kept to the Gunline brand since the start. I do not know if other manufacturer's tools are as good, inferior, or superior, I know that I like the Gunline tool and do not intend to change unless they go are no longer available.

No, their line of tools offered does not fill all of my needs, but with a little modification here or there, and maybe some trimming to make a tight radius, they have worked well for me for many years.

I start a checkering job with new cutting pieces, a spacer, and several new edgers. The cutters are not that expensive, at present less than four dollars, and one in good / new condition cuts much better than one that had been used on a previous job. To me, time is money, and I want a tool to do its job and do it in a quality manner.

In changing the cutters on the tool shank, I have found that the smallest punch of Brownell's Gunsmith set is perfect for the job. When coupled with the Gunsmith's metal bench block, the combination works.

Just a word about sharpening spacers, unless you are really desperate, don't. No matter how good you are with a stone, the angle of cut and the spacing is going to be modified. Checkering is hard enough without placing your work under a handicap of bad tools.

Scrapers

Scrapers have been used for hundreds of years to achieve a smooth finish, or to relive a "little" wood in a difficult to reach space. I use them for a variety of purposes but find them invaluable when inletting the tang area of a shotgun receiver into a buttstock.

My favorite and most used scraper is a copy of a scraper made for me many, many years ago by a machinist that had sworn off wood work. I used the original for over five years before someone felt they needed it more than I did and removed it from my bench top. The duplicate is made of quarter inch drill rod and set into an old checkering tool handle and is the top tool in the picture.

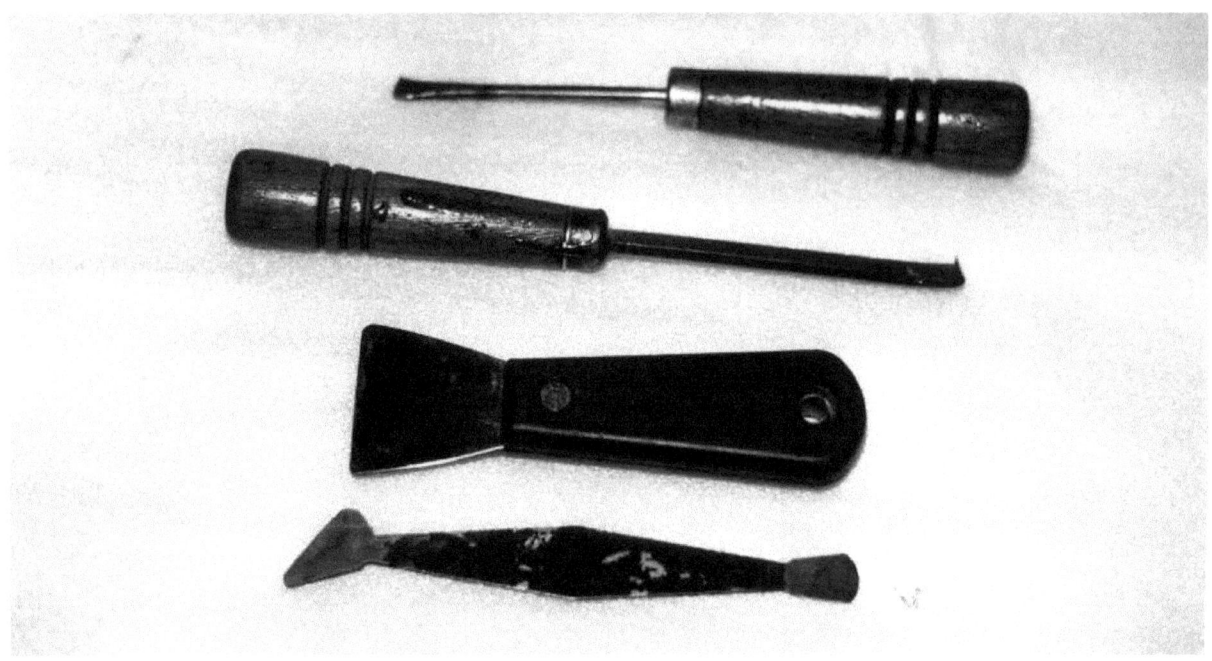

The scraper below it is made on the same design, but using eighth inch flat stock and set into an old checkering tool handle.

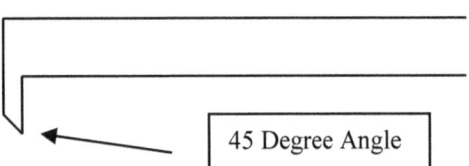

The sharpened angle appears to be the secret of its success, one which I will share for what it is worth.

The large black handled scraper is one I made from an industrial grade scraper intended for another use. I cut the blade off, squared in on a belt sander, and then consulted a very fine book on how to use peen the end of the blade over and true it to establish a scraping edge. It works great, and each time I use it I think of that book on wood working tools that was on the bargain table.

The bottom scraper is a commercial version available from Brownell's. It works very well and is easy to sharpen. I did modify one end to establish a radius which was compatible for removing stripper from the flutes at the tip of the comb on buttstocks. This is one very multiple purpose tool and well worth the money and time needed to learn how to really use it.

Comb Line or Parallel Line Tool

No, I did not originate this tool, but I sure use it a lot. I was having difficulty in establishing a line parallel to the top of the comb when outlining a cut to be made for an adjustable comb. I tried a variety of manner and means, and none felt comfortable. Then I simply placed a ball point pin on a recoil pad box, held it in place, and resting the buttstock on its comb, slipped the buttstock past it leaving a line exactly parallel to the top of the comb.

Not being one to be caught with an empty box around, I brought out a piece of scrap walnut, measured out the most common dimensions I use, and drilled holes slightly larger than the ball point pens I use. Later I rounded the corners and drilled each setting with a threaded hole for a set screw to hold the ball point pin in place. Not satisfied, I drilled another hole lengthways in which I store the pen. And then one to store the allen wrench for the set screws.

Checkering Cradle

Checkering cradles have one primary requirement, as far as I am concerned. They must hold the work securely, they must not damage the work being checkered, and they must be easy to use. By being easy to use I mean that the piece being worked on must be easily moved to the best position to be worked on, and to gather the light.

I have used some very nice checkering cradles over the years, one used connecting rods from a small block Chevy engine as part of the adjustable assembly, and I have used some cobbled-up messes that cost a small fortune to build, and ended up in the scrap yard (the Chevy connecting rod thing) or in my fireplace. I have solicited plans on checkering cradles I have read of, I have taken pictures of checkering cradles used by other stock makers, and rushed home to make my version and I have even come up with a couple of innovative designs myself.

I guess checkering vises must fall into the same category as spouses and significant others, as long as you're happy….

For years, especially when traveling TDY in the military, I used a small electrician's vise (on which I had to replace the threaded screw each year) as my checkering vise. It was a small price to pay for a vise that I could slip into a small carry bag with a few checkering tools, edgers, spacers and desk lamp, and clamp onto any level surface, and be checkering in short order. There are a great many end tables, night stands and corner tables in models in the South that have the small circular clamp marks on their underside from the vise's clamp. It was especially good when used to hold over and under and side by side forearms.

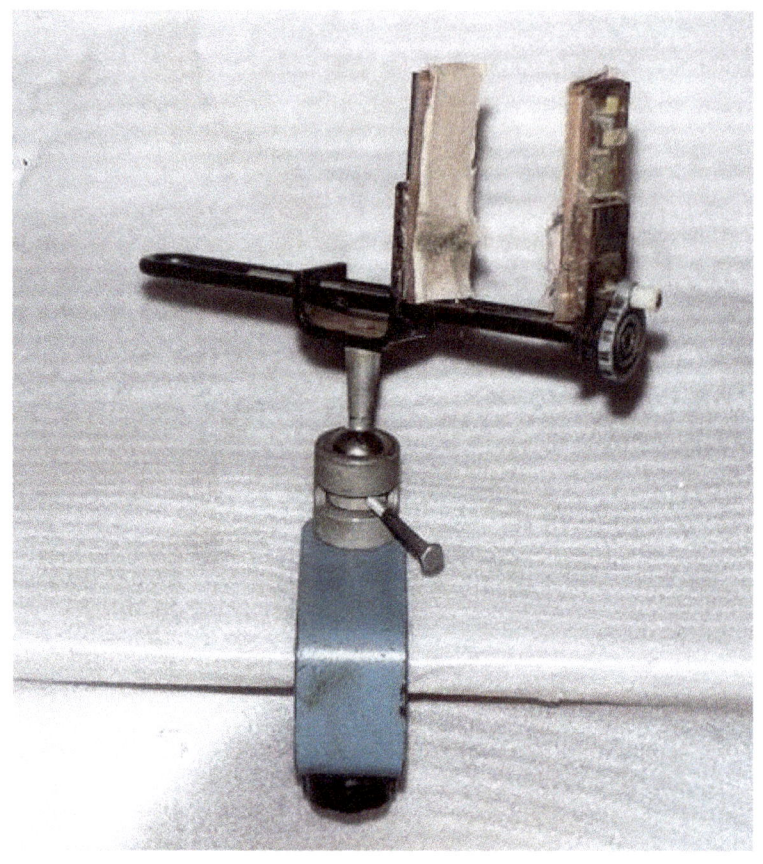

After purchasing it at a yard sale, I believe I paid three dollars, I extended the height of the jaws by welding on a piece of quarter inch thick iron the width of the jaw and several inches higher. A quick visit to the saddle shop resulted in two pieces of thick leather which I epoxied onto the iron extensions and capped the whole thing off with a mole skin covering. It works well, is easily transportable, and has had many functions over the years.

I cannot begin to count the number of buttstocks and forearms that have passed through that vise, and I still have it…

However, not traveling now as I used to, I continued looking for a checkering cradle to use on buttstocks. Having developed the black pipe holder for forearms, I needed something equally secure. So, back to the plumbers I went, and came home with several more pieces of three-quarter inch black pipe and several sets of pipe clamps.

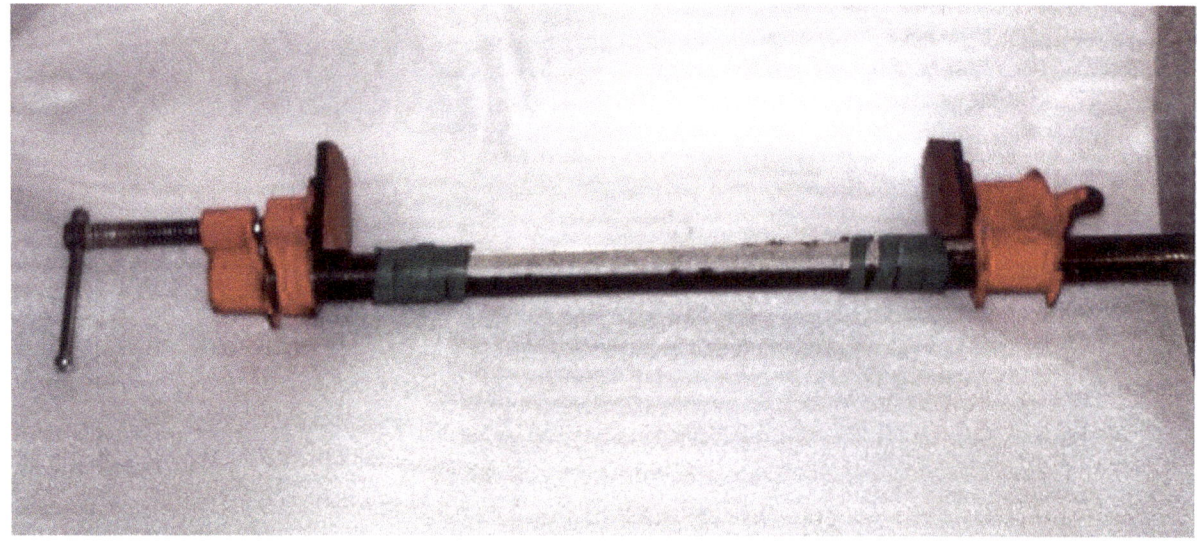

The "jaws" on the pipe clamps are adequate for most tasks, and once a piece trimmed from a rifle pad was epoxied in place, the checkering cradle for buttstocks was almost complete. The pipe is rough, and the length of the buttstocks I work on will vary, I needed something that would serve as a pad between the pipe and the buttstock as well as be easily moved when changing from a longer to shorter pieces.

The problem was quickly solved when I had to break away and repair a lawn hose that had developed a "blowout". I used the short section I had purposely removed during the repair, and made a spiral cut using a box knife. With this spiral of plastic installed on the pipe clamp, I had my answer. It works, although I am looking for one of the older red rubber garden hoses at yard sales to use as a replacement. Just an idea.

Files

Finding a good file, one that leaves a nice smooth cut on a finely grained piece of wood is a pleasure to own. A file that leaves a fuzz on the wood, or glides across the wood without so much as removing dust is a pox on it's maker.

Like so many tools, I believe you will get what you pay for when purchasing files. My files do not come from a discount chain store, and they do not come from China. I spend several years looking for bargain files before I gave up and began buying quality files from name brand manufacturers.

Brownell's, among other quality tool suppliers, offer a very good selection of quality files. Buy a good one and it will last for years. There are other suppliers offering files in their catalogues, but several of the purchases I have from obtained these suppliers originated in China or Pakistan and weren't worth the handles I put on them. Look for a supplier identifying the brand, with a good selection and insure you are well aware of where it is made.

And speaking of handles… There are a great many serviceable file handles out there, but my one requirement is that the handle have a secure ferrule at the point at which the file is to be inserted. A well turned custom handle of fancy American walnut I made several years ago split and resulted in the file sticking in the palm of my hand. I still wanted some fancy handles, but I changed my design to include a short section of brass pipe as a ferrule. All of my handles now have metal ferrules, to include those handles which have been borrowed never to return again..

There are several files, such as the pattern 39 cabinetmaker's rasp that are standards. I have several of the Nicholson brand files which only bear the name "bastard" and not the fineness of cut of angle of the teeth. I am not an expert at identifying the types of files, their correct names nor the difference between the types. I am expert in determining if I like them, if they do the job required of them, and when and how much I will pay for them.

My file selection is small, but those files I have are quality, and I paid the full price for them.

I keep a file card and several stiff bristled tooth brushes on hand and keep my files free of foreign matter, cleaning them in the middle of long jobs, and always cleaning them before putting them away.

For this habit, I would like to thank a very old-time shop teacher that demanded his students turn a three inch section of one inch diameter iron rod into a three inch section of three quarters inch square stock with a file before learning to use a grinder, a mill, or a lathe. He had other little "tests" involving block planes, cross cut saws and nails, but I'll save those for another time – He may still be alive tormenting students, and I don't want him on my case. I spent weeks draw filing that little section of iron rod. Years later, I had it hard chromed and now use it as a paper weight for the papers that I am going to get to, soon, maybe…

Barrel Inletting Scraper

One of the first tools I purchased was a half inch barrel inletting scraper produced by Gunline. I used it for many years as my sole final fitting tool when inletting forearms for single and double barrel shotguns. It is not easy to master, although operating on a very simple principle: just apply a little pressure and either push or pull and the circular discs remove a small amount of wood. The problem is when you loose focus for a moment and the round disks rollover the top of the edge of the wood you are working on – destroying that nice square edge.

Over the years, I have found need of additional tools of this set, and now have all but the largest. Several machinist friends see that the edges of the disks are true and sharp. When a set of disks fail to function as I believe they should, they come off of the tool and go into a small plastic envelope. At a time in the near future they will be placed on a jig in a lathe and "trued up."

Checkering Aids

Laying master lines out on a curved surface, such as a Winchester Model 12 forearm, can be a problem. Getting the mater lines set at the required angle can be time consuming and may not be correct. So, I drew out different sized diamonds on a piece of typing paper, a diamond that was three times as long as it was wide, one that was three and a half times as long as it was wide, and one that was four times as long.

I used a straight edge to insure the lines forming the diamond were absolutely straight and drew them in with a heavy black ink pen. And then I copied the paper onto the heaviest transparency plastic I could find, and then used a paper cutter to cut the diamonds out from the sheet. I then had diamonds of the angles I used mostly and could lay them over a centerline and then use a white pencil to trace along the outside edge.

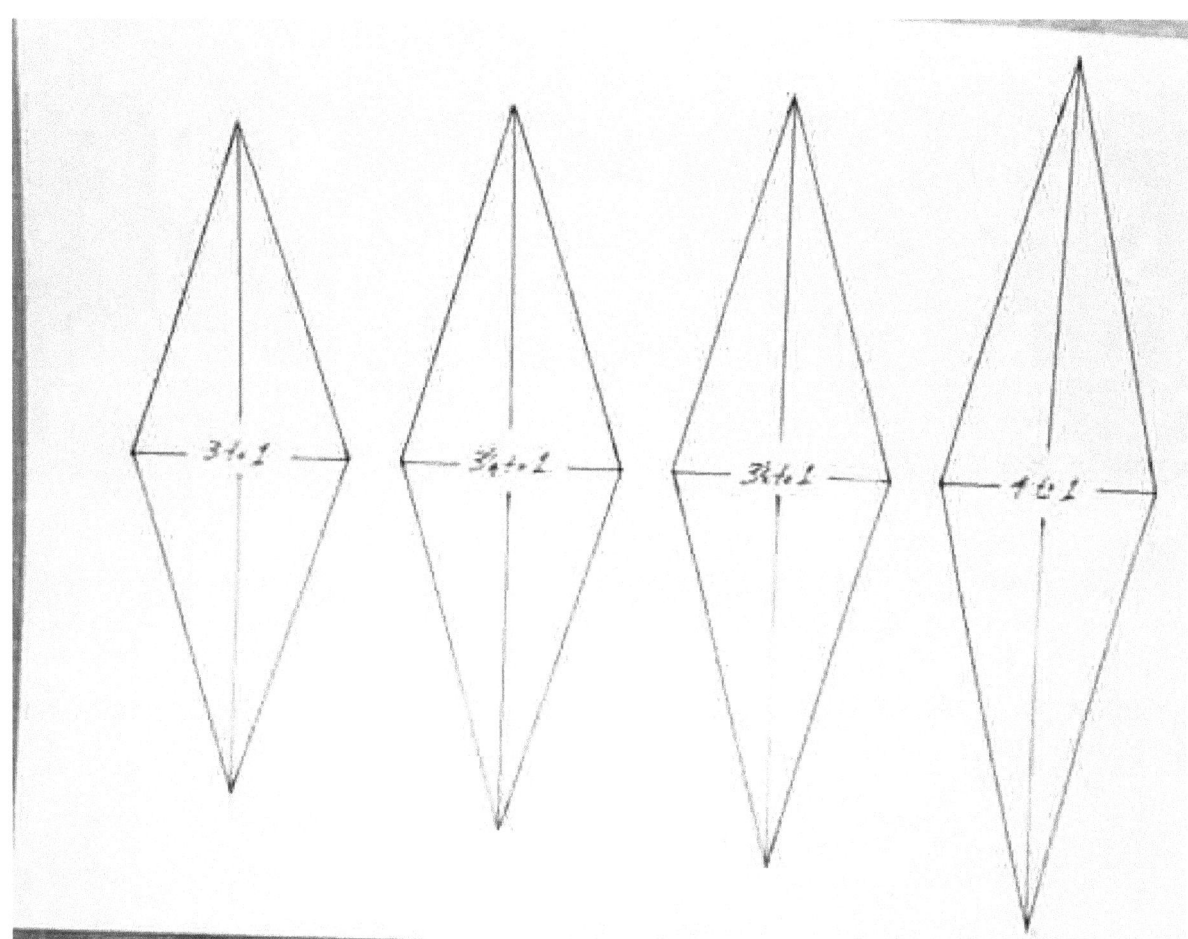

This worked out pretty good but occasionally I found I needed a reference point at the center of the diamond. Back to the straight edge and drew a straight line from opposing points. I have used this simple arrangement for a number of years, have copied the original page onto numerous sheets of heavy transparency, and recommend anyone doing any checkering do the same. A trip down to the local copy store, and a request for heavy transparency stock will yield dividends for jobs to come.

At the same time, having several extra sheets of transparency stock, I used the borrowed paper cutter and made strips of varying widths, everything from three-eighths inch up to two inches, graduating in increments of an eighth of an inch. I keep them on a peg over the bench.

The uses I have found for them are too numerous to mention, but the primary use is to extend the master lines of a checkering pattern by laying on the edge of the line and allowing the strip to follow the contour of the wood.

While transparency stock is available and works well in most applications, I covet the heavy plastic reinforcement that comes in shirt collars. They are really great.

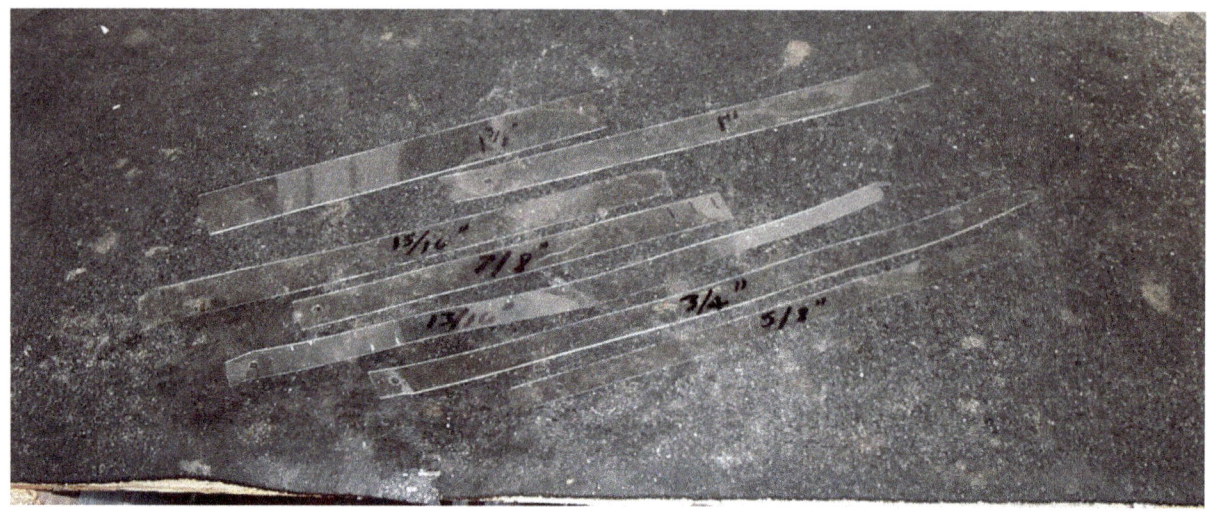

I also use them to help judge the correct path of a line when skipping over a forearm latch hole in the forearm.

Dividers & Calipers

The number of uses for dividers and calipers in stock making has not been determined. I constantly find new requirements for their use and reinforce old habits of making measurements with them.

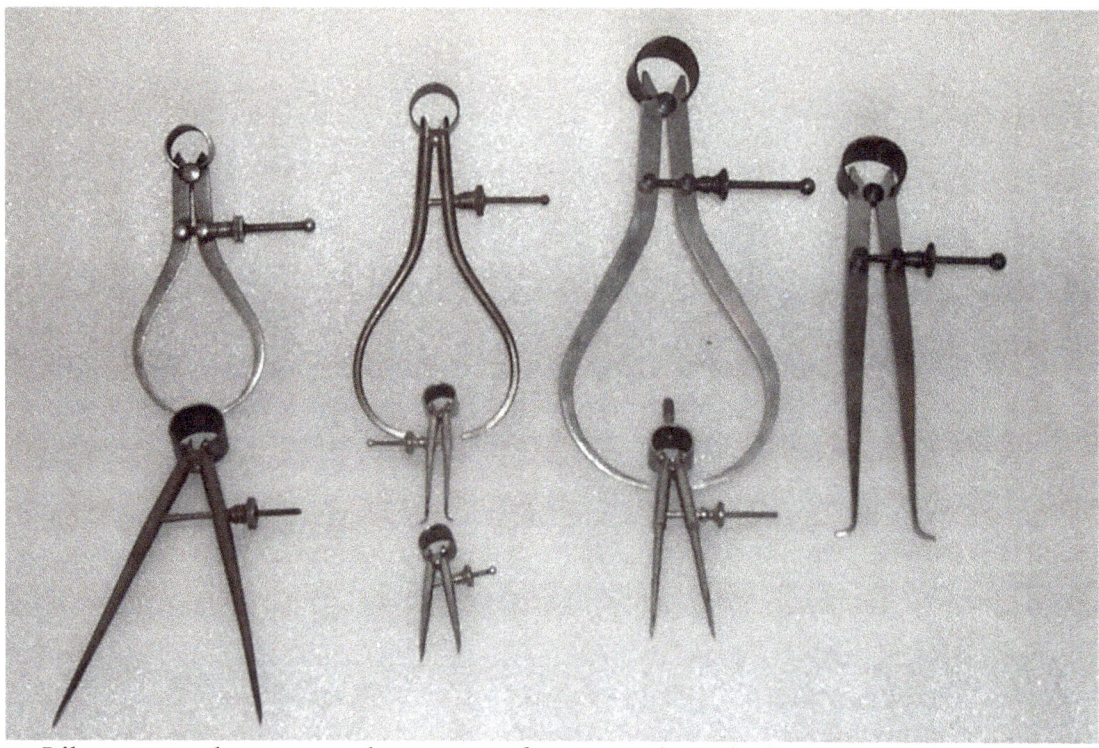

Like most tools, you get what you pay for, so purchase the best you need, not the ones that may be on special or are the cheapest. If the dividers will provide the service and function required, purchase them. Most of mine are very old, having purchased a machinist's toolbox at an estate auction many years ago. However, one pair and I have been together for almost forty years. I purchased them new for my father, and upon his death, retrieved them from his tool box.

For exact, point to point measurements, in my opinion, there is nothing like a good set of sharp pointed dividers.

Other Tools

There are a great many other tools needed from time to time to complete a particular function in stock work. And yes, there are some simple tools which may perform the task in a satisfactory manner in some instances. However, I have found that over the years, many a stock maker has developed some tool which performs the task at hand with greater ease and in less time. Or, maybe he was just having a bad hair day and wanted to do it differently!

The following tool is nothing more than a piece of round stock milled with a hollow ground screw drive, and then hardened and a "T" handle installed. I have had this tool a number of years and it amazes me the amount of torque it can generate in loosening a stock bolt.

This tool is a little more elaborate, and designed for one gun, the Remington Model 1100 buttstock. With the self centering dowel, once the screw driver bit is in the stock retaining nut, the nut is coming off. A friend came up with the initial design almost thirty years ago, and other that being made of slightly larger round stock, is basically the same.

    Again, the following tool is gun specific, the Remington Model 1100. This wrench serves as the stock retaining nut when fitting a buttstock to a Remington Model 1100 receiver, pulling the stock up tight against the receiver.

Whatever the reason, please do not be confined to traditional tools.

SECTION 02
STOCKING SIDELOCK DOUBLES

The first gun that I ever stocked was a L. C. Smith, Ideal Grade, 20 gauge double barrel shotgun. I did it with little assistance or instruction, referencing only a short article in a magazine on the difficulty or correctly replacing the buttstock of a side lock double. As I recall, the restocked gun in the article was to be used as a wall hanger. The L.C. Smith I restocked went right back to the field as a bird gun.

There are few reference texts on the Belgium side lock doubles and the few that are available lack good detail. Some of the best information collected over the years came from the catalogue of Fajen's, Warsaw, MO. Those people helped me identify many an old side lock in years past.

Unfortunately, I did not take pictures of my early work to any extent and have long since lost my notes. I am in the process of collecting information – I am the one with the camera and close up lenses at the gun show bothering vendors for permission to take a picture of an old shotgun. I have however, gone back through some of the old catalogues and gleaned information which I have compiled in the reference section of this book.

The American doubles do have more information, especially with some of the later reference texts being published, on L.C. Smiths, Lefevers, Ithacas and similar guns. I keep the books available and when returning the gun to the customer, provide what information on it that I can, a simple "Made in 1911, middle of serial number range, 2, 061 made."

But I didn't have any reference materials until I had stocked several and had learned many a hard lesson. After the first three, I began to develop tools for certain tasks, assembling side locks for one, removing and inserting the flat springs for another, and techniques for performing tasks such as drilling the hole for the tang screw.

The best instructions that I can give anyone attempting to restock an old side lock are to have a bountiful reserve of patience, and if possible, if at all possible, have the old stock for reference. I have restocked side locks doubles with a stock in excellent condition in place, with the receiver portion of the stock still attached to the receiver the remainder broken off at the wrist, delivered wrapped in newspaper, in a skeet box, in a tool box, and one in a GI laundry bag.

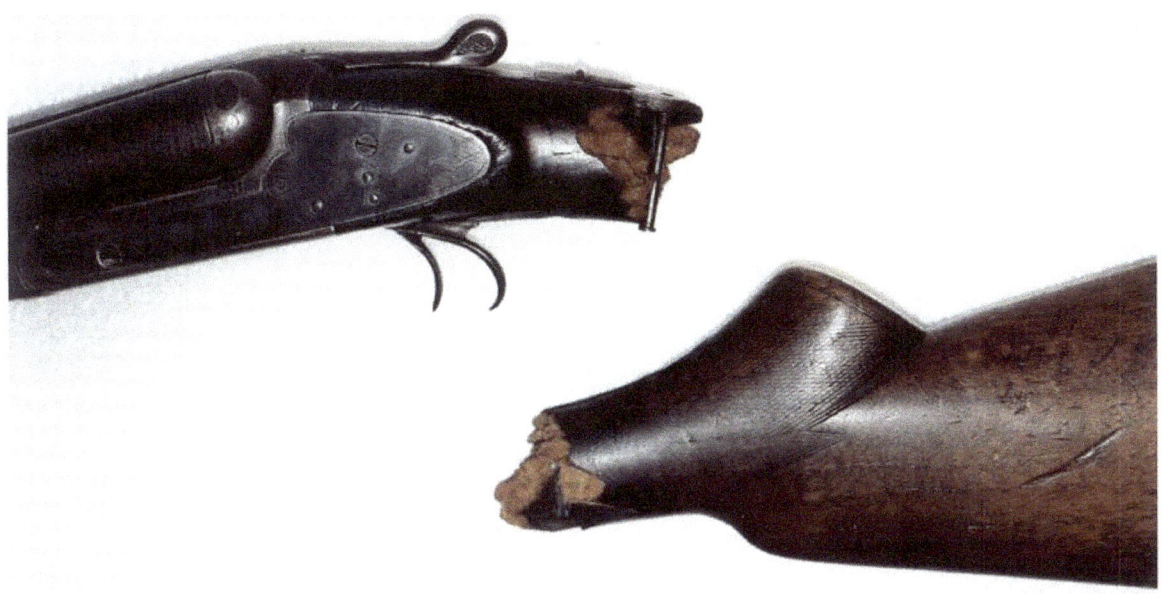

Stocking side lock doubles is one of the most demanding stock jobs to be undertaken by either a professional or hobbyist. There is very little wood to metal contact to absorb the recoil, and for that reason, the wood to metal contact must be precise. Over the years, the vast majority of side lock double butt stocks that I have replaced had been broken at the wrist. But almost every one of them had cracks behind the lock plates, at the end of the upper tang, or at one or more other places…

The most common location for cracks is the wood surrounding the upper tang and at the read of the side plate. The reason is quite obvious after one has taken a few dozen of them apart: the side locks are rounded and upper tang on most side lock doubles is tapered, thus, with age, the wood compresses and the side plate and tang act like a wedge during recoil. The same holds true with the lower tang.

Why does the wood compress? Age, to some degree, but most of the stocks I deal with are not dry from age, rather they are oil soaked. Refinishing them is also a lot of fun, but that will be covered in another section.

For this reason, if the gun is to be stocked other than for an "absolute" wall hanger (rendered incapable of firing – to include welding the firing pins and breach plugs in place), I bed the receiver and the side plates and liberally coat the exposed wood inletting with thinned acra glass. In addition I drill from the tang inlet down into the grip area, but not through it, and bed a threaded rod. This modification is totally hidden, but sure strengthens the grip area.

I have stocked many LC Smiths, both standard and featherweight, that are regularly used for bird hunting, as well as some Lefevers and small gauge Belgian doubles. With Cowboy action shooting increasing in popularity, the number of hammer side lock doubles I am requested to stock is continually increasing. I love it. In my opinion, not only is a side lock double a challenge to stock, but when stocked, is both functional and graceful.

There are three ways to restock a side lock double. The first involves using the original stock as a pattern and sending it out to someone like Wenig Custom Gunstocks, Lincoln MO, as well as others offering a duplicating service. If you have the old stock, and this is the way you want to go, do yourself a favor and make the repairs on the stock before you send it out. Replace missing wood with a bedding compound or an automotive body filler, and use AcraGlas

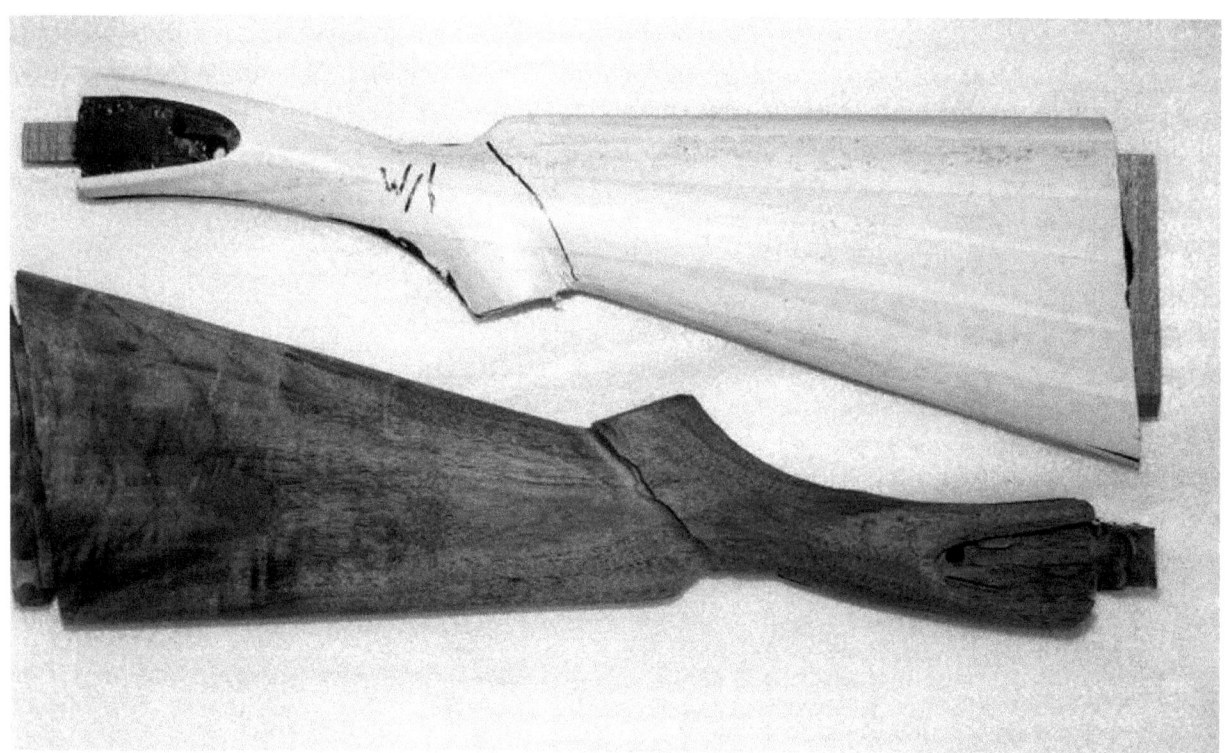

to repair the cracks, dowel or pin them if you have to. If the stock is short, epoxy and screw additional wood or spacers onto the butt. If the grip is narrow, or the checkering is worn smooth, add thickness with thin layers of bedding material.

Some of the old doubles had combs that were sharp, and I mean sharp. I use automotive body filler to increase the radius of the comb, and contour it back into the stock with a course file.

When you are satisfied with the configuration of the stock, then send it out for duplication.

For many years I used this technique and sent the patterns out to Fajen's for duplication, with the demise of Fajen's, I now use Wenig's Custom Gunstocks, Lincoln, MO.

The second way to stock a side lock double involves finding a stock dealer such as Wenig's and ordering a semi-finished buttstock. I would caution you on ordering a stock unless you know the stock you are ordering. Small changes in receiver configurations by the manufacturers years ago that are not identified on the receiver as a model change, often lead to paying for a stock not used, ruining a stock trying to make it fit, or returning it and confessing your ignorance. I have done all three several times. The best way is to package up the receiver and send it.

If I am not absolutely certain about a stock, I send the original, what is left of the original, or at least pictures of the receiver and the original buttstock to the stock dealer.

In most cases, a call to the stock dealer will result in you learning more about the variations of the side lock shotgun you have that you might really want or need to know.

The third and last way is what I call "scratch" and is one I began with. One starts with a stock blank and a pencil, progresses to a saw, goes to chisels and a powered grinder, and then to files and sand paper. This in the way I have begun many a stock job when the gun was turned over to me minus the buttstock, and usually in pieces in a box or bag. Some of these jobs were great guns that were totally serviceable after stocking and some of them made good wall hangers. For all practical purposes, starting a stock from a blank is needless work…

If you have a stock blank and insist on using it, and the blank has been correctly allowed to dry and the moisture content of the wood is in the workable range, you have many hours of frustrating work ahead of you. I have done it more times than I want to remember, and if at all possible, will not be doing it in the future.

Several firms will duplicate your old stock onto your blank at a very reasonable rate and save countless hours. This also provides the opportunity to "add" to your original stock with built up layers of tape or the material of choice. Before I begin a side lock stock job, I inspect the gun, and if I feel repair is necessary, inform the owner of the requirement to have the repairs made, to include screws being replaced.

If the owner chooses to not have the repairs made, and if the failure to make the repairs will cause additional difficulty in stocking the gun, and or detract from my work, I can (a) go ahead, bite the bullet and do the work. Or (b) return the gun to the owner. In most cases I return the gun to the owner, feeling that the end product will reflect back on my workmanship.

If you are not prepared to do some metal work, or have some done, you are going to have a long row to hoe. Most metal work on the old side lock doubles is pretty simple, screw replacement, spring replacement, bending a sear bar, replacing the missing end of a trigger guard, building up the sear notch on the hammer, or in worse case, repairing a broken or missing upper or lower tang.

One gun owner didn't want to repair the broken upper tang on a side lock double, telling me that it had been broken and shot well for many years. He may still be shooting it, but the stock on the gun is not my work…

I stress that I now do only stock work. Earlier in my career, I did all manner of repairs, and constantly searched Flea Markets and Garage Sales for older guns to buy and use for parts. You can't imagine the number of old shotguns that are missing forearm irons, hammers, screws, springs…

As a matter of procedure, I kept a supply of screw blanks on hand, and a reference card for each type of side lock shotgun I worked on. The reference card contained a listing of all the screws on a gun, their length, diameter, thread size as well as head size and depth. The screw blanks varied in quality, with the very best being ones that I turned or had turned. The assortment from Brownell's was a close second, and the ones obtained from an advertisement with a post office box for a contact were volunteered to my son's science project, *How rust forms in Salt Water.*

With the action fully assembled and functioning, and before you disassemble it, take pictures of different views and then several measurements. The first measurement is the distance – outside to outside – between the upper and lower tangs. I recommend using a pair or outside calipers for this task, but a set of simple outside calipers will do. The second measurement is the distance – outside to outside – between the two side places. If you have the screw that passes through the stock and secures the side plates, then your measurement is made that much easier. When taking this measurement, be sure the side plates are flush with the receiver.

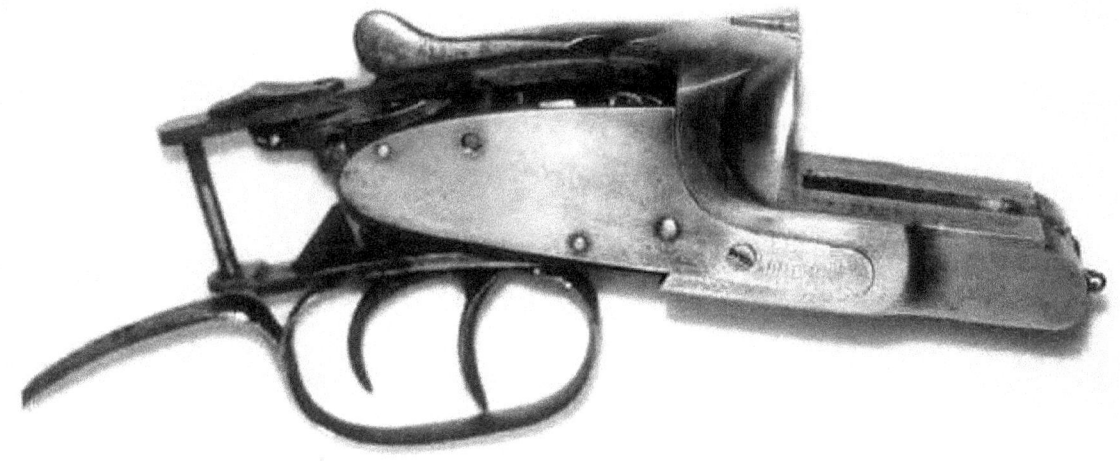

Now take it apart, and I mean all apart. The receiver should be stripped of everything that can be readily removed. About the only thing you might consider leaving is the bradded over cocking rods. Otherwise, take it out. On LC Smith shotguns, the screw anchoring the yoke to the barrel release lever is bradded over.

Over the years, I have found that using a moto tool with a cutting wheel works well in removing just the bradded over metal of the screw. The wheel is easy to control and does a very good job when used as a grinder rather than a cutting wheel as it was designed.

I have restocked several very nice LC Smiths on which the bradded over metal was removed with something, I believe a very large course file, which left scratch marks on the upper tang of the receiver as well as the yoke and barrel release lever.

Regardless of how the bradded over metal is removed, it must be removed before the screw can be removed and the receiver stripped. After all of the metal parts are removed, the next chore is to thoroughly clean the receiver, and I mean really clean it. All of the built up foreign matter, to include dirt, gunpowder residue and whatever else is present, must be removed. A spray can of brake cleaner and several stiff bristled brushed of varying sized work amazingly well.

Why? Built up foreign matter will leave false impressions when fitting the receiver to the buttstock, and this is a problem you do not need when it can so easily be eliminated!

Regardless of your starting point, stock blank or semi-finished stock or maybe a pre-turned blank, the first item to be fitted is the receiver, <u>the stripped receiver</u>. Note: I have found that a plastic container with a snap on lid – similar to those used for storing food – is great for storing all of the parts of a receiver. I go a little further by segregating the pieces of a component such as a side plate in a small "snack" size zip lock baggie.

Assuming you have a semi-inletted blank securely mounted in your padded jaws of your vise, set your inletting black and sponge brush out, as well as your half inch beveled point carving chisel, a 3/8" scraper and your 1/8" chuck moto tool with a #113 cutter in place.

Blacken both sides of the upper tang and the end of the tang as well as the underside and put a light pass on the inside of the receiver. Slide the receiver into the semi-inletted blank until it stops with light hand pressure. Words of advice, hard learned, expensive words of advice, Do not force the receiver "just a little more" into the stock. Most upper receiver tangs are wedge shaped, and when forced act just like a wedge, splitting off a piece of wood. **Not Good**.

If the upper tang is not straight sides or tapered, but has an enlargement on the end, such as an early model Lefever, the forward area of the tang must be inletted first, and then the rear of the tang lowered into place and inletted. These are very difficult to inlet and do a good job.

We are now at the point at which two blind men were attempting to describe an elephant, one with the tail and the other with the trunk, each thinking they were at the rear of the elephant. As the blind man at the rear felt the length of the elephant's tail, he observed that the hairy end of the tail was most likely used to sway flies from its rear.

The other blind man ran his hand up the elephant's trunk and into its mouth and felt it's teeth just before the elephant closed it's mouth. "Watch out," he called to his friend, "this ass hole has teeth." The motto of this story, if you can't see what you're doing, go slow and watch where you put your hands.

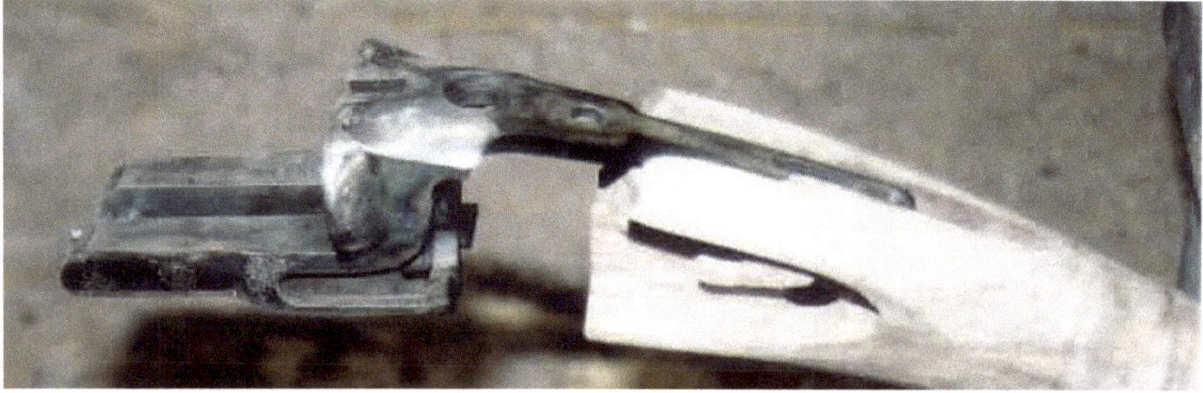

Tap it lightly, hand pressure only at this point. Remove it and you should see inletting black on the areas where the wood contacted the blackened metal of the upper tang. Scrape the blackened – wood – away. Just how much wood do you scrape away will depend upon how the remainder of the tang fits. A good rule of thumb is to scrape away only the black contact points.

After only twenty-seven fitting and scraping sessions, the progress is encouraging, nothing great, but encouraging. So far everything is looking good. At this point remembering to take off only the blackened contact points is very difficult.

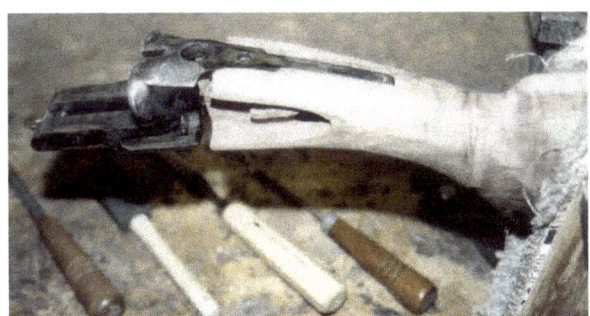 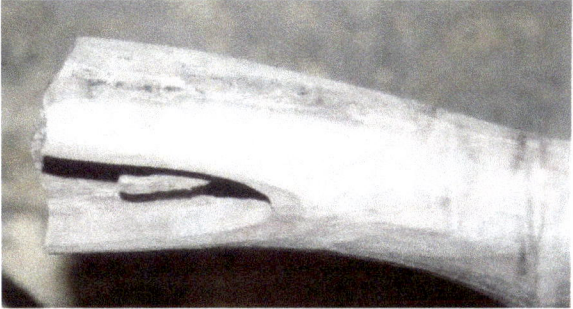

In addition to scraping the "channel" in which the upper tang sits, you will also begin to fit the end of the upper tang as well as the shoulders at the point the tang narrows.

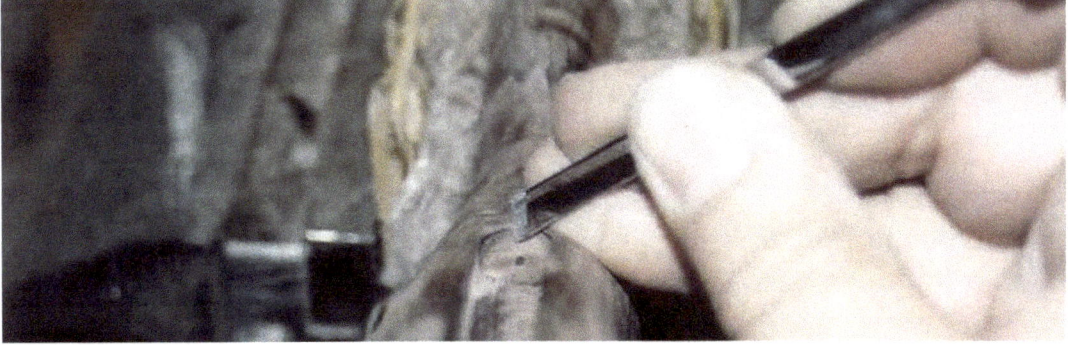

Because of the location and radius of the cuts required I use a skew point chisel.

On the preceding picture, notice the small black "contact" line at the rear of the upper tang inletting... And notice the angle at which I am holding the chisel to remove the contact line...

Remember the cardinal rule in stock making, "You can take it off, but you can't put it back," so be careful, don't take chances, don't get in a hurry, and take a little off at a time. You may have to fit the receiver to the stock fifty or more times before it fits into the stock correctly. Correctly being full depth with the receiver and stock having contact at the stock face.

Take your time, the end result will reflect your skill, and your patience.

As the receiver tang fits further and further back into the buttstock with each subsequent try and removal of the blackening agent at the contact points, blacken the receiver face and check it for contact as well. As I have stated earlier – the contact must be at all points.

During this preliminary stage, do not increase the depth of the inletting for the upper tang – concentrate on getting the upper tang to fit. Once the tang slips back into the stock completely, check to insure the receiver is coming in contact with the face of the buttstock. If there is not contact, slowly seat the receiver back a little more until the receiver does come in contact with the stock face. Remember, the face of the buttstock, combined with the upper and lower tangs, provide most of the recoil transference/absorbing area of the stock.

After getting a good imprint of the receiver face on the face of the buttstock, attach the barrels to the receiver. Because the receiver has been stripped, anchor the barrels in place with a wrap of nylon filament tape, or better if you have some, several wraps of surgical tubing. The purpose of the barrels being placed on the receiver is to establish the stock measurements, or 'drop' of the stock at the tip and heel of the comb.

To take the stock measurements at the tip and heel of the comb, with the barrels held horizontal in the padded jaws of the vise, and the toe of the stock resting on the bench top or other spacer providing a secure platform, begin by insuring the barrels are securely in the receiver, in the same position as if the barrel locking mechanism were holding them in place. This is critical if your measurements are to be accurate, and a whole lot of labor depends on the measurements being accurate.

There are some very impressive fixtures in use for taking this measurement but using a simple straight edge and measuring rule – I do not recommend a steel measuring tape – but do recommend a steel rule, especially the six-inch pocket style which does not have the 'free space' but begins recording measurements from the end of the rule.

Next, extend a straight edge, such as a metal yard stick, on edge, down the rib of the barrels – but not over the sight beads, especially if the barrels have a mid-sight bead. With the straight edge in place, measure from the bottom of the straight edge down to the top of the tip of the comb "A", and then the top of the heel of the comb "B". One person can do the job, but if someone steadies the straight edge on the barrels while the measurements are being taken, the task is much simpler.

From these measurements, you can determine if the inletting for the front or rear of the receiver needs to be deepened, or if you have an acceptable measurement. For instance, is a field stock could measure from 1 1/4" to 1 5/8" at the tip, and from 1 1/2" to 2 1/2" at the heel. A reference of factory stock measurements is contained in the Reference Data Section of this book.

If you are going to shoot the stock, then carefully shoulder the barrels/receiver/buttstock, and look down the rib. Now close your eyes, obtain a good head position on the stock – good being comfortable shooting position – and then open your eyes and look down the barrels. What do you see? Do you have to move your head to see down the barrels correctly? If you do, then great. If you have to move your head, more work is involved.

If the measurement of the buttstock at the heel of the comb, shown as "A" in the illustration needs to be decreased, deepen the inletting at the rear portion of the upper receiver tang. But remove the wood very carefully. A technique I use is to remove about 1/32" of wood from the rear most portion of the upper tang, and then scrape the wood from the receiver between the face of the buttstock and the rear most portion of the upper tang inletting. I use a short machinist square to insure I don't hollow out any troughs between the two points.

If the measurement of the buttstock at the heel of the comb, shown as "B" in the illustration needs to be increased, deepen the inletting at the front of the receiver in the same manner as described above and then scrape the wood from the rear most portion of the tang inlet to the face of the buttstock.

Once the receiver is correctly positioned to allow the correct drop at the tip and heel of the comb, and before inletting the lower tang, I bed the receiver to the buttstock using rifle bedding compound. This not only strengthens the buttstock but insures equal dispersion of recoil through the entire mating of wood to metal.

While I am bedding the receiver, I also bed a reinforcing rod in the grip area of the buttstock to provide additional strength.

In preparation for the bedding, I use a moto tool with a 1/8" cutter to undercut the lower half of the sides of the wood coming in contact with the sides of the upper tang, allowing for a slight buildup of bedding which cannot be seen from outside. By doing this, the perfect wood to metal fit is seen with the receiver in the buttstock, but the bedding compound positioned at the lower half of the tang depth, provides additional strength. This is especially essential at the front of the upper tang where the wood is very thin and the rear of the upper tang which is a recoil absorbing area. In addition to providing an absolute equal contact of wood to metal, the bedding seals the wood and will prevent the wood from being saturated with oil in the future.

Why don't I wait until I have the major components, including the side locks, in place before I bed the receiver? I want the receiver and lower tang to be securely and firmly held in place before I begin inletting the side locks where the slightest looseness can result in a lot of unnecessary work, or in the worst case, starting over. So I bed the receiver.

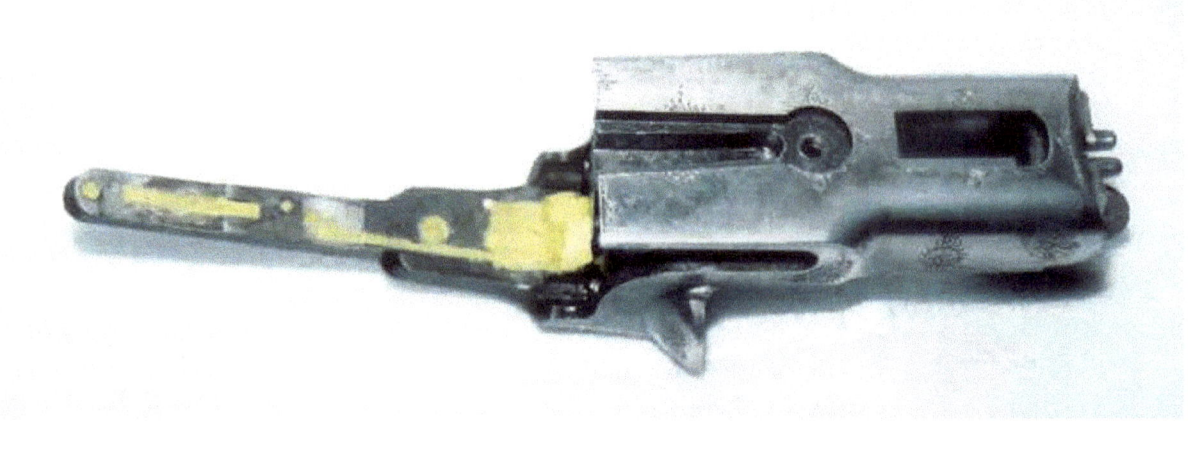

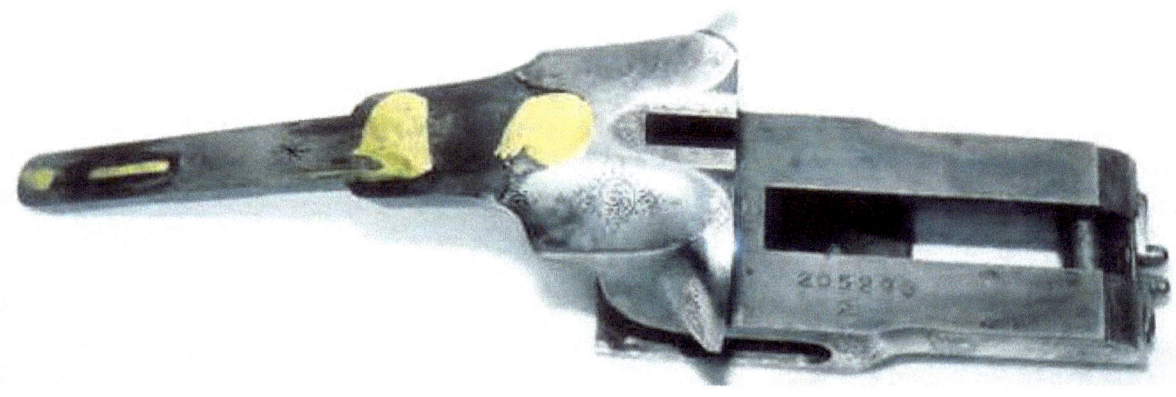

After filling in all of the voids and holes in the receiver which will come in contact the buttstock with modeling clay, and those that might come in contact, I coat the receiver with release agent and set it aside to dry while I mix the bedding compound.

Do just like the instructions say. On Acraglass, the instructions stipulate a 4 to 1 ratio, they don't say "about" a four to one, or "near" a four to one. And they sure as heck don't say a little more of this will make it better. Follow the instructions. The instructions say four to one, and that is what I do, using a graduated mixing cup to be sure. On small amounts I use measurement spoons.

I do slowly stir the mixture a little longer than usual, add just enough flock to slightly thicken it, add the amount of die necessary to match the buttstock wood. Believe me when I say a little of that dye goes a long way. Continue stirring until the graduated measure cup begins to get warm. When it is warm, it's ready to use.

I have use Brownell's AcraGlass to bed shotgun receivers for a whole bunch or years, and have found it works very well. Yes, there are many other types of bedding compounds, some may be very good, but the ability to establish color which will match the wood being used, and the manner in which the AcraGlass flows, well, I am very comfortable using it. And will quit when it is no longer available.

With the material in the cup getting progressively warmer, it is time to use the mixing stick to coat the face of the buttstock which will come in contact with the receiver, and then line the upper tang recess, and slip the receiver into the buttstock. To insure the receiver is firmly set in the buttstock as the Acraglass hardens, I use a donut (circle) or surgical tubing to hold it in place.

One rule of thumb when applying the bedding compound, put more than enough in or on, the excess will ooze out and can be easily removed in its liquid state with the mixing stick. Fail to put enough in or on, and you either have a bad job or you'll have to re-do it.

I let the AcraGlass harden overnight before I handle the buttstock at all. In that time it will set up and really provide a bond. As I am going to inlet the lower tang next, I do not trim away any excess wood at this time, preferring to allow it and the excess Acraglass serve as a holding agent. I do remove the surgical tubing donut. But, if for some reason the receiver releases from the buttstock, I slap the donut back in place.

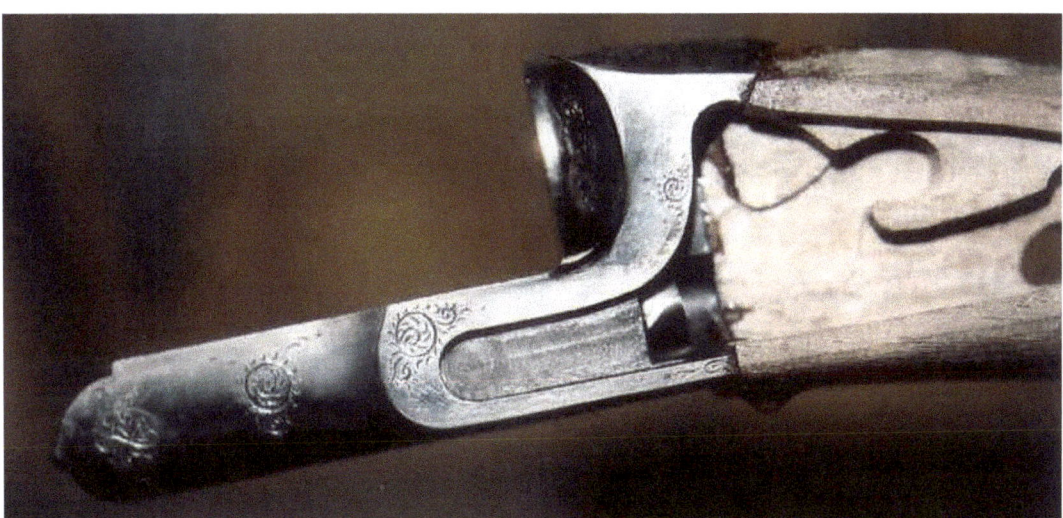

On the preceding picture, please notice the excellent contact established between the receiver face and the buttstock. The bedding insures absolute contact at this point as it does on the upper tang.

With the buttstock firmly held, upside down, in the padded jaws of the vise I get ready to inlet the lower tang. In most side lock doubles, the forward portion of the lower tang is removed from the receiver via a machine screw, in others the lower tang is shaped to fit into a recess in the bottom of the receiver. On the LC Smith I am using as an example, the lower tang is held in place with a screw.

But a note here, before you begin inletting the lower tang, it should be stripped of all parts, to include the triggers, and thoroughly cleaned of all foreign matter, to include old oil deposits. However, there are exceptions to the rule, and one of them is the Hunter One Trigger found on LC Smith shotguns. I have only had the Hunter One Trigger totally apart once, that was enough. I sent it to a "specialist" with the Hunter One Triggers and asked that he re-assemble it.

Shortly thereafter, I purchased some junk parts and as luck would have it, there was a stripped double trigger lower tang in the bottom of the box. Over the years I have collected several and use them as an inletting guide when the final tang will house the single trigger assembly.

Hunter One Single Trigger

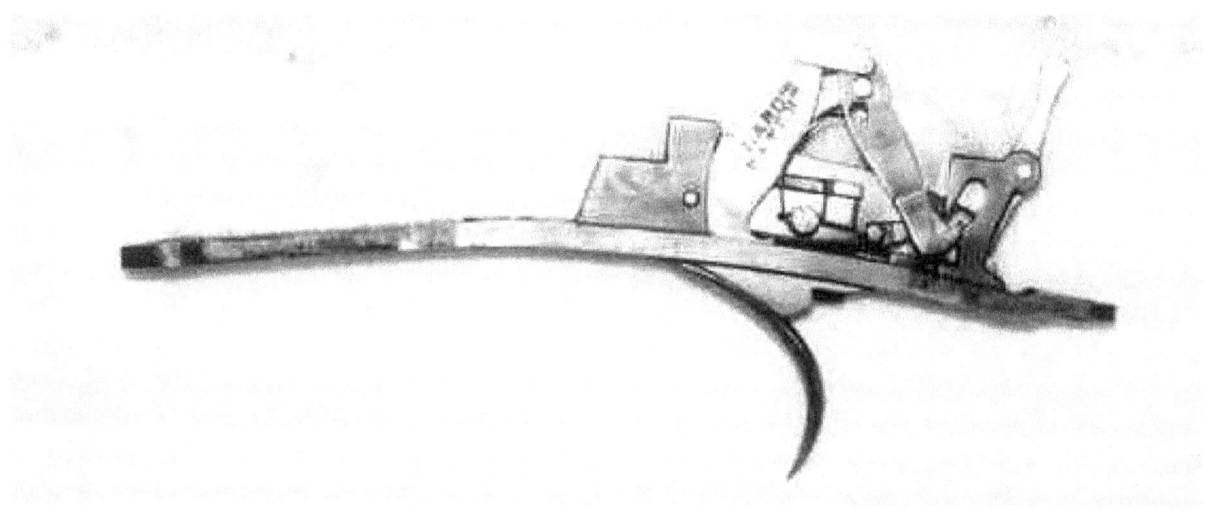

Standard Double Trigger lower tang.

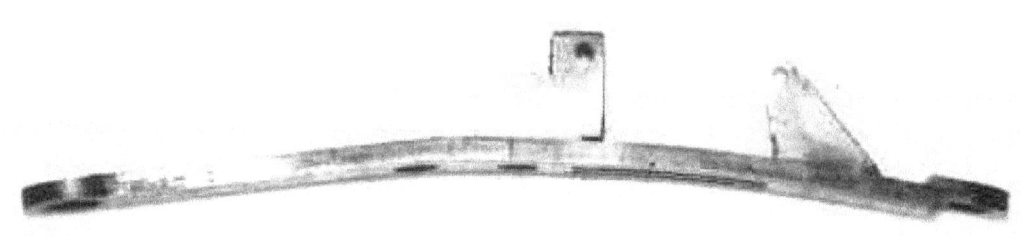

If the wood at the receiver is higher than the receiver, lower the height of the wood to within a sixteenth of the receiver level. This will reduce the amount of inletting required and will allow you to get a better impression of the blackened metal.

Using the inletting black, blacken the inside edges of the tang, and coat any area on the inside that is above the tang surface, such as a rise onto which the triggers are secured. In some shotguns, the forward slope of the area designed to hold the triggers bears against the inside of the stock, providing additional support for the receiver as well as the lower tang.

Placing the front of the lower tang in the recess area, or into the area of the screw, slowly lower it into position until it comes in contact with the buttstock. No pressure, no striking the tang, just remove it. On the buttstock will be the impression of the lower tang as it started into the wood.

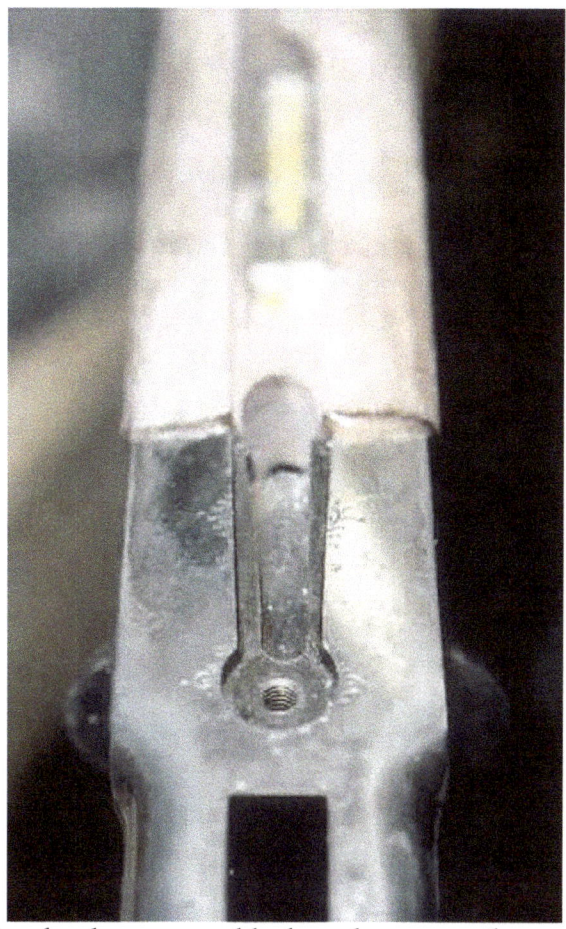

Your task is to slowly remove blackened area on the surface of the wood by removing the wood under it down to the correct depth. And the correct depth is achieved a little cutting and scraping at a time. Depending upon the amount of wood to be removed, you can use a wood chisel or a scraper, or a moto tool if you are comfortable in its use.

I have found that a sharp scraper is the ideal tool for inletting side locks, as is a very sharp carving chisel. For the hobbyist, I would recommend using the chisel set produced by Gunline and sold by Brownell's. The set is not expensive, is of excellent quality, and serves the intended purposes well. DO NOT go down to the bargain counter of the local lumber yard or supermarket and seek a wood chisel. They just won't give you the desired results you need.

If you intend to have future need of a fine chisel, there are many available. I have a friend who has turned me on to the W. Butcher chisels, made in Sheffield, England in the EARLY 1800's. However, a good rule of thumb is you will be paying for what you get.

I do not recommend a moto tool with cutter. They are too hard to control, too difficult to adjust the amount of wood being removed and can get away from you and chew the heck out of the inletting leaving you with gaping holes in your inletting.

Be very careful when removing this wood, take a little off at a time, remember, you can take it off, but putting it back… And do not force the lower tang into the wood.

When inletting a side lock double, as I mentioned previously, you need a lot of patience. Just scrape or chisel the wood a little at a time, until it fits. Patience.

Repeat this process, blackening the metal, placing the front tip in the recessed area or area of the retaining screw, lower it onto the recess, identify the freshly blackened area, and chisel or scrape the blackened area. A little at a time, and gradually it will lower into the tang slot.

There are two good indicators for determining the correct inletting depth of the lower tang. First, the metal joint between the lower tang and the receiver should be flush, one not higher than the other. The second is the measurement between the two tangs you took earlier with the receiver assembled.

The receiver is inletted to the correct depth when the lower tang is inletted sufficiently to achieve that measurement, you are *almost done* with the lower tang. Generally, there are two screws connecting the upper tang of the receiver to the lower tang which holds the triggers.

One screw located at the rear of the receiver tang. In some guns the screw goes down through the receiver tang into the lower tang, in others the screw comes up from the lower tang into a threaded hole in the receiver tang. A few come down from the receiver tang and thread into the trigger guard. I have restocked several Lefevers in which this was the case. The second screw is usually under the barrel release lever, and goes down into the rise from which the triggers are attached. For lack of a better term, I call this rise the "trigger tower." And before you ask, no I did not invent the word, but heard it used by another stock maker and have borrowed it for several years.

The location of the rear tang screw is critical to the tight fit of the receiver to the buttstock. For that reason, if no other, drilling this hole is important. First, mark the exact center of the upper tang hole. You can use an awl, a scribe, or a sharp pencil. If the screw goes down through the upper tang, I use a scribe or awl to make this mark. If the upper tang is threaded, I have a small box of different threaded screws for this purpose, and the end of every one of them is beveled. When I screw it into the tang, the beveled point leaves an exact location of the center. One technique can be used on the upper tang, and the other used on the lower tang. Whatever technique is used to determine the exact center of the hole, it must be the exact center.

Use an awl or center punch to mark the center of the screw holes, and then remove the lower tang. Now is the time to remove the receiver from the buttstock. To do that, we first need to remove the excess Acraglas and some wood. Then the receiver from the buttstock. I begin this process with the buttstock securely anchored in the padded vice jaws, and then use a fine double cut file to take the wood down to approximately a thirty-second of an inch from the metal surface. I use short strokes, and take my time, being careful to watch the amount of wood between my file and the metal.

If I have done a good job of filling in the holes and voids on the buttstock with modeling clay, by placing the receiver in the padded jaws of the vise and pulling on the buttstock and adding a soft tap from a nylon headed hammer to the pistil grip of the buttstock, the buttstock will separate from the receiver.

As soon as it breaks loose, STOP! Carefully inspect the tang areas to insure none of the wood is cracking or chipping. At this point, a repair isn't too great a deal, continue the separation process and a "restart" may be in order.

With the receiver removed from the buttstock, I can now drill the rear tang hole. I have found that to drill the hole accurately, a drill press is almost essential. I use a cross feed vise to hold a short center punch with its point up. In the past I have use a block of wood with a slightly undersized hole drilled in it into which I inserted the punch and then "C" clamped the block of wood to the drill press table.

Regardless, a center punch – securely held in place - must be aligned with a drill bit of the correct dimensions in the chuck of the drill. **A special note, if the tang screw is tapered, the drill bit must be equal to or slightly larger than the larger end of the taper.** The alignment must be absolutely straight.

The rear tang screw indention, made earlier, on the bottom of the buttstock is rested on the center punch point, and the drill bit brought down through the receiver tang to come in contact with the indention made on top of the buttstock. Thus, the area to be drilled is located absolutely between centers and will not be drilled at an angle or off center. True, the buttstock is held in place by hand, but for a stock maker, this shouldn't be a problem.

So, holding the stock in place, drill approximately half way through the buttstock. Reverse the buttstock, placing the start of the freshly drilled hole on the center punch, center the drill in the indention of the bottom of the buttstock and drill the hole. You should come into contact with the first half of the hole drilled, and thus have a hole drilled at the correct angle.

Just be sure the hole is correct, slip the receiver into the buttstock, give it a little tap to insure it is fully seated, and install the lower tang. If the lower tang is held in place with a screw, install and tighten the screw. If it is held in place by a mechanical recess, slip it into the recess. AND then slip the tang screw in place. If everything was accomplished in the correct manner, the screw should slip right into the hole and be positioned to engage the threads at the opposite end.

However, if the screw was tapered, the hole is slightly larger than need be on one end, but that can be corrected.

If the screw does engage the threads of the tang as it should, slowly tighten it to the correct depth. In most instances, the correct depth is the depth required to become flush with the tang containing the threads. But, (remember the measurements? right!) get the calipers and take a reading…

So, with the receiver and lower tang correctly inletted and bedded, the rear tang screw in place holding it all together, It's time to drill for the mid tang screw, usually hidden under the barrel release lever. The exact location of this screw is not critical, it will pull the trigger tower up into contact with the inside of the inletted area as previously described. So, knowing this, if there is an error made in establishing the angle of the hole, the angle of the hole should be positioned to pull the lower tang tighter into the stock, rather than force it out.

Measure the diameter of the screw at a point nearest the head, and select a drill bit slightly larger, no more than a thirty-second. I choose to use a drill press for this purpose, although when I started out I use a hand drill at the lowest possible speed. Very carefully drill the hole from the top, <u>remembering the target is a threaded hole, you don't want to drill into it, just to it.</u>

Install the screw and pull the lower tang up. The tension used to tighten this screw should be sufficient to bring the trigger tower in contact with the inletted buttstock.

Just as you prepared the upper tang for bedding, do the same for the lower tang: Fill all of the holes and voids with modeling clay, apply release agent to the lower tang and the rear tang screw.

Mix the AcraGlas just as you did in the preceding instructions. Apply the bedding compound much as you did, but if the trigger tower bears against the stock, be sure to apply bedding to the area at which the trigger tower will come in contact.

NOTE: If the rear tang screw is tapered, put sufficient bedding in the rear tang screw hole, enough to fill the void between the tapered screw and the hole and use the tapered screw.

*At this point I must confess to having stocked quite a few of the side lock doubles. After fighting the original screws trying to get them out of the bedding, I traded a machinist friend many cups of shop coffee and hours of intelligent gun conversation for a set of actions screws, similar to those used for bedding rifles. He made the long shanked screws with "T" handles in several sizes and thread spacings, and even hardened them for me. I use them constantly, adjusting the length, if need be, with several washers. I even have a tapered tang screw, he made it for me to use when stocking **his** side lock double.*

Never a worry about buggering up one of the original screw heads, I use my action screws. However, for the hobbyist, I recommend taking the rear tang screw down to the local supply store and purchasing a socket head screw corresponding to the diameter and thread spacing – and an Allen wrench to install and remove it. If your side lock double in not of evident American manufacture, the threads are most likely metric. Double check these "new" screws to insure you are not cutting new threads with the new screws. If the heads of the socket head screws, turn them down with your portable lathe – your portable electric drill – and hold them against a fine-toothed file or sanding belt to reduce them.

The bedding process is not meant to cover up errors, although I have seen jobs that reflect it as having used as such. Bedding serves to provide the optimum wood to metal fit, and therefore disburses the recoil evenly, increasing the life of the stock. In addition, it makes one hell of a moisture sealer.

Having left the butt stock overnight to allow the Acraglass to harden, it is now time to remove excess wood from the upper and lower tangs.

With the triggers and trigger guard removed, this is a fairly straight forward process – however – watch the grain flow, do not cut against the grain. I use a small three inch draw knife made by a friend for this purpose, but also use a file and straight cut chisel.

Take the wood down to a within a thirty second inch from the metal. Later, you can file, scrape or sand the wood down to the correct depth. Be Careful, watch the grain flow, cut with the grain.

NOTE: If you are going to have the metal refinished, you can file or sand down to the full level, mating the metal to wood surface perfectly. But unless you know the charge for refinishing the metal, leave about a thirty-second or excess wood. I am seldom lucky enough to get the metal before it is refinished and must be super careful not to disturb the new finish.

So with the receiver and lower tang correctly inletted and bedded, the rear tang screw and mid tang screw in place holding it all together, it is time to inlet the side plates. If you haven't already stripped and cleaned the side plates, please do so. But do so with a word or caution: Most side plate shotguns have STRONG hammer springs, if incorrectly disassembled, parts could fly…

If you do not have the proper tools for safely compressing and removing the hammer springs for disassembly, I strongly recommend that you take the locks to someone that does. Oh, putting them back together is far more difficult that disassembling them, so make a friend during the first visit.

The first thing to do is to remove the excess wood at the face of the receiver down to a level just about the receiver metal level. I remove the wood at an angle, extending the angle back about a half inch.

With this high wood removed, I can then use the blackening agent to coat the bottom of the lock plate as well as all around the edge. A word of caution, the backening agent transfers onto wood easily, almost as easily as it down to cloth and skin… And with the edges and bottom of the side plate covered with blackening agent, a handle would be nice. Just so happens you have one, the small screw which holds the hammer/sear spring in place can be used. Instead of inserting it in its normal position inside the lock plate, screw it in from the outside of the lock plate. While the small screw is handy, I suggest obtaining a longer screw of the same thread and attaching it to a small handle. I have made several using 1/2" plastic tubing and bedding compound left over from the bedding operation. Simple to make, and very handy.

The process of fitting the side plate always begins with placing the forward tip of the side plate in position, in the milled slot in the receiver, and lowering it until it comes in contact with the wood. By coating the edge and underside of the side plate with your blackening agent, when the lock plate comes in contact with the wood, the blackening agent will transfer to the wood, and it is this wood covered with blackening agent which must be removed.

As the inletting progresses, you have made use a soft-headed hammer, or short section of wooden dowel, to **gently tap** the lock plate and establish a contact point between the lock plate and the buttstock. Inletting side plates is critical to the appearance of the entire job, this is where taking only a little wood off at a time is critical.

The side plate will be re-blackened many times during the inletting before it finally achieves the desired level. Remember, when inletting the side plate, take a little off, **do not** get ahead of yourself and decide to save time and make some deep cuts. When I have done this, I have regretted it.

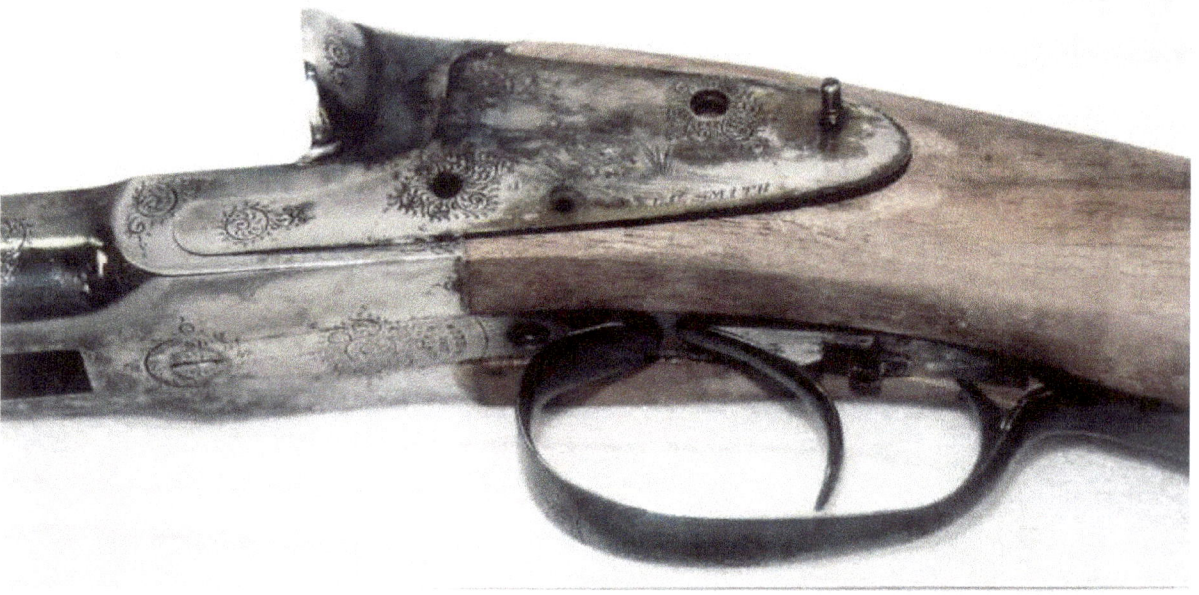

Some areas of the side plate inletting will provide a small shoulder upon which the side plate was intended to rest and serve as a "depth" measurement for inletting, others will not. If you are working from a semi-inletted buttstock, they should be there, at least sufficient amounts to correctly position the side plate. If you are working from a blank in the scratch method, concentrate on inletting the side plate into the wood and leaving the entire area under the side plate level with the side plate. Later, some of this area will have to be removed for the working parts of the side lock.

Exceptions to this are the false side plate guns such as the Beretta 687EL and EELL. The sideplates on these guns are purely for decoration and contain no working mechanisms.

To properly inlet a side plate, I have found that a small, very sharp scraper is great, as is a very sharp straight edge carving chisel. The emphasis here in on sharp. A dull tool will drag the wood and cause more problems, problems you do not need.

Picture illustrating a scraper being used to inlet lockplate on a Beretta EELL

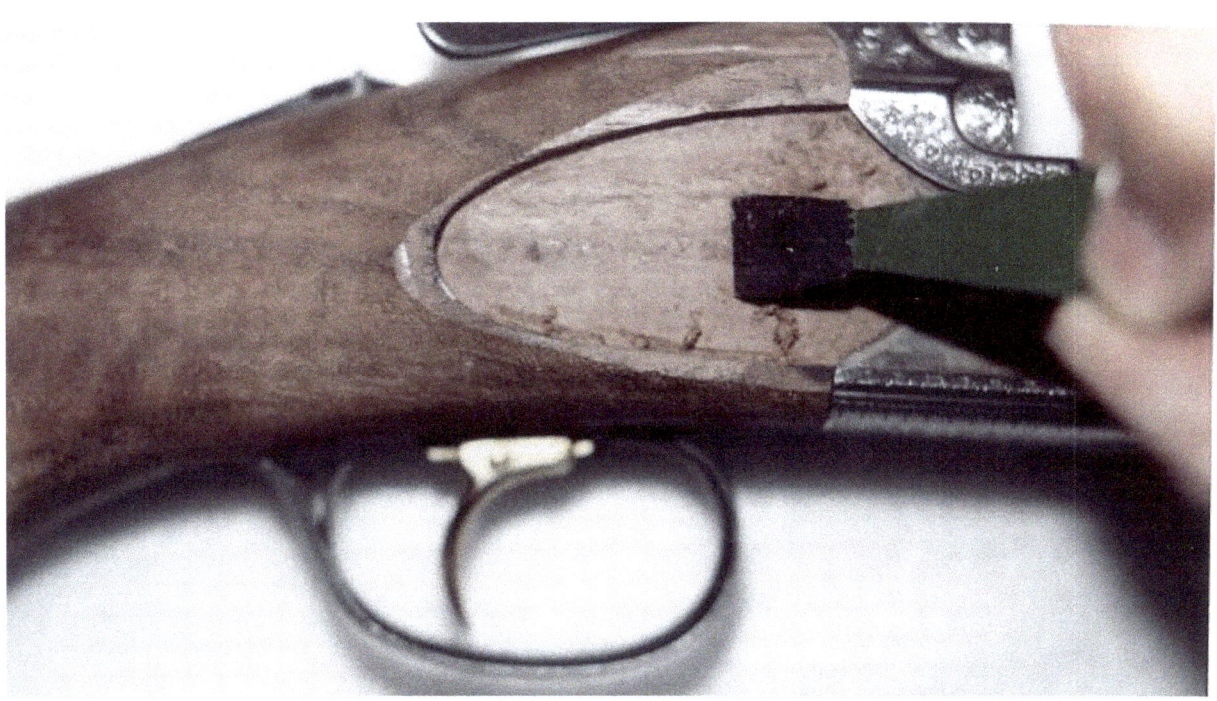

Using the blackening agent as your guide, repeat the lowering of the lock plate onto the wood and removing the blackened wood, repeating the process until you are satisfied that the side plate is inletted to the correct depth.

NOTE: Do not remove the excess wood down to the lock plate surface level until later. If the excess wood becomes a problem, remove down to a sixteenth above the lock plate surface.

How can the correct inletted level be determined? Easily, the matching of the two metal surfaces, the front of the side lock and the rear of the receiver, should be absolutely flush.

With one side plate inletted, begin the other. On this lock plate, the hammer/sear spring retaining screw can be used as a handle, of the longer screw passing through the left lock plate and screwing into the right lock plate can be used by screwing it into the right lock plate from the outside. Either will work, your choice.

When both side plates are fully inletted, refer back to your measurement as to when the correct side plate to side plate measurement should be, and check yours. If the side plates are flush with the receiver metal, you should be close.

Not is the time to drill the hole necessary for the side plate anchoring screw. Identify and mark the centers of both holes by scribing the interior of the hole in the side plate directly onto the wood it is inletted onto. Shouldn't be a problem. With both holes marked, use the same principle to drill this hole that was used to drill the rear tang screw hole.

Many of the older side lock doubles used a piece of tubing set into the stock through which the side lock screw passed. This tubing, acting as a sleeve, insured the correct distance between the two side plates. I have found this to be far more common on single trigger doubles that doubles with two triggers.

Ideally, the side plate anchoring screw should engage the threads of the side plate, and when tightened, the end of the screw should come out flush with the side plate on the opposite side. If there is significant protrusion of the screw, more than a sixty-fourth of an inch, you have inletted too deeply and must correct the problem.

The first thing to determine is which side has been inletted too deep. To accomplish this, look at the side plate to receiver metal fit, is the side plate metal below the level of the receiver? If so, that side is your culprit. If you cannot determine exactly which side is the culprit, split the difference between the two side plates, and establish a false shoulder using a sliver of wood no longer than a quarter inch, and placing it at the rear most portion of the side plate.

With these false shoulders in place, a small dab of wood glue, and I mean small, will hold them in place, attach the side plates and install the side plate anchor screw. It should tighten up and be flush in you have guessed correctly. Leave the side plates installed for a while, to enable the wood glue to set up and secure the false shoulders in place.

After sufficient time has passed to allow the false shoulders to become attached, remove the side plates from the buttstock, and clean all of the blackening agent from them and coat them and the side plate anchoring screw with the Acraglass release agent, and set them aside to dry.

Following the instructions, mix a small portion of Acraglass, no more than a teaspoon will be necessary, stir in sufficient flock to give it body. In this application, you do not want the Acraglass to move too much. When it becomes warm enough to apply, use something to distribute a small bead of Acraglass around the existing shoulder of the inletted area on one side. I use the ice cream stick I use to mix the material. I do take a swipe at the point with a box opener to establish something of a point.

Place the side plate in position, slip the remaining side plate position in place, and tighten the side plate anchoring screw to the desired depth.

NOTE: You have applied Acraglass to one side only, do not do both sides and the same time. Do one, wait for it to dry, and then do the other.

Place the buttstock with the side plate you have just worked on in the up position. In this manner, the Acraglass with hardener and form the needed shoulder. I would recommend letting it dry overnight, and then repeat the process on the other side.

With the side plates inletted to the correct depth, removing the excess wood down to the side plate level is very tempting, and to a point we should succumb. With a half to 3 three-eighths inch wide straight chisel, slowly remove the excess wood down to within a thirty second of the lock plate surface area. We want this small amount of wood remaining so that it can serve as protection of the edge during the handling and fitting yet to be accomplished. Later, when the side plate with the entire mechanism in place is inletted, we will remove the excess wood with a fine file and metal sanding block.

To remove the side plates from the buttstock, remove the side plate anchoring screw, screw it into the side plate with the threads, and remove the side plate. For the side plate without the threads, use a drift punch to gently tap it out of position.

At this point, I like to get away from the side plates and leave them installed in the buttstock and begin inletting the trigger guard.

The trigger guard presents a unique problem not encountered elsewhere on the gun. I have seen many jobs on which the end of the trigger guard was not inletted properly, leaving a large gap between the end of the tang and the wood. Just as the side plate was inletted slowly beginning with the area nearest the receiver, the trigger guard must also be inletted. In this manner, when the tang is inletted, the trigger guard screw will draw the tang into the wood and there will be no gaps. The end of the tang will most likely be beveled, and so should the inletting.

To begin with, most side lock doubles have trigger guards which screw into the bottom of the receiver, however, there are a few which slip into a locking mechanism. Regardless, use your blackening agent to coat the underside of the trigger guard tang and position the trigger in the receiver and let it come down in contact with the buttstock - insuring that the tang is centered in the grip width.

A special note: Trigger guards which have been crudely repaired or have missing portions are common. However, Brownell's Inc, Montezuma, IA, carry a replacement trigger guard which can be ordered threaded, or unthreaded. I have used several of them and have found them to be of excellent quality and a real life saver on more than one occasion. That does not mean that I do not still search gun shows looking for original trigger guards, I do.

Once you have established contact, you can begin inletting the tang into the stock. As with the side plates, remove the blackened wood a little at a time. I use a straight edged carving chisel to remove the wood on the sides, and a scraper to increase the depth, alternating them as required.

At this point a major question comes up: How deep should the trigger guard be inletted? And the answer is two-fold. First, the trigger guard should confirm to the contour of the grip, there should not be a changing of radius in the middle of the grip. If the trigger guard is a replacement, or has been repaired, the trigger guard may have to be bent to conform to the radius of the grip. And second, the wood should come up to the surface of the trigger guard in a smooth contour so as to not create an unsightly matching of the two surfaces.

Regardless of how well you do inletting the sides, unless the end of the tang, the beveled tang – remember – is inletted without a gap, the area will not look good. To achieve this matching of surfaces, as you inlet the tang, remove wood from the end of the tang area very carefully, removing just the blackened area. DO NOT anticipate a depth or angle, just remove the slimest thickness of the blackened wood.

To achieve this process, as I begin inletting the rear of the tang, I drill the hole for the tang screw, and use it to pull the tang into place and in contact with the wood, leaving the blackened wood to be removed. Yes, it is a very slow process, but the end result will be a trigger guard tang inletted into the grip area providing a smooth continuation of wood to metal, without gaps.

There are some trigger guards, such as the older Lefever's, on which the end of the trigger guard is squared and ends at the bottom of the grip cap. Fitting this trigger guard and grip cap arrangement can provide some interesting moments.

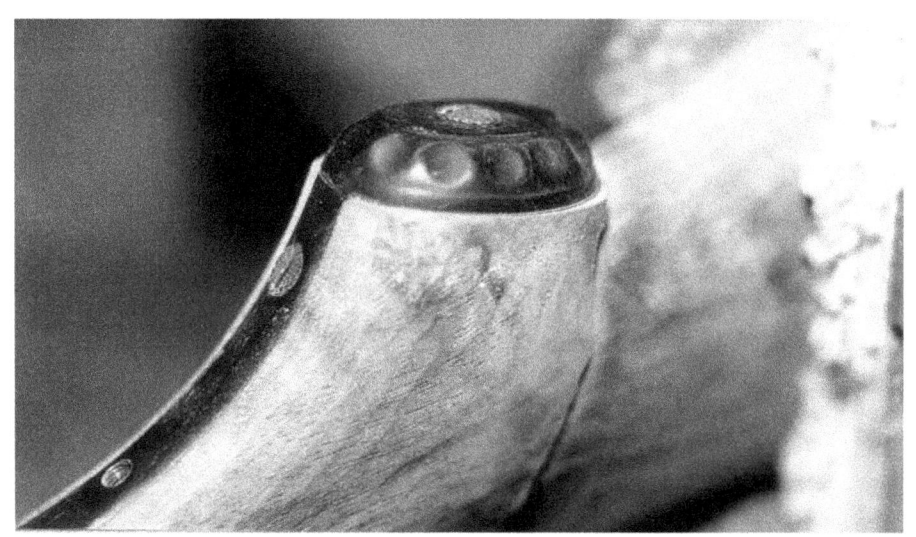

SECTION 3

STOCKING SEMI-AUTO AND PUMPS

Semi-automatic shotguns most likely will have an "action" tube in which some spring mechanism is housed whose task it is to absorb the action of the bolt when the gun is fired. The diameter of this tube will vary from a half inch to over three quarters of an inch, although I am sure there are exceptions on both ends of the spectrum.

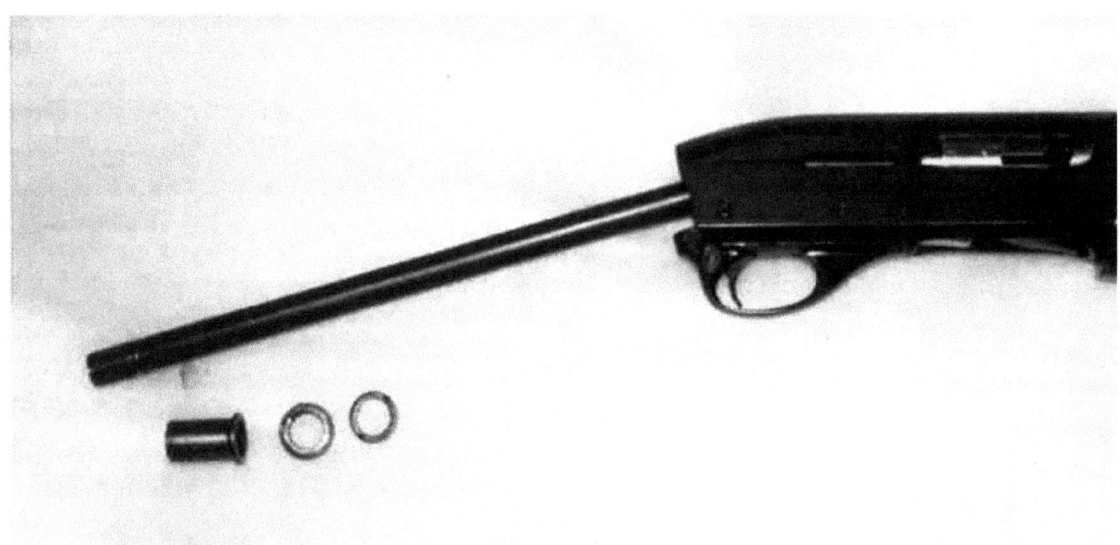

The angle of the action tube will vary between guns, comparing Beretta 390 to the Remington Model 1100, and in some cases, vary some between guns of the same model. This single factor has the greatest impact on the initial measurements at the comb of the semi-finished buttstock you are about to install. The buttstock is held to the receiver by a nut arrangement attaching to the action tube.

On most pump action shotguns, the buttstock is held to the receiver by a stock bolt coming in from the rear of the buttstock and engaging some type of threaded arrangement at the rear of the receiver. Notice I said "most", there are some which are secured with an action screw between the upper and lower tangs of the action

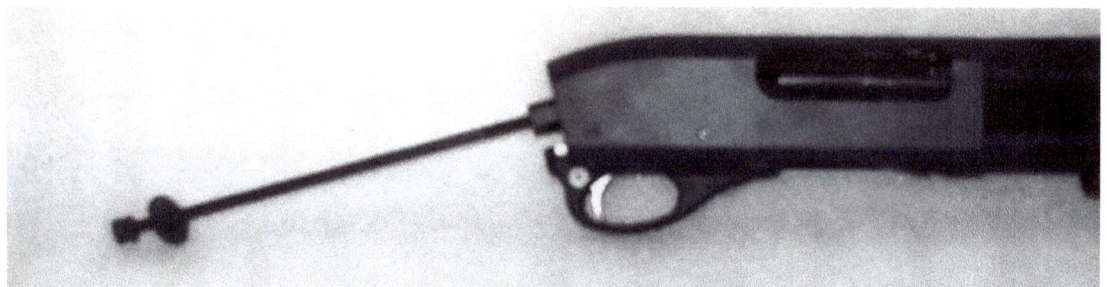

When fitting a pump action shotgun buttstock, I create a dummy stock bolt, about six inches in length, without a head, and screw it into the action. I use this as my guide to insure I am placing the buttstock against the receiver the same each time.

When trying to determine the comb measurements of a semi-auto buttstock being fitted to a receiver, there is some comparison to getting married. You don't really know how it is going to turn out until you try it. Problem is, at what point in the "trying" process can you throw your hands up and walk away? So, fit the buttstock to the receiver.

Most providers of semi-finished shotgun wood provide an excellent product, copied to very close tolerances. Some of the very best work on the market comes from Fred Wenig at Wenig's Custom Gunstocks, Lincoln, Missouri. They also duplicate a customer's pattern such as he did on in the photo below.

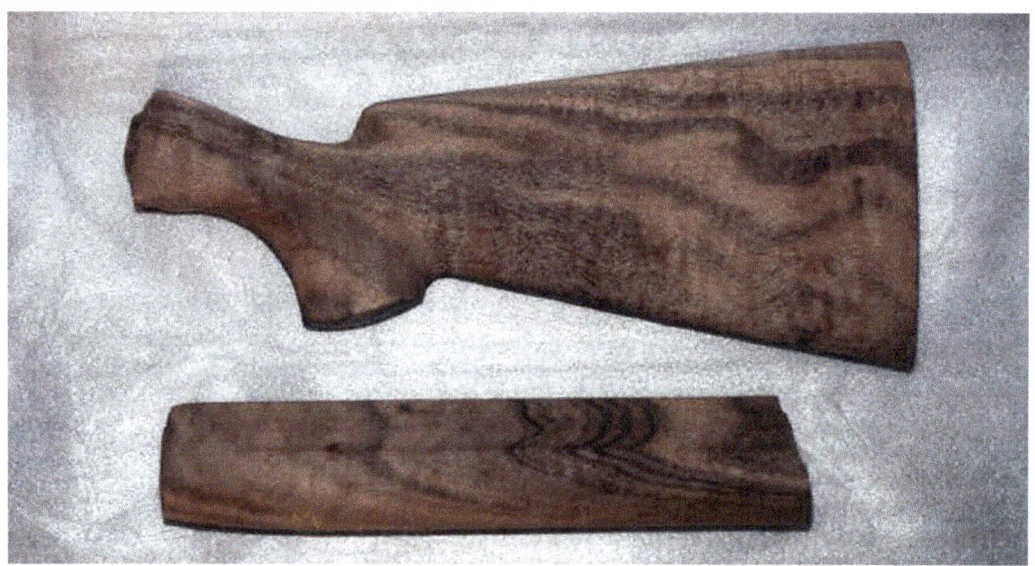

As I just happen to have a Remington Model 1100 set on hand from Wenig, I will make them the sample woods for this section. At this point I do not get many calls for restocking pump guns such as the Remington Model 870, but if one should come in, I will include it also.

First thing, trim off the obviously excess wood. This is a bit of wood at which the buttstock was held in the duplicator. Look at the old stock to be sure you are not cutting off something that should stay. Most butt stocks come with the excess wood removed from the receiver area, just check and be sure. It can save a lot of work later on.

Assuming the action tube hole in the buttstock is the correct diameter, the first thing we need to do is use the sponge brush to apply the blackening agent to the rear of the receiver and trigger guard where it will come in contact with the buttstock.

Note: after establishing the correct contact between the buttstock and the trigger guard or trigger housing, we will relieve this area of the buttstock to insure the trigger housing can be removed without removing the buttstock.

As tapping on the receiver can lead to other problems, I like to place the receiver between the padded jaws on the vise, secure it, but with only enough force to hold it, not crush it. With the receiver secured, slide the buttstock over the action tube, keeping the vertical alignment with the receiver, until the buttstock comes in contact with the receiver. Tap the rear of the buttstock lightly, the blackening agent will transfer to the wood, identifying the contact points between the wood and metal.

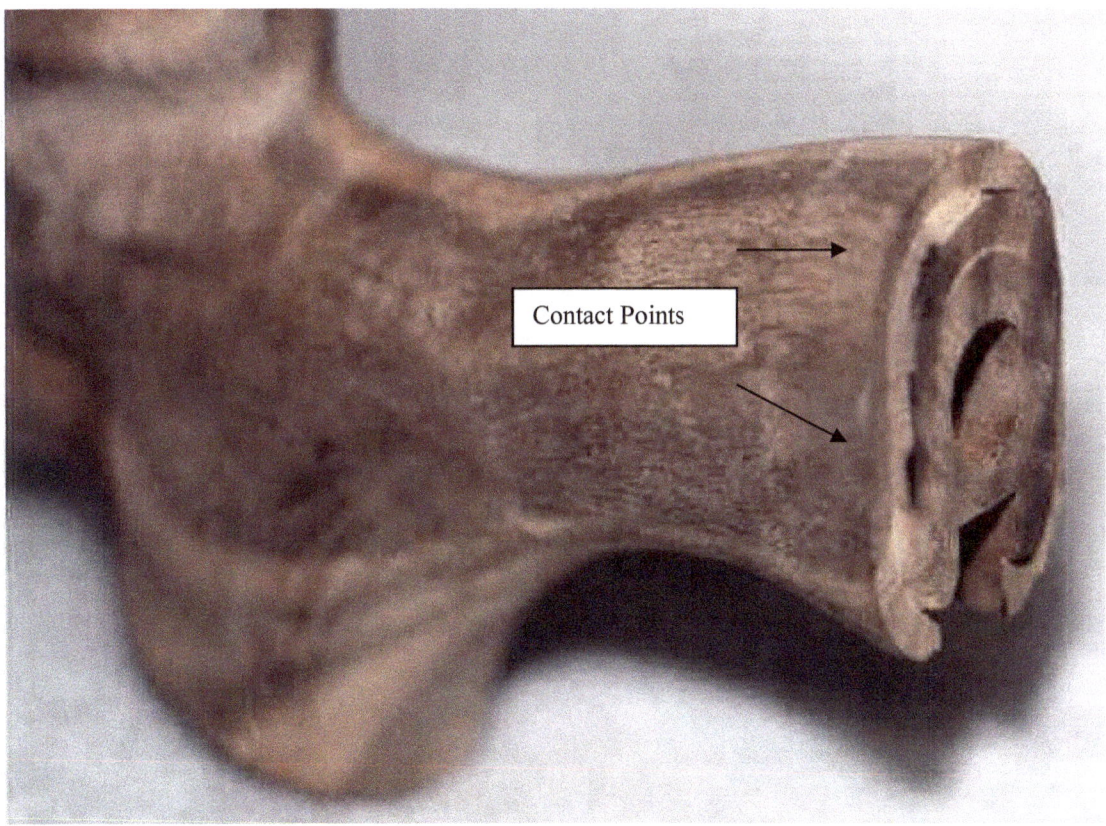

If this were indeed the perfect fit, evidence of a clear and complete fit would be the blackening agent appearing on the buttstock at every wood to metal point. But, this isn't a perfect world, and there is work to be done. However, the improvement in the quality of duplicating over the last twenty years is truly astounding.

As the contact is at the end of the grain, we are somewhat limited as to what tool can be used to remove the blackening agent. A scraper is normally used when inletting the tangs into a buttstock, but in this case, we are not working with the grain. Please do not use a power grinder, either a moto tool or hand held high speed grinder. These tools take off a lot of wood very quickly, and are difficult to control when used on end grain wood, and can leave you with a repair job or a joint not repairable.

My tool of choice is a carving chisel with an angle cut, something less than a forty-five degree angle has worked best for me in the past, and I just happen to have several in varying blade widths. The chisel in the Gunline starter kit is very good for this task and is slightly narrower than one I made years ago. Both hold an edge very well, and the one I use is the one closest at hand.

With the initial contact made after several "tries", the blackening agent needs to be refreshed on the receiver, and the buttstock needs to be cinched up tight with the action tube nut, or in the case of a pump action, the stock bolt.

As the buttstock will be slipped onto the receiver in this manner several times, I have developed several tools which make the task easier. For Remington Model 1100 and 11-87's, I use a tool made of round stock that has been drilled and taped with the appropriate thread for the action tube to secure the stock to the receiver. I also developed a "Tuff Tool" which I use to remove the action tube nut of the Remington Model 1100. It is without a doubt – in my opinion – the best tool on the market as it WILL NOT SLIP from the action tube nut and had a "T" handle to apply torque.

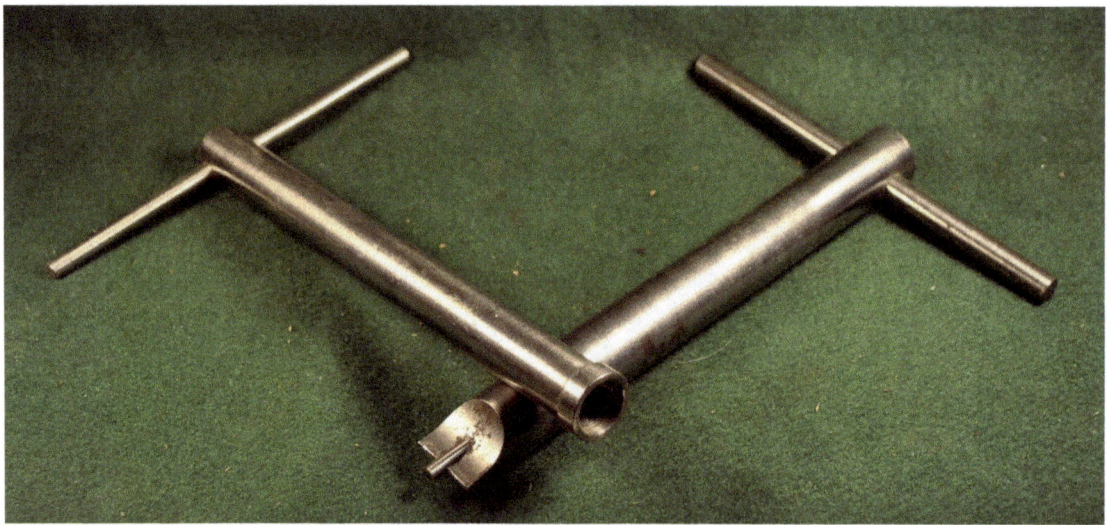

For others, I used oversize socket head bolts, shortened to the correct length and with the diameter turned down to the required measurements and threaded as appropriate. I find using a "T" handle allen wrench much easier to use when cinching a buttstock and receiver together than when trying to use a screw driver.

For the hobbyist, the use an appropriate sized screw driver is an acceptable practice, but be careful. The number of times the buttstock must be cinched down to the receiver will vary, but fifteen to twenty is average. Once the butt stock is correctly fitted to the receiver, the next step is removing the excess wood.

    With the face of the buttstock fitted to the receiver, and comfortable in the fit, we can now remove some of the excess wood around the joint between the receiver and buttstock. The amount of wood to be removed varies with each supplier with some leaving a lot, and others leaving very little.

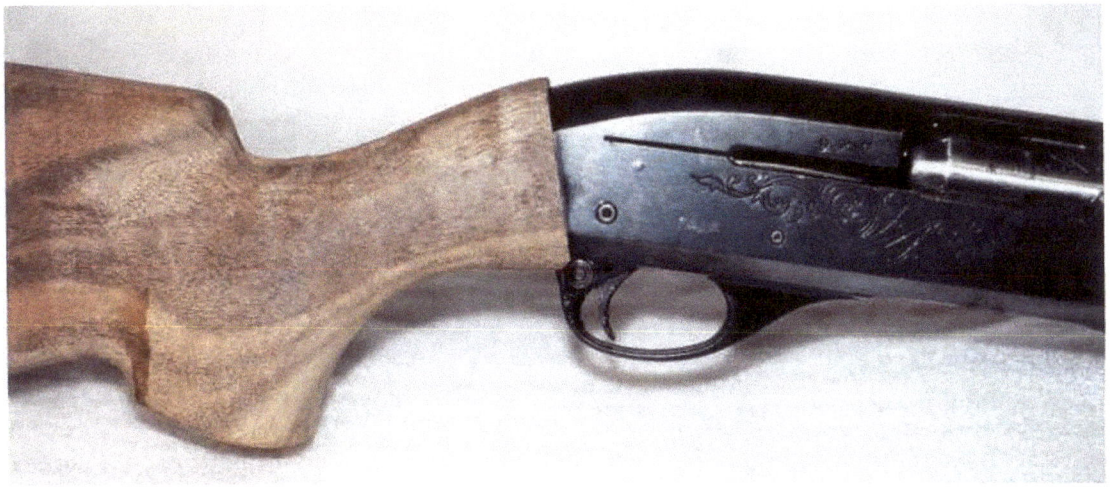

    The excess wood should be removed to a point at which about a thirty-second of wood remains above the receiver. I begin identifying the wood to be removed by using a #2 pencil with a flat point and trace a line onto the wood around the receiver.

    I then remove the receiver from the buttstock, place the buttstock in the padded vise jaws, and slowly begin removing the excess wood

Depending upon the amount of wood and its hardness, I use the method most suitable for the amount of wood to be removed. For a lot of wood, I will start with a small block plane or draw knife, for less, I would go directly to a cabinet makers file, for just a little wood, I would use 150 grit sand paper on a sanding block.

The rule here is to be sure of not taking too much wood off and creating a situation in which the wood level is lower than the receiver level. Again, take a little off at a time, and be sure to leave about a thirty-second yet to be removed during the final fitting and sanding phase.

Once this is accomplished, the receiver is ready to be bedded to the buttstock.

As previously stated, I bed all of my work. The bedding seals off the end grain of the wood on the buttstock, preventing oil from permeating the wood in years to come, and it provides absolute 100% contact between receiver and buttstock.

I prefer to use Brownell's steel or aluminum bed compound to bed rifles and recoil lugs of over and under shotguns. However, when bedding pump and semi-automatic shotguns, I use Brownell's Acraglass bedding compound. I cannot emphasize enough the need to follow the directions when mixing the two ingredients to form the bedding compound, and stirring the mixture the required length of time – four minutes is just not that long.

The Acraglass can be dyed to a variety of shades making it almost impossible to detect. Bear in mind, we are not substituting good bedding for poor inletting. Our goal is to augment good inletting with superior bedding, as well as provide an excellent seal for the end grain of the wood.

I use a spray cleaner to remove the blackening agent from rear of the receiver before coating it with release agent. The mold release agent marketed by Brownell's has been my favorite for years – be sure to coat the action tube and, if the gun is a pump action, the stock bolt as well. Release agent is very inexpensive and is easily removed, don't be afraid to use it.

One very important item, **plugging holes**. Many receivers offer the opportunity of creating one piece receiver-stock combinations by having small holes into which the bedding compound can migrate and cure. I use old fashioned model clay to plug these holes. The type of model clay used in grade school - at least when I went to school. Some could actually fashion something from it.

On Remington Model 1100 and 11-87, a thin steel plate, the stock plate, is inserted between the stock and the receiver, do not forget to have it in place before starting the bedding. Other guns have similar "buffers" which need to be considered in the bedding process. With the stock plate in place, and the holes filled, and the release agent covering everything which might come into contact with the bedding compound, we are ready to bed the butt stock to the receiver.

Apply a sufficient amount of mixture to provide the seal and bed needed, remember, the excess you put on is the excess you must take off. I like a very small "bead" around the joint between receiver and buttstock. To achieve this, and reduce the around of work I will later have to devote to trimming the excess bedding and wood from the buttstock, I remove most of the excess bedding while it is still in the liquid stage. At this size, I am sure the bedding I want has been established, and the wood sealed, and there is not a lot of excess to be removed later.

Allowing the bedding to "cure" overnight, I continue the process by removing the stock nut assemble, freeing the receiver from the buttstock. To remove the receiver from the buttstock, after the stock bolt or action tube nut has been removed, holding the receiver up, with the toe of the buttstock an inch or two over the work bench, I use a nylon faced hammer – not plastic as it will compress the wood – and lightly strike the inside of the grip several times. This breaks the bond between the receiver and buttstock which can then be slid from the action tube.

If the buttstock does not break loose easily from the receiver, do not continue to beat on it, but determine the problem. Look for bedding compound around the safety area – such as on Remington Model 1100's – before using additional force. When I have this problem, and yes, it does happen, I place the receiver in the padded jaws of the vise, trigger guard up, pull on the buttstock, and use the nylon hammer to strike the inside of the pistol grip. The force of both striking the buttstock and of pulling on it, seems to work well. There have been few buttstocks over the years for which this removal did not work.

Looking at the receiver end of the buttstock, you can readily see the bedding ring left by the receiver. The next task is going to be reducing the excess wood down to the slightly larger than receiver dimensions.

Some people advocate placing a piece of tape at the rear of the receiver and sanding the excess wood down to the tape. <u>I do not advocate using this technique</u>. Many of the guns I stock cost thousands of dollars, and the engraving on many is… Anyway, I am not going to take a chance on damaging a customer's gun, not when I can take a little more time and do the same, if not better, job without the risk.

Years ago, experimenting with the capabilities of my first "large" vise, I found that I could secure a buttstock between the padded jaws. I did this by placing the comb against one jaw and moving the buttstock to a point at which the pistol grip and the belly of the buttstock touched the other jaw. Remembering to only tighten the buttstock only tight enough to secure it, knowing that to tighten it "too" tight would indent the belly of the buttstock, it has worked for me for years.

Removing the excess wood down to the receiver outline is best done with a good file and a lot of patience. As there is a definite "ring" of excess Acraglass identifying the boundary of the wood to be removed, I use the flat of the file to begin removing the wood.

When the removal process comes to the underside of the buttstock, switch to a half round file.

I keep the receiver nearby, and with wood still to be removed, I slip the receiver on, and mark those areas from which more wood needs to be removed. I may repeat this process ten or twelve times. Each time marking the area for wood removal, and then using 320 grit wet and dry sandpaper on a steel block to sand only those areas. The time spent on this process pays big dividends in appearance later.

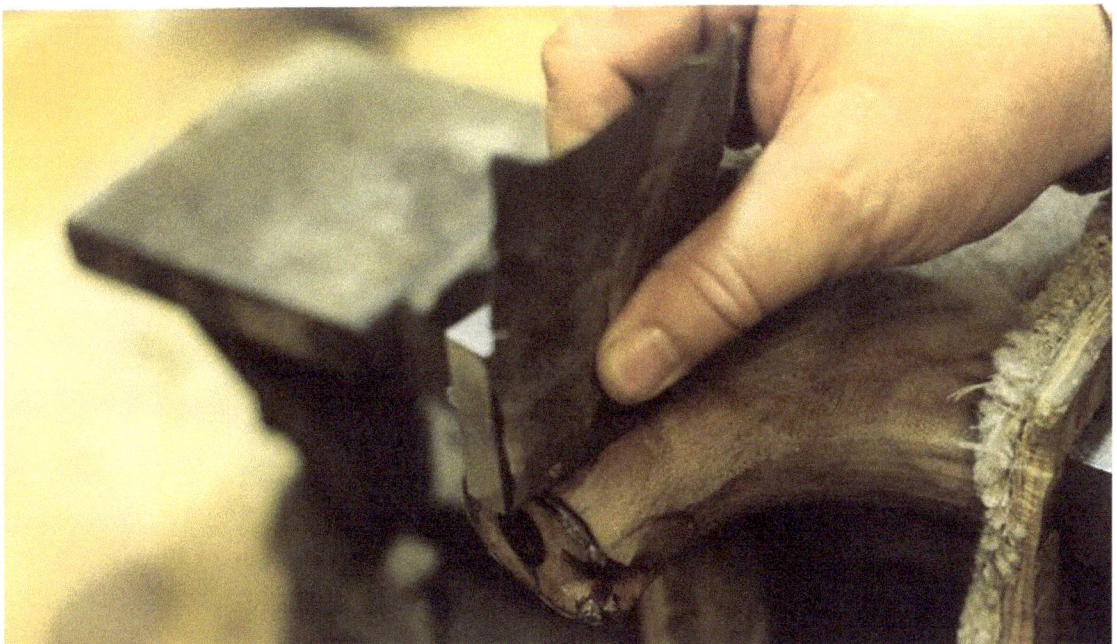

SECTION 4

STOCKING BOX LOCK SHOTGUNS

The receivers of box lock shotgun receivers are secured with a stock bolt, or with screws securing the receiver tang with the floor plate. I am going to go through the stock bolt secured actions first, and then cover the tang screw type.

The receiver of most box lock shotguns is secured to the buttstock with a stock bolt coming from the rear of the buttstock and engaging a threaded area between the upper and lower tangs of the receiver.

The angle of the stock bolt, the diameter and thread of the stock bolt, not to mention the length of the stock bolt vary with not only the make of the shotgun, but in some cases, with models of the same make. In some cases, I have had to turn and thread a piece of drill rod to obtain a dummy stock bolt, the worst case was a "drop by visit" to the hardware section of the parts store. While the length of my dummy stock bolts vary from three to six inches, I have found that four to five inches is the easiest length to work with.

I NEVER start inletting a box lock receiver to a buttstock without a dummy stock bolt. The dummy stock bolt is no more than a correctly threaded bolt section, without a head, which I screw into the receiver, and then insert into the stock bolt hole from the semi-inletted receiver end and use as a guide. For years I have continued to add to my collection of dummy stock bolts and have found them invaluable when fitting receivers to buttstocks. Most have a flat spot ground into the shank with a make and model number scratched into it.

This insures the receiver is sliding into the SAME position each time it is inserted into the stock for fitting. The use of this simple devise can save not only hours of time, but a nice piece of wood from the scrap pile.

The voice of experience speaks – I've done it.

Speaking of experience, did you know the Stock Maker's definition of "experience" is having done something wrong, and remembering not to do it again?

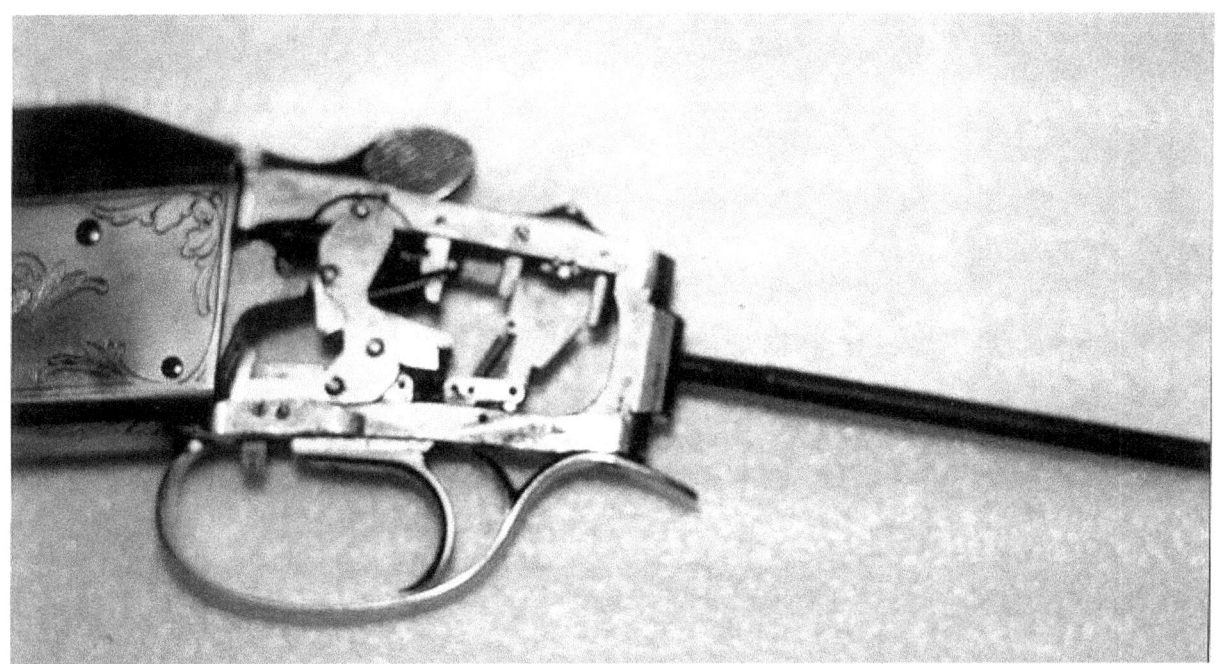

Did you notice in the above picture the trigger guard <u>has not been</u> removed? It will be before the receiver fitting is begun. Reason? The trigger guard is just one more thing that can cause a false impression or cause more work than is necessary. Fit the receiver to the wood, and then install the trigger guard onto the receiver – with the receiver anchored in the buttstock, - and then fit the trigger guard to the stock.

If the old butt stock is available, take a good look at the wood which comes in contact with the receiver, then look at the wood on the semi-finished butt stock. In most cases there is excess wood at the point at which the receiver matches the butt stock. A lot of time can be saved here with some judicious trimming of the excess wood but be careful. If there is a question at all as to how much wood to take off, leave it on.

I recently finished correcting a customer's error when he tried to fit an excellent piece of wood up to his Perazzi. Trouble was, he had removed far too much wood from the front of the buttstock, and in doing so almost lost several hundreds of dollars invested in the semi-finished butt stock. Take a little off at a time. And if the old butt stock is available, use it as your guide.

So, with the dummy stock bolt in place, use the sponge brush and inletting black to coat the sides and rear of the receiver tangs as well as the rear face of the receiver where it will eventually come in contact with the buttstock. And slowly slip the receiver into the inletting as par as it will go with only slight hand pressure. DO NOT force it, especially if the tangs are stepped or tapered, you could end the job before you get started if one side of the butt stock cracked or just fell off. Take your time, go slow and easy. If the wood has not been properly dried, or has too much or too little moisture, it is unstable and subject to be brittle of crack under pressure.

When inserting the action into the buttstock for the first time, take it slow, DO NOT FORCE it. Slide it in only as far as you can with hand pressure. DO NOT WIGGLE it, insert it straight in, and then remove it straight out. Unless the action is inserted and removed straight in, and straight out, the action will come in contact with the stock and leave false impressions.

You want to identify the points of contact between the receiver and the buttstock as will be indicated by the blackening agent. Believe me when I say you will be inserting the action into the buttstock many more times, the key here is to be patient. If there is any doubt about having created a false contact point, remove only the slightest amount of wood under the blackening agent, just enough to remove the blackening agent.

On this first time, you just want to get an idea of what to expect. How far into the buttstock will the receiver fit? Where are the points of contact? How dominant is one area over another? This is just an informational fitting, don't get excited – getting excited comes later.

Each stock maker, depending upon his preference, likes and dislikes, and in some cases, the phase the moon, uses a different technique and/or tool for remove the inletting black indicating a contact point between the wood and receiver. I use a scraper in a design given to me by Major Tom Martin and Hillary Burton. Brownell's carries scrapers similar, and when mine wear out, I will probably buy a set from them. The tool was simple to make, and is described in *Section 1,*

Tools. I have been using a tool of this design for over twenty-five years and wish someone would make them for sale.

Just remove the black area, no more than a few thousands should do the trick, and then insert the action again. Most of the time, the location of the black marks will change, repeat the process with the scraper and try it again. The hardest part of fitting a receiver to a semi-finished buttstock is to not get in a hurry but take your time and remove very little wood at a time.

For removing wood where the face of the buttstock comes in contact with the receiver, I have found that a very sharp chisel works really well. And I mean sharp. You will be cutting across the grain, and only a sharp chisel will make the cut and not drag the wood. Just for insurance, I always pass the chisel point across the leather strop loaded with yellow or green compound. Just gives the chisel that final edge which makes cutting the face of a stock easier.

With the receiver sitting in the buttstock just as it should, use an appropriate chisel, or Dremel Tool with a #115 cutter, to relieved the area inside the buttstock which will come in contact with the recoil shoulder of the receiver. This is the area in which absolute contact is essential, and I will make the statement which may upset some: No stock maker – regardless of his experience – can inlet this area and establish contact as well as bedding compound. On all competition guns I stock, I bed the recoil shoulder of the buttstock with Brownell's Steel Bed Rifle Bedding Compound. The following picture is of the area inside the buttstock into which the recoil shoulder of the receiver has been bedded. This will insure absolute placement of the received in the buttstock each time.

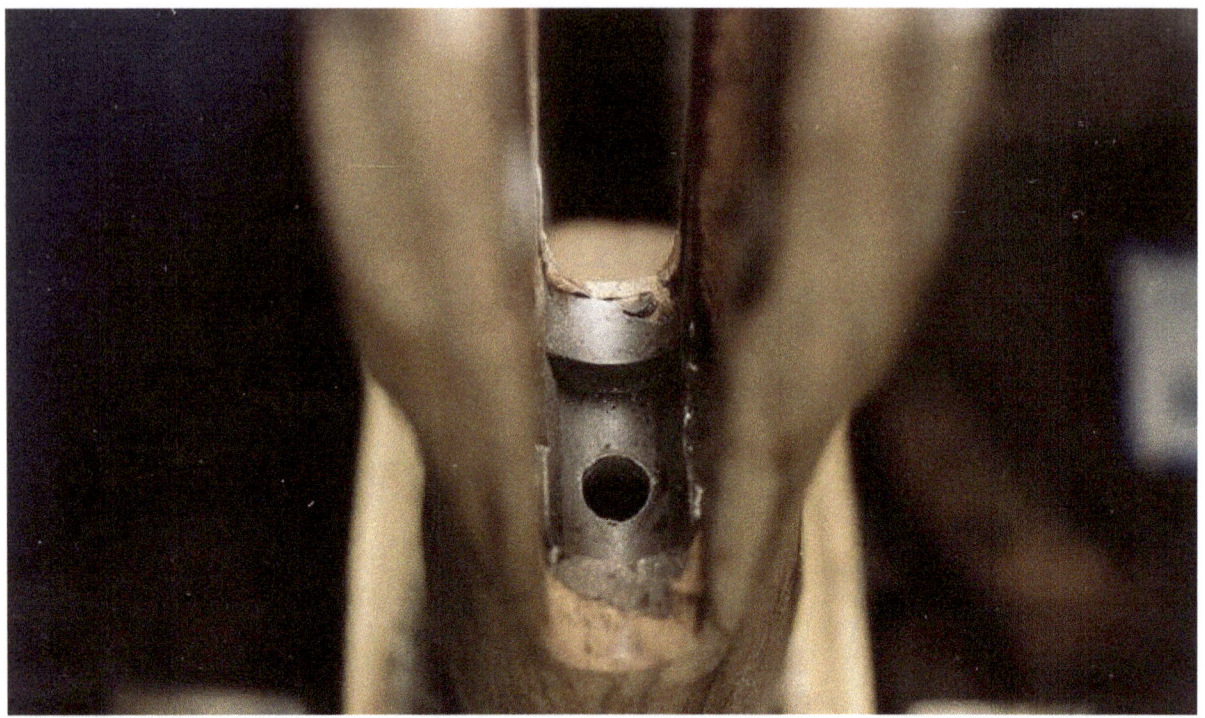

With the receiver fitted and the recoil shoulder bedded, now is the time to fit the trigger guard to the stock. I screw the trigger guard onto the receiver, then blacken the bottom of the trigger guard, and then turn and lower the tang down onto the stock. Tap it lightly, and move the trigger guard aside, leaving a darkened imprint of where the trigger guard will be.

No, the imprint is not the exact imprint of the trigger guard tang, it is the imprint of the part of the tang which touched the wood. Just as we have done on other parts of the inletting chore, use a appropriate chisel or scraper to remove the blackened area. One thing, this is one area where I DO advocate the use of a small burr on a Dremel tool to remove the necessary. But remember, be careful, go slow. The tool can make some drastic jumps and really mess up some wood.

With the receiver all inletted and the recoil shoulder bedded, and the trigger guard inletted, it is time to start getting rid of some wood. I like to use a good sharp chisel to take the excess wood level almost down to the tang level. Be very careful in which direction you remove wood, always go with the grain of the wood, and in cases of highly figured wood, or wood with fiddleback such as a fine grade of claro, take very slight cuts.

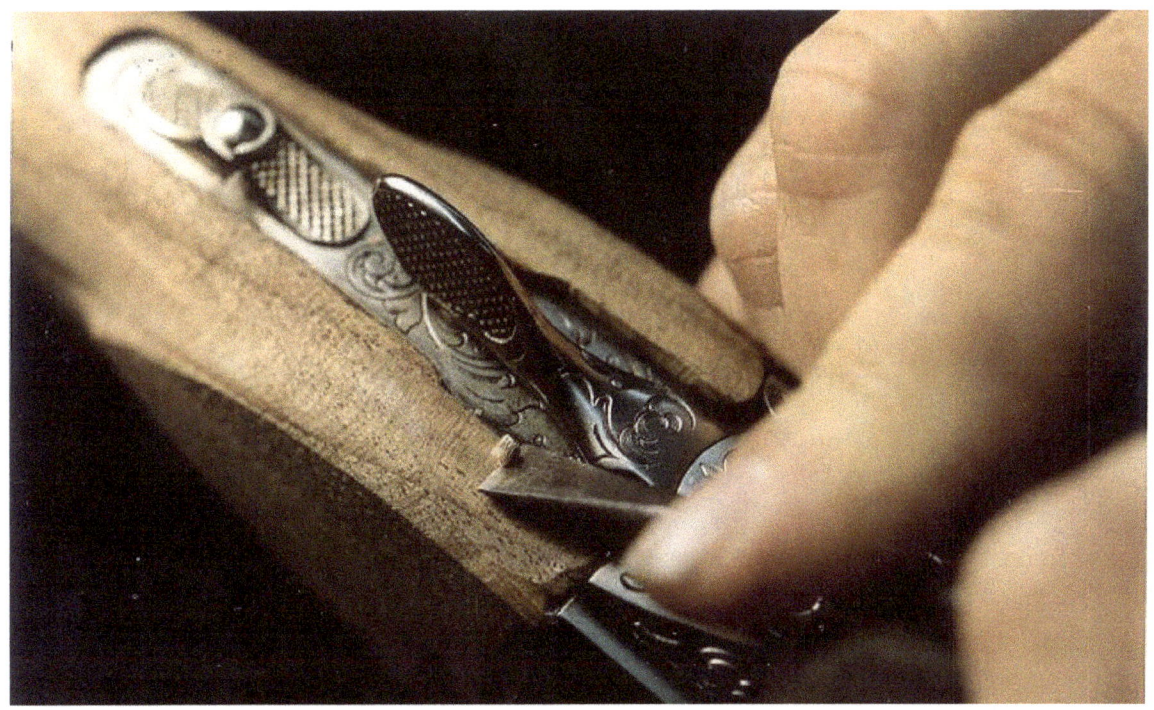

I leave enough wood above the surface of the tang to require a thorough sanding with some 100 grit paper followed by 220 grit paper. Before I remove the receiver from the buttstock, I use the fine point of a very small knife to track a line into the wood at the exact depth of the tang height. I simply lay the point of the knife across the top of the tang and cut / scribe a very faint line into the wood.

This is the marker I will use when filing or sanding the wood down to the final level, matching the tang height. There is not a lot of wood to be removed, and on highly figured stocks – I like Claro with a lot of fiddleback – there is not a lot of room for error. If the wood does not respond well to a file, I use a one-inch wide piece of self adhesive sandpaper – start with 100 grit – on a thin piece of scrap wood to "sand" the wood down. All the time I am sanding, I keep checking the cut / scribed line on the inside of the wood to insure I do not go below it. The ideal level is to barely remove it with the final sanding using 320 grit paper.

With the buttstock fitted to the receiver, the excess wood around the tangs removed and the trigger guard inletted, now comes the interesting part of shaping the outside of the buttstock. The one task that has eluded many just starting out is the raised wood to the rear of the receiver. As previously stated, I prefer to fit the receiver to the buttstock and leave the wood a little proud, about twenty to thirty thousands above the surface of the receiver at this stage.

If the original stock is available, I use a piece of paper from my note pad and cut a small rectangle or diamond from the center of the paper. Over this hole in the paper, I place a piece of masking tape or nylon filament tape. The purpose of this tape is to hold the paper in place while I use the flat of a pencil to trace the outline of the raised wood onto the paper.

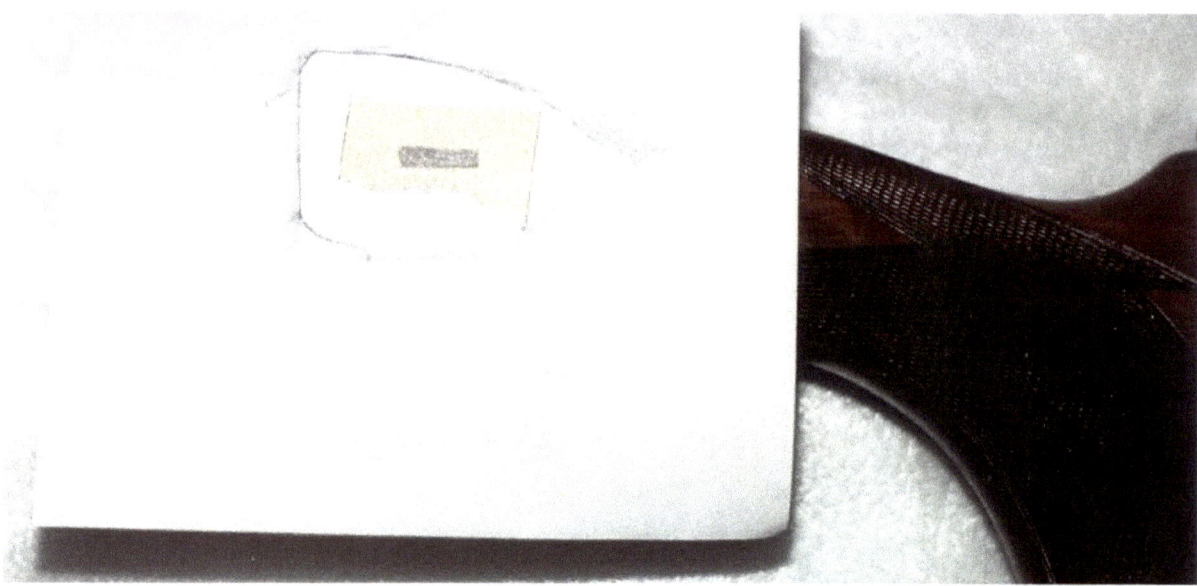

Now use a little care and the outline created should be very good. With the outline on paper, use some scissors or knife to cut the outline needed from the paper. You should end up with an exact copy of the outline of the raised area. Double check the piece you have traced and cut out, insurance that it is the correct shape and you have not made an error.

Using the front edge of the stock, position the paper copy on the replacement buttstock, and the outline traced onto the replacement buttstock with a pencil

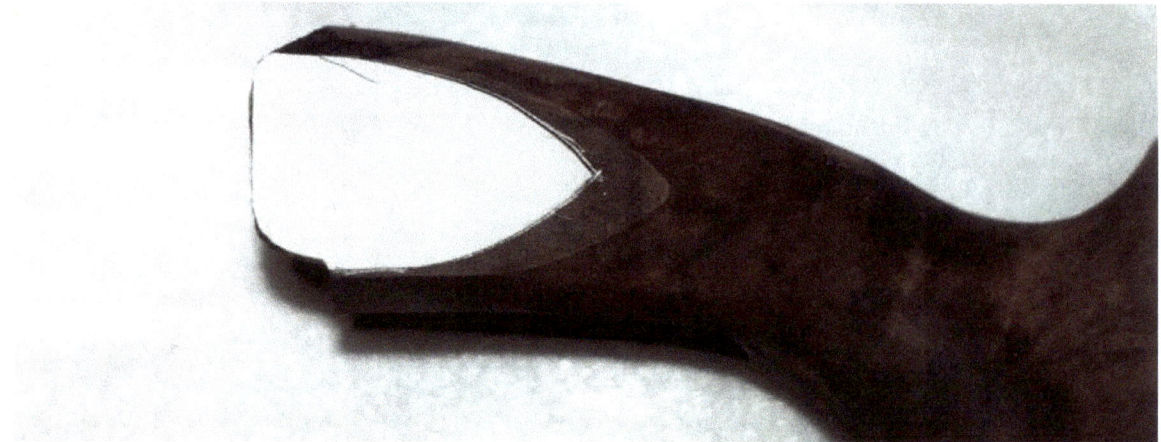

Just as you used care when copying the outline onto the paper, use the same care when tracing the outline of the paper onto the wood. For safety's sake, I use the rounded tip of a #2 lead pencil. In this manner, it I make an error in the tracing – yes, it does happen to the best of us – the time required to correct the error is minimal and does not include a deep mark into the wood.

On the picture below, please note how much excess wood was left on the semi-finished buttstock, lots of wood to remove, or to enlarge the area.

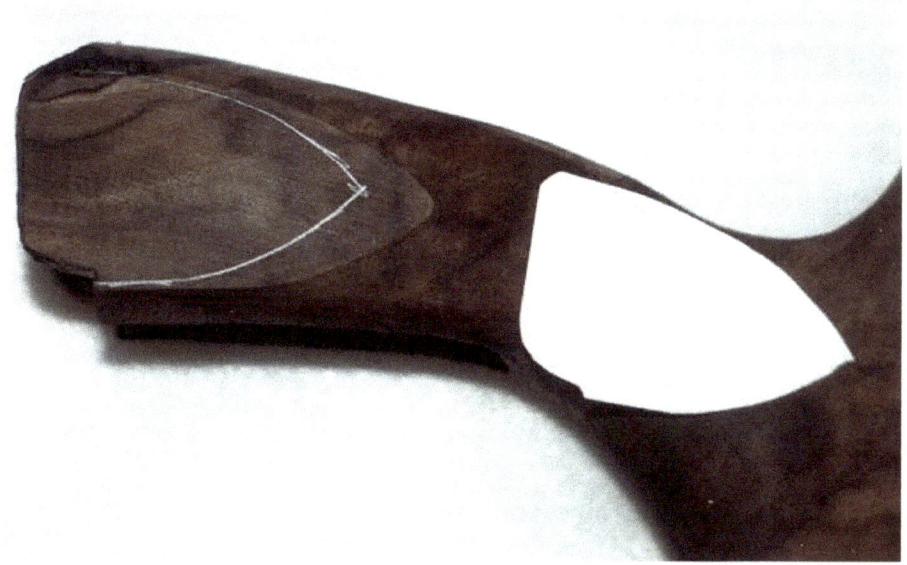

To establish the same pattern for the opposite side, just reverse the paper, laying it face down, and the same pattern will be on both sides. I do not view this "mirror" effect as being essential to a pleasing contour of the receiver, close? Yes.

The next part of the task requires some familiarization and practice with the tools to be used– relieving the wood around the proposed raised area. The tool I use, the Gunline half inch barrel inletting tool, does the task well when controlled, or it can create an unsightly rounded over mess if not controlled. I also have several "non-standard" size barrel inletting tools on which the cutter discs have been removed from the tool and resized on a mandrel on a lathe. The assortment of these tools allows me to vary the radius being cut to in the wood.

I have observed others using the same technique, but the California Stockmaker that selected a short-handled gouge from his bench and made quick work of the task most impressed me. Perhaps in another ten or fifteen years, I will be comfortable enough with his technique to use it. At the time I observed him, he had been making stocks longer than I had been alive! I keep telling you it just takes patience…

Working slowly and carefully, from the outside in towards the pencil line, and cutting with the grain. Make one short cut at a time, always cutting with the wood. To cut against it can increase your sanding time several fold. The time you take will result in a quality product.

The next type of received will be one in which the upper and lower tangs are held to the buttstock with several screws passing through the wood and anchoring in the tangs. There is no stock bolt coming through the buttstock and screwing into the receiver and pulling and holding it in the buttstock. On these actions, the lower tang comes loose from the receiver. A Fox Sterlingworth is an excellent example of such an action.

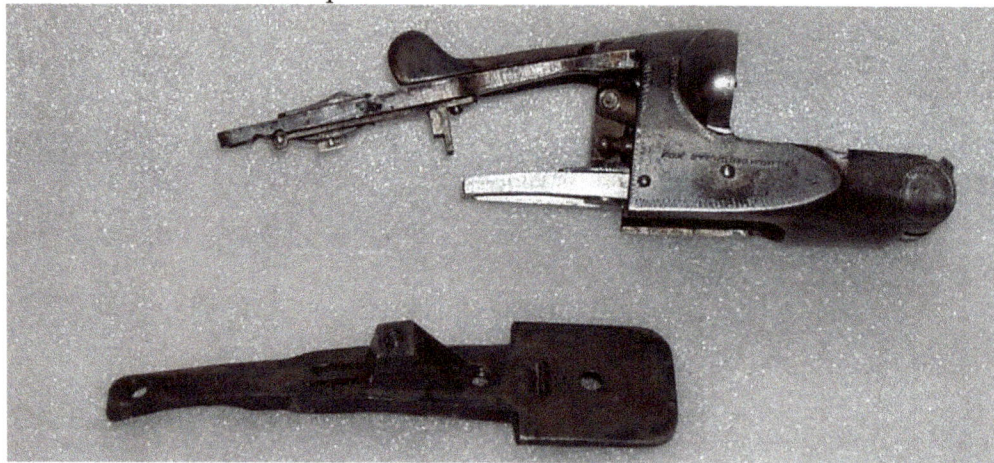

The first step is to inlet the upper tang into the semi-finished stock, but before anything is even started, the receiver must be stripped and thoroughly cleaned. The older actions will build up a lot of material which needs to be removed before it either gets inletted for as metal, or come off during the inletting and causes a "Huh? moment.

Strip it and clean it. Even the trigger plate! I have found that a stiff bristled toothbrush and some brake or carburetor cleaner works well.

This is a prime example of someone having attempted to stock a Fox Sterlingworth and failed to insure moving parts clearance below the wood surface. The picture below is how I received the gun.

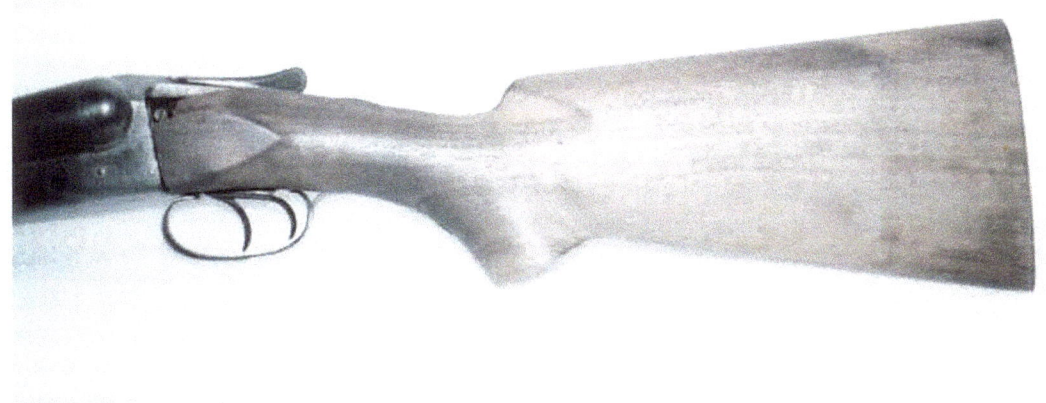

SECTION 5

Fitting Forearms

A forearm on a shotgun can make or break both your spirit and your job cost. Forearms run the gauntlet from fairly easy, to being one bad task, to something just short of impossible. This is especially true when the forearm is from the same blank as the buttstock, mess the forearm up and replacing it with matching wood will create gray hair and stomach problems even the best anti acid can't touch

While I will cover forearms for side by side, pump and semi-automatic shotguns, the vast majority of my work in making replacement forearms has been over and unders for competition trap and skeet shooters as part of an upgrade of the wood on the gun.

I prefer to obtain semi-finished forearms from a reputable firm, such as Wenig Custom Gunstocks, Lincoln, MO. They have an excellent inventory of patterns, and their duplicating is very close. Should the customer want something special, the use of bondo or built up layers of tape on the customer's forearm can create the dimensions the customer wants. The pattern is then duplicated into a semi-finished forearm.

The key word is *semi-finished*. The wood is not going to fit directly onto the metal without a lot of scraping and fitting. There is a lot of work remaining.

I will cover fitting three types of forearms to the forearm iron and then to the receiver and barrel. The Over and Under (O/U) first, then the side by side double and finally the pump and semi auto forearms.

The semi-finished forearms received from a firm such as Wenig's, will still have a lot of fitting to do, but the vast majority of it has been done.

KRIEGHOFF MODEL K-80

The first example of an O/U I will use is for a Krieghoff K-80. Fitting the forearm can be divided into several stages of work: The first is to remove the excess wood left over from the duplication process.

In the tools section, I cite the importance of the small block plane, removing the excess wood from a semi-finished forearm is a prime example for its use.

With the excess wood on the outside removed, and the small pieces of wood on the ends used to connect the forearm during the duplication process also cut off – I use a band saw with a fine toothed blade – there is still additional excess wood to be removed and/or blended into the forearm shape.

As with all other tasks involving the removal of wood, remove a little at a time.

    Be very careful before making any cuts to remove the excess wood. Make a very small cut to confirm which way the grain of the wood is running. At this stage of the task at hand, attempting to make too large a cut, with the grain running the wrong way and splintering out the wood, could relegate the semi-finished forearm to the kindling pile. I have found that in most cases, cutting from the top down is a safe way to start the removal.
    I remove the excess wood with a series of shallow cuts – sometimes I follow my own advise and take a little off at a time – completing one side before going to the other. for the purpose of the picture I am holding the forearm with one hand and the chisel with the other. As a rule, I like to have the forearm secured in a pipe vice or directly in the jaws of the vise.

At the front of the forearm, there will usually be an excess of wood remaining. In this case a small nub on either side of the forearm. With the forearm secured vertically in the vise, I remove the excess wood with either a file or chisel, depending upon the grain of the wood. I remove enough wood only far enough to blend in with the contour of the forearm. At this point I do not begin shaping the forearm to final contour, that will come later, much later. Although there is also excess wood in the barrel channel, I leave it.

With the excess wood removed from the forearm, it is time to begin fitting the forearm iron into the wood. After using the blackening agent to coat the sides of the forearm iron, I try inserting the forearm iron into the wood. In most cases, it won't even begin to go into the wood. In the case of this Krieghoff forearm, I "spread" the wood a little, and I mean **little**, and start the forearm iron into the forearm.

Inserting the iron into the wood no more than a half inch, I removing the iron. I can readily see the black contact agent that has transferred to the wood. Depending upon how much contact agent, and where it is located, I use either a scraper or chisel to remove it, no more than a few thousands.

Insert the wood again, don't force the iron into the wood or it will split and you will have a two piece forearm very quickly. After several insertion and scraping sessions, usually ten to fifteen, the forearm iron will begin to start in alright, but quickly become tight, leaving contact agent on the wood. This is good, just keep scraping or cutting it off.

As the forearm iron begins to go in full depth, the forearm iron will come in contact with the wood at the rear of the forearm, and about the same time, make contact with the forward area of the inletting. Do Not anticipate anything and begin "saving time" by taking out a large amount of wood. Take off only what has black contact agent on it.

The Krieghoff forearm has a small ridge of wood which fits into a recess cut into the forearm iron. This little ridge of wood is critical in the fitting process, be very careful to retain it when contouring the rear of the forearm to match the forearm iron.

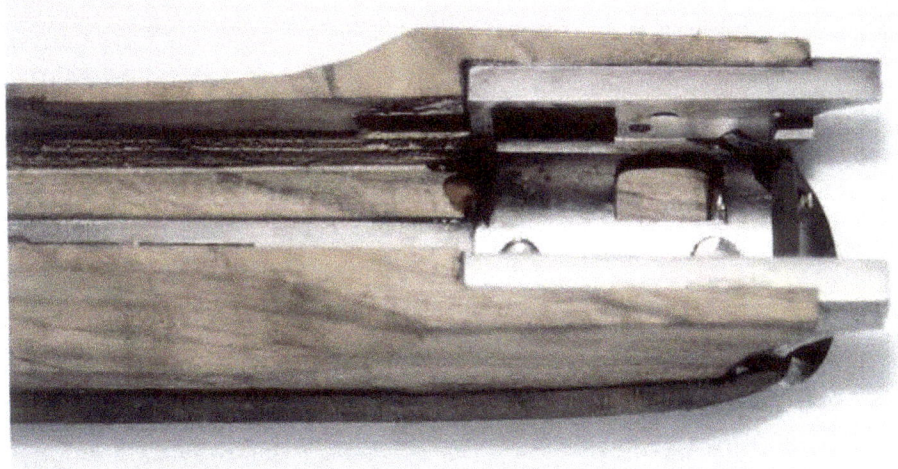

    With the wood fitted to the metal, you are at a point at which everything you are about to do, if not done properly, can make a mess out of your work. The two holes for the forearm iron screws must be drilled into the wood.

    Go through your drill index and select the EXACT size drill for the holes in the metal forearm iron. If at all possible, use a drill press to insure the holes you are about to drill are perfectly vertical.

    Drill down through the wood FROM THE INSIDE of the forearm.

    Now comes the fun part, <u>the small forearm rosettes must be inletted</u> into the bottom of the wood.

    First, I will tell you how I accomplished this task for many years, and then I will tell you how I shortened this task to a two minute no risk job.

    With the just used drill still in the chuck of the drill press, align the drill so it will once again pass through the hole, and secure the forearm, metal down, to the bed of the drill press. A cross feed vise works well.

    Remove the drill from the chuck, measure the shoulder diameter of the rosette, and select a drill of this diameter or just a few thousands larger. Enlarge the hole in the forearm – the drill you are using should self-center into the already drilled hole – to the <u>thickness</u> of the rosette, approximately 3/16". But measure the rosette you are using as there are several variations.

    Remove the drill from the chuck, measure the diameter of the rosette, select a drill of this diameter of just a few thousands larger. Using this drill, enlarge the hole in the forearm once again to a depth equal to the thickness of the cap of the rosette.

    The rosette should fit down into the hole, and align with the hole in the forearm iron. And it should look good, no gaps and the forearm wood should still be perfectly to the forearm iron. The preceding is how I accomplished this task for years.

    I now remove a custom ground stepped drill from my fixture box and chuck it up.

I use the first step to drill down through the forearm iron into and through the wood. Then turn the forearm over, metal down, and insert the first step down through the hole just drilled, and use the second step to drill the enlargement for the shoulder and then on down to for the larger hole for the cap of the rosette. Done.

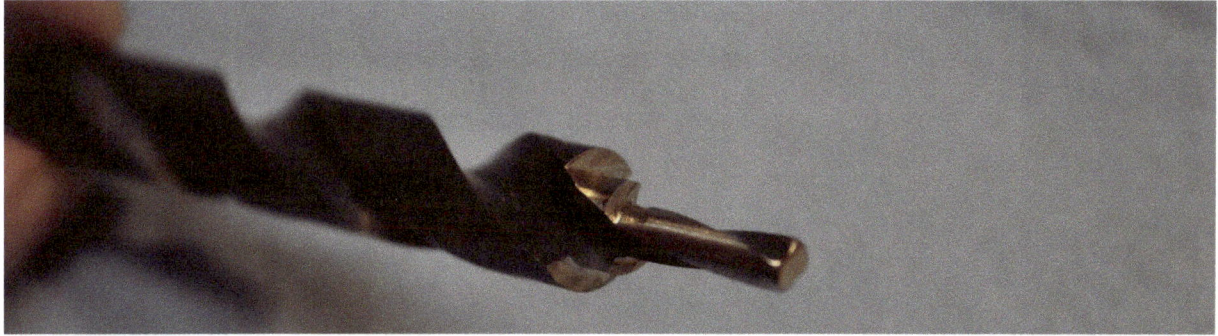

I traded a recoil pad and installation to a machinist for the custom ground drill made to my specifications.

Just a note here: I use the Krieghoff Forearm Rosettes for most of the forearms requiring them.

REMINGTON MODEL 1100

The semi-finished forearm in standard grade American Walnut for the Remington Model 1100 or Model 11-87 will look much like the one pictured.

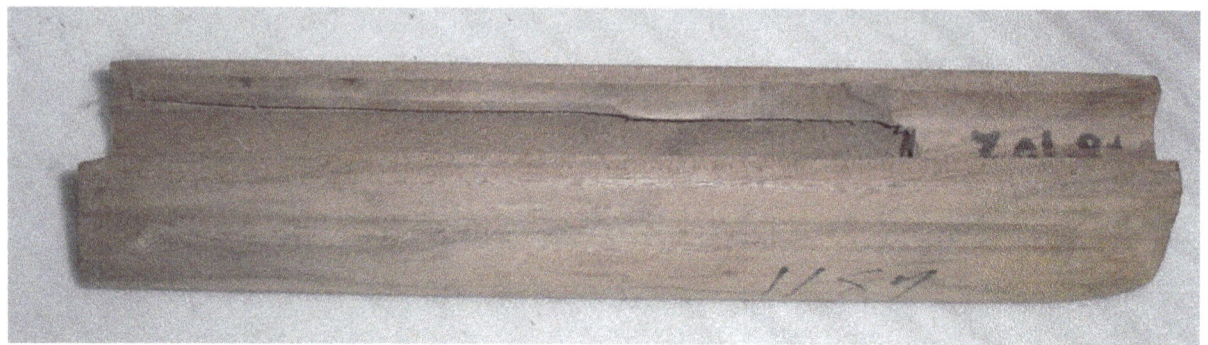

One of the first tasks at hand is to remove the excess wood from the rear of the forearm. It usually consists of a small ridge remaining from the excess wood which allowed it to be held for turning in the duplicator. This wood was separated from the forearm with a band saw cut. This ridge of wood and is seldom thicker or higher than an eighth inch. But unless approached with caution, can create an unsightly mess which is difficult to straighten out.

I use a sharp wood chisel carefully remove it, <u>cutting from the inside of the forearm towards the outside</u>, thus eliminating the possibility of wood chipping off.

After the ridge of excess wood has been removed, I prefer to use a flat steel block with 220 grit paper to smooth the wood. However, a hard rubber sanding block will work, as shown.

With the excess wood removed, the end of the forearm leveled and smoothed, the process of fitting the forearm to a barreled action can begin. On the Remington Model 1100 Semi-Automatic shotgun, there are several contact points which will become apparent as the forearm is fitted to the shotgun.

First, with the sanding block holding the 220 grit sand paper, lightly smooth the top of the forearm, removing the duplicator cutter marks and smoothing out the surface to receive what is to follow.

With the barrel installed on the receiver of the shotgun, after being certain the weapon is unloaded, slip the semi-finished forearm over the magazine tube. Do not force the wood, light hand pressure only. In this case, the forearm slid down within an inch of the receiver. Good. Some I have had wouldn't fit over the magazine tube without opening up the hole.

Time for the Inletting Black. As previously mentioned, I use a one-inch sponge brush to spread the inletting black over the metal surface to be fitted. In this case, I spread it lightly along the barrel, around the barrel ring, and the forward edges of the receiver. And then…and then…slip the forearm over the magazine tube to the rear with only hand pressure. If it binds, stop. Do not force it. In this case, the forearm went back within an inch of the receiver, but the barrel channel of the forearm was making solid contact at several places.

Using a soft lead pencil, lightly trace down the sides of the barrel leaving a thin pencil mark on the top of the forearm wood that you have smoothed with the sanding block. Now the thin pencil line will show clearly.

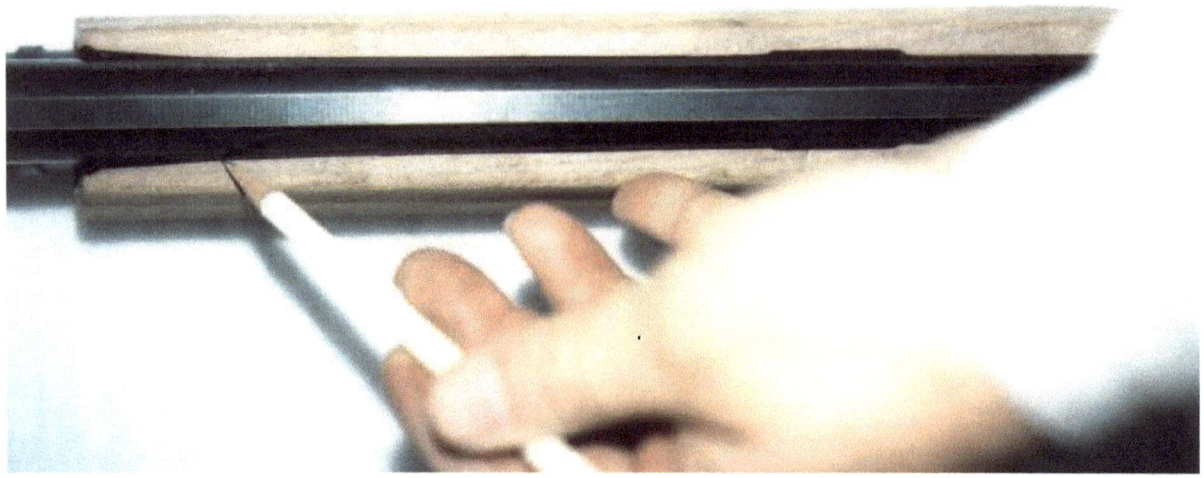

Remove the forearm from the metal, and look for contact points at which the inletting black transferred from the metal of the barrel and receiver to the forearm.

The best tool, in my opinion, for removing the inletting black and inletting the forearm for the barrel, is Gunline's Barrel Inletting Tool. It is offered in several diameters – I have them all – and choose one which will fit the barrel radius of the channel I am working on. I cannot tell you of the times the tool has gone over the edge of a barrel channel and ruined a perfect edge. Using this tool is like milking a rattle snake, be careful, go slow, and do not take anything for granted and the results will be rewarding.

WINCHESTER MODEL 12

The Winchester Model 12 shotgun had had a variety of styles of forearms over the years. The one pictured below was obtained at an auction. I am not certain who turned it, but believe it was Fajen as I came into possession of it about the time they were going out of business. I am a great bargain hunte and have several large boxes of used and semi-finished forearm and have little or no idea of what they fit. The common thread between all of them was their price – They were a bargain!

Regardless, I came into possession of the pictured forearm, and have held it back for a number of years, hoping to find a buttstock with the matching fiddleback – no buttstock yet.

The Model 12 forearm appears very simple, and for the most part it is, however, once the connecting wood at the front of the forearm is removed in the fitting process, the forearm is easily cracked – the voice of experience speaks!

The first step in the fitting process is to fit the forearm to the action slide assembly. The action slide assembly tube should slide into the forearm with little of no resistance. Under no circumstances should you have to force it, much less use a wooden block or nylon hammer. If the slide assembly does not slide into the forearm, the hole in the forearm must be enlarged. This is seldom the case. The most common cause for the failure for the forearm iron to not go to full depth is the action arm at the side which goes back to the action.

With the forearm iron installed, it is time to assemble the receiver and barrel assembly and insure the forearm wood allows free movement of the slide assembly.

BERETTA MODEL 682

The Beretta 682 and associated models, such as the 680, 686 and 687 present a unique problem when fitting the forearm, the entire forearm latch is attached to the forearm iron, and must fit precisely into the hole in the forearm, while at the same time, the forearm must match the contour of the forearm iron. The first time I fitted a forearm to a forearm iron such as this was a test of will. It was about as much fun as juggling flaming balls of cat turds while wearing white gloves. And there is no easy way to do it, other than having patience and taking it slowly.

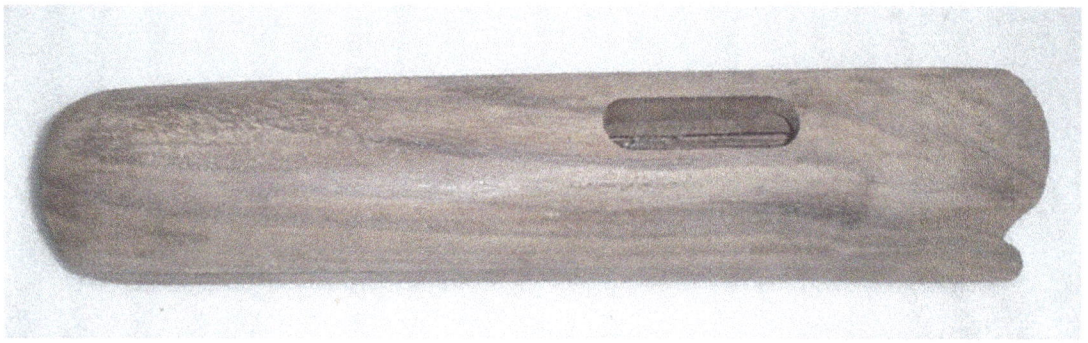

The forearm iron, does not slip directly into the forearm. First, the rear inside of the forearm iron must be given a coating of black contact agent. This will provide a good reference as to how much wood must be removed to accommodate the forearm iron.

The rear of the forearm must first be fitted to the radius of the forearm iron, and once done, the rear of the forearm latch hole must be beveled ever so slightly – FROM THE INSIDE – to allow the forearm iron to lowered into position through the hole. Use of the blackening agent will be a great aid in determining how much wood must be beveled.

With the forearm inletted to the forearm iron, the holes for the forearm screws must be drilled and the rosettes installed in the forearm. To insure the forearm does not move during this process, a surgical tubing donut is used to hold the forearm iron in place.

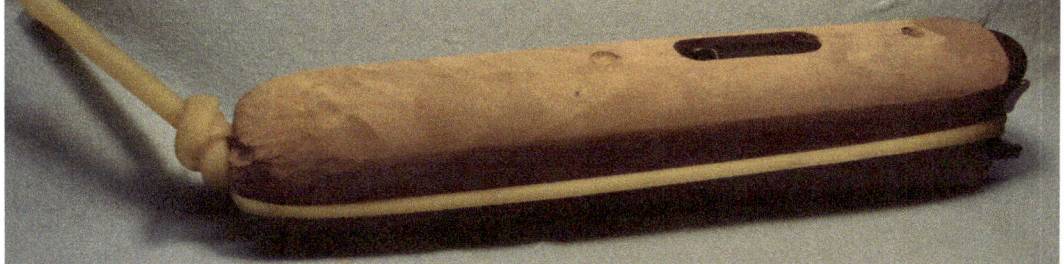

A drill the exact size of the forearm hole is drilled down through the forearm iron and through the forearm.

With the pilot hole drilled through the forearm, the piloted drill is used to drill a hole for the rosette.

When starting the hole, go slowly so as to not tear the wood, but to follow the pilot hole

Check the depth of the shoulder frequently, drilling too deep can cause additional problems in seating the rosettes.

And this is what the finished product should look like. The rosettes are seated to an appropriate depth and the edges of the holes illustrate a very clean cut.

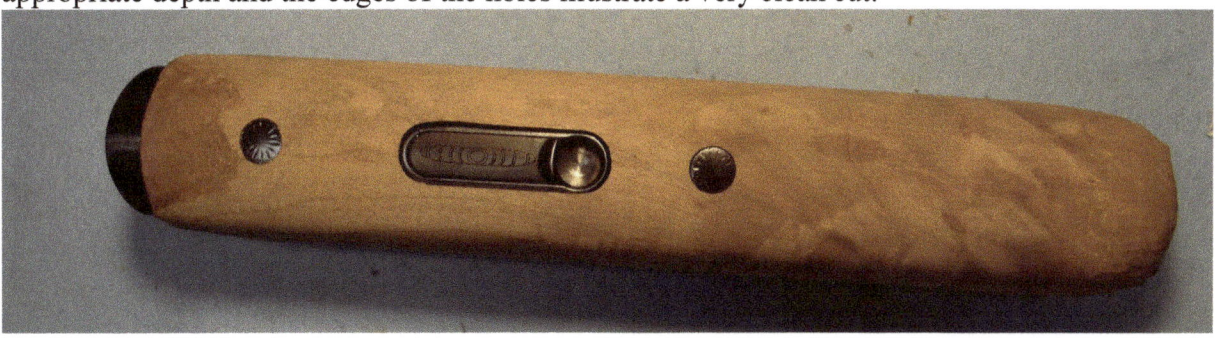

L.C. SMITH Splinter Type

The first thing to do is to remove the excess wood from the rear of the forearm. This is the area which will have contact between the forearm iron and the wood of the forearm. There are several ways to quickly remove the excess wood. One can use a file, a chisel, or a powered disc or belt sander. I have used them all, and have toyed with the idea of a trained beaver…

But I prefer using a sharp wood chisel to gradually remove the excess wood. On a snap on splinter forearm, where you are not concerned with the forearm latch coming up through the bottom of the forearm, the amount of wood removed from the rear of the forearm is not critical. But where a forearm latch is present, the distance from the rear of the forearm to the forearm latch hole is critical for a neat appearance. I leave the method of removal to your imagination, but I will stick with a sharp chisel and recommend you do to.

With the excess wood removed, it is time to square the rear of the forearm. I, on occasions, use a ten-inch mill bastard file to do this job, but in this case where the surface area is so small, I ise a flat steel plate with 220 grip sandpaper over it. Do not use a rubber sanding block for this task. The sanding block will not give you a flat surface needed to match the forearm iron. Use a small piece of flat steel, or on worse case, wrap the sand paper around a 12 inch mill bastard file and use it as a sanding block. I cannot emphasize enough to be very careful when squaring the end of the forearm. Inattention to detail here can reflect poor workmanship and / or cause a lot of extra work straightening it out later.

With the end of the forearm squared, slip the forearm iron into the wood using hand pressure only, as I have done in the following picture. Look at that! The forearm iron only lacks a quarter inch to fit up to the wood! Oh, this forearm came from Wenig's Custom Gunstocks, Lincoln, MO. I have fitted many forearms over the years on which the forearm iron would not even begin to enter the wood. Makes for a lot of scraping and cutting.

After removing the forearm iron, I coat the sides and bottom of the forearm iron with a blackening agent and slip it in again. After removing it, I scrape the blackening agent from the forearm. Remember, just scrape the blackening agent, do not get handy with a chisel or worse yet, a hand held high speed grinder. When the end of the forearm iron comes in contact with the back of the forearm, you are close.

Carefully, and I mean really carefully, remove the blackening agent, recoat the forearm iron, and try the fit again. Keep doing this until black contact is shown across the back of the forearm.

Decision Time: If you are attempting to restore the weapon to museum quality, the screw hole in the forearm iron is meant for a wood screw. Be absolutely sure to pre-drill the hole for the screw accurately, because if it is not drilled correctly, when the screw is installed, it can destroy the fit of the forearm iron to the forearm. I put a drop or two of AcraGlass in the screw hole before installing the screw.

If, however, the gun is to be a hunting gun, I use the Krieghoff Technique and install a rosette in the forearm. This ensured do problems with the fit of metal to wood, and the forearm will not come loose from the forearm iron.

L.C. SMITH Splinter Type
(with oval latch)

The first task at hand is to remove the excess wood, and on this forearm, there is excess wood at each end. At the front of the forearm, there is a "rise" that needs to be removed. I have removed similar wood in the past, and have used a block plane, a wood chisel, a file and a belt sander. As the block plane is the most direct, and I happen to believe the most controllable, it will be used to remove the excess wood.

But before anything is done, the wood must be secured. I use the pipe vise – my checkering cradle – to hold the forearm and apply the sharp blade of the block plane.

The wood at the rear is removed in the same manner as the previous described forearm, and the rear of the forearm squared off. In fact, the entire process of inletting the forearm iron is the same. Once the forearm iron has been inletted, the difference and most of the work begins. On this semi-finished forearm, the inletting for the forearm latch cover has been roughed out.

But before the final inletting takes place, a reference point must be established on where you want the forearm latch to end up on the forearm. And that reference point if the forward hole in the forearm iron through which a forearm machine screw comes through and anchors the forearm latch cover. If this hole is drilled correctly, the placement of the forearm latch cover will likewise be positioned correctly.

With the forearm secured, and the top (where the barrels will contact the forearm) level, select a drill the exact size of the hole, and – using a drill press preferably, with the forearm held in a machinist's vise – drill down through the forearm wood into the inletted area.

At this point, you have a hole through the forearm which should line up with the threaded hole in the forearm latch cover. Placing the forearm latch cover over the roughed-out hole in the forearm, you can either "eyeball" the alignment of the screw hole to the forearm latch cover, OR, secure a threaded screw at least a half inch longer than the existing screw and use it as an inletting guide. I prefer the latter method, and have a small bottle (formerly held my "patience pills") in which I store different sizes of screws used for this purpose.

With the forearm iron fitted to the wood, it is time to begin the fitting to the barreled action. First, give the lower part of the barrels, all of the way back to the receiver, a good coating of inletting black. Mine can be clearly seen on the picture below. With forearms with a latch, the forearms will usually snap into place with a good loud snap. But they can be easily removed with finger pressure. It is the forearm latch which will engage when the forearm is correctly fitted that will keep the forearm attached to the barreled action.

The forearm latch on this forearm is appears much like a roller, and when fitting the forearm it is difficult to judge your progress. To monitor my progress when fitting this type of forearm, I use a simple means of judging my progress. Lay a narrow piece of tape across the forearm latch cover and over the latch. I then use a cutter to separate the tape covering the roller from the tape covering the latch.

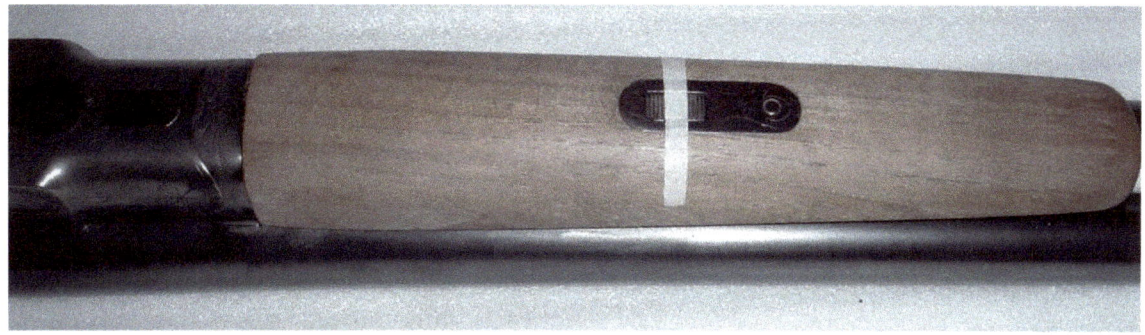

As the fitting progresses, the tape on the roller will move as the forearm latch comes to full engagement with the forearm lug. When in question as to your progress, just consult the position of the roller tape in proximity to the tape on the latch cover.

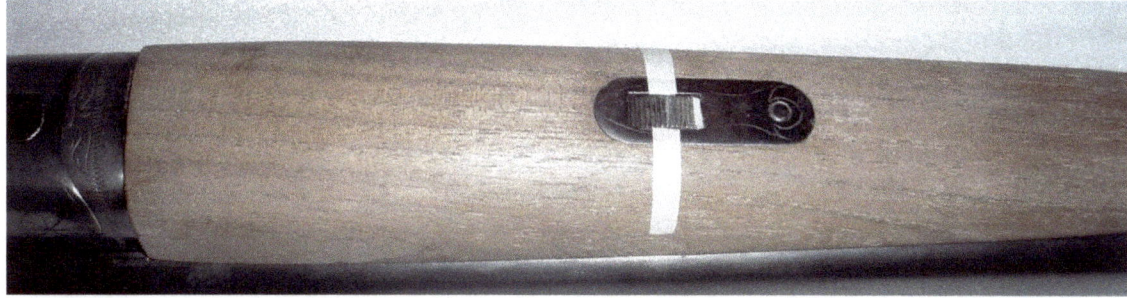

The edges of the forearm must be maintained, without a run over from the tool used to remove the inletting black from the barrel channel of the barrel inletting tool. As the barrel inletting tool takes some time to get used to, for the novice, I suggest a tool I used for several years and still find cause for occasionally. It is a small piece of adhesive sandpaper – I prefer the 100 grit – wrapped around a piece of wooden dowel slightly smaller than the diameter of the barrel being fitted. I cut off just enough to go half way around the dowel, place the dowel in the middle of it with the end of the dowel right on the edge of the paper, and press fit the adhesive sand paper to the dowel. If I am not going to use it right away, I will wrap a rubber band around it to "help" the adhesive adhere to the dowel. Makes for a nice makeshift tool.

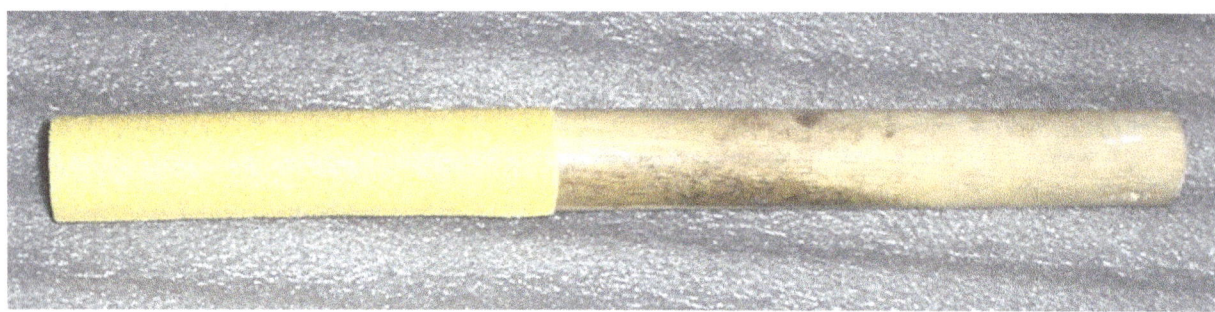

With the forearm fitted to the barreled action, and the exterior of the forearm shaped and sanded down to 320 grit paper, disassemble the forearm metal from the forearm. Before starting to finish the forearm, use another deep penetrating finish to seal all of the "inside wood" of the forearm. I use a fine texture toothbrush for this purpose, the kind on sale for $.49 at most department stores. Works well for getting the finish down into the inletted areas.

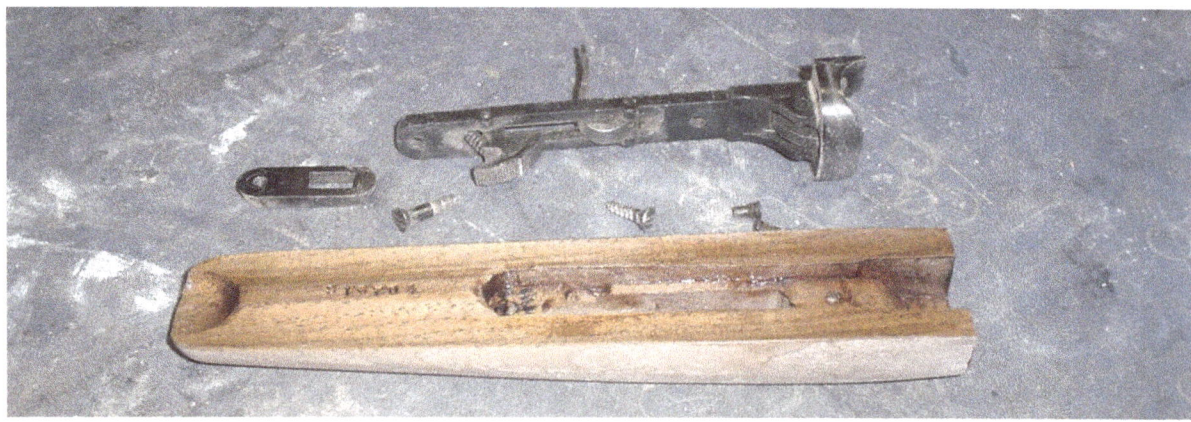

L.C. SMITH Beavertail Forearm
(with oval latch)

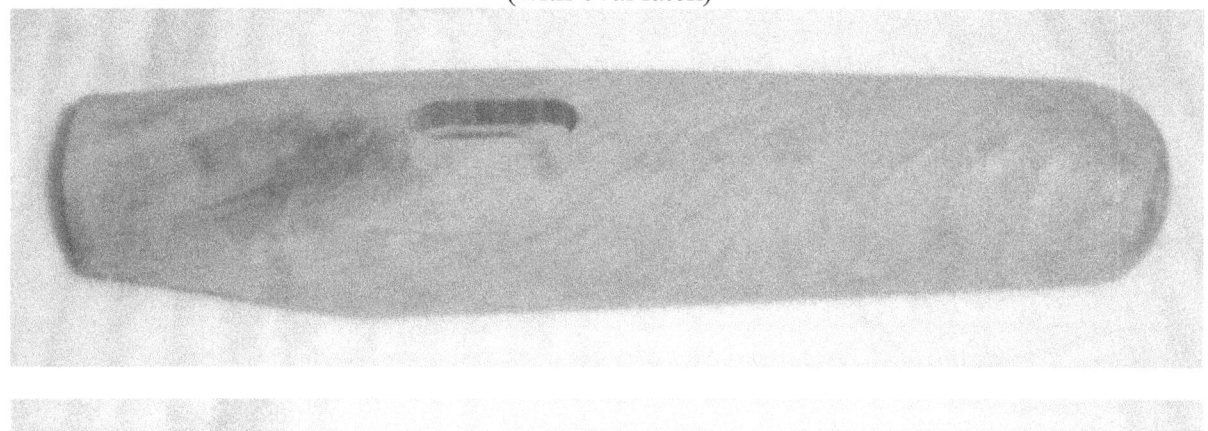

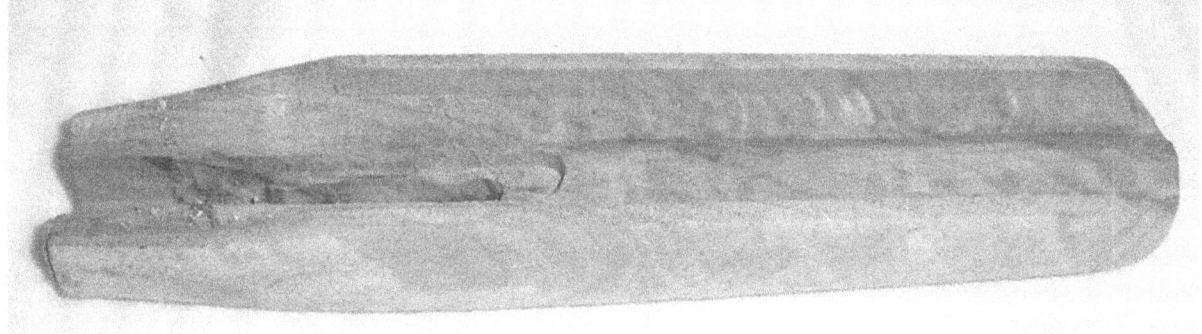

As with the previous versions of the L.C. Smith forearms, the rear of the forearm must be square, the forearm iron inletted and the latch plate cover inletted. But the really fun part is inletting the forearm to allow it over the barrels – and to inlet it closely, leaving no gaps. So, I will skip over squaring the rear of the forearm.

SECTION 6
Finishing Semi-Finished Stocks and Forearms

At this point, the buttstock and forearm have been fitted to the metal, all excess wood removed, and the wood rough sanded with 320 grit paper. If you are not at this point in the restocking/stocking process, go back to the Section of stocking the type of action you are dealing with. **This section deals only with applying the finish to the wood**.

Comfortable that the stock is thoroughly sanded and ready for the sealer in preparation for the finish, a little knowledge is necessary. First, which finish will be used? This decision should be made based on the expected use of the gun, NOT which finish is on hand, or which finish is the least expensive.

But go back a moment, a major question to be answered first is how the stock, or buttstock or forearm is to be held while the finish is being applied? The following are some suggestions:

I am fond of using the wire from heavy duty clothes hangers and different diameters of hard wood dowels as a mean of hanging stocks which are anchored to the action with a stock bolt of action tube nut.

I drill a 1/16" hole in one end of the dowel, and insert the wire, secure the wire in a vise and drive it a little deeper into the dowel until it is securely held in place.

I insert the dowel into the stock bolt hole from the butt end and use it as a handle with the wire protruding through the face of the stock.

I also keep an assortment of different sized dowels on hand for just this purpose. Most are about a foot long, some a little shorter, some a little longer.

If the fit is loose, but the next size larger dowel is too large for the hole, I use a little masking tape or duct tape to increase the size of the dowel until it provides a snug fit

With the wire protruding through the stock, I bend the first half inch or so of the wire into a hook from which to hang the stock in the drying box. A very simple manner of handling the buttstock when applying finish as well as handing it up to dry.

For forearms such as the Krieghoff Model 32 and K-80, I have an eighteen-inch length of black pipe drilled with holes spaced to the forearm bushing measurements, and use two screws of the appropriate thread and size to secure the forearm to the metal. I not only use this "tool" for holding the forearm for finishing, but also for holding it when checkering it. To keep the screws in place when not in use, I place a small piece of nylon filament tape over the screw hole, cut a very small slot in it, and shove the screw through the slot. The tape keeps the screw in position for the next use.

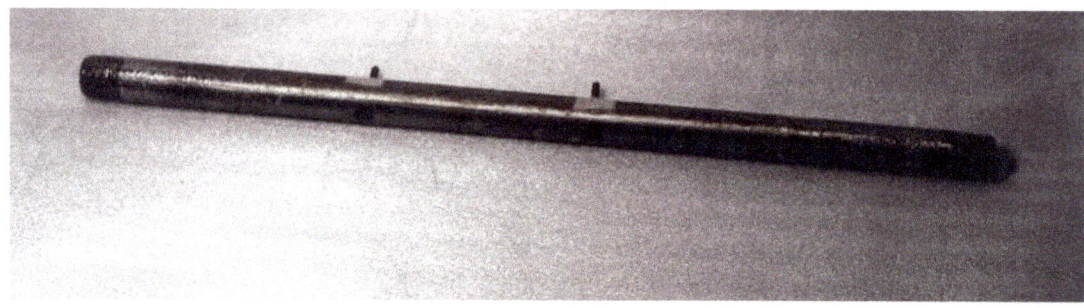

For finishing a forearm, a section of wooden dowel can be used and the appropriate holes drilled for the anchoring screws. The dowel can be cut, shaped and sanded to fit a variety of contours and the holes are easily drilled in the wood, and if an error is made, easily corrected. On the pictured example, notice that the wire from which the project is suspended is passing through a hole in the dowel and then securely twisted into a permanent position. It works!

For forearms such as the Remington Model 1100 with the huge hole in it for the magazine tube, I use a large dowel that fits snuggly into the hole, and then place a screw into the dowel to keep it from slipping off. Just the need for a little insurance, learned the hard way.

Forearms such as the Perazzi and KOLAR, I have several small threaded discs which I secure in place with a correctly threaded screw through a section of black pipe. It works well and provides a secure means of holding the forearm for a variety of tasks.

On rifle stocks, such as Mauser, Rem 700 series, Winchester 70 and most bolt action rifles, I use a piece of ½" dowel laid in the barrel channel and extending back over the receiver area with a screw coming through the forward action screw hole into the dowel. A wire through the end of the dowel protruding from the forearm of the stock, bent as previously described, serves as a means of hanging the stock while applying the finish and hanging it in the curing box to dry.

To ease you into that decision, let's first identify some of the more common finishes available to you.

I have requests from customers for the use of a variety of finishes to be used, and for the most part, where I have experience in their use and knowledge of the appearance and wear of the finished product, I use them. However, my recommendations are Pilkinton's Classic Oil finishes, SB McWilliams Classic Oil and for a heavy use stock, FullerPlas Satin or Gloss. No, these are not the only finishes available, and there may be some out there which are better. These are the ones that I am confident in using, and in effect, willing to put on my work.

While the application is similar in each case, there are differences in applying them. For that reason, I will be finishing three different projects: One will be finished in TruOil, one with Alkanet Oil, one with Pilkinton's Classic oil finish and one with FullerPlas Satin.

PROJECT #1 TRU OIL

The buttstock had an application of TruOil and been in the drying box for two (2) days. Using the 0000 Steel Wool, after it is rinsed in a solvent and allowed time to dry, use the steel wool to remove the TruOil from the surface of the stock.

  It will become readily apparent where the TruOil to be removed is, just look for the "shady spots" in the finish. After sufficient rubbing, the "shady spot" will disappear leaving the wood surface. That is the goal for the entire stock.

Always rub with the grain. Very little pressure is required on the steel wool to remove the finish from the buttstock. Just take your time and be patient. During this process you will quickly learn why thick applications of TruOil during the early stages of application are a no-no. The stuff is not easy to remove.

Once the buttstock has been thoroughly clean of the previous application of finish, wipe the buttstock down with a clean shop towel. Because some of the steel wool can get into the pores of the wood, I put a small magnet in the shop towel when rubbing a stock down. It is amazing how much steel wool residue it picks up.

With the first application of TruOil removed from the stock, it is time to apply another coat of the finish. I use the bottom of a medicine cup as the receptacle for the TruOil, pouring in a small amount – remember, what goes on must come off! – being careful to pour only what I anticipate needing.

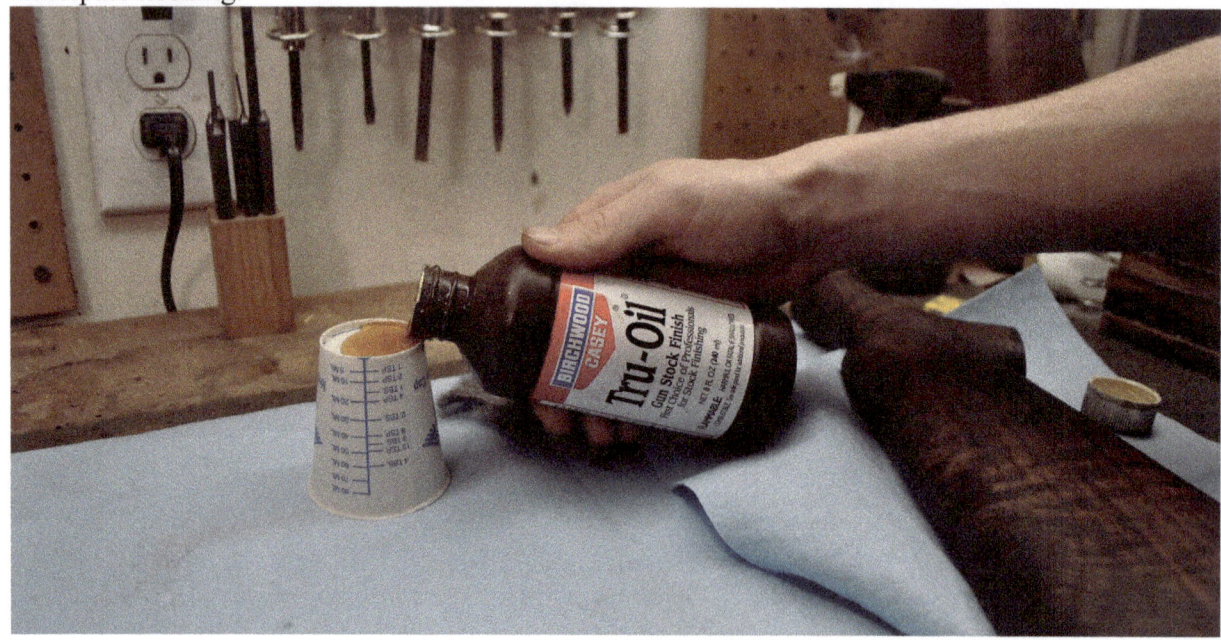

Yep, one little finger dab at a time. It is amazing how far a little TruOil will go. The "dab" technique…

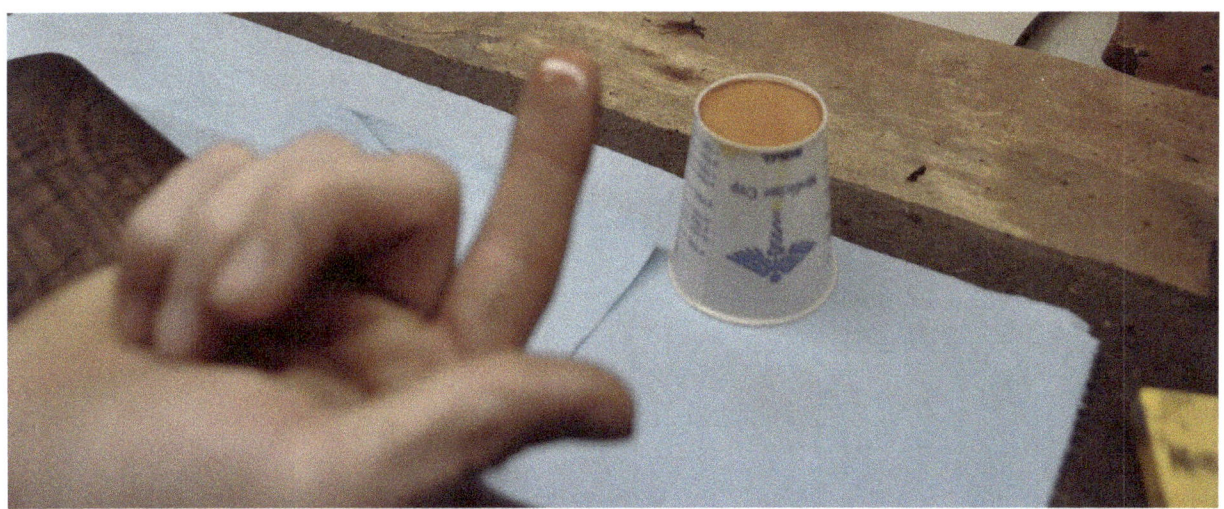

I prefer to apply the finish to the neck of a buttstock, apply it near the face of the buttstock and then spreading it forearm. I have found this technique allows sufficient finish on the wood and makes maximum use of the finish.

I then do the underside of the grip area, and then work my way around the grip cap and back.

When I begin applying finish to the sides of the buttstock, I use two or three fingers to spread the finish, wanting to get it on the wood before it becomes tacky. It is at this point I want to point out that once the finish begins to become tacky and hard to spread, you have spent too much time in one area. To continue to work the same area will leave fingerprints and splotches of heavy finish.

After several days in the hot box, the wood was removed and I found the wood had continued to absorb the finish.

Notice the unfilled grain at the light reflection. This is a clear indication – no pun intended – that there are still applications needed.

The check in the butt of the wood is still there, but has not increased. So, it will be left alone and repaired when the stock is cut to the proper length.

Taking the finish back to the wood was a chore, using both steel wool and 400 grit sand paper, but the grain was still showing nicely and looking better with each coat.

Using the dab and smear technique, I applied another coat of TruOil and put the wood back in the hot box. The forearm was in much better condition, with almost all of the grain filled. After taking the last coat of finish down to the wood, I applied a generous coat of finish and hoped it would be the last… but maybe one more for insurance before polishing.

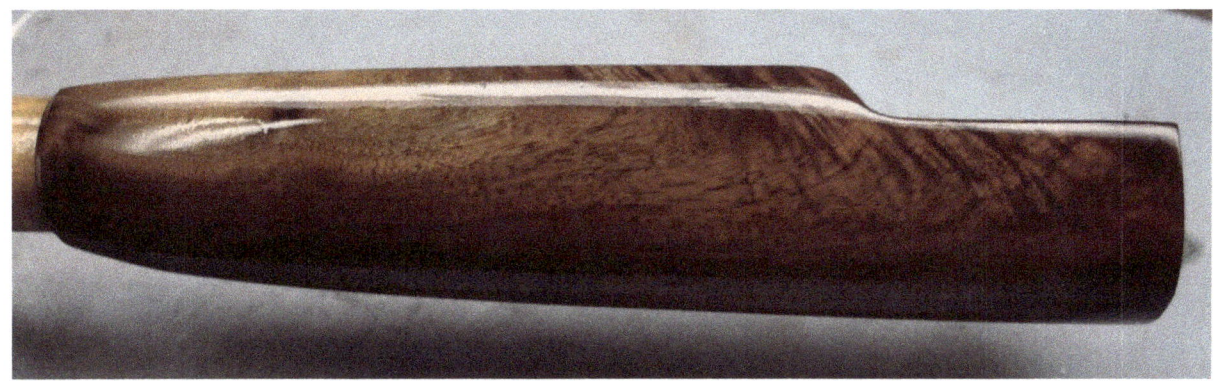

PROJECT #2   ALKANET OIL

Some time back, I was familiarized with Alkanet oil when a customer brought some work, and a refinishing kit obtained from a shooting periodical. He asked that the kit be used in finishing the wood on the gun I was restocking. Interestingly enough, before that gun was done, another customer brought in some work, and requested that the Purdey's Refinishing kit he had brought in be used. The kits were very similar, but one ingredient was the same in both kits – Alkanet Oil. Or Red Root Oil as it is sometimes called. I did as the customer's requested, and was very satisfied with the finish, but was aware that the finishes involved a lot of time. Much more than I would like to spend on a job for the fee I quoted.

About that time, I met a man that was marketing a new finish kit which contained Alkanet Oil. I obtained a small supply from S. B. McWilliams and am convinced that it is the best of the three.

With the wood sanded down to 320 grit wet or dry sanding paper consistency, I whisker the stock, removing the whiskers with 320 grit sand paper. I then whisker the stock a second time with Lacquer Thinner, having found that this really gets the sanding dust out of the grain. It also shows the wood grain to the extreme.

Always wanting to "tweak" a finish to my own style and desires, I continue to use the product, but use the following procedure to apply an Alkanet Oil finish.

I use a 1/2" soft bristle brush to apply a liberal coating of Alkanet Oil. By turning one of the medical measuring cups up-side-down, the recess in the bottom of the cup provides a secure means of access to the oil.

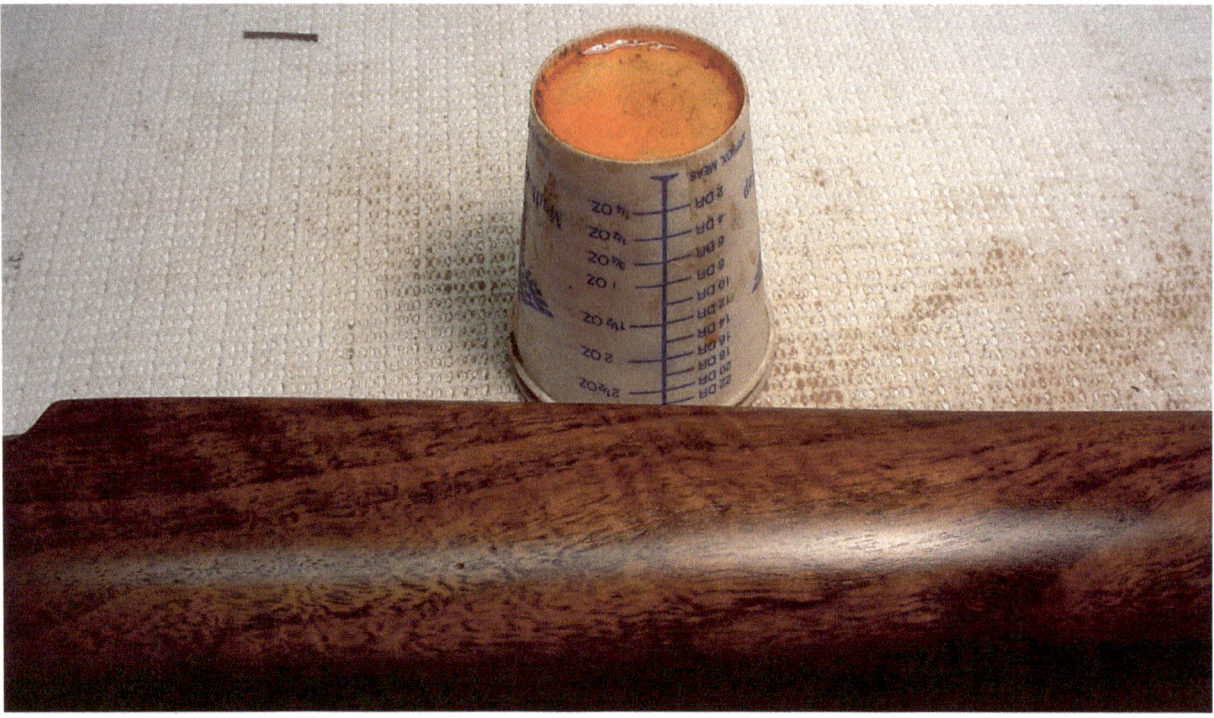

Using the dowel as a handle I make sure to cover the entire stock. If I detect a "dull" area – meaning the oil has quickly soaked into the wood – I apply a little more.

Oh, did I tell you that the Alkanet Oil will give the wood a deep rich reddish tint? It does, and it brings the grain out better than most finishes I have used. Especially on Claro and English Walnut.

With the stock thoroughly covered, and no dull spots, set it aside for half an hour. If there are dull spots in which the oil had penetrated deep into the wood, apply more.

At the end of the time, use a soft cloth, or a better quality paper towel, and wipe the finish from the wood WITHOUT drying the stock out. You want the excess oil off of the surface – give it time to settle in the pores – not totally out of the wood.

Now put the stock away for at least a full day, two days is better. I have a box made of plywood heated with two 60 watt light bulbs, in which I hang my wood to dry. The two light bulbs keep the temperature between 85 and 95 degrees. For many years I used a box that was made entirely from one sheet of wall board with the joints reinforced with fiberglass from a Corvette repair kit. It too was heated with two light bulbs.

After a minimum or one day, but preferably two days, repeat the process – covering the stock with Alkanet oil, waiting a half hour, and then wiping it off of the surface of the wood. And then back in the hot box. If I use the term "hot box", it is just another name for the wooden box I use for curing some finishes and drying others.

After two more days, it is time to go to the next step in obtaining a great oil finish. Closely examine the surface of the wood, look for any areas which might show the results of some overzealous sanding, or possible a file mark. Once identified, use 320 grit wet or dry sand paper to sand the areas down - removing the marks. When the marks are removed, use a very little bit of oil on the tip of your finger to apply oil to the sanded area.

Once the oil is on the area, lightly sand the area with the 320 grit paper. You will immediately notice that the grit on your sandpaper fills with a mixture of oil and sanding dust – I call it "stock mud" for the lack of a better name.

That's good!

You are putting a mixture of the oil and the sanding dust from the stock down into the pores of the wood, and that is what it is all about!

With the few areas taken care of, sand the entire stock in that same manner. Just a little bit of oil on the tip of your finger, spread over a small area – I divided the length of the forearm in half and work on one half at a time – and then sanded until the pores begin to fill. Yes, you are going to use a lot of sand paper, I normally use 5 to 7 1/8 sheets for every sanding. No, I do not fold my sand paper from a full sheet. I fold it into halves cross ways, and then quarters also cross ways, and then tear the quarters into 1/8 sheets. These I fold over in half and use.

With six coats of hand rubbed Alkanet Oil on the wood, I have become well aware of the potential of the finish in bringing out the grain.

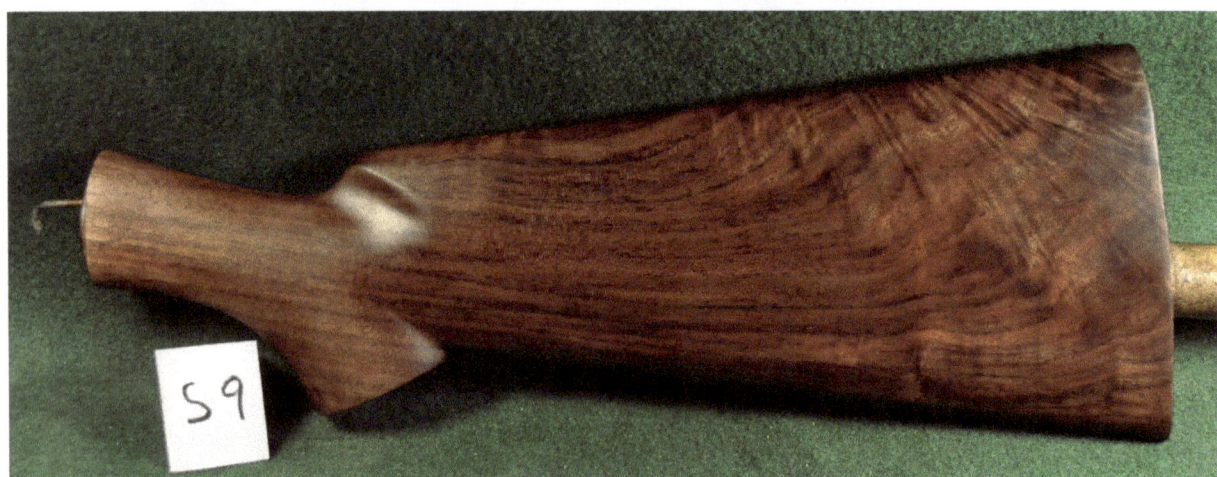

The forearm was a little more porus wood, and after the sixth coat of Alkanet Oil, I again wet sanded the wood with 600 grit wet /dry sand paper.

Even with some small areas of open grain, the wood is definitely looking great. As I rub on this wood, I glance over to the "Almost" rack and begin selecting the Model 12 barreled actions just back from Simmons with their rib and blue. This is going to be one fine gun.

Continue using a dab of the oil and wet sanding the stock, allowing two full days between applications. The denseness of the wood will determine the number of applications necessary to fill the grain of the wood and to provide a nice satin sheen to the wood.

The top forearm in this picture is the original forearm from the Ithaca NID 12 Gauge with all of the associated metal still installed. The lower forearm is the forearm I received back from Wenig's Custom Stocks after sending out the original and asking them to duplicate it. No, the metal was removed before the original forearm was sent out for duplication. Notice the screw through the forearm near the rear – I thought this was someone's major mess up until I saw several of these screws and the related cracked forearms. I determined my forearm would not crack, even with so much figure, I was determined that it would not crack.

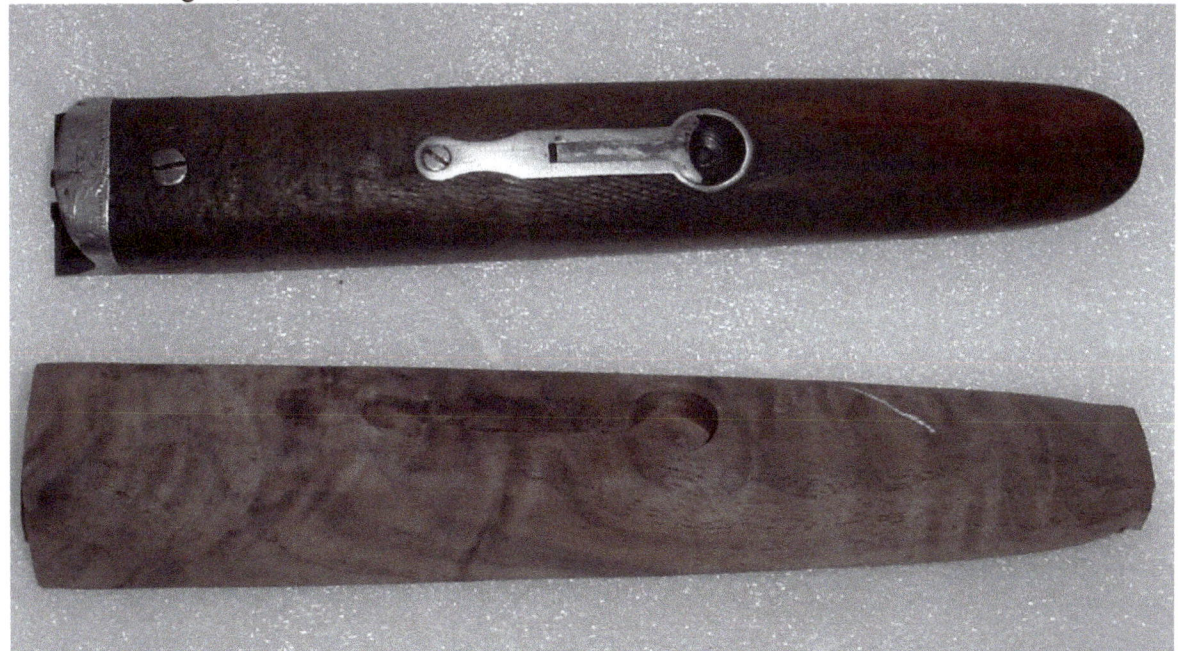

Please notice the inletting for the forearm latch.... that is really excellent work. It is this quality of workmanship that allows many to take on a task such as this with confidence, and complete the project with the end product being something to be proud of. When I started out, detailed inletting such as this was not available and many a forearm was relogated to the fireplace as kindling. The forearm latch is the first metal inletted. I will go into this more later on. I guess Stockmakers are lucky, we get something out of our mistakes – Heat!

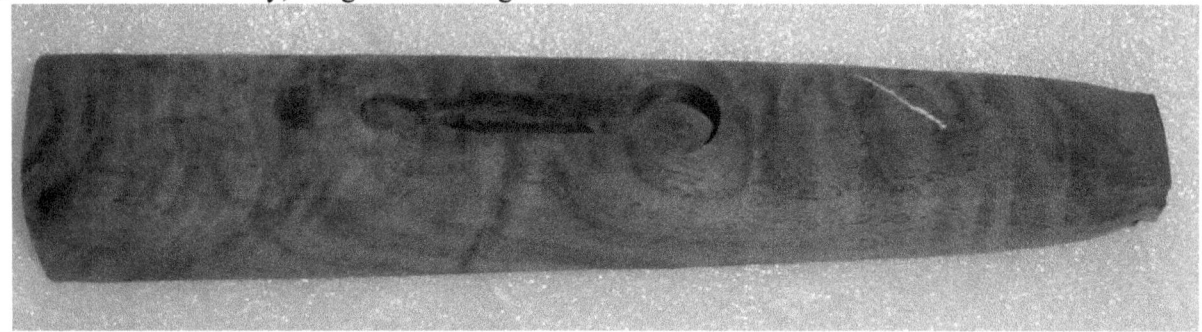

The new semi-finished buttstock sits below the replacement buttstock that was on the shotgun when I purchased it. It appears to be a very early Bishop . As this gun is expected to go back to a hard life in the firld, I wanted a little figure n the butstock, but none near the action area. Wenig's filled the bill to perfection.

Wetting the buttstock with a little lacquer thinner gave witness to some small amount of figure hiding in that great, strong, straight grain. Just enough to make the wood noticeable, but not enough to weaken it.

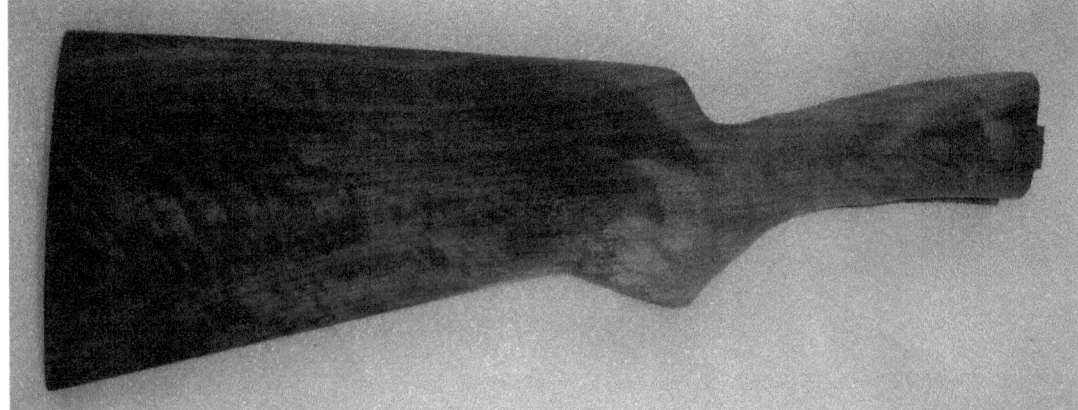

The forearm doesn't need anything to enhance its grain, it shows plenty well.

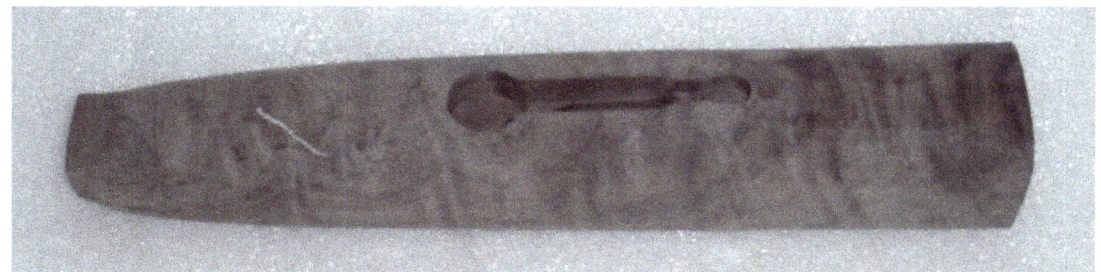

I had asked that the nose of the original forearm be extended an inch – I dislike short forearms – and the duplicate came back with the requested modification.

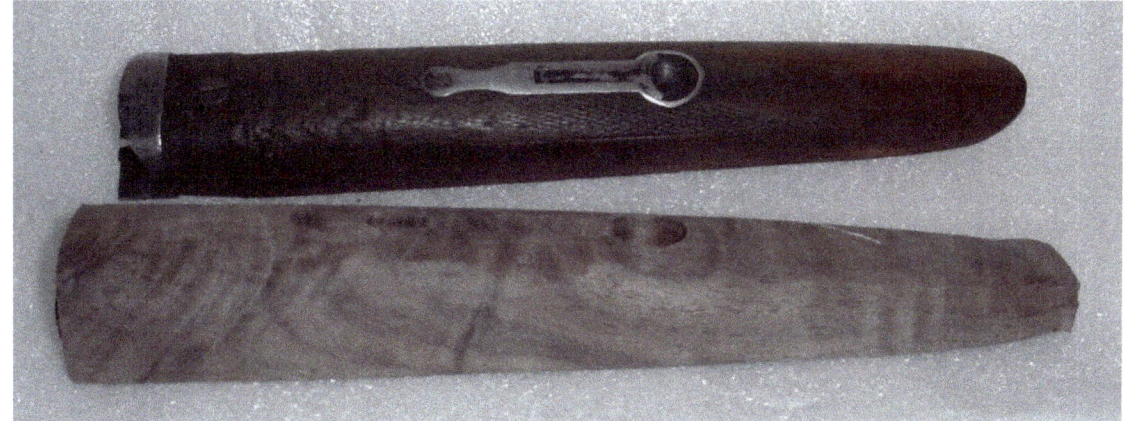

The pictures below show the forearm "soaking it in." The "it" being the S. B. McWilliams stock finish, first part, the red root oil. I had coated the forearm with the material using a soft bristled brush and following instructions, left it sit for a few minutes before wiping off the excess with a soft cloth. The shiney areas are those indicating the wood has absorbed all of the oil it is going to – for the first application – while the dull area indicate itthe wood has soaked in everything provided and could soak in a little more.

Please note how the forearm is held to the handle – a single wall board screw through an existing forearm iron hole. Really secure and not a problem to remove.

The picture below illustrates all of the wood is currently saturated and ready for wiping down. It seems a shame to wipe off such expensive finish – is there another way? Something to be tested at another time.

The photograph below illustrates the completed forearm without any checkering. Please note the beautiful contrasting grain of the wood. This is the result of the use of the Red Root Oil – six applications – and then the final finish, FullerPlas, over it.

Please note the steel bushings for the rear forearm screw. The use of this bushing will preclude cracking the highly figured forearm caused by overtightening the screw.

PROJECT #3
Pilkington Gun Co Red/Brown Gunstock Finish

Well sanded, the buttstock shows promise of some unique wood grain, if the finish lives up to my expectations, this could be one really nice set of wood.

I like the grain flow on this piece of wood, and while it is not outstanding, I believe it will end up being a very nice stock set and represent the Model 12 Winchester it goes on well. Being cut in the Winchester factory field style, it will lend itself to a variety of applications and customers. I chose to leave the grip cap area plain, no grip cap at all.

Just a note, you will notice that the vast majority of my stocks <u>have not</u> been cut for length, I choose to do this after they are sold and the correct length of pull for the customer has been determined.

There are cases in which the customer selects a stock from the semi-finished inventory and we fit the stock to them before sanding and finishing the wood.

I only have one bottle of the finish on hand, and forgo using the medicine cup for the "direct dip" method and hopefully save a little material,

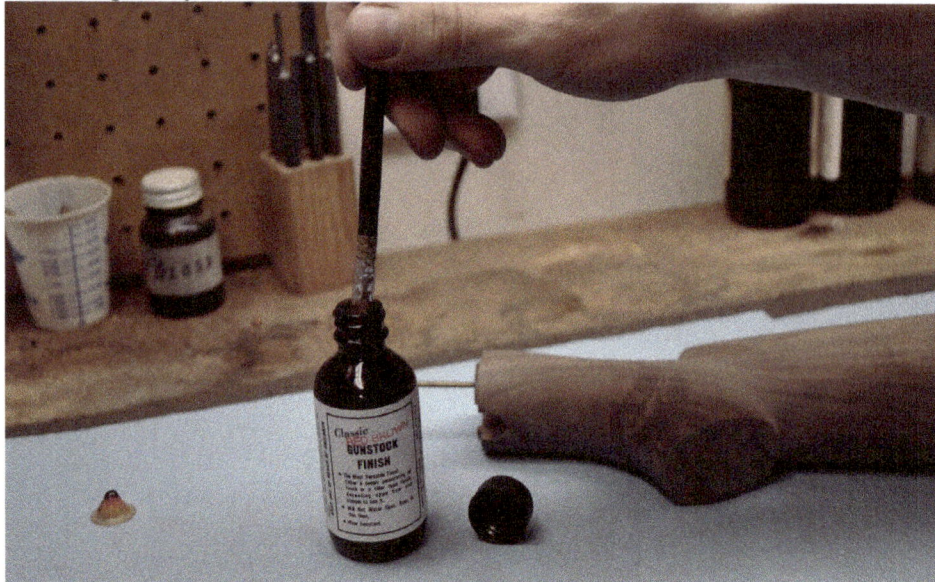

My first impression – WOW! The grain on the buttstock popped out like Christmas tree lights on a dark night. This is going to be something nice.

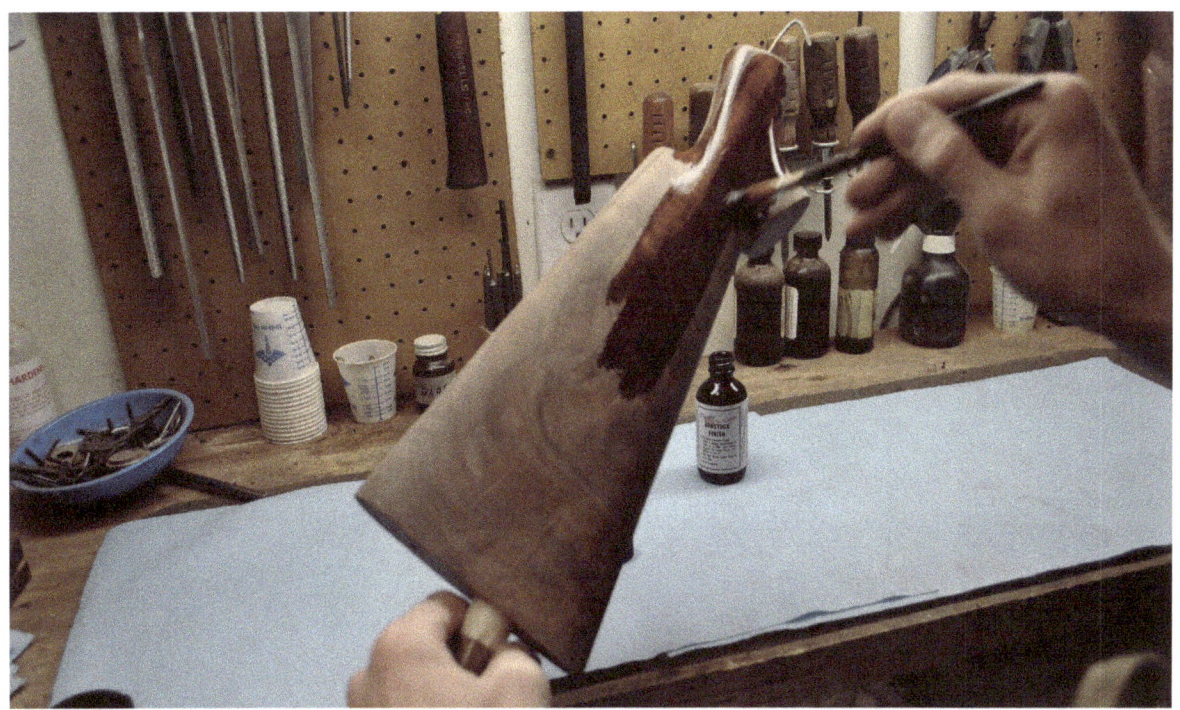

With one side covered, and the off side almost done, I began thinking of a checkering pattern I would use on the buttstock and forearm. The grain of the wood was unique, and to some shooter, this would be the wood he would want on his Model 12. If not, I could always purchase another Model 12 and use the wood on it.

Completely covered in the finish and ready to hand, I was more than satisfied with the initial appearance. But I had been fooled before, the test would be later.

After half an hour, the buttstock was removed from the box and wiped down with a shop towel.

Wiped down, and ready to go back into the hot box. At this point I began to be a little concerned about the open pores behind the pistol grip. But this was just the first application of the oil, there was lots of time to get to them.

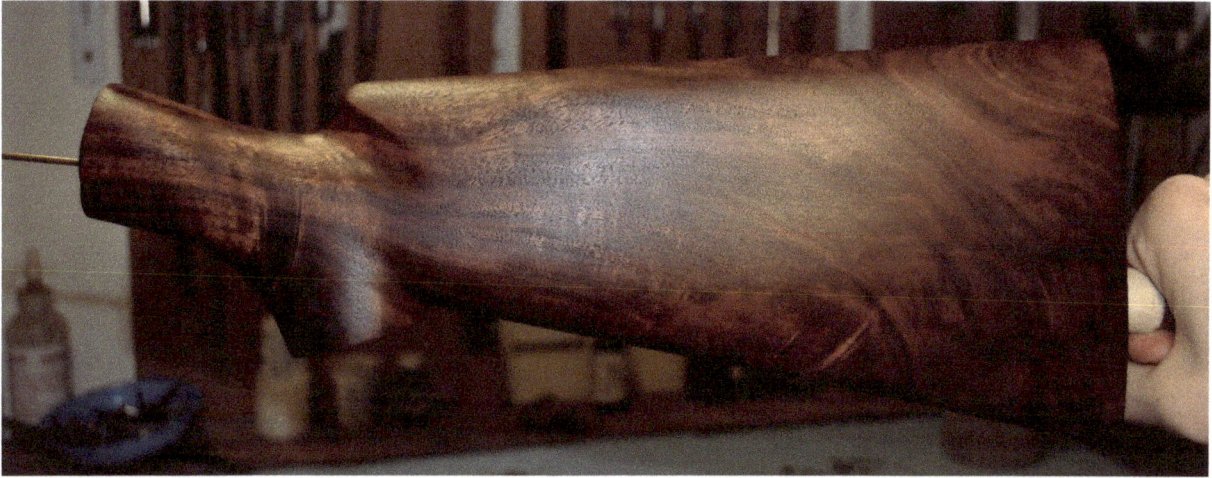

Into the drying box it went. The following day, I checked the buttstock and was surprised to find that it appeared to be a little darken than I remembered, but the grain was really strong and getting more and more desirable.

After two days, I pulled the buttstock out, sanded it very lightly with 320 grit paper, and then applied just enough finish to cover the wood, and sanded the wet finish with 320 grit paper. The stock mud built up with the sanding eliminated my concerns over the pores of the wood – they began filling. I knew that when the oil and sanding had progressed through several coats, the pores in the grain would be filled.

The fourth coat of Pilkington's consisted only of a few drops and spread and rubbed into the wood for a good ten minutes. The result was a great looking low luster.

The grain in the forearm was a little more open than I would have wanted, but after the experience with the finish, I felt confident it would come out nice.

The following picture is one of the forearm after the finish had been applied, allowed to set a half an hour and then placed in the hot box for two days. Nice, huh.

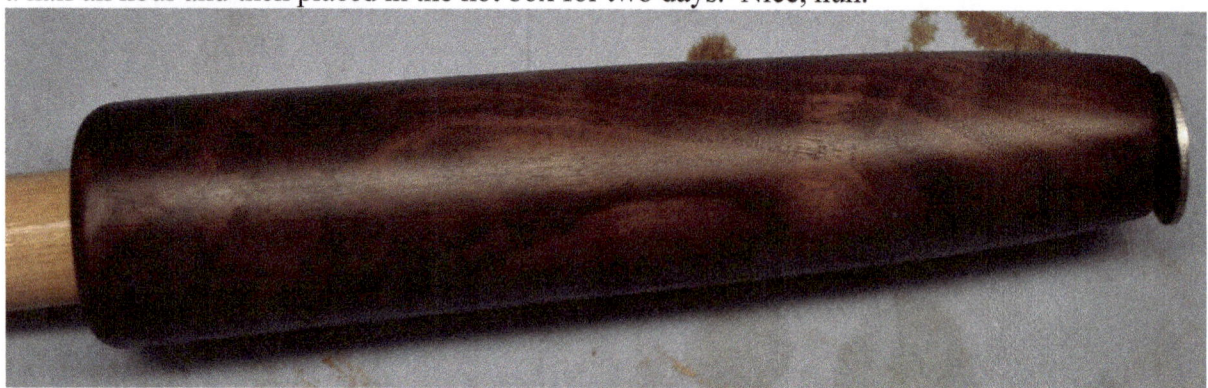

The second Pilkington's was applied after two days, and then the excess wiped off as previously illustrated, and the forearm and buttstock were sanded with 320 grit sand paper, and then they went back into the hot box.

The next day, the buttstock and forearm were removed from the hot box and a very small amount of the finish was rubbed into the stock. The results were amazing… The grain in the wood had taken on new life and looked great.

The weekend came up and the wood stayed in the hot box uninterrupted. However, on Monday morning a very few drops of the finish – the fifth coat - was applied and back to the hot box it went.

Two days later, I removed the buttstock and forearm from the hot box, and as the following photo's illustrate, the wood looked very nice.

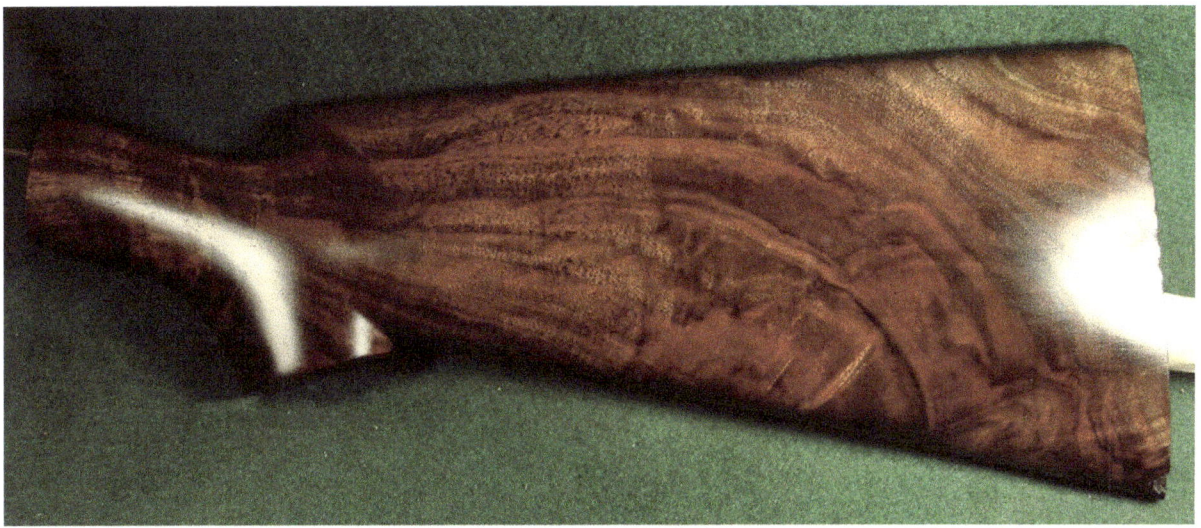

I am especially satisfied as to how the finish brought the grain out, but still displayed in an appearance that reflects a traditional oil finish. The finish has brought out the grain of the wood to a level I could only imagine, it is absolutely great. I can already imagine this set of wood with original Winchester pattern checkering on a solid rib Model 12, in my hands and walking across the field hunting pheasants. And when my companions mention my "missed shots" I will tell them I have the best looking gun in the field. And that's what counts.

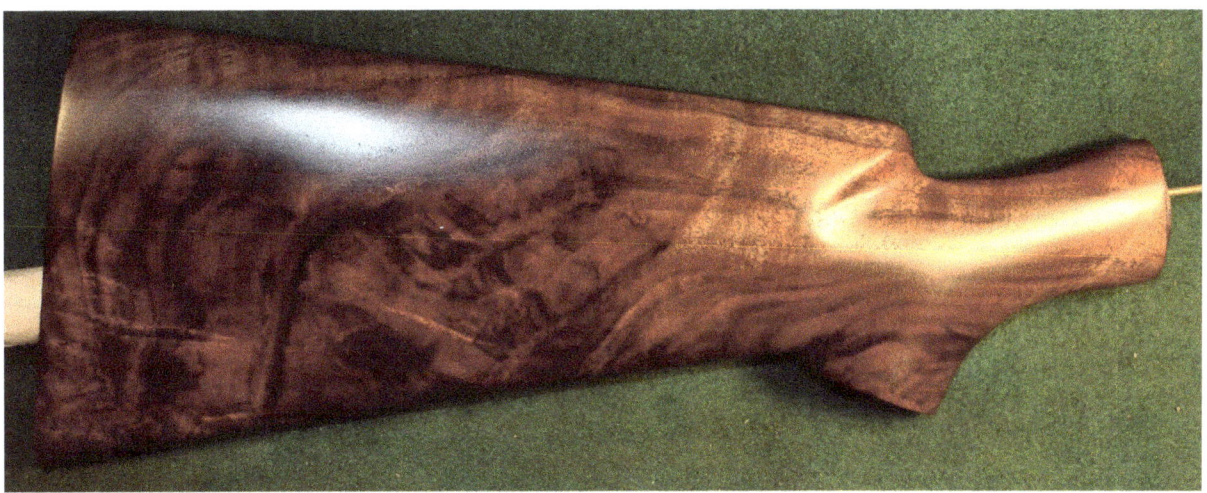

And look at that grain in the forearm – It is filled. And it looks great.

PROJECT #4   FullerPlas

FullerPlas is one of the hardiest finish I have used and still use. It is not difficult to apply, and it shows the wood very well. In addition, as I do a lot of stocks and refinishing for Skeet shooters, it is easy to repair to a like new gloss. The following wood set is for a Winchester Model 12 shotgun destined for the Vintage Trap Matches being held in conjunction with many major trap shoots.

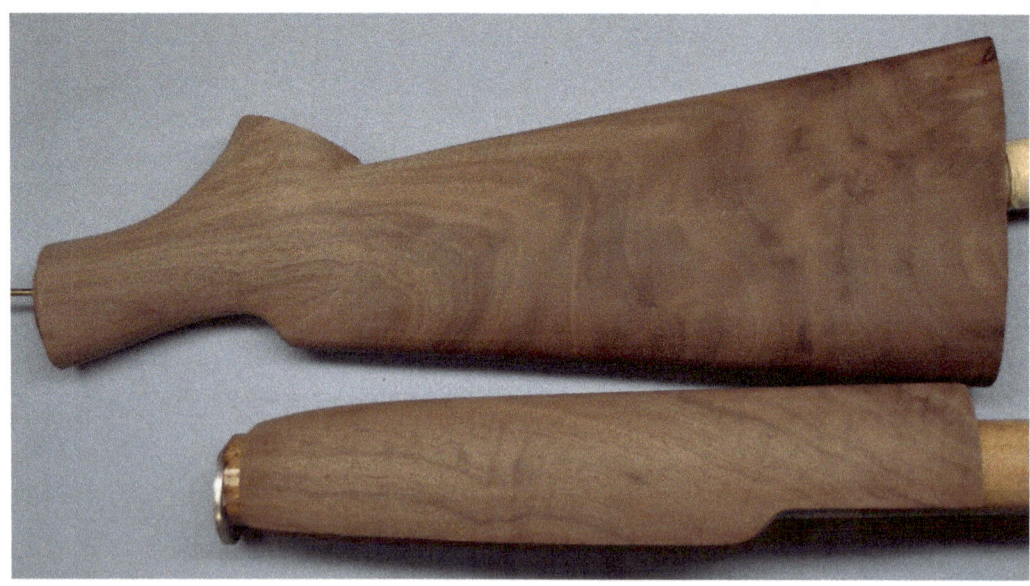

    I do not use fillers, other than a thinned version of the finish to be applied to the wood. Why? Compatability. I once had a stock returned to me after several months because the finish was flaking off. It took a while – I keep a card on each stock set, complete with pictures and a listing of work performed and materials used – but I isolated the cause down to the filler the customer had requested was not compatable with the finish I used.

    On FullerPlas, I thin the mixture by one third, and use it as a filler. When adding additional coats of finish, I use the unthinned FullerPlas. I like to apply six to eight coats of FullerPlas, allowing at least a day between each coat, <u>and then wet sand it.</u>

    I start with 400 grit wet/dry paper to eliminate any foreigh material and insure the grain of the wood is filled. If for whatever reason I go through the finish and down to the wood, the wood gets an additional coat of finish with emphasis on the area sanded through.

    I then resand the wood with 600 grip wet/dry sanding paper and then jump to 1500 or 2,000 grip wet/dry sand paper, being very careful to only sand the surface lightly, using lots of water, and wiping the residue off the wood frequently.

    The sanding and polishing procedure for FullerPlas is contained in Section 14, Refinishing Stocks, so I won't duplicate it here.

PROJECT #5   Gun Sav'r

    A customer asked that the two stock sets he wanted refinished be refinished with a product I hadn't tried before. Respecting the Customer's wishes, I ordered a can of it, and several weeks later – it had been out of stock – it arrived. I am very apprehensive about introducing new products into my shop. So I found a couple of small "proofs" of stock wood, sanded them as I would a stock or forearm, and actually read the instructions on the can.

    Following the instructions, I quickly discovered I could use and obtain an acceptable finish on the proofs. However, selecting another proof, I use the new product and the technique we had developed in the shop for the finished we used.

On the proofs, we stopped at four coats, wet sanding each coat and rubbed the final coat well into the wood. I let the proofs stay on top of the bench for several weeks, just to see how resilient the finish would be to dings and dents. Suffice to say, it did well.

But better yet, the few dings I repaired were a quick fix with the repair finish blending into the original finish. Thanks to the Customer, we now use this finish and display finished product for the potential customer to select from.

As part of a teaching point, I ended up with a forearm for a Beretta 682 Gold E without a matching buttstock. I selected it as the project piece for the Gun Sav'r finish. To illustrate the changes as the process is applied, the first picture is of the fitted, shaped and sanded forearm.

With a little corrective work, caused by shop handling, I applied the Gun Sav'r with a brush.

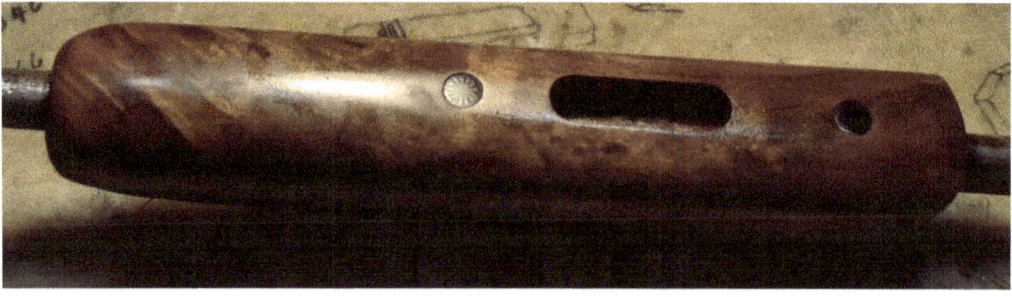

After one day in the hot box, I removed it and lightly sanded it with 400 grit wet/dry sand paper.

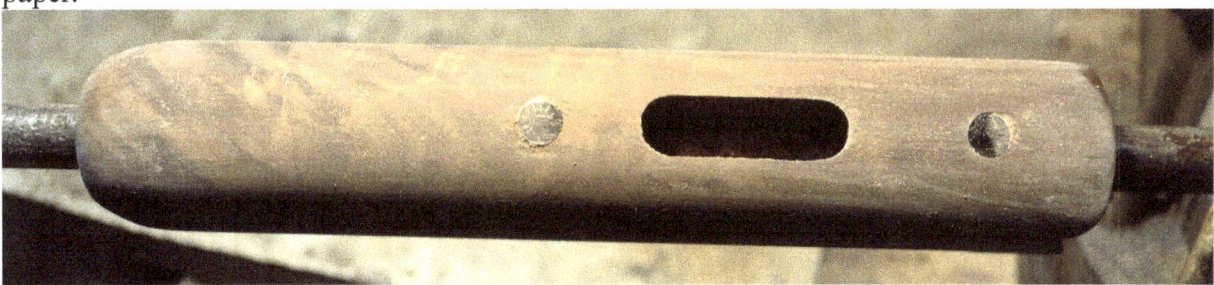

Other than the rear rosette being slightly canted, I was more than a little happy with the result. What you can't see in the picture is how fast the pores of the wood are filling.

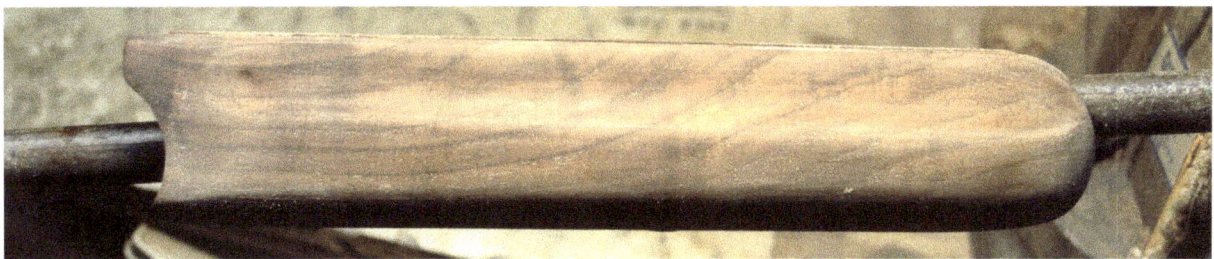

So, out came the Gun Sav'r for a second application. Using the dab and rub technique, I put oil on the entire forearm. Just compare the pictures of this view, and then take a guess at what the completed forearm is going to look like with some paneled 26 lines per inch checkering.

Even the odd side of the forearm is taking nicely to the finish. Uh oh, just caught an error at the rear of the flute, there is a small place that was not sanded out properly. So, lets use this as an opportunity to how easy it is to repair the finish.

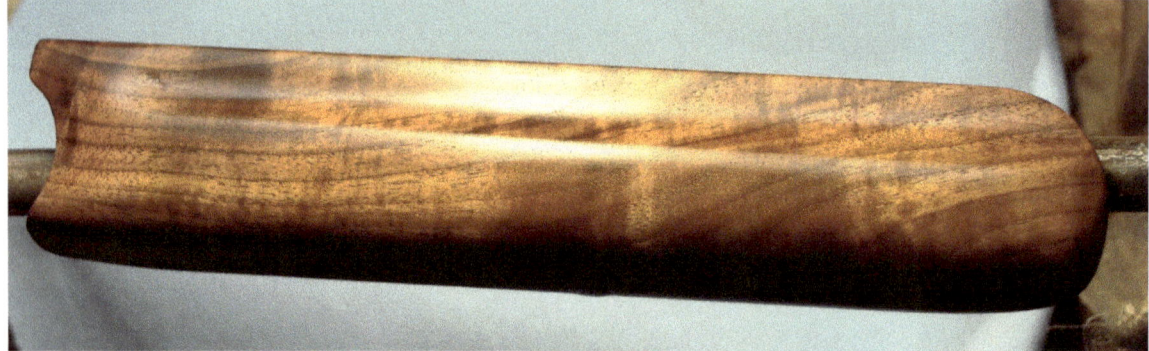

And here is a close-up of the repair made to the right side of the upper flute.

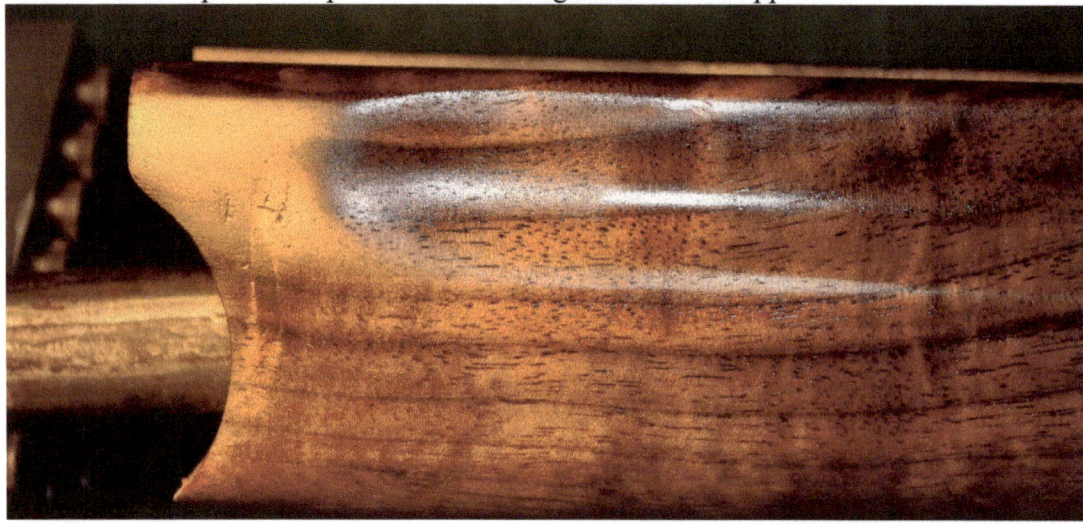

A few more coats of the finish, a little sanding to fill the pores, and the repair should disappear.

Take a look at how the grain of the wood pops out. That, at this point, is an indicator of just how good the finished product is going to be.

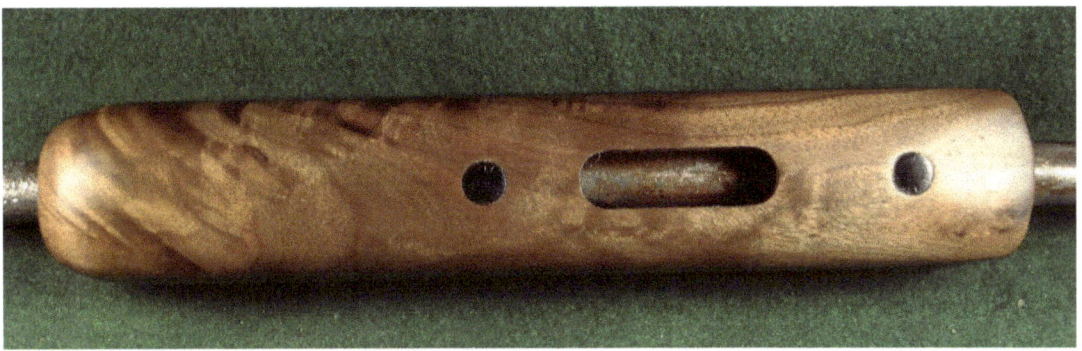

With four coats of Gun Sav'r finish on the forearm, and just a few small places in which the grain is not filled, back to the hot box in preparation for another coat.

SECTION 7
Recoil Pads

     I attempted to put my first recoil pad on a shotgun with a drum sander mounted in a quarter inch electric drill. I couldn't make up my mind to put the drill or the stock in the vise, so I tried it both ways. Neither worked and I ended up taking the mess to a gunsmith, asking him to repair my gouges so that I could sand down and refinish the stock.

     I picked the buttstock up several days later and rapidly determined that he had done his job well. He showed me a small bench sander he had made which used a two-inch wide belt, explaining that was all that was necessary to mount a recoil pad. I was transferred soon thereafter, and never saw him install a pad, but will always be thankful for the opportunity to have met with him and viewed his small shop.

     That Christmas, I received a small bench sander which used a 1" x 42" belt, but it came without an electric motor. I spent the day after Christmas fighting off people returning unwanted presents and searching for an electric motor with the correct base to mount to the sander. I was successful and before the sun went down, I was assembled and running.

     I would like to say that my first installation was flawless, but it wasn't. I nicked the finish of the buttstock, and the angle of the pad at the toe was too square. One side was below surface level, and the other was above. However, the person that purchased it from the gun shop where I traded it several weeks later probably didn't notice, if they were blind.

     My father was fond of saying something to the effect that if you didn't know, find someone that does and make a friend. In my case, I approached a person that I considered a gun butcher, rather than a Gunsmith, as he advertised his services. I wasn't too surprised to find that he was using homemade drum sander to install pads.

     But the manner in which he approached the task was one that I picked up fast. He had several rolls of very thick nylon filament tape on a hook over his bench. He would make several wraps of tape around the butt in the general area where he was going to shorten the stock, (or near the butt if he wasn't), and then hold the stock in his miter box with one hand and the saw it the other. The first time I watched him do it, I cringed, thinking of the chips that would be missing from the other side of the area around the cut.

After completing his cut, I was more than a little surprised when he made a few fast swipes at the butt with a course file, proclaimed it square and screwed the recoil pad in place. I watched as he removed the excess rubber of the pad, and actually sanded into, but not through the outer layer of tape. When he removed the tape, I was surprised to find that the area around the cut was smooth – no lost chips or finish. And other than a defined gap between the recoil pad and butt, not a bad job. I expected him to use a smoother grit of belt to smooth the pad base, or at least square up the butt, but all he did before pronouncing the job complete was to heat up a filler stick or the approximate color of the buttstock and fill in the gap.

I learned the value of nylon tape that day, a lesson that I still observe to this day and have taught many people. I tried the miter box twice and sold both of them at reduced prices at a yard sale. Just couldn't do a good job that didn't require a lot of time to square the butt up. A neighbor had a small bench mounted band saw that I used several times, before purchasing a large twelve-inch band saw which, with a short pass across the sanding belt, gave me a nice square butt.

I used a band saw with a pass across the belt sander for a lot of years, but when Major Tom Martin, a long-time friend, great gun smith and fine shot, told me of a new way, I listened. I found that not even a truing pass at the sanding belt was necessary. Straight from the saw, the buttstock was ready for the pad.

I have changed to a carbide blade in the last year, when I found one that I could afford, but that is the only change.

The following is the procedure that I use when shortening a stock to compensate for the added length of a recoil pad. The length of pull – distance from the center of the trigger to the center of the butt – must be established. A good tape measure is fine, and I have used one. But for years I have used an aluminum yard stick and found it fills my needs.

If for example, the length of pull is to be 14 5/8", I place the end of the yard stick directly over the center of the trigger, and allowing for the thickness of the recoil pad, 1" in this case, and make a mark with a black felt tip pen at 13 5/8" line.

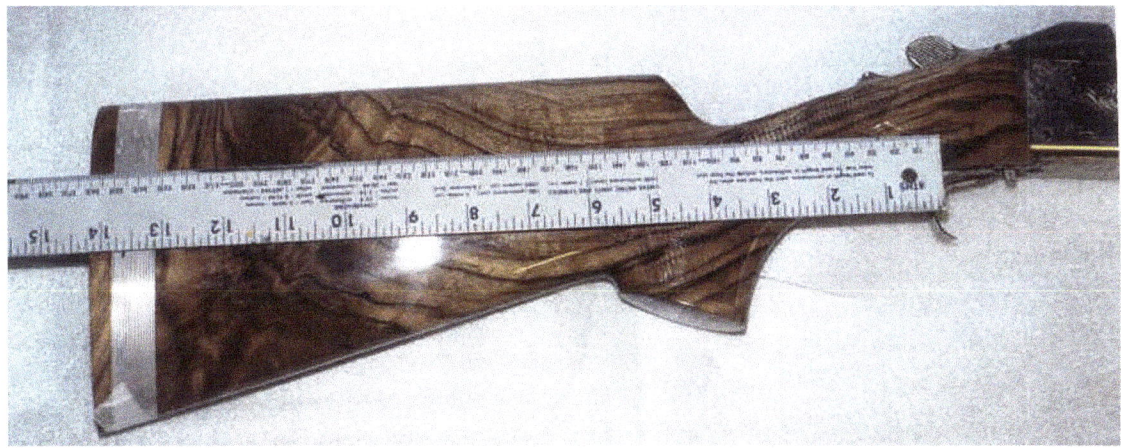

Using nylon filament tape at least an three-quarters inch wide, I carefully lay a wrap around the buttstock covering the area where the cut will be made. I am very careful to lay the tape on and have no wrinkles.

The area under a wrinkle in the tape is not in contact with the finish on the wood, and the finish on the wood may chip off when cut. Don't take a chance, lay the tape flat. I start at the top of the comb, go down the sides, and then cut the tape off at the bottom/toe of the stock.

In most instances, the mounting or replacement of the recoil pad involves maintaining the same pitch from the original measurement. Using the compound miter saw, I achieve this by loosening the table lock, moving the saw blade down until the blade is in a position at which I can slide the butt of the buttstock back into the side of the blade.

With the comb of the stock against the fence, I then move the rotary table until the end of the buttstock is flush against the blade. This often necessitates using some shim stock made from three by five cards under the receiver area of the stock. I have a friend that is always thinking up an easier way to do things – you should hear his explanation of balancing the Federal budget! – and will soon – I hope – come up with an elevation devise on the saw table to take the place of the three by five cards. When the entire butt is against the side of the saw blade, I raise the blade, and prepare for the cut.

I place the buttstock in position, wanting only the faint reminder of the line indicating the cut location to be left on the buttstock. If I am going to error at all, I will cut too little wood and have to make a second very thin cut. It has happened, but not often.

Naturally, if I want to change the pitch, I move the saw to the correct angle to achieve the pitch desired and make the cut. Until something better comes along, I will continue to use the compound miter saw for shortening butt stocks as well as changing pitch. Who was it that said the best ideas he had ever had were the ones "borrowed" from someone else. Thanks, Tom.

Before you go any further on this project, check your recoil pad over. I have received a recoil pad which had a void in the exterior, and I have received recoil pads which are not flat enough to mount. The following picture is of a new recoil pad.

The following picture is a quick pass over a belt sander to discover if the recoil pad was acceptably flat and ready for installation. The sides were high and then ends were shallow.

The following photo is one of the recoil pad after several passes over the belt sander. It is really flat and ready for installation.

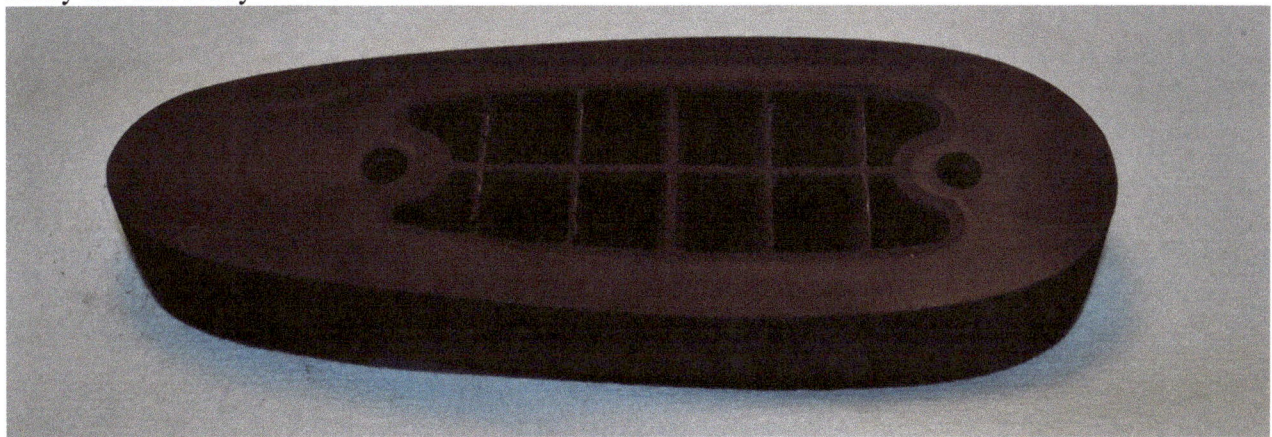

As the screws which hold the recoil pad to the butt stock must be inserted into the back of the recoil pad. Holes must be made to accommodate the screws. I have a small punch which I use almost extensively. However, recently, a customer brought back to recoil pad jobs, requesting small "slits" be made in the replacement recoil pads. From now on, I will ask the customer which type they want.

When putting the recoil pad on the stock, check out the original holes for wear. If the screws to be used are loose, you have several options. First, you can drill and plus the old holes with furniture dowels. Second, you can use a larger or longer screw. Dripping and plugging the recoil pad screw holes is covered in the Repair Section.

If you are applying the recoil pad to a new or cut off stock in which there are no screw holes, I insert the top screw into the recoil pad, position the pad on the stock – insuring the pad is centered vertical and horizontal – and tap the screw head which will leave an indenture in the butt of the stock.

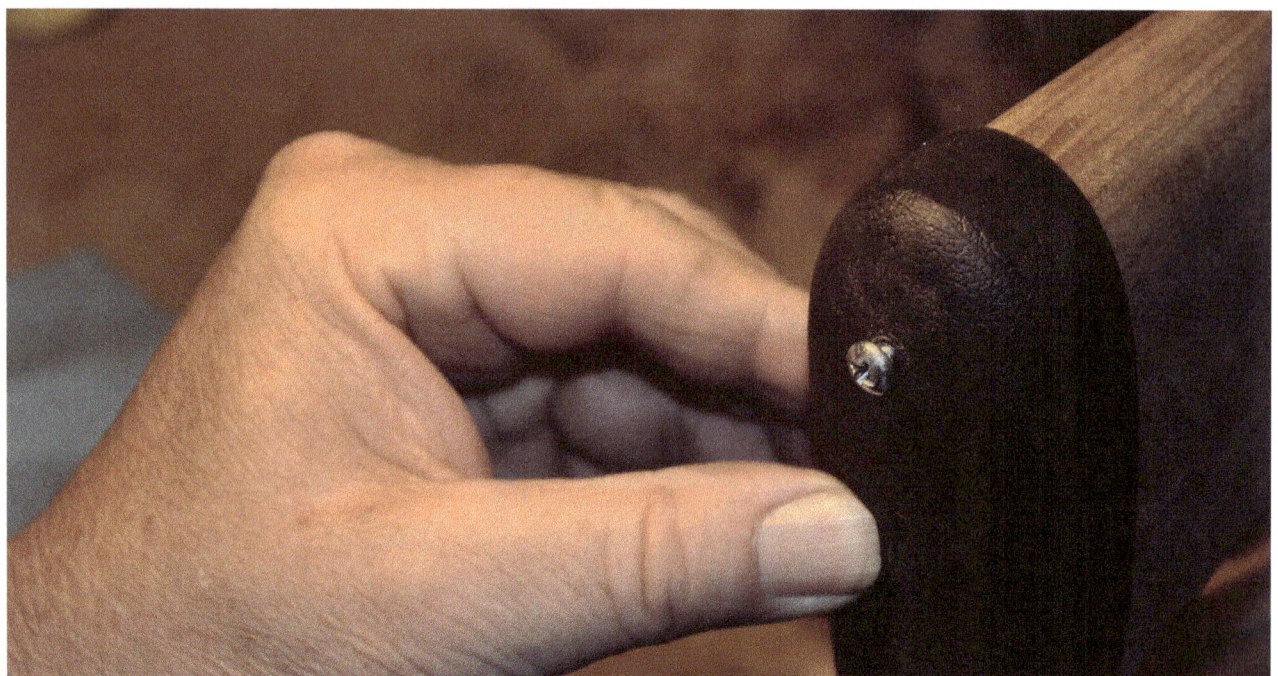

Depending upon the size of the screw to be used, select a drill bit the same size as the BODY OF THE SCREW. This will allow the full threads of the screw to cut into the wood. If you are in question as to the size of the drill bit, drill a hole with it in a scrap piece of wood.

After insuring the correct size drill bit is being used, drill the hole in the butt of the stock, being sure to drill the hole at a right angle to the butt and not raised, lowered or canted.

With the first hole drilled into the stock, screw the recoil pad onto the stock using the top screw. With the recoil being held in place by the top screw, insert the lower screw into the recoil pad, align the recoil pad correctly, and when it comes in contact with the stock, tap the screw hard enough to leave an impression on the butt of the stock.

Leaving the pad on the stock, but moving it up to expose the second impression, drill the second hole in the stock, insuring it is at a right angle to the butt.

Inserting the lower screw into the recoil pad, align the pad to the lower hole in the stock, and tighten the lower screw and then the upper screw. There should be no gap between the recoil pad and the butt of the stock.

With the recoil pad in place, use a VERY sharp pointed awl to scribe the outline of the stock onto the recoil pad surface. To insure a good picture, I have used a Marks Anything white pencil to highlight the scribed line.

At this point, the method of removing the excess rubber from the recoil pad comes into being. I have used the same fixture for a number of years and have found it to serve my needs. In the past, I would tape the stock and remove the excess rubber with the recoil pad in place. I have also used several other fixtures but didn't like them as well. And in a few hard-pressed cases, have done them free hand – a practice I DO NOT RECOMMEND.

Attaching the recoil pad to the fixture with the 2 supplied socket head screws, you are ready to remove excess rubber.

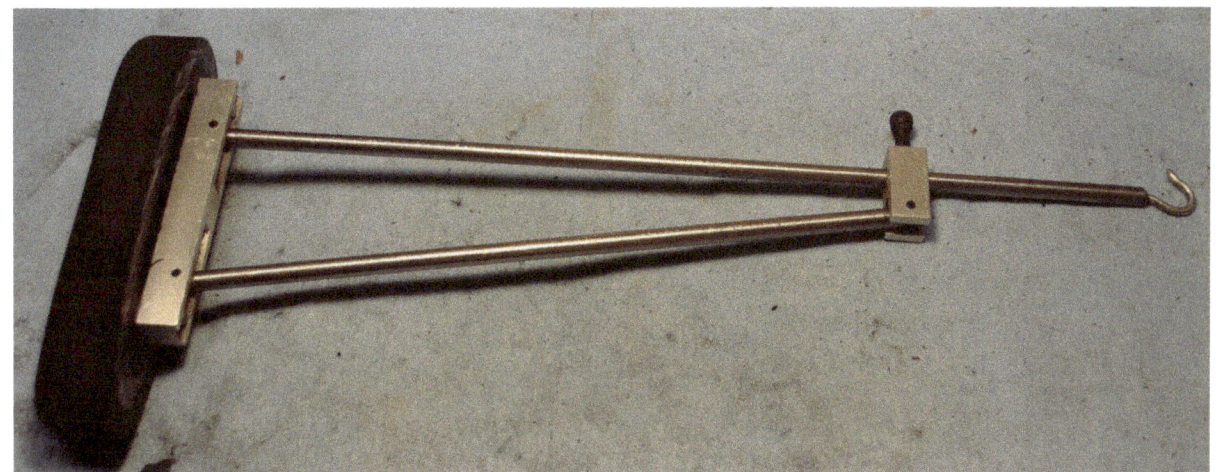

I move the fixture to the 2 x 42 belt, 120 grit, 1/3 hp sander. Check the alignment of the fixture to insure the bottom tip of the recoil pad will follow the line of the belly of the stock.

I take away only enough rubber to establish this line, and then remove the fixture and align it with the butt of the stock.

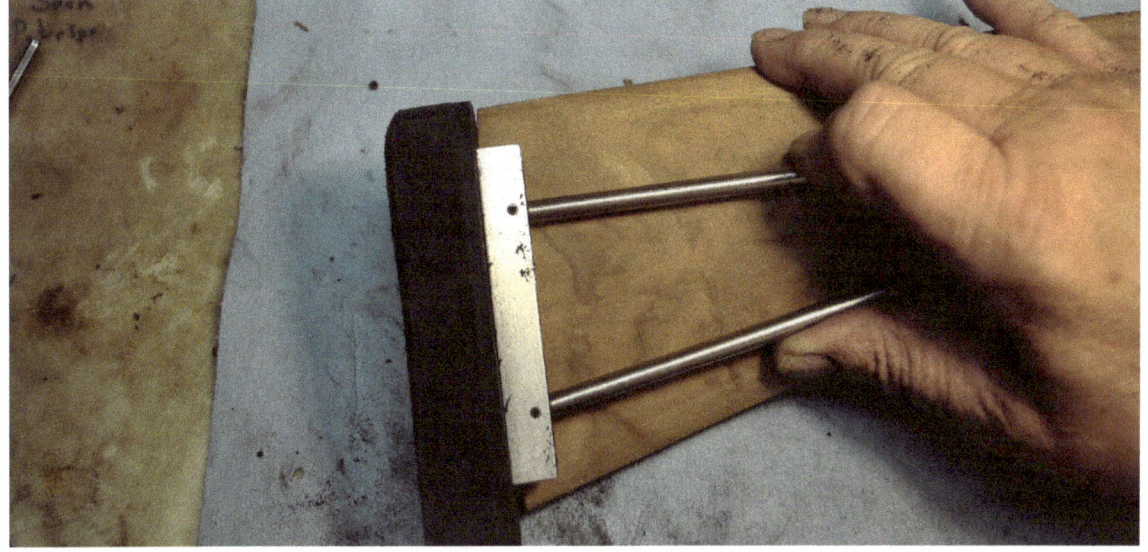

If the stock line is consistent. If it is not, I correct the settings on the fixture and take off only enough to establish the new line and check it again. When the fixture is properly set, I begin removing the excess rubber from the recoil pad.
SAFETY: DO NOT perform this task without wearing safety glasses. And I would recommend the use of a surgical mask as well. That black rubber residue needs to be a consideration.

At this point, I am going to stop with the application on a "conventional" wooden buttstock and address the procedure for a synthetic buttstock.

Mounting recoil pads on shotguns with synthetic butt stocks can present a variety of problems, to be dealt with by a variety of solutions. However, some of the solutions are much more difficult than others. I recently had a customer, a local Gun Shop, bring in two shotguns with synthetic buttstocks on the same day. One was a well worn Browning BPS with traces of mud from at least three different duck hunts, and the other was a new, in the box, Franchi. Pachmayr Presentation recoil pads were to go one each of them.

The Browning BPS was not difficult, instead of using my compound miter saw to reduce the stock length to the new length dictated by the customer's requirements, I used the band saw with a twelve tooth per inch metal cutting blade. As usual, I taped the stock where my cut was to be, squared the end of the buttstock to the saw blade by using card stock taped under the grip area of the buttstock, made the cut, used the belt sander to "flatten" the cut area. The recoil pad holes in the synthetic buttstock matched the recoil pad holes and proceeded with the pad installation – the recoil pad holes in the synthetic stock matched the screw holes in the recoil pad.

The Franchi was a stock requiring special attention and procedures. For a starter, the buttstock held an aluminum tube in which the action tube came into from the receiver, and the action nut held everything together. And the buttstock was filled with a foam insulation.

Calling the Customer, I informed them that this installation would require additional time, and thus an additional charge. I was asked if I could even do it, as they had been told by others it could not be done. I really dislike being second choice and told them I could do it. At that point I would have used ten penny nails to install it, just to get it on.

The great thing about a synthetic buttstock is how the white pencil I use to mark my length of pull / cut line. Really stands out. In making the mark, and then covering it over with the nylon filament tape, I decided to begin taking pictures of my work on this project and illustrate to the customer how it was done.

Using the comb marking tool, some describe it as a block of wood with a pencil sticking through it, I made a line I was to follow with the band saw.

Knowing I was to use the band saw, I wanted to level the buttstock for the cut. Knowing the band saw blade is at a right angle to the band saw table, I used a small machinist square to insure the butt of the buttstock was square. I did this by placing a series of three by five index cards, folder or cut in half, under the grip area of the buttstock. When the butt was at a ninety degree angle, I taped the cards in place. Thus, with the cards in place, I was ready for the cut.

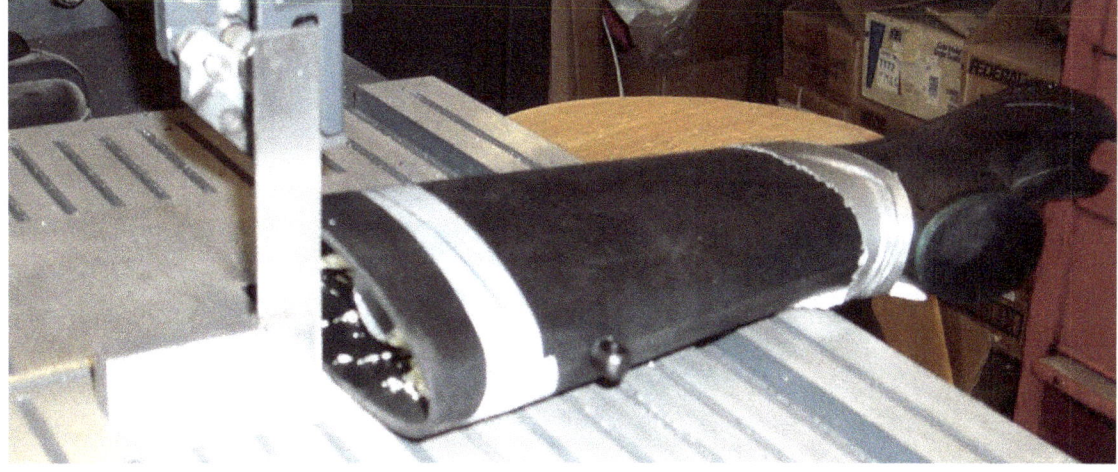

For the hobbyist, this same cut could be made using a miter box and a large hacksaw with a sixteen-teeth per inch blade. If this manner is used to make the cut, I would suggest securing the buttstock in the miter box. If it can move around during the cutting, the line will not be anywhere near straight, and will require a lot of time to achieve a flat upon which to mount the recoil pad.

The band saw made short work of the cut, including the aluminum tube, and the cut was pretty clean, thanks to a recently installed band saw blade, and the foam didn't smell like burning gym shorts as I had been told. Not really difficult. But the fun was just around the corner, no pun intended.

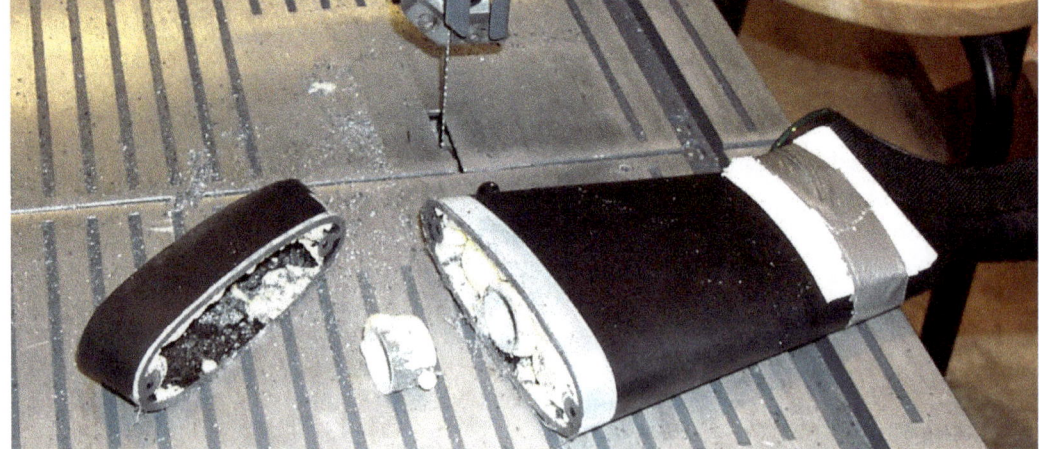

Just lift the tape off and the residue of the cut comes off with it. Nice, quick cleanup. The great part about taping the area to be cut on a synthetic stock is cleaning the stock residue.

My intention from the beginning was the devise a "filler block" to fill the void in the buttstock and provide a means of anchoring the recoil pad with screws into the filler block. As there was no longer any hope of securing the pad directly to the buttstock, as I had done on the Browning BPS buttstock, the filler block was imperative. I needed something which would fit into the buttstock, provide a base for the screws, and most important, stay in place…

Using the 2 x 46 belt sander, I quickly established a flat mounting surface at the butt. If a belt sander or disc sander isn't available, a good wide file, such as a very large mill bastard double cut would have done fine. It would have taken a lot more time, but the results would have been just as good.

Placing a piece of copy paper – we used to call it typing paper when people used type writers – over the butt of the buttstock, I held it firmly in place with one hand, and rubbed a pencil lead around the INSIDE edge. This effectively transferred the dimensions of the inside to paper.

Cutting the paper outline from the paper, I then transferred it to a piece of scrap walnut from one of my many "scrap wood buckets." Realizing the tube would have to fit through the filler block, a couple of quick measurements placed a tentative location of the filler block. A forester bit just a little oversize went through the walnut in quick fashion and then a trip back to the band saw was in order.

Note! I drilled the hole in the walnut while there a lot of wood to surround the hole once drilled. In this manner, I did not risk cracking the wood during the drilling process as the edges of the wood would be very thin.

With the filler block cut, it was time to reduce the height of the foam insulation. I decided to use the foam as the base upon which the filler block could rest, but reduce the tube by a quarter inch, just enough so it would not come in contact with the recoil pad. Using a carbide cutter in my hand tool, it quickly routed out the foam just a hair deeper that the thickness of the filler block. Again, I was disappointed, no aroma from the grinding of the foam. I believe I have friends that may not tell the whole truth sometimes. Know what I mean?

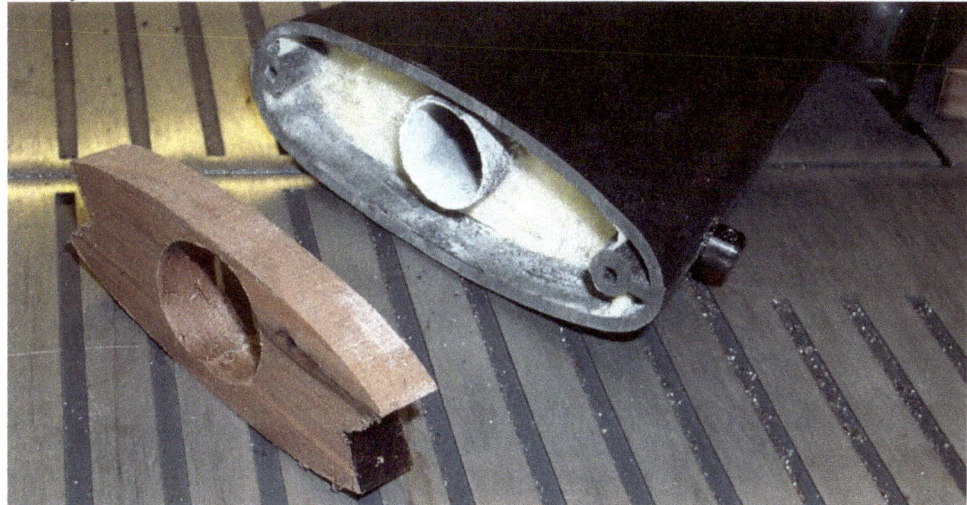

With all of the pieces ready for assembly, I placed the buttstock butt up in the padded vise jaws, eyeball leveled the butt, and pulled out the AcraGlass. AcraGlas is a constantly used product in my shop, and I would recommend it to anyone that does stock repairs, home repairs, or just needs something to stir. The stuff is great when mixed per instructions and used as intended. Well, I mixed a about an ounce of the stuff, added some floc – comes with the product – a little dye to give it color, and stirred the required four minutes.

As is my habit, I let it age a minute or two as I taped the area around the butt, letting the tape overlap the cut area by a quarter inch or so, effectively forming an enclosure to catch any excess AcraGlass. Then the thought hit, maybe the foam had a few voids into which the AcraGlas would flow into the never to be seen or heard from again, land. A quick check found two such locations, which a little modeling clay soon eliminated.

Pouring in enough mixture to cover the foam, I inserted the filler block and watched as the AcraGlas rose around the edges of the block, other than for a few small areas. I let the mixture settle, and then filled in the voids, hoping that the AcraGlas would not find an undetected void in the foam and begin to vacate. But for the second time that day, I got lucky and still had some AcraGlass left over when the seeping stopped. The first time? When a customer called, saying he had changed powders for his twelve gauge, did I want the "old" Green Dot. All four pounds of it…

I know what the instructions say, and I still like to let AcraGlas set overnight. I advise this practice wholeheartedly.

The next day, I peeled the tape off, used the belt sander to once again establish a flat, being careful to remove the AcraGlas, not the buttstock, upon which to install the recoil pad. From this point, the recoil pad installation was like any other recoil pad.

With the buttstock cut to the correct length and pitch, it's time to prepare the recoil pad for mounting. Take a look at the recoil pads on shotguns for a few years, and one can see a variety of means which allow the recoil pad screws to be inserted through the face of the recoil pad. For years I used an Exacto knife to cut small slits in the recoil pad face at the screw locations. It seemed to be the accepted practice. To reduce chamfering by the screwdriver when installing the recoil pad, I would dip the screws in a little liquid soap. I put many a recoil pad on in this manner, and for the hobbyist, it is certainly an acceptable means of accomplishing the task at hand.

And then I saw a pad that had two small circular holes in the face which looked like a leather punch had been used, but the pad was too thick for a leather punch. And then I remembered seeing some hole punches in a tack room when I was small. Drilling an 1/8" hole in the end of a three-inch piece of 5/32" drill rod took a few minutes.

Remember, I am a stock maker, not a machinist. Quickly beveling the outside of the drill hole, I had my punch. I have seen this type of punch identified as a *post punch*, a *standing punch* and a *hollow punch*, and have found several sources of supply for this type punch. However, I have never found the exact size needed for recoil pads, and thus, I make them. I also use a slightly large punch for punching a hole in the recoil pad for a shotgun the owner wants to insert the takedown tool through the recoil pad and engage the stock bolt. This is basically the same punch I offer for sale to the Gunsmith trade and those hobbyists I come in contact with. It leaves a nice clean round hole and makes the whole job of putting holes in rubber a lot neater.

At this point, let me describe the three types of recoil pad screw holes. The first are the holes that are in the correct location and can be used with existing/available screw. The second are the holes that are in the correct location but have been wallowed out and cannot be used. The third are screw holes that cannot be used because they are in the wrong location.

The first variety, in the correct position and in good shape, are a minority for whatever reason.

The second variety are the most common, and the solution is perhaps the easiest, I can go to a longer screw, or a screw of a larger diameter. I keep a compartmented tray of screws for this purpose, ranging from #8's to #12, from an inch long to two inches long. Or I can plug and re-drill them.

For the third, I keep a supply of quarter inch diameter hardwood furniture dowels in inch and half lengths. When I need to fill a screw hole, I chuck up a nine sixty-fourths inch drill and plug the hole. This little operation is covered in the **Repairs Section**.

When I am ready to put the recoil pad on the stock, and the buttstock has had a recoil pad mounted on it previously, I dip the first third of the recoil pad screw into a small jar of liquid soap on the bench. Insert it through the face of the recoil pad and screw it a couple of turns into the old hole. The liquid soap is a great lubricant for this purpose. If the pad is positioned well enough to allow continuing the belly line of the stock, and if the stock has not been shortened, insert the lower screw and check the fit once more.

However, if the buttstock has been shortened, remove the screw, and deepen the recoil pad screw holes with a drill the diameter of the body of the screw. This allows the threads of the screw to "thread" into the wood. When the screw is screwed into the wood without benefit of a pilot hole, the screw can act as a wedge, and succeed in cracking or breaking off a piece of the buttstock. Take the time to increase the depth of the screw holes.

If new holes must be located, I use a small punch made of drill rod. It is slightly less than the diameter of the holes in the base of the recoil pads, about two inches long, with a point ground onto one end at about a 115 degree angle – a very blunt point indeed. I am interested in securing a center point, not sticking a rod into the butt of the stock.

Dipping the end of the recoil pad center punch into the little liquid soap, I insert the punch through the face of the recoil pad, through the base of the pad, and position the pad on the butt, and tap the punch. With the close fit of the punch to the recoil pad base hole, the resulting punch mark in the butt is well positioned. I then drill the pilot hole for the recoil pad screw and insert the screw to its full depth into the wood. I know this is an extra step most do not perform, but I like seeing the screw full depth in the hole, and later, it makes putting it in a lot easier.

Removing the screw, I insert it into the recoil pad, and secure the pad to the buttstock with the top screw, insuring the toe of the recoil pad is correctly positioned before tightening the top screw. Inserting the punch through the lower hole, I again use it to mark the lower hole location on the butt. With the buttstock still in the vise, loosen the top screw, rotate the recoil pad out of the way, about forty-five degrees is good, and drill the lower hole.

Let me go back a moment. If I am not going to use the original holes for any reason, I plug them. An extra hole in the buttstock is just another avenue for moisture to enter the wood. Just takes a few minutes, plug them.

With the recoil pad holes drilled, I am not ready to grind the recoil pad to fit. I begin this process by attaching the recoil pad to the buttstock. When I have both recoil pad screws installed, I loosed then a quarter turn, move the pad sideways until I find the center of the movement, and then tighten the screw, and then repeat the process with the remaining screw. In this manner I have provided myself some latitude when positioning the recoil pad on the buttstock after fitting.

For many years, I fitted the recoil pads while attached to the buttstock.

Whenever the wood at the end of the buttstock is disturbed, such as in shortening for a recoil pad installation – SEAL the wood. The following picture is of a buttstock on which the wood was not sealed. Over time, moisture came in between the wood and the finish, raising the finish. It also went into the wood and caused more problems.

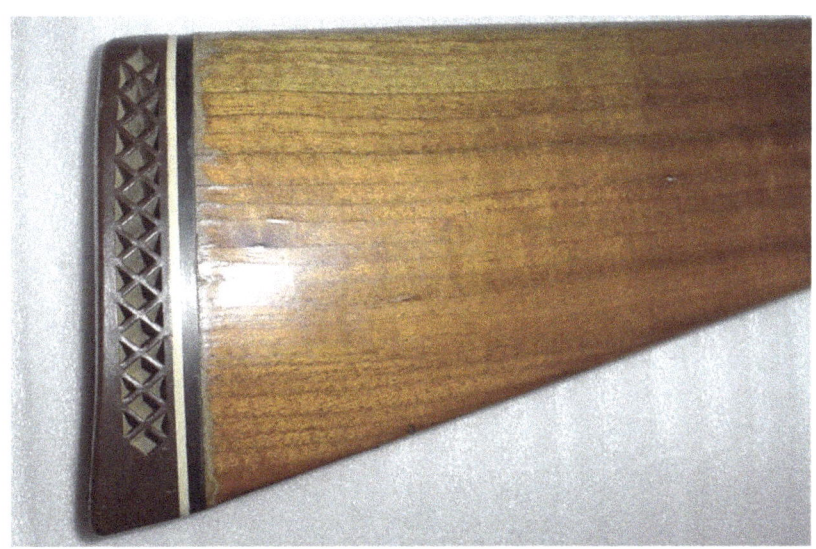

When I am called upon to add length of pull to a stock, and a thicker recoil pad is out of the question, I attach the spacer to the recoil pad.

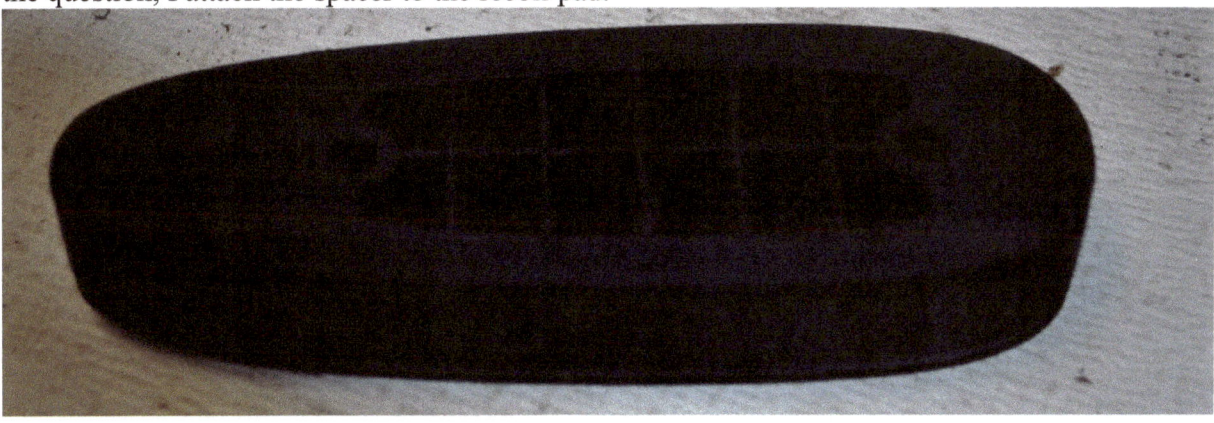

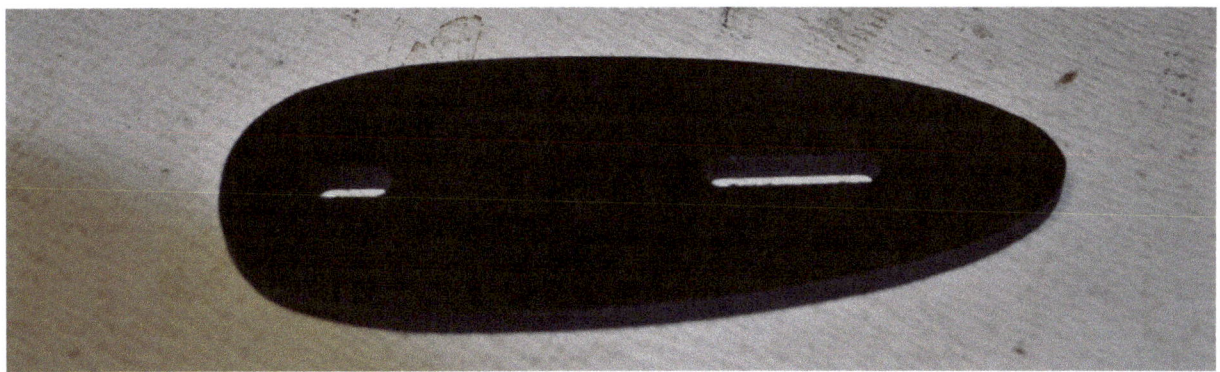

A little black dye in the AcraGlas mixture will be used, and it really works well in hiding the joint.

On my bench, at one end, there are two outlines of recoil pads, and two holes drilled into the bench top. I mate the spacer to the recoil pad, and then anchor them to the bench top with two extra-long – 1 ½" – screws, pulling them tight to the bench. When you do this, use something – I use the ice cream stick used when mixing the AcraGlas – to remove the excess AcraGlas coming from the joint onto the bench. Failure to perform this step could result in a permanently mounted recoil pad on your bench…..

SECTION 8
Installing Adjustable Combs

A friend came home from a local gun show enthused about an old commercial Mauser rifle he had purchased. While it did have the original claw mounted telescope arrangement, the lack of bluing and dings in the worn wood did not impress me. The three-leaf folding express sight was nice, but when he pushed that little button that released the catch on the spring loaded adjustable comb, raising it to scope height, I just plain old fell in love with that rifle.

Adjustable combs on a buttstock can provide a "custom" fit without considerable fitting expense. Adjustable combs allow a rapid transition from one discipline to another; skeet to trap for instance, or to sporting clays or field shooting. If accomplished in a tasteful manner, the adjustable comb can enhance the appearance and value of the stock, but most important, it will allow the shooter the comfort of a stock that fits.

Components common to adjustable comb hardware can be identified a (1) circular base, (1a) bar type base, (2) post, (3) screw and nut, (4) bushing. The hardware can be made of aluminum, bronze or stainless steel. It can be frosted, polished or given whatever finish the metal will take. On bar type installations, I also offer to have the bar engraved with the customer's name.

Not only does it add something to a "piece of metal", it provides the name of the owner of the gun as well as where the work was done.

There are several makers of fine adjustable comb hardware, the one I began with and have found to be consistent in appearance and quality, uniform in size and function well, is the line offered by GRACO. I do however, upon request, make hardware of similar dimensions from Stainless steel.

The components can be modified to be anchored in a variety of ways, and to accept or provide depth adjustment screws. Depending upon the wants of the shooter, I make the modifications requested. Illustrated is a bar type base, drilled and tapped for set screws to be used in establishing comb height adjustment.

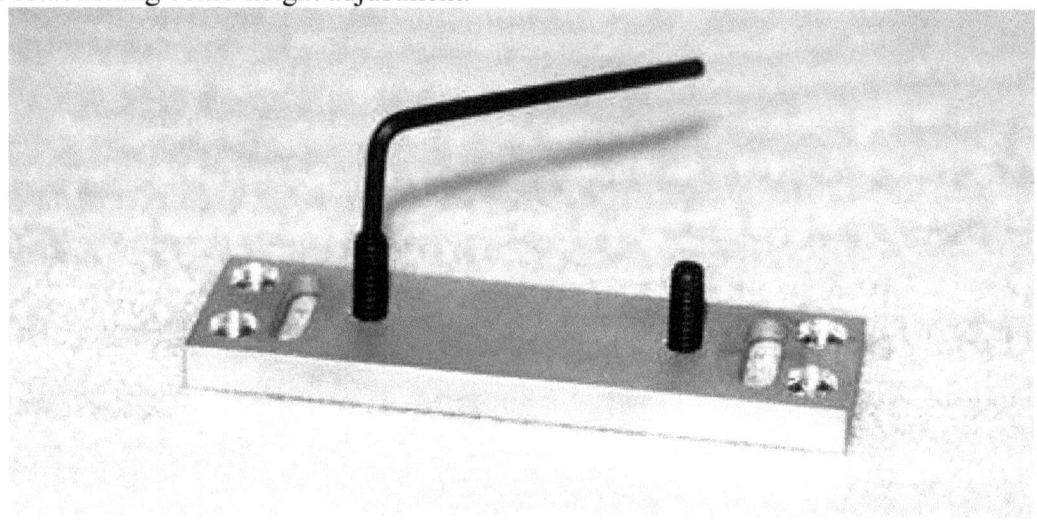

As I do a lot of refinishing and stock repair, I have seen a variety of adjustable comb hardware, most of it functional, some of it appeared easy to install, others looked difficult and would require jigs and fixtures. For the hobbyist, I would recommend using the GRACO adjustable comb hardware in disc form, the Model 870 and 1000. It requires the least amount of tools and functions well.

GRACO offers both the circular type, and several sizes of the bar type, and I am sure that everyone that installs them has a favorite, just as I do. I love them little circles. But like so many of my vices, others do not share it, and request that the bar type be installed on their buttstock. In some cases neither the circular base nor the bar will fit my requirements, especially on the older Remington 1100's which have a very narrow comb. In these cases, I pull out one of the "special bases" that I have made – the base is narrower and thus has less lateral movement – but will set well in the narrow comb of the buttstock.

At this point let me bring out an important fact: ***Not all buttstocks are capable of accepting an adjustable comb***. Because of "hollowed out" buttstocks or most common, the action tube position – such as the Remington Model 1100 or the Beretta 303 and 390 – there is often insufficient area available to install the required hardware.

One of the primary problems associated with installing an adjustable comb on a stock attached to the action with a stock bolt is the thickness of the wood from the top of the comb down to the stock bolt hole. Several gunsmiths have told me of their "requirement" to have 1¼" to 1 3/8" of wood as measured from the top of the comb to the stock bolt hole, as an absolute minimum.

Anyway, however the determination is made, it must be made. I have seen several techniques used and depending upon the type of stock and size/location of the stock bolt hole or action tube, tailor my technique to the need at hand.

I have seen several tools designed specifically for the purpose of determining the thickness of wood between the top of the stock bolt hole of action tube hole and the top of the comb, they work and are amazingly accurate. The number of adjustable combs to be installed, as well as the variety of stocks upon which they are to be installed will determine the sophistication of the tool to be used.

A simple technique, one I started with and continue to use, applicable to the hobbyist who is going to install one or two adjustable combs, involves placing the buttstock on it's side.

First, at the rear of the receiver inlet, measure the distance from the top of the wood down to the center of the stock bolt hole. Place a tic mark (a), on the side of the stock corresponding to the location of the stock bolt hole as it comes through the stock at the receiver. I use Brownell's White Pencil but a grease pencil of almost any color would do.

Second, locate the center of the stock bolt hole in the butt, and make a tic mark (b) on the side of the buttstock corresponding to the center of the stock bolt hole. Use a straight edge to connect the two tic marks – I use a piece of heavy plastic document protector about an inch wide.

Measure the depth of the larger portion of the stock bolt hole, transfer that measurement to the side of the stock (c). I use a length of half inch dowel for this purpose.

Measure the width of the larger portion of the stock bolt hole, divide it in half and make parallel lines to the stock bolt line (d). The lines on the buttstock should correspond very closely to the actual hole in the stock, their size, position and length.

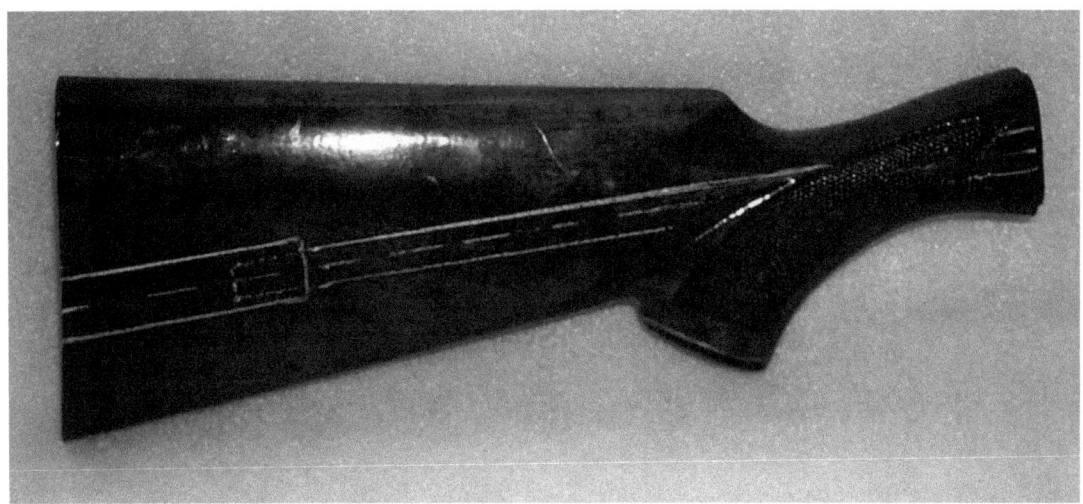

As previously stated, the comb cut should allow between 1 1/8" and 1 ¼" comb thickness. To make this line, I place the stock comb on a flat surface, and use a simple tool to slide along the flat surface and leave a mark on the wood. The comb line tool is a 1" by 2" by 4" block of wood with holes drilled into the side into which a ball point pen can be inserted and serve as a marking device. The pen can be held or wedged in place, but I drilled holes from the top of the wood down into the holes meant for the pen, and then threaded the wood with 12X/24 threads and use allen head set screws to secure the pen in place. The holes are drilled, and identified as spacings of 1", 1 1/8" and 1 ¼" and 1 3/8". For the hobbyist, this simple tool can prevent serious errors. Take the time, make one.

With this information drawn out on the stock, a decision can be made if sufficient wood is available for the installation of an adjustable comb. The whole process takes little more time to complete than it does to write it down or read it.

One of two circumstances will be apparent: The hardware will intrude into the stock bolt/action tube hole, or the hardware will not intrude. It is that simple. For the sake of argument, let's say that sufficient wood for a normal installation – 1 1/8" to 1 ¼" of wood ***is not available***.

If the gun has an action tube, you have two alternatives. First you can stop, wipe the marks off of the stock, reassemble the gun, and go about your business.

Or, you can determine that absolute minimum amount of wood needed for a modified installation. My absolute minimum is 1/4" wood remaining between the action tube and the adjustable comb hardware AFTER the comb cut of 7/8" has been made. Insert your marker/pencil into the 1" spacing hole in the block and make a line representing a one inch distance from the comb. If sufficient wood is still not available for this modified installation, wipe the marks off, reassemble the gun and go about your business.

If sufficient wood is available, great.

Next scenario, if the gun has a stock bolt hole, rather than an action tube, and the lines indicate that the hardware will intrude into the stock bolt hole. First, how deep does it intrude? Does it intrude into the area of the bolt diameter? Or does it intrude into the large portion of the stock bolt hole in which the stock bolt head, retaining washer or stock bolt guide resides?

If the lines indicate the adjustable comb hardware will intrude into the smaller hole of the stock bolt diameter, wipe off the marks, etc, and go about your business.

In most cases, the lines will intrude into the area in which the stock bolt head, stock bolt retaining washer of stock bolt guide resides. If this is the case, great, we can do it. We do, however, have to compensate for this intrusion.

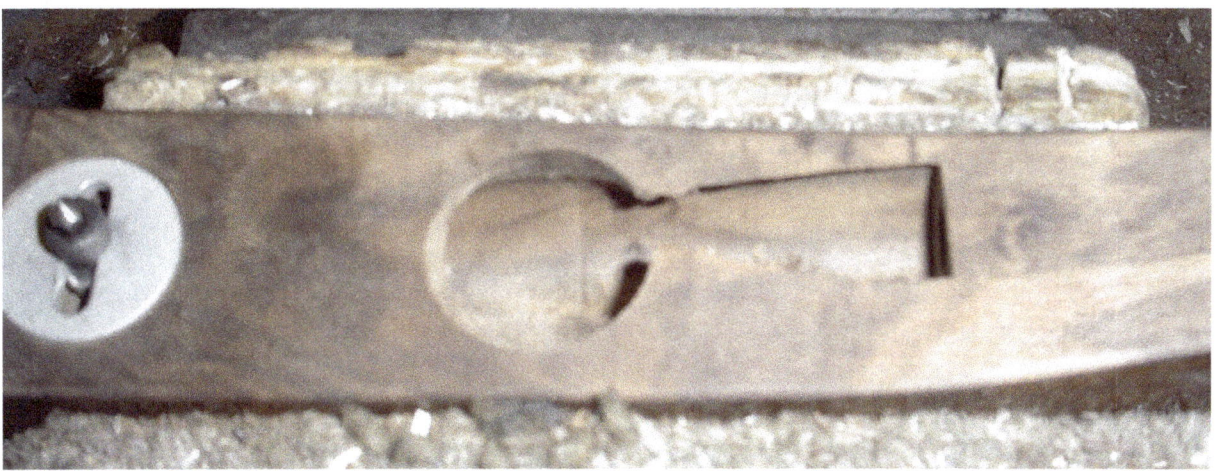

We can do this in two different ways, first, we can epoxy a hardwood dowel which has been center drilled in the stock bolt hole and use a longer stock bolt.

Or we can insert the stock bolt assemble into the hole and insert a hardwood dowel which has been center drilled with a hole sufficient to allow a tool to pass through the dowel and engage the stock bolt.

A special note. If I use this technique and the stock bolt is a screw slot head, I convert the stock bolt to a socket head and provide a "T" handle allen wrench of the appropriate size to the owner.

If the situation calls for an extended stock bolt, I search my stock of stock bolts. If one of the correct length is not available, I have one made to my specifications by a local welder who will use a socket head bolt of the appropriate thread and diameter and weld in an extension, dress the weld and cold blue the completed bolt. Many times, bolts which can be modified to fit – primarily shortening them – are available at a Mill Supply outlet.

The hardwood dowel I use is of oak, and available locally. I have seen soft wood dowels available in the large chain stores and would use them if nothing was available. If you have elected to use an extended stock bolt, and need a center drilled section of dowel, first measure the distance from the stock bolt shoulder in the stock out to a location past the point at which the adjustable comb hardware will intrude into the stock bolt hole.

    With this measurement taken, transfer this measurement to the dowel of the appropriate diameter and cut the section of the dowel to be used. Drilling the hole through the dowel can become a problem even in the best of times, but here is how I do it.

    First I center punch the exact center of both ends of the dowel. For the hobbyist with only a hand drill, drill a pilot hole using an eighth inch drill bit in from each end, keeping the drill centered as much as possible. Next, go to the larger drill bit will allow clearance of the stock bolt, I usually use an 11/32" and find that it works well in most instances. But the drill bit size should be determined by the size of the stock bolt plus a thirty-second for clearance.

    If you are skilled, the two holes will meet in the middle and you will have a straight hole, if not, use a slightly larger drill to enlarge the hole and allow for the free passage of the stock bolt. A somewhat cheap tool that makes this task easier is an extended drill bit, something 10 to 12 inches long. As you are not going into production, purchase a drill of sufficient quality to drill the hole you need drilled. Purchasing a carbide drill for this purpose would be a waste.

    With the dowel inserted into the stock, slip the extended stock bolt into the whole and engage the threads on the receiver. If you can tighten the receiver into the wood, you are ready for the next step, if not, why? This check and confirm activity insures the stock bolt is of the correct length, and the hole in the dowel is functional. Imagine shoving the dowel covered with acra glass into the hole, and then determining the stock bolt to be too short.

    Dowels usually comes in three-foot sections, try again. When I first tried this years ago, I came close to using the entire section of dowel before getting one with an acceptable hole.

For those that want a hole in the dowel through which a tightening tool could be inserted, use the same technique in drilling the dowel, but depending upon the head – screw slot, hex or socket head – the drill used might need to be larger to accommodate the desired tool.

The length of such a dowel would be the distance from the butt to the head of the stock bolt, MINUS two inches. One of the two inches is intended to be between the stock bolt and the dowel – this space can be used for a PVC spacer - which will allow the stock bolt to move back as it is unscrewed from the receiver. The other inch of space is reserved for the butt end.

For the shop that has need of center drilled dowels on a re-occurring basis - I keep two, six and eight-inch lengths of 3/4, 7/8 and 1" dowels on hand - I have found that to drill the hole accurately, a drill press is almost unbeatable. I use a cross feed vise to hold a short center punch with its point up and the punch vertical, and then align the center punch to the point of the drill.

In the past, I used a block of hardwood with an undersize hole drilled in it and the center punch forced into the hole and then the block "C" clamped in position.

Regardless, a center punch – securely held in place - must be aligned with a drill bit of the correct dimensions in the chuck of the drill. The alignment must be absolutely straight.

If the center drilled dowel is to be used in combination with an extended stock bolt, begin the process by coating the stock bolt with release agent. Setting the stock bolt aside to dry, begin preparing the dowel for permanent placement in the stock by cutting grooves lengthways of it. These grooves are evenly spaced around the circumference of the dowel to allow the excess epoxy to flow, as well as provide a means of carrying the epoxy deep into the hole. I use a hacksaw with a course blade to make this cut – only a little deeper than a sixteenth – and make five or six of them.

For most of my epoxy needs, I use Brownell's AcraGlas and use it for this project also. Mixing up a small batch – I use the measuring cup also from Brownell's to mix only what I need and still insure the instructions are followed – I then use a mixing stick to lightly coat the inside of the stock bolt hole. Then coat the dowel, and inserting the stock bolt through the dowel, drop it in place.

Use the tightening tool – screw driver or "T" handle allen wrench – to lightly tighten the buttstock onto the shotgun receiver. I am trying to secure the dowel in place, not assemble the weapon, and tightening too much can cause problems with the dowel sitting in place properly. Set it aside to harden.

If the dowel is to be used in conjunction with the old stock bolt, and the tightening tool must pass through it, I like to place a spacer between the stock bolt hold shoulder and the dowel. Most frequently, I use a one-inch long piece of PVC pipe of the correct diameter.

First of all, assemble the stock onto the shotgun receiver being sure that the washer under the stock bolt head is present, then insert the PVC spacer if used. Check and confirm the center drilled dowel will work by inserting it into the stock bolt hole until it comes to rest against the PVC spacer, and then insert the tightening tool through the dowel. If you cannot engage the stock bolt with the tightening tool, find the problem and correct it before proceeding.

If it works, great. Remove all of the parts from the stock bolt hole and on to the next step.

First, coat the head of the stock bolt with release agent and set it aside to dry. Prepare the dowel by cutting length way groves around its circumference. These grooves are evenly spaced around the circumference of the dowel to allow the excess epoxy to flow, as well as provide a means of carrying the epoxy deep into the hole. I use a hacksaw with a course blade to make this cut – only a little deeper than a sixteenth – and make five or six of them.

Insert the stock bolt and tighten it, securing the receiver to the buttstock. Drop in the PVS spacer, insuring it falls to the bottom of the hole and comes to rest against the shoulder of the stock bolt hole.

Mix up a small batch Brownell's AcraGlas using the measuring cup also from Brownell's to mix only what is needed. Insure the instructions on mixing the AcraGlas are followed. I then use a mixing stick to lightly coat the inside of the stock bolt hole, then lightly coat the dowel.

Insert the dowel into the stock bolt hole until it comes in contact with the PVC spacer. Now, as we want to store the buttstock receiver up, the dowel would have a tendency to slide back down the stock bolt hole unless we provide a stop. I use one of two methods of providing a stop. The first and most preferred, is a chunk of modeling clay I use when filling voids in receivers when bedding actions. Made a ball of it and shove it in until you are certain it will hold the dowel in place.

The alternate method involves much the same principal, but I use those little styrofoam peanuts that always seem to be blowing out of boxes. I shove several into the stock bolt hole, wedging the dowel in place.

Then place the combination aside to dry, receiver end up. My thoughts are simple on this practice, if excess AcraGlas comes back down the hole in the dowel, I can drill it out. If storing the combination receiver down allows excess AcraGlas to puddle around the stock bolt, I may have a problem and a one-piece gun…

We should now be prepared to mark and cut the comb for the adjustable comb. In preparing to make the cut for the comb, I have found that by using a heavy-duty nylon filament tape to cover the area of the stock to be cut, (tape on both sides and across the top), I do not have chips in the finish or wood separation.

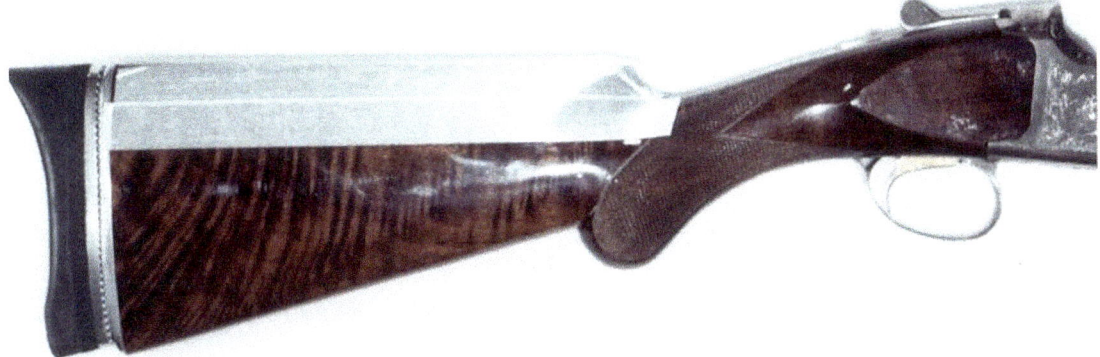

As a matter of course, and after having tried several different band saw blades, some would make straight cuts but couldn't make the radius I wanted, others were uncontrollable, and some … I have chosen the *Craftsman Aluminum Cutting* blade for this purpose on my band saw. This blade gives me a smooth cut, is easily guided and allows a nice radius on the ends.

With the buttstock taped up, and the stock bolt hole properly supported with the dowel AcraGlassed in place, it is time to make the line upon which the adjustable comb will be cut. Using the comb line tool previously described, insert the ball point pen in the appropriate spaced hole. I prefer 1 ¼" if possible, hold the buttstock comb down on a flat surface, butt vertical, and slide the comb line tool across the flat surface, allowing the pen to leave a line on the tape.

With the primary line drawn on the tape, another decision must be made, unless the owner of the buttstock has already determined what they want. That decision is the position of the two cuts freeing the comb from the buttstock. Some adjustable combs are cut with both cuts being made from the top of the comb.

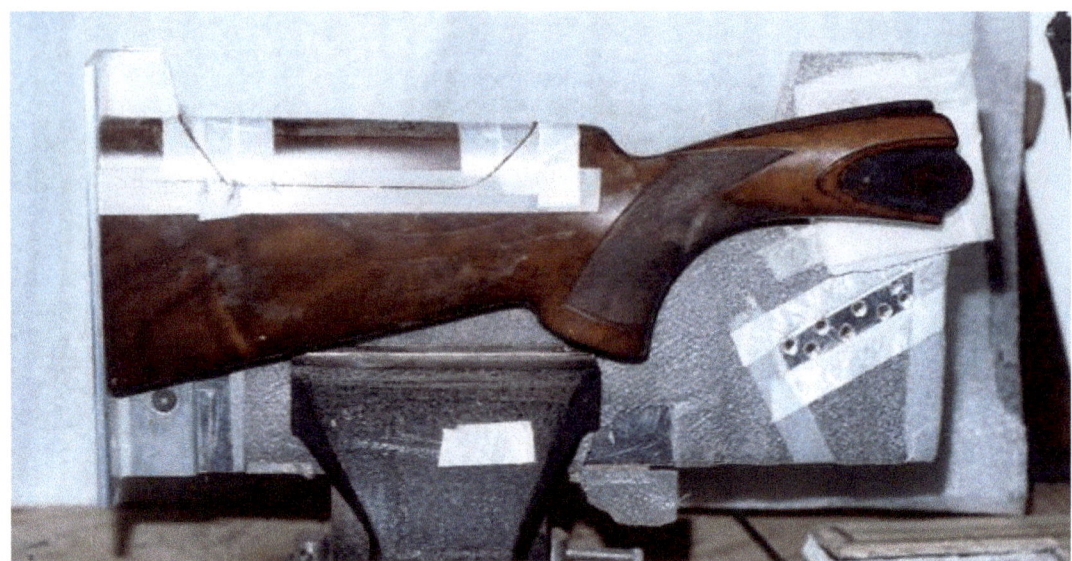

Other cuts are made with the rear cut coming from the top of the comb, **but the front cut entering the wood at or very near the tip of the comb.** I use the later style with skeet shooters who "crawl" their stock and need the additional room. I actually prefer this cut, feeling it does not distract from the lines of the stock as much as the dual comb cut.

Assuming the rear cut will be standard, regardless of the front cut, I use a 1" radius cut from a piece of plastic transparency. Positioning the overlay to connect the top of the comb approximately 1 ½" from the butt, and the comb cut line, I use a ball point pen to trace around the radius. Why do I go through this?

I have found that I get less blade bind, and make a smoother cut using this radius. In addition, I use a oscillating sander to finish the interior of the cut on the buttstock and have found that the 1 ½" sanding drum works well.

I do the same with the front cut, unless the cut comes in from the tip of the comb.

To insure the cut is square, I mount the buttstock in a jig after insuring the recoil pad holes are vertical. If they are not, I drill one hole to compliment an existing hole, and mount the buttstock in the fixture.

For the hobbyist, a simple fixture can be quickly made. A 1" x 2" x 6" of scrap can be used quite effectively. The key is insuring the two recoil pad holes in the butt are vertical. If they are not, drill an additional hole to compliment an existing hole. I use a simple test to determine if the recoil pad holes in the butt are vertical, I place a combination square in the workbench, and align the top recoil pad screw hole with the edge of the square. If the bottom hole falls in line, great. If not, I place a mark on the butt above the bottom screw hole which is in line. I then drill the additional hole.

To correctly space the holes on the board to be used as a fixture, I determine the width of the butt, (2" for example) divide in by 2 (equals 1") and then add ¼" for clearance. I then use a pair of dividers to determine distance between the two holes to be used.

Using the combination square, I mark off the centerline distance to be used, (1 ¼" in our example) and then the spacing. Use a drill that provides clearance for the screws to be used but does not allow additional movement. As the screws which will hold the fixture to the buttstock must first pass through the fixture, a longer than normal screw must be used. I use and recommend the use of the same size as the recoil pad – usually a #10, but sometimes a #12 - but ¾" longer.

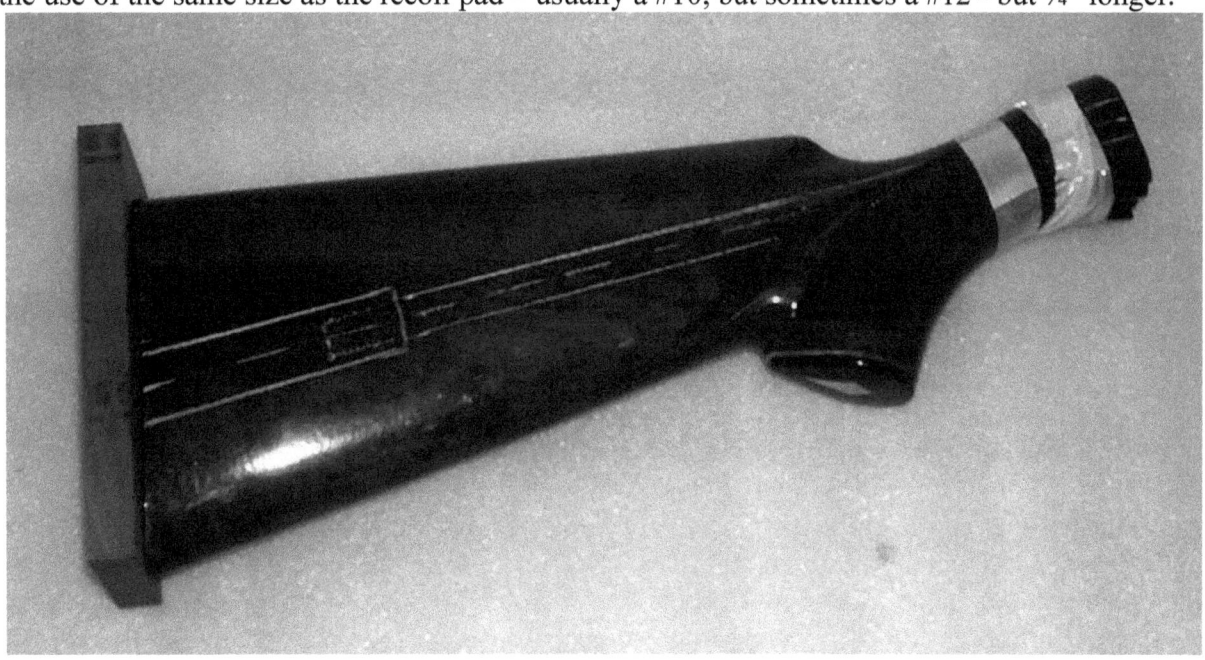

With the rear taken care of, the front of the buttstock must also be supported. I have used and advocate the used of a simple piece of wood of a thickness sufficient to level the butt stock, and secure it in place with several wraps of nylon filament tape.

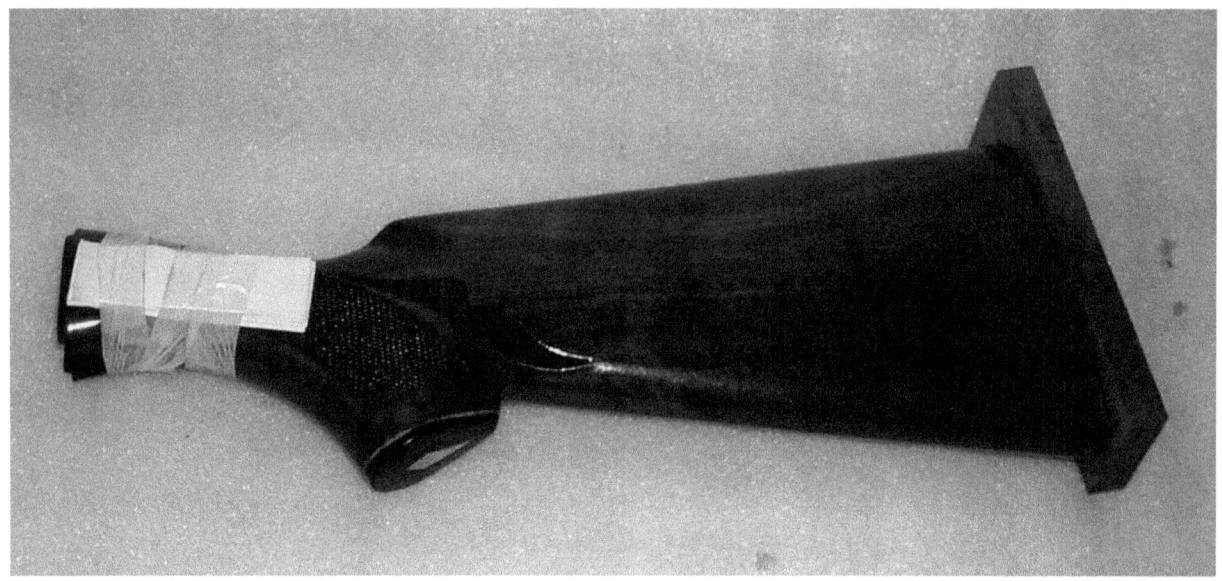

For a shop installing several adjustable combs per day, a fixture holding the buttstock while the comb is being cut, and for subsequent operations, is a time saver and enhances quality. I have seen few stock makers do the cutting freehand, without a holding/leveling fixture of some type, I admire their skill. I will not do it nor do I advocate it. I have seen a variety of fixtures used to secure the buttstock for cutting, some rather elaborate, but all functional. The one I use was made from scrap aluminum, it is light, easy to use, and versatile.

With a short straight edge surface, two inches is sufficient, use a ball point pen to lightly make index marks on the side of the buttstock on the tape, crossing the anticipated line to be cut. I make my index marks about an inch long, split over the two sides of the line to be cut.

Before beginning the cut on the buttstock, make sure that the vertical guide on the band saw is elevated sufficiently for the buttstock to clear it. Then with the buttstock secured, make the comb cut.

After making the cut, I flatten the bottom of the comb on a 2" x 42" belt sander using a medium grit (120) belt. I use the 120 grit belt because it removes the wood well, but does not leave deep sanding marks, even on highly figured wood. I remove as little wood as possible in erasing the saw marks and providing a flat surface. I then block sand the freshly cut areas with 240 grit paper and then 400 grit paper.

For the hobbyist, instead of a belt sander, coarse sandpaper on a sanding block will do the job. Keeping the edges sharp and the flat level is very important. *Please note that the nylon tape put on the stock before we cut it is still in place.*

Sanding the buttstock can be much more difficult, especially for the hobbyist. For the hobbyist, I recommend starting with a wood file, such as a pattern makers file, and after removing the saw marks, then wrapping sandpaper around a wooden dowel or at least 1" in diameter, but no more than 1 ¼", and using it to "draw sand" the cuts. When the file marks are erased, go to a finer sandpaper, then lightly hand sand with 400 grit paper.

For the commercial shop, I highly recommend an oscillating sander using a medium and then fine sanding drum before doing a final hand sand with 400 grit paper to sand the end cuts. When the forward cut begins at the tip of the comb, the oscillating sander can still be used, just be sure of controlling the pressure of the stock against the sander.

Sitting the comb back on the stock should confirm the quality of one's cutting and sanding. If there are large gaps, and there shouldn't be, remove the high spots until the two surfaces match very closely. I then fully sand the flats and remove the edges, rounding them slightly with a double cut mill bastard. For the hobbyist, a conventional metal file will do the job.

As I have stated elsewhere in this book, properly sealing exposed wood is essential to the long life of the wood, and the comb area needs sealing and finishing. I dilute a small amount of Deft Semi Gloss Cabinet finish four to one, with lacquer thinner. And then brush it sparingly onto the exposed wood. For those with the later need, Deft also puts their semi-gloss in spray cans which work well in this application if you are familiar with using a spray can. As Deft dries in 10 to 12 minutes, several sealer coats can be applied in a short time.

After three to four sealer coats, depending upon the grain of the wood, use 400 grit sandpaper to smooth the surface, and then go over it lightly with 0000 steel wool. The finish should reflect a grain filled semi-gloss wood surface.

Although I have recommended Deft Semi-gloss, I have used and seen used a variety of materials used as sealers, including Tru Oil, Tong Oil, quick dry epoxies and several clear finishes. The main requirement is that whatever you use should bond to the wood and "compliment" the finish already on the stock.

The next step is to select the type of hardware to be used, and depending upon the stock, how it is to be installed. There are two types of hardware, bar and circular, that are commonly used, each presents it's own problems and solutions. For the person wanting to put an adjustable comb on his gun, or just installs a few, I would definitely recommend the circular or disc type hardware. The expense of the required tools to install it is minimal, so I will address the installation of the circular hardware first.

There are also two ways to install the hardware, the hardware can be held in place with screws, or it can be epoxied in place. The type anchored with screws is illustrated on the left of the picture, the type anchored with epoxy is illustrated on the right.

On some stocks, especially Remington Model 1100, Model 1187 and Beretta 302, 303 and 390, but actually any semi automatic shotgun with an action tube, there is no room to use small wood screws coming down through the hardware into the stock, on these I epoxy the hardware in place.

To provide a good surface to which the epoxy is to bond, I drill a series of 1/8" diameter holes approximately 1/16" deep around the circumference of the disc type hardware, approximately 3/8" apart.

On others, most over and under and pump guns, I drill the hardware - both disc and bar styles - to accept small wood screws, countersinking the heads into the metal. I prefer this method because if the wood has to be refinished at a later date, the hardware can be removed.

As there are two basic types of adjustable comb hard ware, bar and circular, that are commonly used, each presents its own problems and solutions. For the person wanting to put an adjustable comb on his gun, or just do a few, I would recommend the circular / disc type hardware. The expense of the required tools is minimal, so I will address the installation of the circular hardware first.

A furniture repairman that befriended me years ago explained how he was so accurate in positioning hidden dowels for some of his repair jobs. He showed me an aspirin bottle full of very small lead shot. He would make a small tick mark with a scribe on the larger of the two pieces to be joined, place on shot in the tick mark, place the other piece of wood in position, and strike the wood over the shot with his open hand. The shot would imprint both pieces of wood, providing the man the centers he needed for drilling the dowel holes. If more than one dowel was needed, he would install the first dowel without glue, and repeat the process in finding a second location.

When I started installing adjustable combs, this is the technique I used. It works. Locating a shell with #10 shot was only as difficult as a visit to the ammunition counter and purchasing several shot cartridges for a 357 magnum revolver. For the person installing the adjustable comb on his stock, or perhaps a small shop installing them infrequently, I would recommend this procedure for determining centers.

But first, the approximate locations for the discs must be determined. It doing this, I place the rear disc in a position approximately ¼" in front of the bottom of the radius, and using a ball point pen, mark the approximate location of the center of the disc on the tape at the side of the buttstock. The second disc, I place approximately 2 ¾" - measured center to center – forward of the first disc, and make an identical mark on the tape at the side of the buttstock.

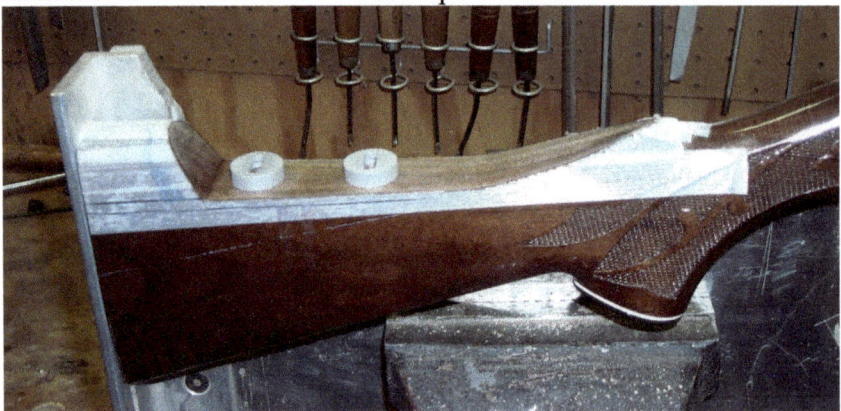

Removing both discs and setting them aside temporarily, I then measure the width of the buttstock at the point indicated by the rear most ball point pen mark. This mark indicates the center of the lateral position of the disc, divide it in half, and using a scribe, make an indenture on the flat surface indicating the point at which I want to drill. This indenture should be at the center of the width of the buttstock at that point.

I can then effectively drill the buttstock to accept the disc hardware the customer wants used. Please note, this customer also wanted the rear to be a straight line cut, rather than the radius I prefer. For the hobbyist, if you can't borrow a Forester drill of the correct diameter to accommodate the disc, buy one. When drilling the holes for the disc, maintain the drill vertical, enlist the aid of a buddy, or in a real tight, ask your wife to help. She will relish the idea of telling you what to do and get away with it.

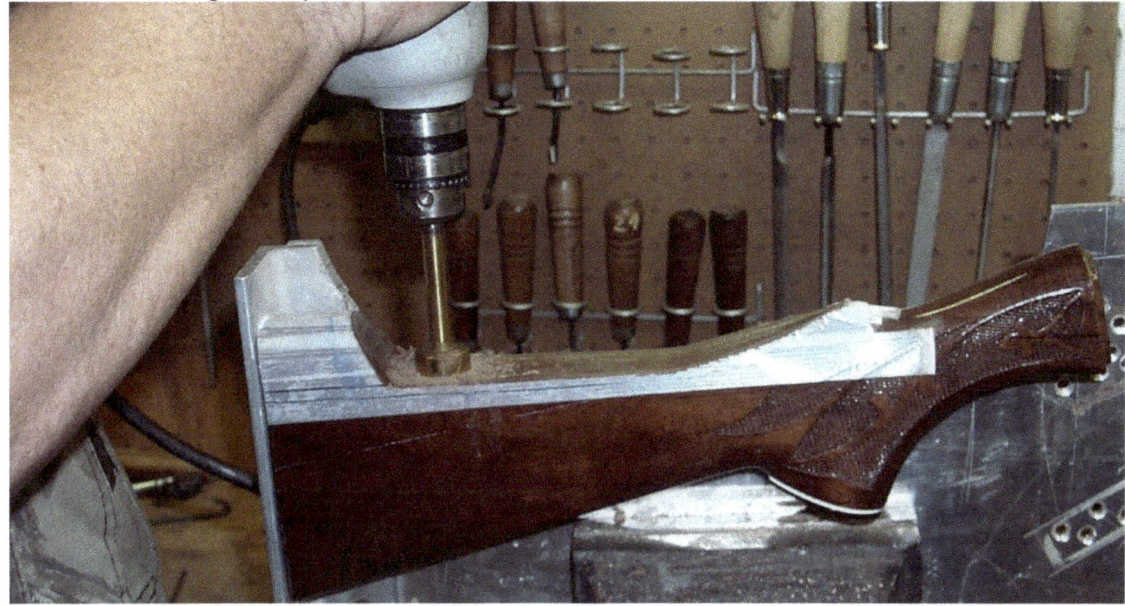

For drilling the hole in the buttstock for the adjustable comb disc, I strongly recommend the investment in a forester drill bit of the appropriate size. Not only will the width of the hole be correct, the sides will be straight, and the bottom true to the sides. I have drilled several sets of holes using a forester bit and a hand drill. It works. However, care must be taken to insure the drill bit is vertical. In addition, the depth of the holes must be checked carefully to insure the correct depth – thickness of the disc – is not exceeded. This may mean inserting the discs in the hole several times to determine the correct depth. The goal is to have them just a hair below the comb surface.

This is where I begin using a technique I have developed to indicating the drill position on the comb. I have several 10 x 24 socket head screws just a quarter inch long. I used this screw and the nut provided in the adjustable comb kit and assemble the disc, the short screw and the nut. The screw is short enough it will not protrude through the nut and bottom out.

As the allen wrench used for the post screw - 5/32" – is the same as the short screw, I cut off a piece about a quarter inch long from the end of one of a 5/32" allen wrench, chucked it up in my hand drill, and ground a ninety-degree point on the small piece of allen wrench. Realizing that the shop was infested with *squirbells* – invisible animals that eat small screws and springs dropped on the floor, most gun shops have them – I made several of them. Effectively using almost the entire allen wrench.

Insert the assembled disc in the holes, place the small piece of Allen wrench in the head of the screw - point up - place the comb over the cut.

Aligning the vertical lines on the two pieces and tap the top of the comb with the flat of your hand. The tap will result in an imprint in the comb of the point of the allen wrench in the head of the post screw. The first hole position for the comb is thus determined.

Now some people will insert both assembled discs in the buttstock, insert a pointed piece of allen wrench in each one, align the pieces, tap the comb, and have the position of both holes at the same time. *It you are really good in perfect alignment, this might work. I do one at a time*.

The next step is to drill the rear bushing hole in the comb. Again, I would strongly recommend the use of a forester drill bit for this purpose. I have a small fixture into which I place the comb for drilling. The fixture holds the comb in place, with the surface to be drilled level, insuring the holes to be drilled will match the alignment of those in the buttstock.

For the hobbyist, without a drill press and using a hand drill with the appropriate forester drill, this step can cause you a lot of problems. First, you must worry about the hole being drilled in the correct place, then the alignment of the hole, and finally, the depth of the hole as if the hole is too deep, it will come through the top of the comb. And yes, I have repaired several combs customers have brought in with the bushing hole drilled through the comb.

When I first used a hand drill to drill the bushing holes in the comb, I enlisted the aid of a friend to hold the comb, check the alignment of the drill, and determine the depth of the hold by watching the depth mark on the drill bit. If at all possible, perform this function on a drill press.

After drilling the rear comb bushing hole, insert the bushing into the comb and try it over the rear post in the buttstock. If it glides up and down, great, if the comb must be held at an angle to rise or fall on the post, a "small" problem exists.

The location of the second bushing hole is critical to the success of the project. The location of the center must be exact, and it must be drilled precisely at this location if the bushings in the comb are to accept the post of the base and provide the vertical movement without excess movement. To insure the correct location of the second bushing hole in the comb, leave the post on the rear hole, and insert the pointed piece of allen wrench to the front disc.

The comb, with one hole drilled and bushing slipped in place, is slipped in place over the rear post, and down to make contact with the locator pointer. Insuring the comb is centered over the buttstock, strike the top of the comb lightly. The resulting indenture in the bottom of the comb by the location pointer identifies the exact point at which to drill the second bushing hole.

With the second bushing hole indicated, carefully drill the hole. Again, you want the hole only deep enough to allow the busing to sit flush to the surface of the comb. Take your time, correcting an error at this point can be both time consuming and expensive. With both bushings slipped into the comb, it is time to continue.

Slip the comb over the two posts. If all went well, the bushings in the comb should slide over the posts to the depth of the holes drilled. At this point, the posts are taller than the bushings holes are deep. Slip the comb over the two posts. If all went well, the bushings in the comb should slide over the posts to the depth of the holes drilled. At this point, the posts are taller than the bushing holes are deep.

If the comb does not slip over the posts, we must correct this problem, and it can be corrected unless the holes drilled are totally away and gone. Perhaps you noticed that the bushings fit over the posts with little slack? Right. And that is why care must be taken to drill the holes so precisely. The procedure I have outlined is quick, utilizes few tools, and is not expensive. So let's make the assumption that something disturbed you when drilling the bushing holes in the comb, and the comb does not slip easily over the posts.

Correction Time…First, we must secure the bushings to the comb. This is accomplished by installing the set screws which – when tightened – will lock the comb in position on the posts. But first, we have another task for them. The set screws I use are 10 x 24. I use a #21 drill to drill a hole through the side of the comb and through the bushing. The placement of the hole, and the edges of it have a lot to do with how the overall appearance of the installation is perceived.

I identify a location for the hole first. With a fine point pencil I place a mark approximately 5/16" above the bottom of the comb, and centered with the bushing hole. Here again, care must be taken in drilling this hole. First, I use a small center punch to identify the location.

I place the comb in a compound vise to drill the holes needed. For the hobbyist, I recommend the use of a drill press, rather than a hand drill. If you have to use a hand drill, enlist the aid of a buddy to help keep it aligned, or significant other, providing she is still talking to you.

If a drill press is available, the bottom of the comb must be at parallel to the drill. I have insured correct alignment by lightly clamping a short piece of angle iron to the comb – using a piece of scrap soft wood between the top of the comb and the clamp - and also insured the edge of the comb to be drilled is at a right angle to the drill.

I know it sounds like a lot of trouble for just a hole. But that hole can make a nice looking job or something else.

With both holes prepared, I use a #19 drill to continue the hole and drill through the bushing.

With the holes drilled through the bushing, the hole now must be threaded. I thread the wood as I am going into the bushing. A good sharp tap makes this task an easy one.

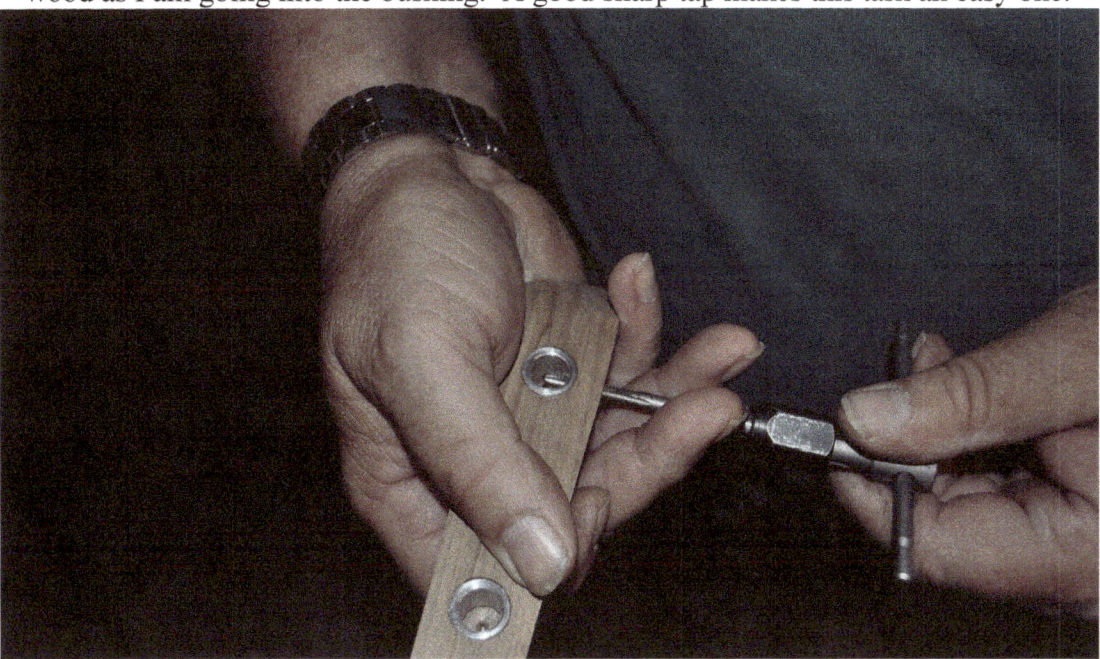

With the holes and the bushing taped, insert the set screws, and tighten them until they just begin to come through the bushing, and back them out a half turn.

With both bushings so secured, we are ready to correct the error in hole alignment. To drill the hole, I use a drill 1/64th" larger than the post diameter.

First the discs must be attached to the buttstock. Most buttstocks do not have sufficient wood to use small wood screws to hold the hardware to the stock. I have found that a very good epoxy will do the job IF the hardware is prepared. To provide this insurance, I use a #19 drill to drill holes approximately 1/16" deep around the circumference of the hardware. In this manner, I am providing something for the epoxy to grasp.

With the holes drilled, and the hardware prepared, one final step, call it insurance if you will, must be made. The GRACO circular/disc hardware is open on the bottom where the cut was made to accept the nut. The chance of accidently getting some of the adhesive agent in this cut must be prevented.

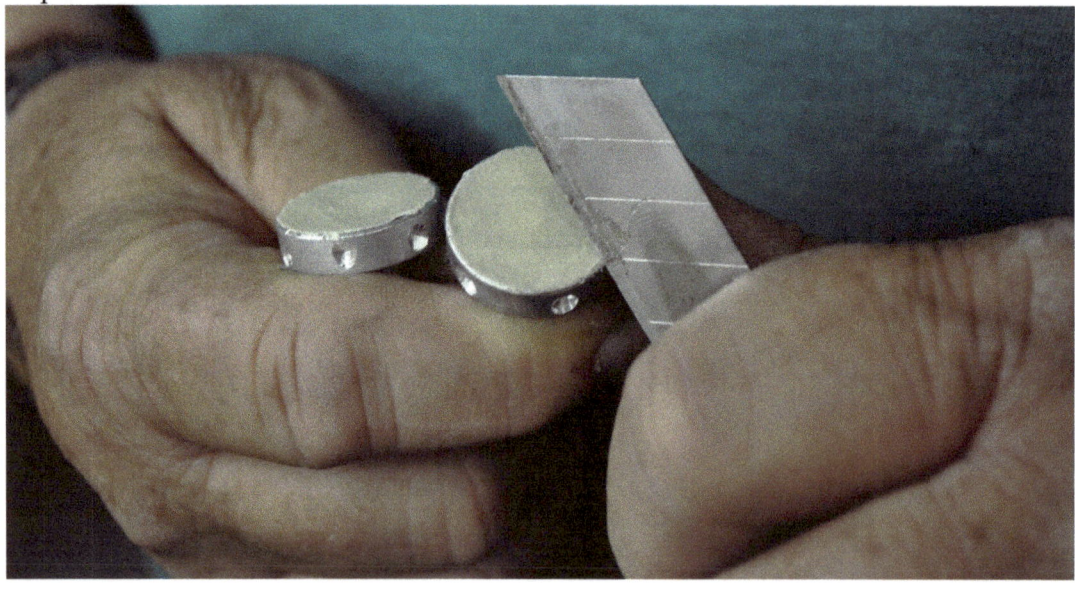

I coat the inside of the holes drilled in the buttstock for the hardware…

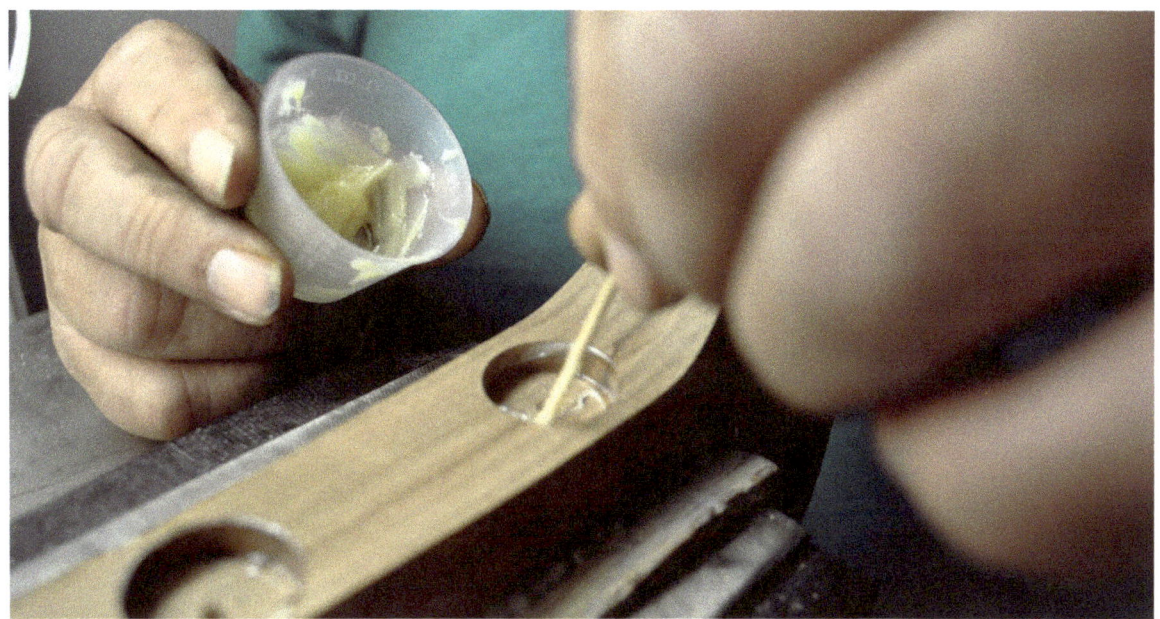

And then apply epoxy to the hardware.

before seating the hardware in the buttstock.

I have found the easiest way to remove the excess epoxy is to wipe it off with a finger tip and deposit it on a paper towel. It works very well, thank you!

To insure the hardware dries in an upright position, compatible with the hardware in the comb, I place the comb over the hardware/posts….. *Just a note here: There are rules and guidelines for almost everything. A Plumber friend told me in his business there are two. Liquid runs downhill and don't lick your fingers.*

And hold my breath until it slides easily down the posts. Please note that the comb is not resting on the buttstock. The holes drilled for the bushings in the comb were only bushing depth for a reason – to keep the comb from coming in contact with the buttstock epoxy and rendering the job a waste of time.

The holes in the comb will be deepened after the epoxy has set, enabling the comb to slide down and make contact with the buttstock.

SECTION 9
Adjustable Buttplates

There is an incredible selection of adjustable butt plates on the market, and many gunsmiths and stock makers have their own design. However, most adjustable buttplates have one thing in common, they are made of aluminum, they have a base plate and a pad plate, and a means of joining the two which allows for adjustment.

For our purpose, the installation of the Stock Shop Single Point Adjustable Buttplate will be accomplished. The Single point adjustable buttplate is unique among most of the other adjustable butt plates in that all adjustments, vertical, horizontal and diagonal, are controlled by a single screw accessible with an allen wrench through the face of the recoil pad. Adjustments are very quick and positive.

The single point adjustable buttplate is comprised of three primary components: a base plate which is attached to the buttstock with wood screws, the pad plate onto which the recoil pad is secured with an allen head machine screw, and the offset button which provides the adjustment when secured in place by an allen head machine screw serving the function as the tension screw. To complete the kit utilizing the 1/8" plates, there are two 10 x 32 x 7/16" allen head machine screws, the two used to secure the recoil pad to the recoil pad plate and one 10 x 32 x 5/16" allen head machine screw used as the tension screw which locks the two plates into position, a small washer for the tension screw and two 10 x 1 1/2" wood screws. For the kit utilizing the 1/8" plates, the three allen head screws are longer to compensate for the thicker plates.

A special note here, when assembled, if the recoil pad plate does not move freely, check to see if the screws holding the recoil pad to the recoil pad plate are not the slightest bit long and are dragging. If this is the case, shorten then by one thread at a time until clearance is achieved.

The first step in installing the adjustable buttplate is to determine the length of pull (distance from trigger to center of buttstock butt) and the recoil pad to be used. If for example, the desired length of pull (LOP) is 14 ¼", and the recoil pad to be used is a Pachmayr Presentation with a one-inch thickness, the buttstock should be cut to a length of 13".

How was this figure determined? The adjustable buttplate is ½" wide – comprised of two 1/8" plates - and the recoil pad is one inch thick: thus, recoil pad of 1" plus adjustable buttplate 1/4" plus 13" stock equals 14 ¼" length of pull. Remember, the length of pull is measured at the center of the recoil pad's height.

Unlike a recoil pad, the base plate of the single point adjustable butt plate, or most adjustable butt plates, is made of metal, is flat, and will not easily conform to a butt which is not straight / flat. For this reason, if no other, I strongly recommend the use of a ten-inch compound miter saw when shortening butt stocks. When combined with a carbide tipped blade, the cut will be absolutely great. In addition, a compound miter saw can duplicate the pitch existing on the stock, or even increase or decrease it exactly. Yes, a powered belt sander can be used to "true" up a cut made by a band saw, but so can a large file.

Once the buttstock has been cut to length, double check your measurement, insure it is the correct length. If additional wood needs to be removed, now is the time to do it. Assuming the length is correct, and the cut is good, a determination must be made if the existing recoil pad screw holes are sufficiently deep for the screws that will be used. As the kit comes with two 10 x 1 ¼ wood screws, I use an eighth inch drill to insure the holes are deep enough. I drill them approximately 1 ½" deep. I do not relocate the holes if they are standard, 3 1/10". If, however, the holes present are not original, or if they have been enlarged, I will plug them using ¼" hardwood furniture dowels and Brownell's AcraWeld, and re-drill them. This procedure is covered in Section 11, Repairs.

After drilling the holes, I run a screw in each hole and then remove it, insuring they will accept the screw with no problem. Placing the base plate on the butt, I use the provided screws to secure it to the buttstock. With it on the stock, I make sure that sufficient metal is available at the toe of the stock to continue the stock line.

I then seal the exposed wood on the butt. Open grained wood is an invitation for moisture. I have seen several Very Expensive skeet and trap guns whose stocks had been shortened and recoil pads or adjustable butt plates installed and the finish had separated from the wood around the joint. It could easily be flicked off with a fingernail, revealing the bare wood beneath it. One case I had the opportunity to repair, the butt had not been sealed after the buttstock had been shortened. I would guess the same condition existed on the others. I seal ALL stocks that I shorten or true. I use the same sealer mixture for this task as I do when applying a satin finish: A mixture of two ounces of Deft Semi Gloss and a half ounce of lacquer thinner. It permeates the wood well, dries quickly, and other than the smell, is great to work with.

With the base plate secured to the buttstock, I then use a sharp pointed scribe to trace the butt outline onto the base plate. I am careful to use a single continuing line, achieved by moving both the scribe and the buttstock, and not press against the wood on the buttstock hard enough to damage the finish. Success is one continuous line on the base plate. Remove the base plate from the buttstock.

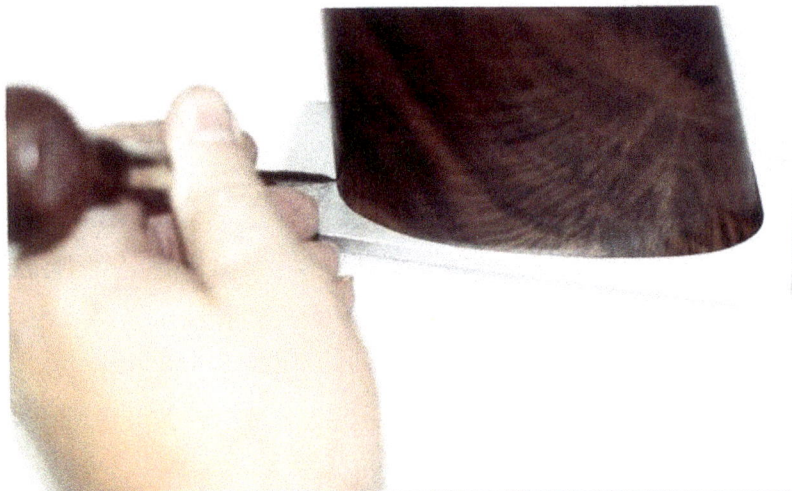

As I get older, and my glasses have more lines, I find that I need assistance in accomplishing some of the finer tasks encountered. One of them is following the line on a base plate with a metal band saw, the other if using the belt sander in removing the excess metal down to the line, and then polishing the line out. So, with a good single line on the base plate, I use a grease pencil to fill in the line, and then a shop rag to wipe off the excess. Sure makes seeing the line easier. At one time I used iron chalk for this purpose, just as I do for recoil pads, but on the aluminum background, the black or red grease pencil works better.

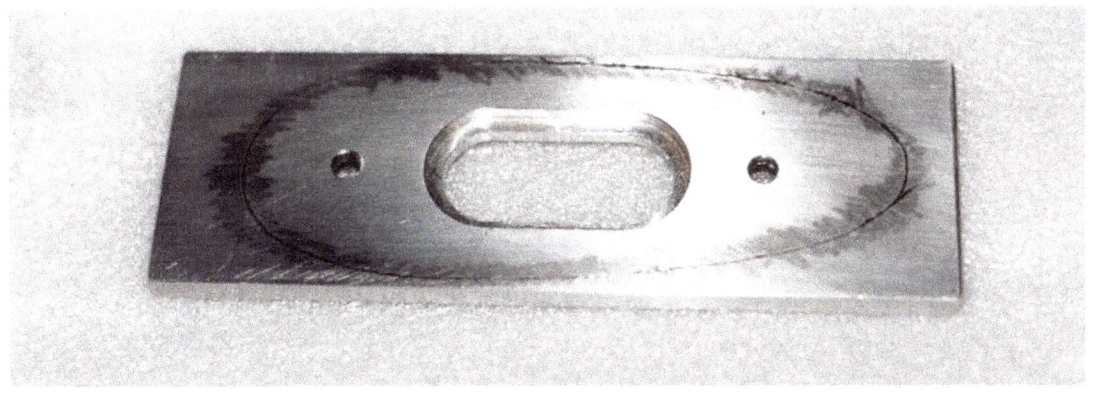

    I use a band saw with a metal cutting blade to remove the excess metal down to within a sixteenth of the line, except at the toe where I leave about 1/8". When cutting the base plate, I am careful not to cut into or go over the line: do that and you are going to have a scar on your base plate that is going to detract from the final product. I cut out both of the plates while I am on the saw. In the past, I have used a metal handsaw to perform this task, a lot slower, but basically the same result. For the hobbyist, before attempting to use a hack saw, I would strongly recommend securing the base plate in a sturdy vise whose jaws are padded to prevent scarring – but will secure - the base plate.

As I use a one-inch wide belt sander for removing the excess metal down to the line, I start out by insuring that the table of the sander is 90° to the sanding belt. No, don't eyeball it. I have a small four inch machinist square, but for years used a combination square.

I begin by using a course sanding belt on the sander, take the metal down to the line, and then switch over to a 400 grit belt and slowly remove the line. Remember to leave the toe of the base plate alone.

With the toe of the base plate needing further metal removal, we get into an area that reflects the skill in application. The stock line at the toe should be maintained. For the professional, mount the base plate on your recoil pad sanding fixture, establish the correct angle, and take it down to the line. After taking the base plate down to the desired level, mount the recoil pad base onto the base plate and with the same setting, establish the toe angle on it.

For the hobbyist, establishing the stock line gets a little more time consuming. If your belt sander has an adjustable table, place a piece of tape down the stock line, and then place the butt of the stock on the sanding table. Loosen the sanding table and move it up until the tape on the stock line of the buttstock comes into full contact with the sanding belt and set your table. This is the correct angle.

Another way of establishing the stock line angle on the base plate is to use a devise to determine an angle. By placing the butt on the square base and bringing the pivoting arm into contact with the bottom of the stock line, tighten the tension piece, and you have the stock line angle. To make use of it, it must be transferred to a block of wood, such as a two-inch section of 2 x 4. I cut the block with the small end about and 1 ½" thick, insuring adequate room for the recoil pad screw. After marking and pre-drilling the holes, use the recoil pad screws to anchor the base plate onto the block, insuring that approximately a ¼" of the toe overhangs.

Before mounting the base plate on the buttstock, put a small radius on the edges of the plate where you have sanded. Not a lot, just enough to break the sharp edges. I use a fine file and barely drag it across. Remember, just enough to break the sharp edge.

With the base plate mounted on the buttstock, check the fit, especially the continuation of the stock toe line. I sharpen one of my black or red grease pencils and use it to locate high points by dragging it along the base plate and buttstock junction, must the same as I did with the scribe. Removing the base plate, I then know exactly where and how much to remove, and I do so. Remember, we are going to polish the edges of the plates as a final act, so don't go below the stock line.

With the base plate completed except for the final polishing, and with it still mounted to the buttstock, mount the recoil pad plate to the base plate with the Tension screw. Position the recoil pad plate in the center of it's adjustment range – that being with the threads in the adjustable button centered vertically and horizontally. However, if you anticipate needing the maximum adjustment in one direction rather than another, shift to a position which gives you this advantage. Scribe the outline of the base plate on the recoil pad plate just as was done on the base plate.

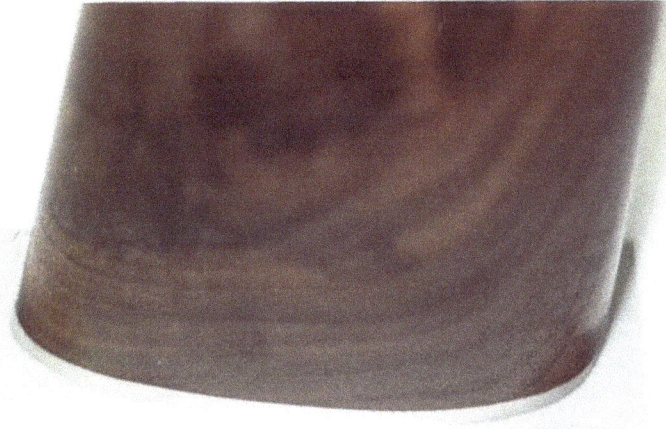

Follow the same technique for removing excess metal from the recoil pad plate as was used on the base plate, to include the sanding process. When complete except for finishing out the toe area, I mount both plates to the same fixture and complete obtaining the stock toe line.

We are now ready to mount the recoil pad of our choice. There appears to be recoil pads for sale of every description, size and some colors. And most of them have the standard 3 1/10" spacing between recoil pad holes. This is the assumption we will make for this installation, although recoil pad plates drilled and tapped for other spacing's are available by contacting the Stock Shop, located in the Supplier's Section. Drilling and taping the existing plate by moving the new holes a quarter inch – both holes in the same direction please – is a quick fix to the spacing problem. Another opportunity is to fit several recoil pad plates with recoil pads for different events.

Placing the recoil pad to be used on a wooden surface with end grain, with the furnished recoil pad punch, punch the recoil pad holes through the face of the recoil pad. I use a short section of pine two by four for this purpose. By using the end grain, the cutting edge of the hole punch is maintained

Removing the recoil pad plate from the base plate mounted on the buttstock, remove the tension screw. Using the furnished allen wrench, shove the recoil pad machine screw through the face of the pad and allow it to protruded through the recoil pad base. With both screws installed, mount the recoil pad to the recoil pad base plate.

From the underside of the recoil pad plate, use a scribe to go through the tension screw hole – center hole in the plate – and scribe and outline the hole on the recoil pad base. This is the location at which a clearance hole must be drilled to provide clearance for the tension screw. Remove the recoil pad from the recoil pad plate, leaving the two allen head screws in the recoil pad.

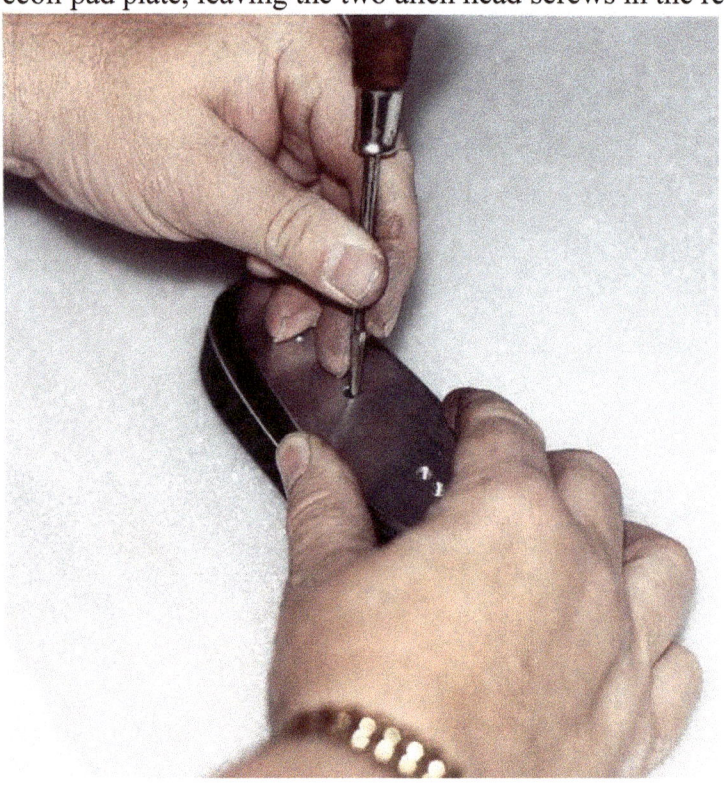

If the clearance hole in the recoil pad base is not sufficiently large to allow clearance for both the tension screw and the washer, the recoil plate will buckle, creating a major appearance error. So, with the center of the hole identified in the base of the recoil pad. I use a 1/2" drill to drill the washed clearance – about a 1/16" deep – and then switch to a 3/8" drill to drill through the recoil pad base and into the recoil pad. DO NOT drill through the face of the recoil pad. But DO drill almost through, approximately 1/8". At this point use the recoil pad hole punch to punch a neat hole through the face of the recoil pad.

Please note that there are recoil pads which do not required this procedure as their construction allows a hollow base. Recoil pads which fall into this category are the Pachmayr Presentation Recoil Pads

Inserting the Tension screw and Washer into the recoil pad place, mount it on the base plate and then mount the recoil pad onto the recoil pad plate, how does it look? You're not through yet.

For the professional, polishing out the edges of the aluminum plate adds the final touches to the installation. I use a blending wheel on a 1/3 hp bench grinder for this purpose but have finished many an aluminum plate with 400 grit wet and dry sand paper and 0000 steel wool. Some use a buffing wheel impregnated with polishing compound, but whatever is used, let the polishing reflect the time and care that went into the installation.

SECTION 10
Installing Recoil Reducers

Recoil reducers come in a variety of sizes, types and effectiveness. There are basically three types of recoil reducing devices.

The first is one that adds weight to the weapon. The heavier weapon, the less recoil, or so it seems. This type can be as simple as the insertion of a cylinder of lead or steel, or even filling the stock bolt hole – or other drilled hole – with lead shot.

On rifles, the barrel channel of the forearm can be "deepened" and filled with a mixture of shot and Brownell's AcraGlas.

The second type is one in which there is not only weight, but a cushion effect as the weight moves during recoil. Those tubes filled with mercury that abut against a spring baffle during recoil seem to function the best.

The third is one in which the recoil pad / buttplate moves forward during recoil and a spring / hydraulic or air cushion cylinder absorbs most of the recoil.

All three of them work to some extent, but the effectiveness between the three varies greatly, and the installation of any of the three will enhance or reduce the effectiveness of the item.

I have found that if the hole for the recoil reduction devise is drilled in the buttstock parallel to the barrel – in all cases in which a device is inserted into the stock – it seems to have an improved functionality over a device inserted into an angled hole such as the stock bolt hole.

A word of caution - and I have made the mistake – be very careful with the alignment of the drill to insure you do not drill through the side of the stock. The drill will "wonder" around, beware!

Is there a correct depth to place the recoil device? If there is a formula, or a rule of thumb, or a standard, I do not know it. I may insert the device, shoot the gun, and then drill a little deeper seeking to enhance the balance of the gun. If I still do not feel comfortable with the installation, I will ask the Customer to come in and shoot the gun and check it for balance.

There are however, limits to how deep the hole can be drilled. If the hole is drilled on the lower part of the butt, be careful to not drill through the belly of the stock.

So lets install the third type. In this case a very nice Grayco unit which acts under spring compression to absorb recoil. More tension on the spring the more recoil felt. The less tension on the spring, the less recoil felt. I have found that this unit is very popular with the Junior shooting group and the older shooters.

Because I install quite a few of these units, I purchased the installation kit comprised of the positioning bar, the drill and the drill collar. Before purchasing the kit, I installed several without the kit and believe me, the kit is worth the money. You are assured that the holes will be positioned correctly. I would advise taking this installation to a Gunsmith that has the installation kit.

The first thing to do is apply the drilling fixture to the buttstock, preferably using the recoil pad holes.

With the fixture in place, insure the drill and drill guide move easily in the fixture.

I use a 3/8" drill for this purpose. I really like the keyless chuck and the time it saves me. Just wish it was a little more positive.

The depth of the hole will need to me measured to insure it is deep enough for the housing, but not too deep. I measure the housing and the fixture for a reading. I have found that once the measurement is known, I can insert the steel rule into the hole and determine the status of the hole.

Just a note: I took these pictures and getting everything in line and touching off the camera was an exercise akin yoga!

With the hole drilled to the appropriate depth, the guide rod holes in the fixture are used to drill the guide rod holes in the buttstock. Although it is tempting to use the base plate of the unit as a guide, please do not. Any deviation from a true ninety degrees with the drill will elongate the nylon bushings of the base plate.   With all of the holes drilled to the appropriate depth…

Attach the base plate to the buttstock. It should fit flat to the buttstock - NO gap.

Using a scribe, scribe an outline of the buttstock on the base plate.

The scribed outline of the buttstock on the base plate is to be followed when removing the excess metal. To save time, I attach the adjustment plate to the base plate. To illustrate a small problem, notice the gap between the two plates…. This gap is caused by the shoulder of the spring housing guide. To overcome this, I place a 3/8" washes over each post of the guide rods when assembling the two plates. This provides a secure platform on which the grinding or sawing – I use a band saw with a metal cutting blade – is to take place.

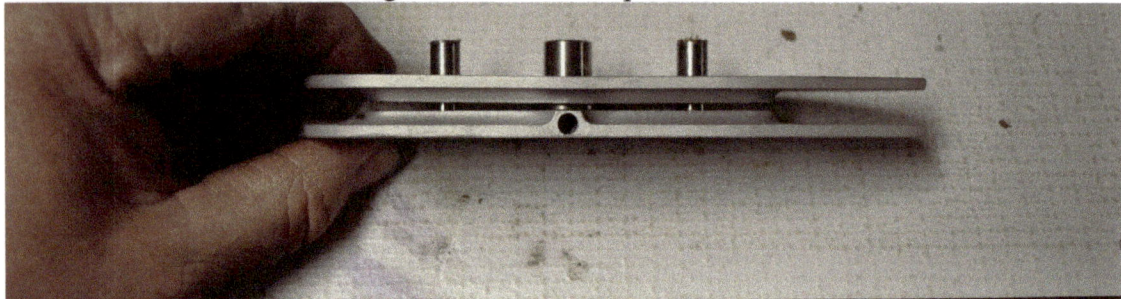

With the excess metal removed, and the edges of the plates smoothed – I use 320 wet or dry sand paper after using a small file to smooth the rough edge left by the saw blade – assemble the spring housing onto the base plate.

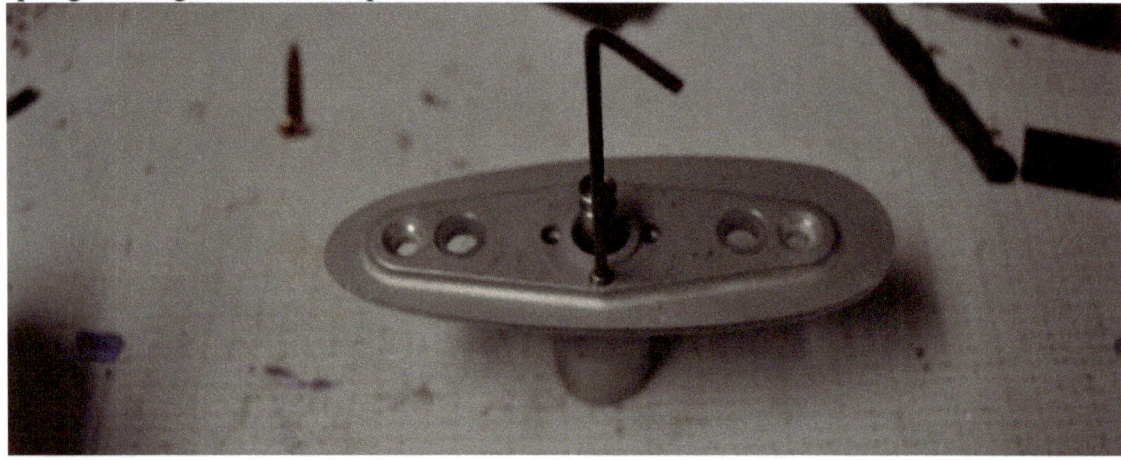

Slip it into place, and anchor it with the two intended screws.

On this particular installation, the customer wanted to use his old recoil pad, with the recoil pad attached to the plate, I use a sharp pointed scribe to scribe the outline of the recoil pad onto the plate.

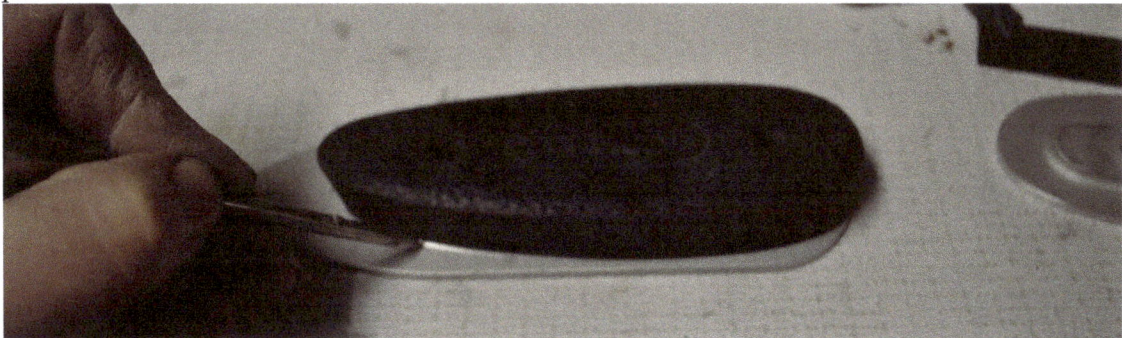

If a new recoil pad is to be used, the recoil plate is attached to the adjustment plate, the outline of the adjustment plate is then scribed onto the recoil pad plate and it is shaped according to the scribed lines. At that point, the shape of the recoil pad plate is scribed onto the recoil pad and the recoil pad is ground to the contour of the recoil pad plate.

After shaping the recoil pad to the appropriate contour, I assemble the unit, check it for functionality, and declare the task completed.

SECTION 11
Stock Repairs
Enlarged Recoil Pad Screw Holes

The most common repair I perform is the plugging and re-drilling of recoil pad screw holes. I have removed steel wool, tooth picks, slivers of wood, wood putty, and part of a business card from enlarged recoil pad screw holes. I have also spent several frustrating minutes trying to find the screw slot of a recoil pad screw only to find that a cut down ten penny nail had been used to secure the pad to the buttstock.

The procedure I use to fill enlarged screw holes is quick and simple, and it works. I use ¼" hardwood furniture dowels an inch and a half long to plug the holes. First I pull out my trusty recoil pad hole repair drill, which is no more than a 17/64" drill. The drill has a piece of tape wrapped around it at an inch and nine-sixteenths inch from the tip.

At this point I am not concerned with the spacing of the holes, that will come later, my concern is getting them filed. I drill the existing holes to the depth indicated on the drill by the tape, and then shake or blow any residual shavings from the hole. The dowels are a tight fit to start with, so I do not test them in the holes.

If I have a project on the bench and am using Brownells AcraGlas, I use it in the holes, if not, I use Brownell's two part epoxy and mix up a small batch, no more that a tea spoon at the most, following the directions on the dispenser. For efficiency sake, I have used a three inch by five inch card as my mixing surface for years. They serve the purpose and are easily disposed of. The epoxy is too thick to pour down the hole, so I use my scribe / awl to divide and transfer the epoxy to the holes.

The dowels have grooves cut into them through which the excess epoxy can come out of the hole, and as I slowly shove them into the holes, using a large drift punch, I let the excess come out. Try to shove too fast, or hammer them in, and the excess epoxy serves as a cushion, and the dowel will not bottom out in the hole. It is important that the dowels fit flush with, or ever so slightly below the surface of the butt.

Past practice has educated me in allowing the epoxy to dry a good fifteen minutes before I proceed. If the same recoil pad is to be installed, I insert the top screw through the face of the pad until it protrudes slightly, about a sixteenth of an inch, through the pad base. Holding the pad in place, I tap the screw lightly.

I then drill the hole at the point indicated by the indenture of the recoil pad screw. I only drill the hole approximately a quarter inch deep. Let me stress that drilling the holes at a ninety degree angle is essential for a recoil pad that will lay flat when the screws are tightened. My father called it "drilling them square."

Start the screw into the hole, taking only a few turns. If the pad lines up with the wood correctly, I remove the screw and drill the recoil pad screw hole to the correct depth. Because I use several different screw sizes and types, depending on what I am anchoring to the buttstock, a recoil pad, or an adjustable base plate, the drill diameter used is keyed to the screw to be used.

I drill the recoil pad holes a little longer than the screws themselves, about a quarter inch longer. Why? Years ago, I split the toe off of a beautiful stock on a Browning over and under.

The screw was a little too big for the hole I had drilled, and not deep enough. For whatever reason, I kept turning the screw, and it acted like a chisel, and broke the piece off. It was an expensive lesson, but one which I remember. Take the time to use the correct drill, if you have questions on the size of drill to use, use the drill of choice to drill a hole in a scrap piece of wood and try the screw in it.

I then screw the top screw to full depth, and back off just a quarter turn, enough so I can move the recoil pad around to insure it is correctly positioned on the buttstock. With the pad aligned correctly, I tighten the top screw to keep it in place.

Using a scribe, I insert it through the face of the pad until it comes in contact with the buttstock, and then scribe the interior dimensions of the screw hole onto the buttstock. Removing the recoil pad, I set it aside, and make a punch mark in the center of the scribed circle on the buttstock. If the scribed circle is not clear, repeat the process. While you do have a little leeway in screw hole placement, there is very little, be sure of the hole location before you drill.

Drill the hole the same way you did the first one. Install the recoil pad, but leave the screws a quarter turn from tight, move the recoil pad around into alignment, and tighten the screws, top one first.

I do not subscribe to the theory of using longer screws or larger screws to compensate for enlarged recoil pad screw holes. Plugging and re-drilling is the technique I use and advise.

Chips, Dings and Dents

Stock repairs are not the basis of my business, but they are the most interesting, and provide the most satisfaction. I receive stocks with all manner of chips in the finish, dings and dents. Some have very interesting explanations, most beginning with "you're not going to believe it, but…" or "I don't know how" and end with 'Can you fix it?"

First, let me offer my definition of a chip, a ding and a dent. A **chip** is missing finish from the edge of the wood, such as the end of the buttstock where it matches the recoil pad or adjustable buttplate, or where the buttstock meets the receiver.

A **ding** is an indention in the wood and finish caused by being struck by an object such as a clay target, gun rack or another shooter's weapon. A ding most likely has wood grain damage associated with it.

A **dent** in an indention in the finish and wood but the finish is still present, just dented in. A dent does not have wood grain damage. A lot of these are caused by gun racks at the ranges, but conditions are getting better as I see gun racks with a four inch centered spacing for guns to rest in. Friendship is great, but guns shouldn't touch.

Now these explanations may not be in Webster's, or those subscribed to by any professional stockmaking person or company, but I use them, and my customers seem to understand what I am saying.

When a customer brings a shotgun in with a chip in the finish, I immediately start looking for the cause. Most of the time the chip occurred when ***something*** caused the finish to lose hold of the wood beneath it. The variety of **somethings** I have found are legend, however, the most common cause is moisture getting into exposed wood which had not been sealed. A failure to use the correct method in shortening a stock can often result in bits of finish chipping off.

I can't emphasize how important sealing exposed wood is to a buttstock and forearm. A little Tru Oil on a toothbrush will do the trick in most instances, but I know people that have put recoil pads on for years and still do not seal the fresh cut buttstock. I guess one could call it building in job security! The following picture is of a buttstock on a Remington Model 1100 gun I purchased. The stock had been cut and not sealed, and a recoil pad installed. The finish was not only pulled away from the wood, but the stock was split is several areas.

The first thing I want to do is clean the wood surface to insure the new finish will stick to the wood. I do this with a small short haired brush, I believe it is sometimes called an acid brush, and denatured alcohol and sometimes acetone. I don't get emphatic about scrubbing the area, I just want it clean.

If the wood below the finish is oil soaked, I will mix and apply some 'whiting', let it set several hours and depending upon the oil in the wood, and may repeat the process several times.

So let's assume the oil is all out, and we have good wood to work with. For a small chip or series of chips, I use Deft Semi-gloss finish and a tooth pick to apply it. Letting it fill the chipped area, often applying several coats over an hour or so, letting each previous application dry before adding another. If the chip is at the butt, I remove the recoil pad, buttplate or whatever is screwed on, and coat the area of the object with a release agent.

The material I use to fill a chip will vary, depending upon the type of finish and the size of chip. But for the most part, I use a semi-gloss cabinet finish produced by Deft. If the area is large – defined as being over a quarter inch in any direction, I use acra glass to fill the void

No, I don't have a 'gloss' and a 'semi-gloss' I use the semi-gloss for both gloss and semi-gloss finish repairs. Read on, it works.

For whatever reason, this finish really latches onto the wood and other finishes. However, for the first application on new wood, I mix three drops of finish to one drop of lacquer thinner, stir well, and apply the mixture to the chip with a scribe. Using the fine point of the scribe or toothpick, I can lay the mixture right into the edge of the chip without depositing any substantial amount on top of the good finish.

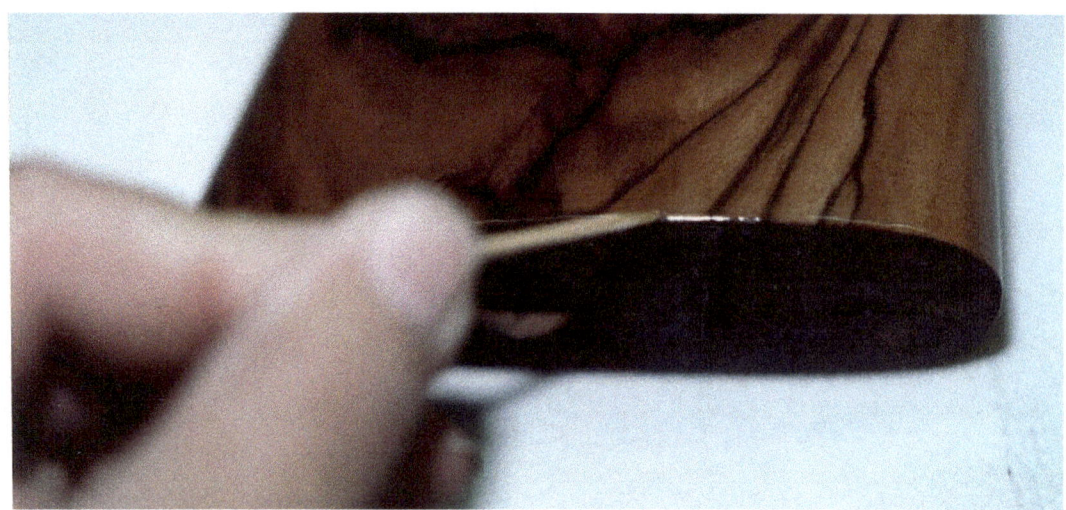

Do not apply a lot at any one time. Plan on applying at least six to ten applications to fill the chip. In this manner, the filler will dry in a flat layer, not as a pool with a sunken center.

A special note: Deft Semi-Gloss finish will dry to a sanding hardness in fifteen minutes. As you do not want to sand until the chip is filled, an application can be made every ten minutes. Naturally, you want the chip surface to be flat, and that is sometimes difficult. To keep the chip area level, I use modeling clay wedges under the buttstock. They work.

When you think you have filled the chip, apply one more coat. The chip area should reflect a slightly 'overfilled' condition, and that is exactly what you want.

I am going to stop the process at this point and begin resolving a ding and later a dent to the same stage. The final resolution of the problem is the same for all three.

So, a **ding** is an absence of finish caused by being struck by an object such as a clay target, gun rack or another weapon and a ding usually has wood damage associated with it.

Because of the wood damage usually associated with a ding, the area to be ultimately involved in the repair is larger. Begin by using a scribe or awl to lift the loose finish away from the ding, allowing clear access to the ding. If bits of finish are impregnated into the wood, carefully remove them with the fine point of your tool. When performing this task, be careful not to damage or scar more wood, take your time, go slow.

If the wood is intact – no cut edges – but compressed, or if the wood has cut edges, the wood must be raised. To do this we use a steam iron and a small water-soaked cloth, I usually end up using one corner of a cloth shop towel that has been folded over several times. You know the kind… They are sold in bundles in the discount chain stores. Yep, auto section.

Lay the corner of the cloth over the ding, apply the tip of the steam iron to the wet cloth, allowing the steam from the iron to heat the water in the cloth and force it down into the wood. Control the area exposed to the steam by having the iron over the remainder of the cloth. DON'T let steam come directly down on the exposed finish of the stock or forearm. To do so may result in the finish turning white, crinkling up, or just turning loose of the wood.

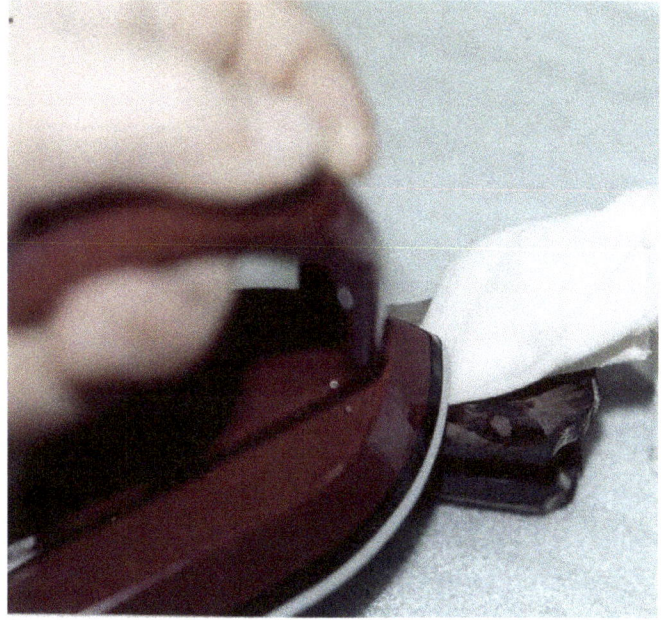

Slowly, the damaged wood will rise up as the wood cells are filled with hot water and expand. It is a simple process but takes a little practice to make it work well. Once the wood is up, check the finish around the area to determine if there is any additional loose finish, if there is, it needs to be removed. It is a lot easier to remove questionable finish now than to discover it halfway through the refinishing process.

After a several days have passed, allowing ample time for the wood to dry out, you are ready to begin filling the ding.

For the first application of the repair mixture to be used on the wood and edge of the existing finish, I mix three drops of Deft Semi-Gloss finish to one drop of lacquer thinner, stir well, and apply the mixture to the ding with a scribe or tooth pick. Using the fine point of the scribe, I can lay the mixture right into the edge of the ding without depositing any substantial amount on top of the good finish. This mixture has proven successful in bonding with the old finish and providing a good soaked in base for the new finish yet to come.

Knowing the normal dry time is ten to fifteen minutes, I apply successive coats every ten minutes until the ding is filled and the filler has created a slight mound indicating it is a little higher than the surrounding finish.

I am going to stop this process at this point and proceed on the repairing a dent. After all three types are covered, I will go into the last steps of the process common to all three.

A **dent** is an indention in the finish and wood but the finish is still present, just dented in.

On small dents, I do not remove the finish of the dent. On large dents, I do remove the finish, usually with the point of a scribe or Exacto knife. I then follow the procedure outline in the ding portion to replace the finish.

If the dent is very small, I first mix the three parts finish and one part lacquer thinner, and apply it to the entire dented area with a scribe. I allow it to dry about ten minutes, and apply successive applications, each ten minutes until the dent is slightly over filled.

Now, with all three types identified and filled, to the next step…

A small object with an absolutely flat surface is needed to be used as a sanding block or bar. The surface area should be approximately one-half inch thick, an inch wide and an inch and a half long. Once you have developed a "feel" for the procedure, you will discover what size surface area is best for you. My "Sanding Bar" is a piece of one-half inch thick by inch and a half wide by three-inch long ground steel bar. One of the three surface areas seems to fill every need I have come across. For this task, the surface of the block must be non-flexible.

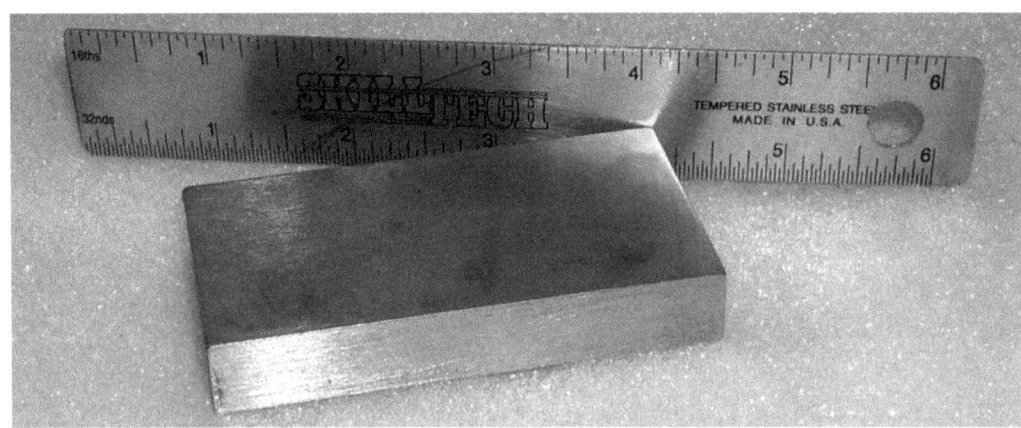

With a piece of 600 grit wet/dry sand paper wrapped around the sanding bar, carefully – very slowly – take the mounded surface of the filler down to the original finish level. Be careful to sand a surface area only as large as needed to contour the mound into the surrounding area. Stop often, look at the area, see where you need more sanding, and identify the areas which do not require additional sanding. Do not sand more than is needed, or you may end up applying additional finish to the area.

Once the filler has been leveled, remove the 600 grit wet and dry sand paper from the block, and replace it with a piece of 1500 grit wet /dry sandpaper. Carefully, WET SAND the repaired lightly. All that you are seeking to do is to remove the 600 grit scratches, and replace them with 1500 grit scratches. Use very little water in the sanding process. Just enough to provide a medium for the sand paper. I use a small atomizer, works well.

Now comes the fun part, for those that were in the service and had to spit polish those inspection boots, well, welcome back. But instead of black boot polish, we will be using the 5F Polishing Compound available from Brownell's. Yes, there may be other compounds out there that may do as good a job, but for absolute consistency and use, the Brownell's 5F Polishing Compound is my choice.

Just as the label on the container instructs, shake the small container well, mixing the ingredients. Using a soft cloth, such as a undershirt, stretched over the finger tip - a shop rag *will not do* in this case – or corner of a folded paper towel, and just touch the material to the residue of the 5F in the lid of the container.

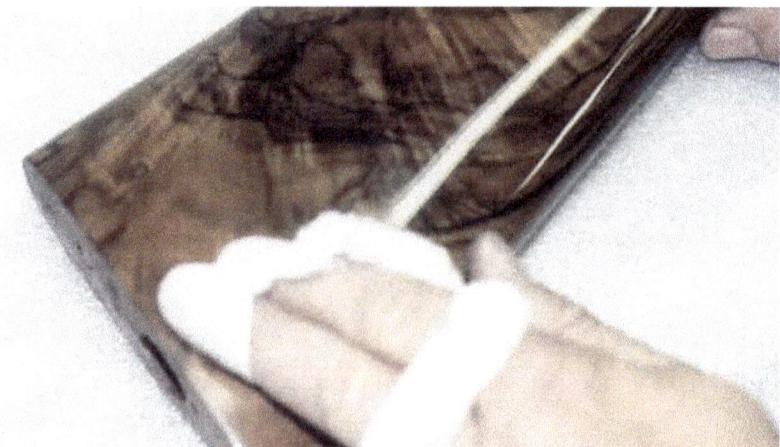

Using a small circular motion, "polish" the repaired area and old finish immediately adjoining the repaired area. Continuing the polishing process until the surface shine begins coming through the polish haze and then rub the polished area with a clean cloth. View the repaired area for flaws in the repair such as sanding paper marks.

Repeat the polishing process until the repaired area blends in with the old finish. Please note, on many repaired areas, I eventually end up polishing a much larger area, sometimes the whole piece, to insure the repaired area is not readily identified because of the shine.

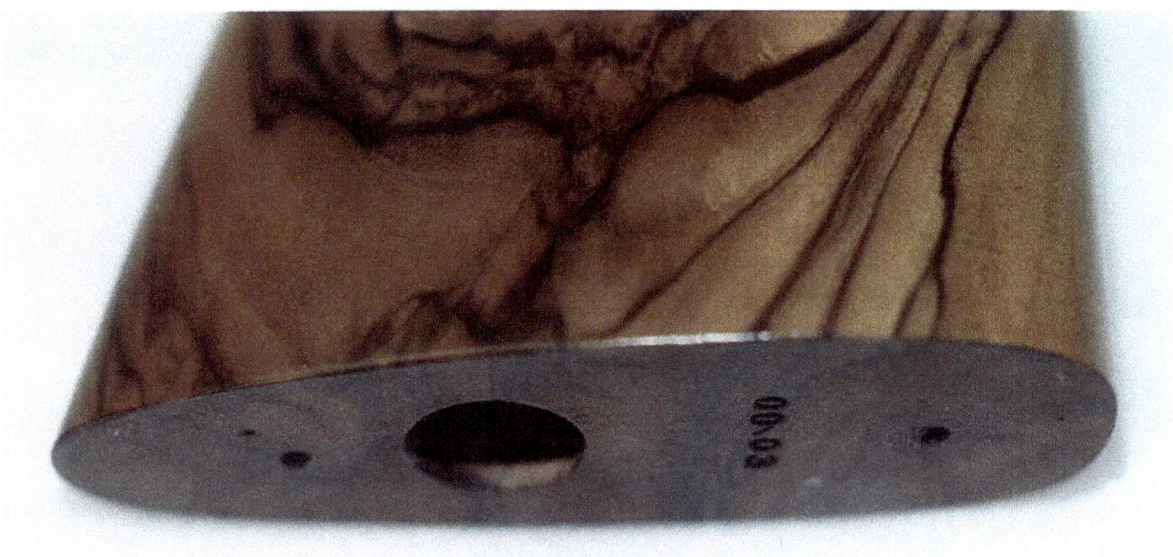

Missing Wood

Many years ago, I watched an elderly man replacing the missing wood from the toe of the buttstock of a very high-grade Browning over and under shotgun. When he was through, I could not find the line separating the two pieces of wood, nor could I identify the add on in any way. In talking with the elderly man, I was informed he was a "retired" piano refinisher. The level of craftsmanship I observed that day has been my goal for over twenty-five years.

I had watched as he rambled through a large bucket of pieces of old buttstocks looking for wood that would come close to matching the buttstock. I watched as he shaped it, attached it, stained and 'grained' it with India ink on a toothpick and finally finished it.

Many of the techniques I use today were learned that day, others were picked up through experience over time. That reminds me, you do know that *experience is that activity not often successful and seldom resulting in pay.*

Repairing missing wood can be divided into categories: The first is when the missing wood is available, such as the broken toe on a buttstock, but it can also be the side of the receiver wood. A quick rule of thumb, the longer the piece of wood has been separated, the more it has been handled, the more difficult it is to replace properly. So, before I do anything, I place the broken piece back in its correct position to see how much damage has been done. If the wood fits back and the joint is all but indivisible, great. I don't get many great jobs…

On most cases such as this, the piece has been broken off for some time, and after hunting season, or skeet season, or trap season, or when the owner remembers, or his wife gets tired of seeing the piece of wood laying around, it comes to me.

When I open the box and unwrapped the two pieces, I knew I was facing a challenge. After looking the pieces over, I took the following pictures and established my game plan. My first impression was someone tried to tape the pieces back together, and then I realized that the tape was intended to serve as a protector against the repair agent to be used. Good planning.

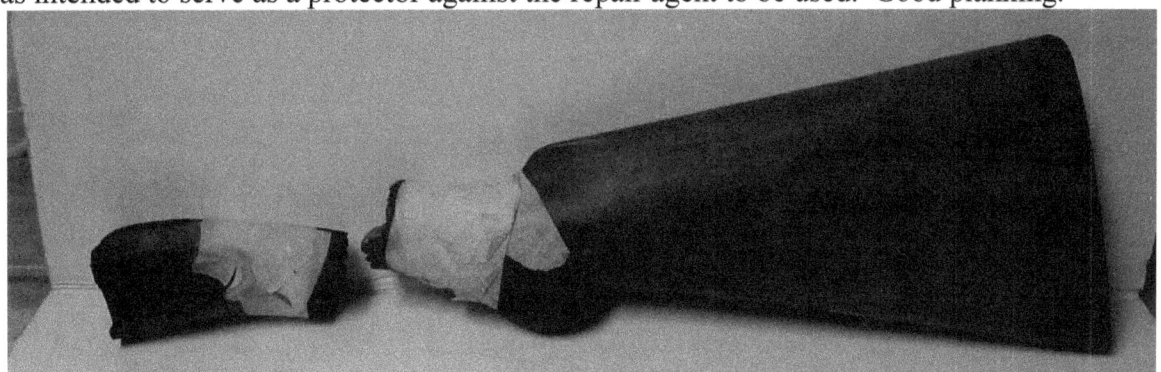

Other than the break, the wood looked in remarkable shape. There were no cracks or compression areas, just signs of use over many years. The break occurred at the point at which the rear tang screw came up from the trigger plate to the upper tang of the receiver.

Looking at the ends of the two pieces, it was evident the wood was very old and had suffered a heck of a blow to sever it.

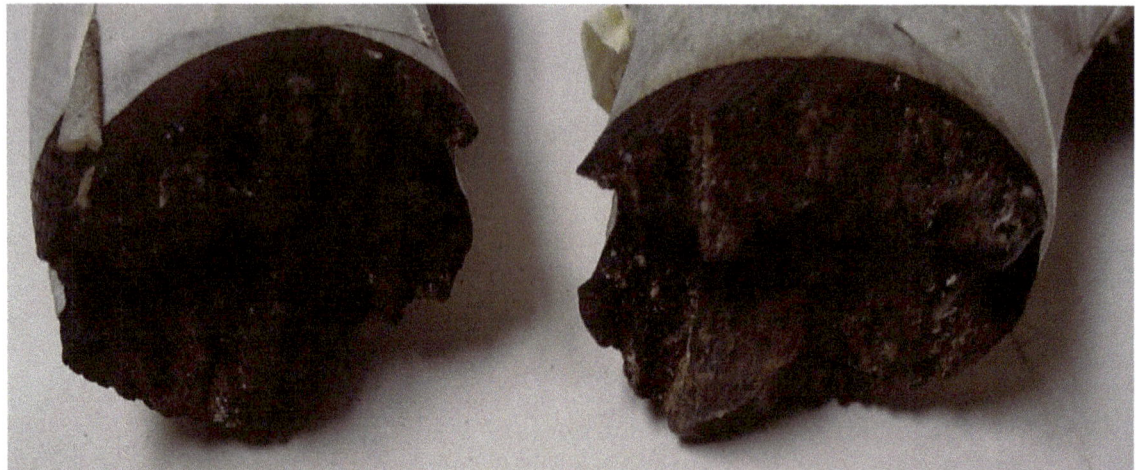

Wanting to insure noting was hidden beneath the tape, as well as preferring to do my own taping for the same purpose, I stripped all of the tape off – someone had done a good job – prior to cleaning the surface wood with a strong solvent.

One thing to remember when making this type of repair is the checkering lines. Unless the repair is made with the checkering lines continuing is a straight line – as they were prior to the break – the repair will be unsightly. And speaking of unsightly – at this point in the plan, I intend to use four (4) small hard wood dowels on the inside of the break. They should not be visible when the job is complete. The first thing I will do, after cleaning all of the foreign matter and chipped wood from the interior and then check the fit of the two pieces. It is better to discover fitting problems before installing the dowels, much less applying the bonding agent. The initial fit, shown below, looked good so it went onto a pipe vice for a little pressure fit. This also looked very good.

Just for information's sake, if the fit does not look good – as in the checkering lines do not line up – double check the break for chipped wood or wood that had been distorted.

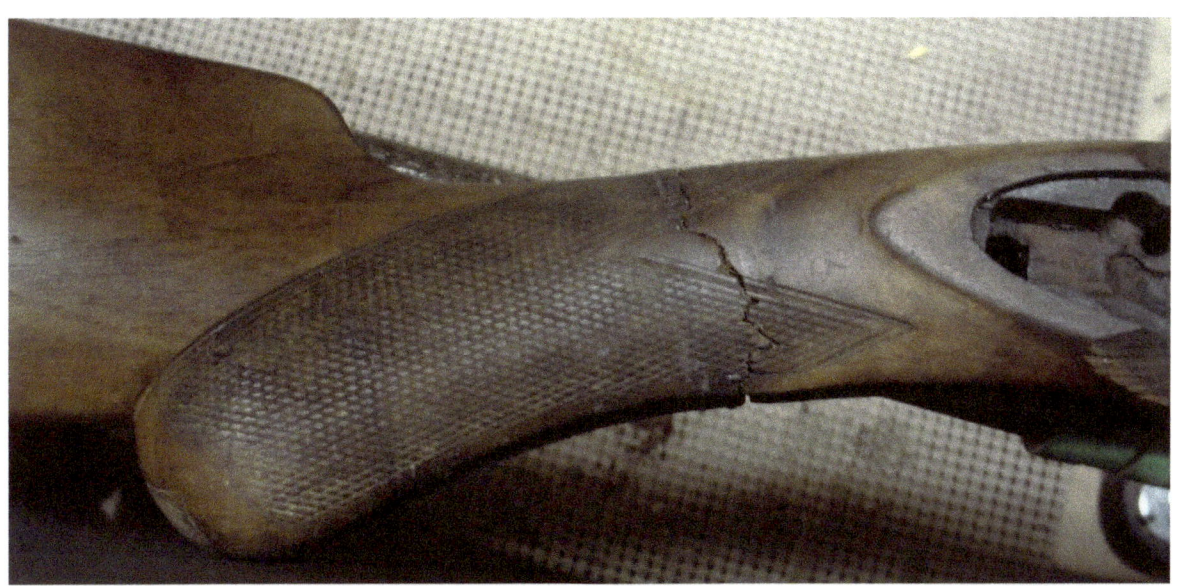

In this case, a small amount of wood has been dislodged and will not allow the two pieces to mate correctly. A skew point chisel quickly removed the problem wood. The small white areas are remnants of a bonding compound. I use a sharp pointed awl to remove more of these from the wood. When this tool fails, I use a small skew pointed wood chisel to remove the material, and is necessary, some of the wood it is imbedded in.

Now comes the fun part. Locating the small hard wood dowels. I use a technique I learned from a piano refinisher many years ago. Using a small center punch, I identify two potential locations on the face of the buttstock break just large enough for a # 7 ½ shot to sit in. And before you ask, I used the 7 ½ shot because I did not have any 9's or 8's. But it is the largest size shot I will use for this purpose. Just a note, when replacing the toe of a buttstock, and want a secure joint, this technique will allow the use of hidden dowels and assist in a really good joint.

With the exact location of the two lower holes made, the next step is to drill a hole in the face at the identified location. I use a drill almost half again as large as the wooden dowel – I use hard wood tooth picks obtained from a Japanese market as dowels – to drill the two identified locations with a hole approximately ½" deep in each piece of wood.

I then insert a piece of dowel approximately 15/16" long into one of the holes, and then try a test fit to insure the two pieces of stock will line up.

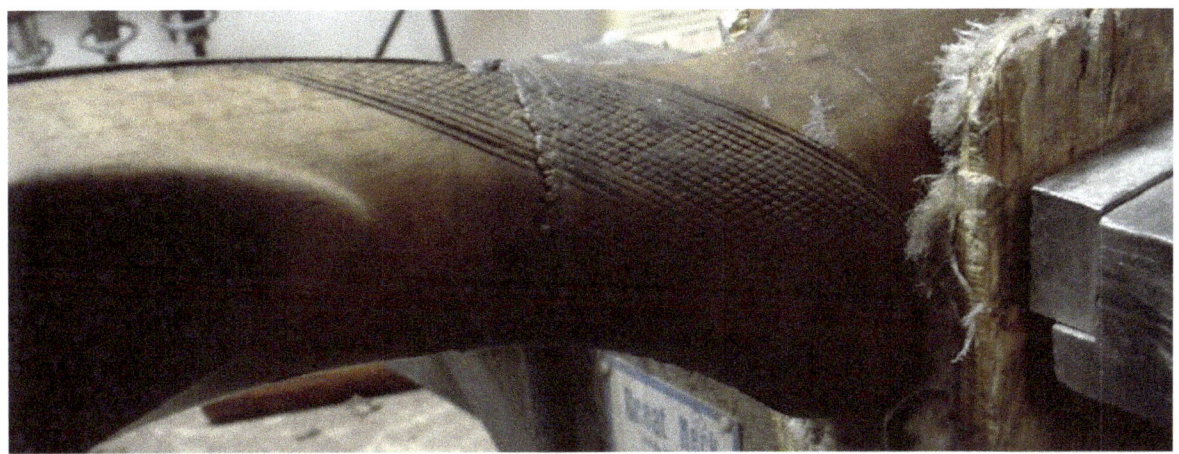

I repeat this procedure with the second dowel, insuring I am getting a good fit. The way I judge the fit is if the checkering lines line up correctly. I they do not, the cause will most likely be the angle of the drilled hole is incorrect. To correct, I use the drill bit to slightly "funnel" the hole and try the fit again. Yes, this takes a little time, but you are insuring that the joint is going to line up correctly. If there are any problems in the alignment, now is the time to address and correct them. Do not assume the alignment is going to correct itself, or that you can twist it into alignment when the bonding agent is applied and the pieces are placed in the clamp. Do it now!

Ok, now insert the second dowel and repeat the process. To include the alignment test.

With the alignment complete with two of the dowels in place, it is time to identify two more locations on the face of the buttstock, and center punch them. When choosing locations for the dowels, use care to identify a location with plenty of wood on either piece of wood to accommodate the dowel hole. The last thing you want to do is drill through the exterior of the stock.

Insert the shot, I use a pair of clamps I was given many years ago and find constant uses for. I have tried several tools for this function, but the clamps work the best of all.

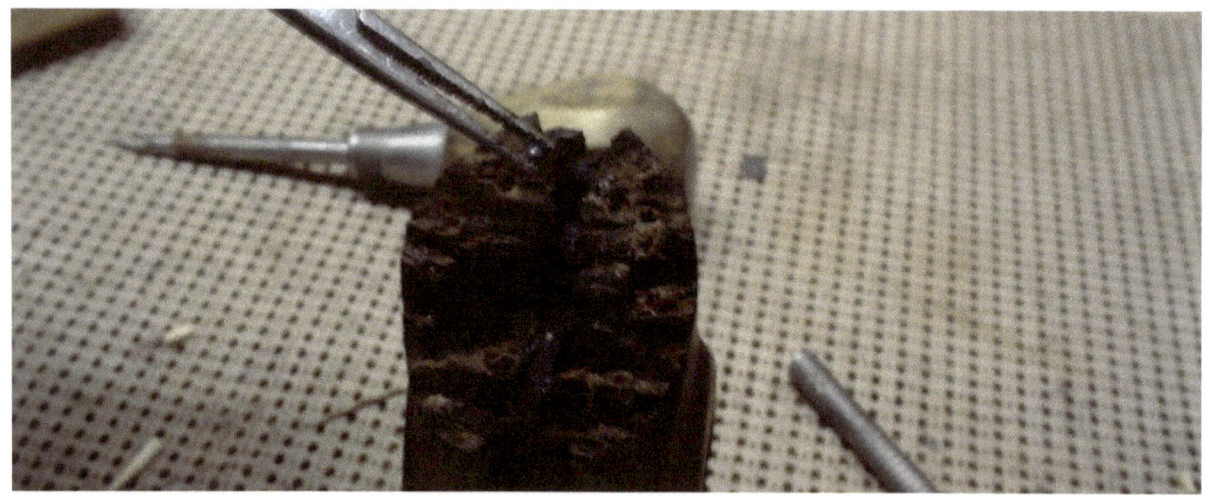

This next picture is one of the best and most explanatory in this section – I just got lucky! The two shot are in place and the two previously drilled holes are evident. As the man said, "I would rather be lucky than good."

Match the two pieces of stock together, leaving the impressions of shot in the face of the buttstock. At this stage, I use a pipe clamp to get the pressure fit of the two pieces of wood and the needed impressions.

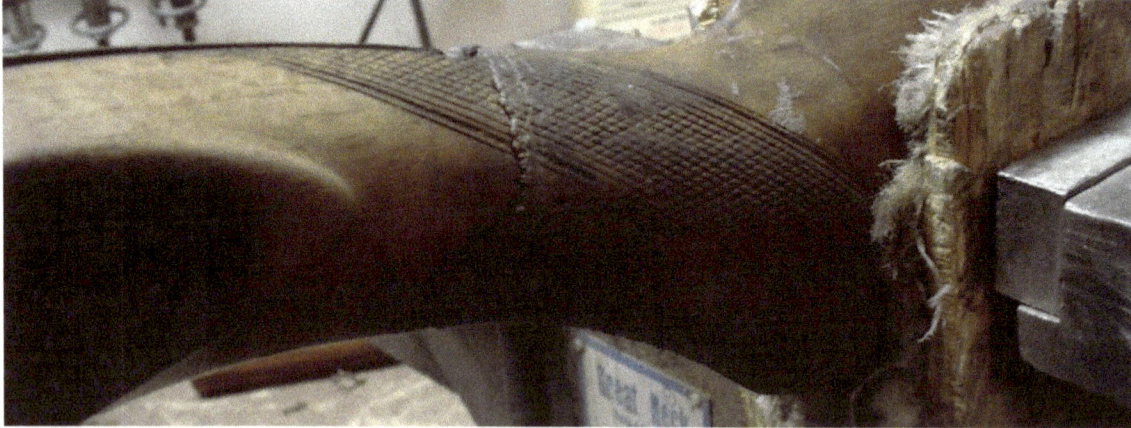

Time to drill the remaining two holes. This is about the time that the opportunity to really mess up the job comes about. Use caution when drilling the last two holes, and just for insurance, funnel them just a bit.

Insert three of the four dowels, try a fit, make adjustment until you achieve a good fit and alignment. Repeat the process with all four dowels in place.

Use the pipe clamp to provide the pressure necessary. Check the alignment of the checkering lines, and make adjustment to your dowel holes.

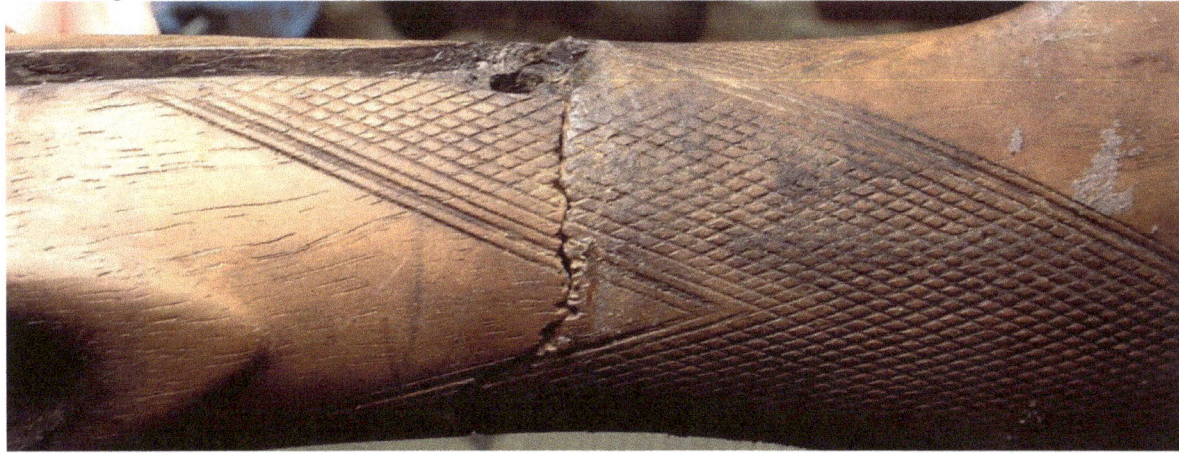

Remove the dowels, and for luck, place them on the bench in such a manner that they can be replaced in the same holes. A variety of bonding agents can be used for this purpose, but I happen to like AcraGlas for this purpose. Mixing up a small batch of it, I actually stir the full four (4) minutes and apply the mixture. First filling the dowel holes – using a tooth pick – and then applying a liberal coating to both pieces of wood. Notice the dowels on the bench?

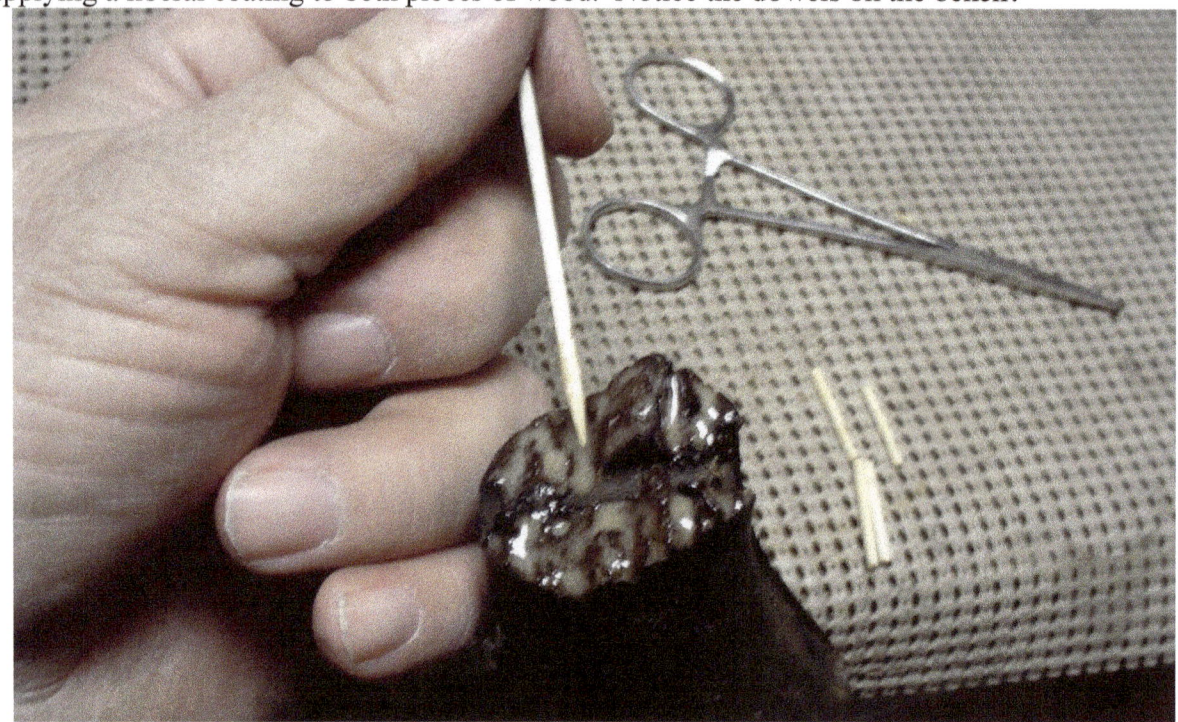

The next step – joining the two pieces and placing the complete stock in the pipe clamp – is almost a two person job. One person can do it, but a second set of hands is really a plus.

When applying the pressure of the clamp, watch the excess joining agent come out of the crack, this is good. If none comes out, there is <u>insufficient</u> bonding agent for the task. Take it apart, add bonding agent, fit it back together. You have done far too much work to this point to let the project come out less than great.

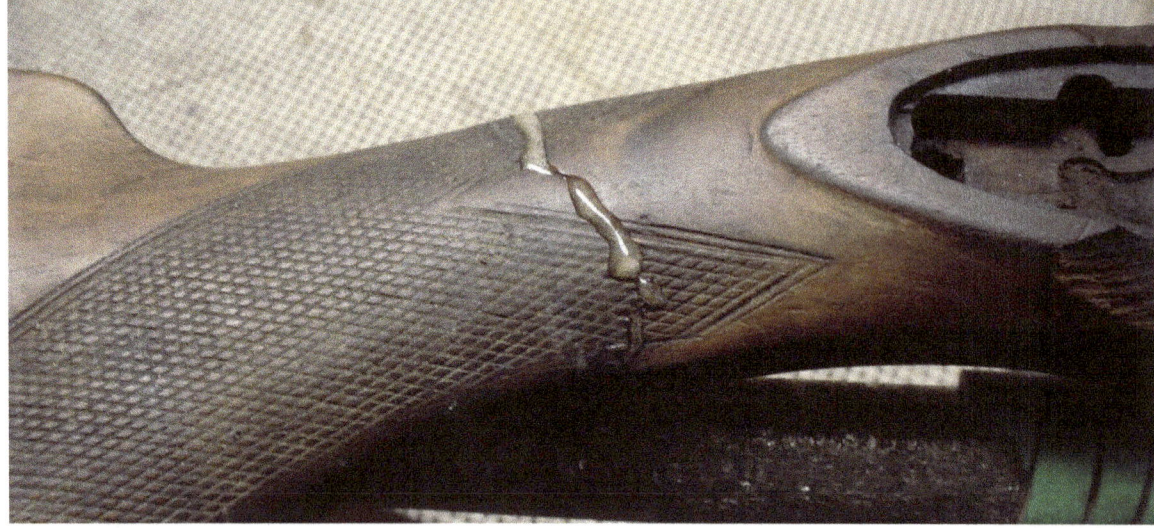

Remove most of the ecess bonding agent, but be careful not to remove any from the surface of the crack.

Once the bonding agent dries, the "down side" will have excess pooled, as shown in the following photograph.

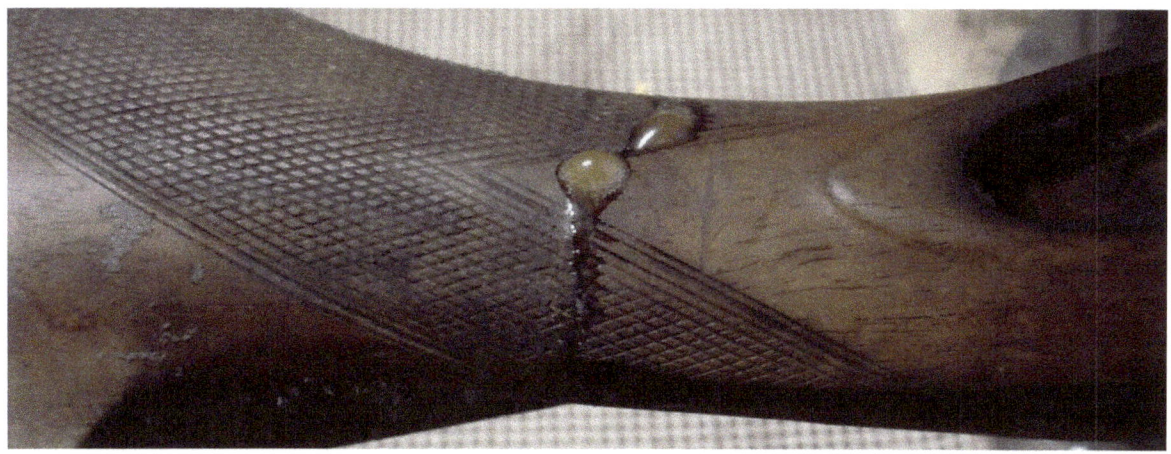

I have a short – eight inches – double cut mill bastard that I have found very good in removing excess bonding agent. It is fine enough to remove the agent slowly, and course enough to remove the bonding agent. I suggest its purchase and use.

When you are removing the excess agent, check the results of your efforts often. You DO NOT want to remove excess wood and or destroy the existing / remaining checkering. A good example is the following picture.

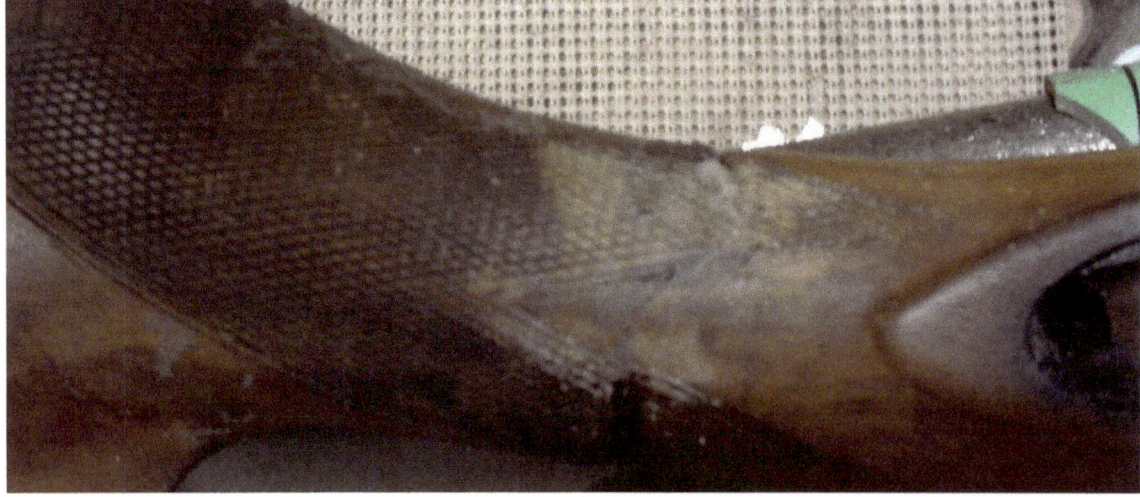

After the file, go to 320 grit wet and dry sand paper and carefully sand the area. Again, use caution not to destroy the checkering lines, leaving a fine line at the joining point.

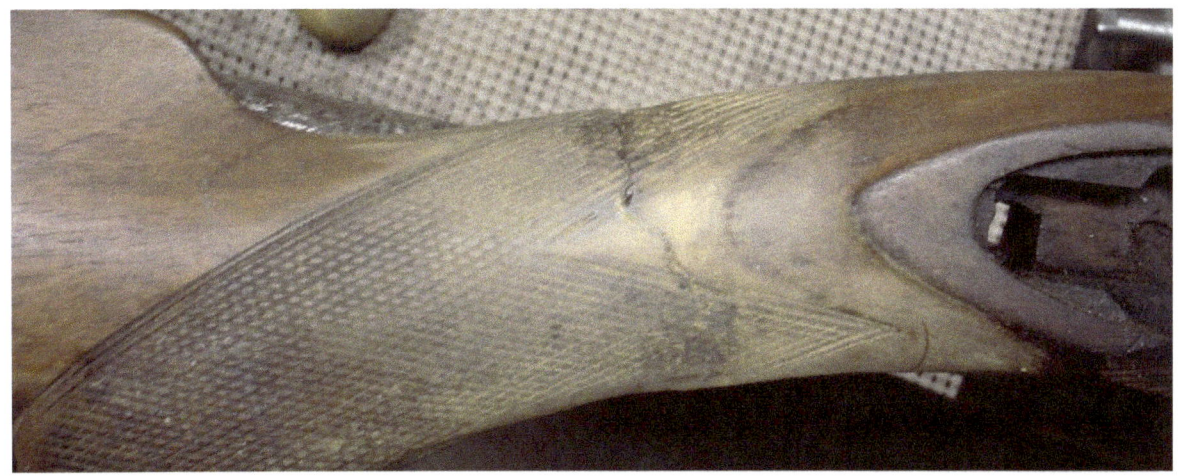

There will be small holes in the compound which need to be filled. For this purpose, I use either thinned down bonding agent, or a quick dry grain sealer. In this case, I am using the S B McWilliams Stock Sealer. It really works great.

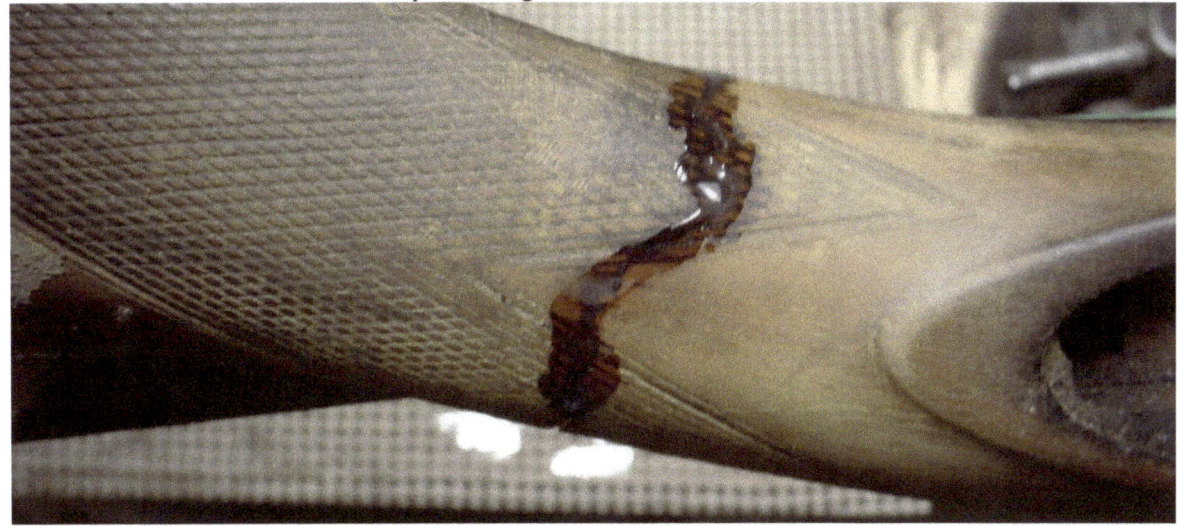

The secret to using it is to apply several very thin coats over the period of several hours. Only after the small holes – bubbles – are filled should sanding take place. Again, the 320 grit wet or dry sanding paper is used, but this time I wrap it around an art gum eraser. I have found that the art gum eraser is pliant enough to follow the contour of the stock, but solid enough to provide a solid backing.

The filler in the checkering lines, and especially the border lines, will become troughs for the bonding agent and the filler. Don't worry about it. Yes, control it to some extent, but don't be upset when it happens. Please note the continuation of the checkering: This is the mark of a correctly made repair.

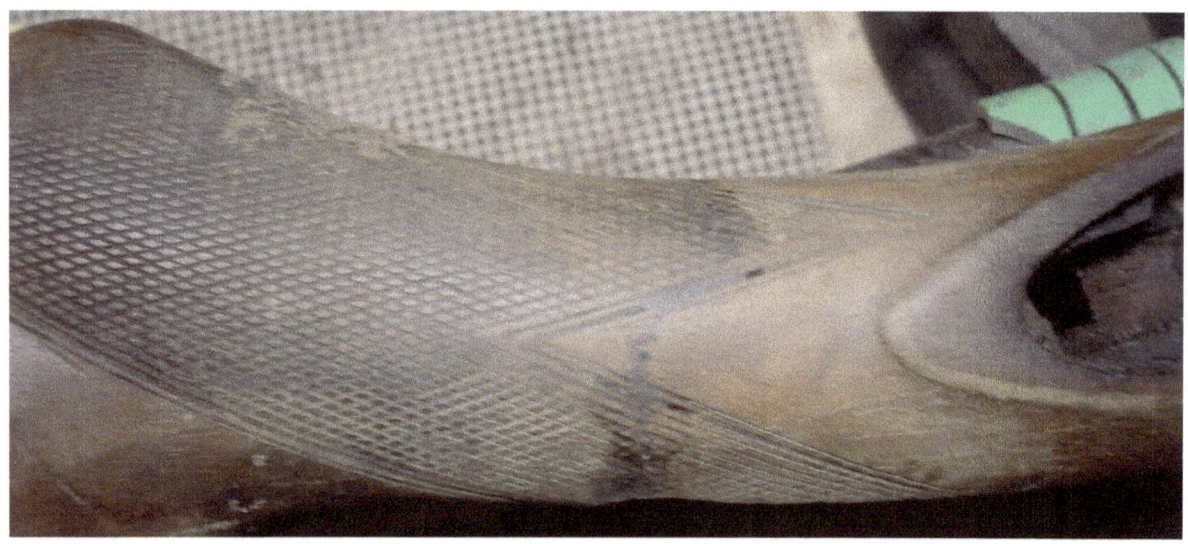

It seems like there is always one hole that acts like a sponge and needs repeated fillings to bring it to level. I continue the use of the tooth pick dipped in the filler to apply a small amount to a specific area. The filler I use dries very quickly and I am able to apply several applications within an hour. It seems that this skill is acquired very quickly.

Now is the time to deepen the existing checkering lines and bring the grip area back to life. To do this, I use a medium cut pointer, and go very slowly. Sometimes the old checkering lines are very faint, or in heavy wear areas, none existent. Do not attempt to use a spacer as most spacing tools used originally were made by the checkerer and were seldom to any measure standard. Just follow the existing lines. If the original contains an error, be very careful when attempting to correct it.

Establish your "tracking lines" first, just lightly cutting into the old lines. You do not want to take any line to full depth at this time. When you have "tracked" the old lines one way, do the opposing lines. In this manner, you will have good lines to track for the entire area to be checkered.

There are times that someone in the weapon's distant past, decided to add their touches to the gun. This gun is no exception. On the bottom of the grip area there is a concave diamond outlined and the interior checkered. Checkering this area is extremely difficult.

For this task I use a fine cut pointer, and proceed slowly, reversing the buttstock in the vise frequently.

When replacing the missing toe of a stock, select a piece of wood of the same type and grain structure. Flatten the two surfaces and check the fit. If the two pieces do not fit well, here's a little hint: Only the exterior of the wood shows. When the two pieces do not fit well, I use my moto tool with a round burr to reduce the height of the interior wood. I leave a ring of wood around the outside of approximately an eighth inch, taking only about a thirty-second of an inch from the interior surface of the largest piece.

Remember, the holding agent must come in contact with <u>both</u> pieces of wood to get a good bond. With the pieces fitting together well, and if the pieces are large enough, I like to add a little insurance. With the larger of the two pieces firmly in a vise or other fixture, I use a scribe to make at least one small indenture near the center of the width and towards one end. Into this indenture, I place a small piece of shot, as shown earlier in this section.

Carefully, position the smaller of the two pieces of wood, and when in the correct position, tap it lightly with the palm of your hand. This will leave an indention on the smaller pieces of wood corresponding EXACTLY to the position of the indenture on the larger piece of wood. Depending upon the size of the two pieces, I drill a small shallow hole, seldom more than a quarter inch deep, but depending upon the thickness of the wood, it may be more or less deep. I then put in whatever dowel material I have chosen to use, check the position of the two pieces of wood with the dowel in place, and may make another indenture in the larger piece and position a second dowel.

Checking the position of the wood again, I use nylon filament tape to mask the sides of the joint and protect the remainder of finish from any excess bonding agent, and shorten clean up tremendously.

I am very fond of using Brownell's AcraGlas as a bonding agent and use it almost exclusively on crack and joint repair. Mixing a small batch using the measuring cups, I follow directions to the letter, to include a timer set for the four minutes of required stirring. When ready, I fill the dowel holes, coat the surface of the larger piece, insert the dowels, and position the smaller piece. And then comes the fun part.

I have found that a joint wrapped with surgical tubing provides a better bond, all but eliminates the presence of a crack, and can often be an experience in frustration to apply. I begin with a section of surgical rubber about two feet long, make a positive tie well ahead of behind the joint by holding the end of the tubing and bring several wraps over the area near the end, securely holding it under pressure.

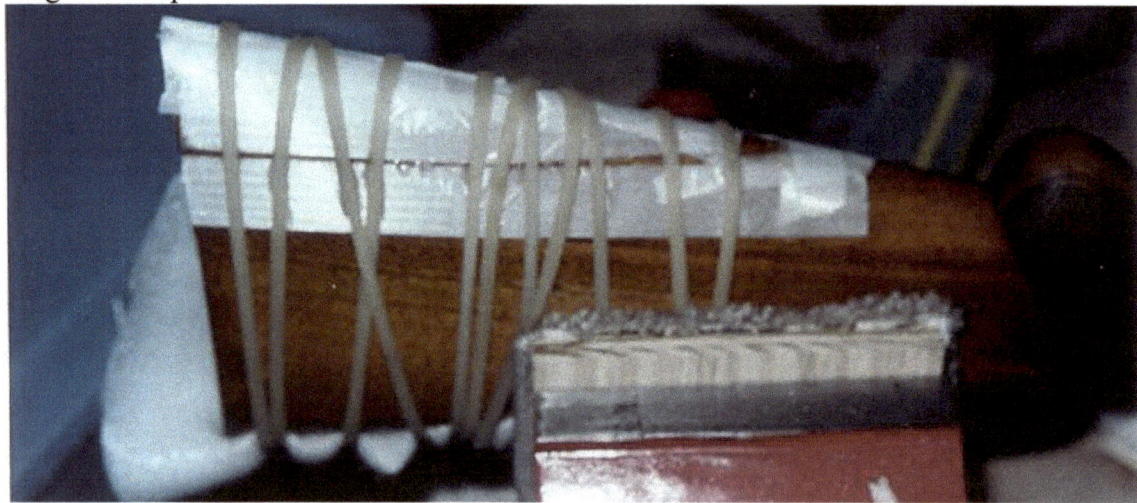

The Remington Model 1100 forearm is prone to cracking at the rear from use and abuse. Remington recognized this many years ago and added a small step in their manufacturing process. They lay a piece of what appears to be a fiberglass or nylon cloth in the rear of the forearm and then use fiberglass to set it in place. I have seen a variety of older forearms with this modification without cracks. For this reason, on all Remington Model 1100 forearms that come through the shop, without this modification, I offer to modify the forearm. On all forearms I make for the Remington Model 1100, I modify them. The following is a very simple step by step procedure I use for achieving this modification.

First, after securing the forearm, I use a dremel # 9 cutter to cut a trough at the rear of the forearm. I judge the depth of the trough by allowing the cutting her to cut down to a point at which the shaft of the cutter is riding against the inside of the forearm. This appears to be the most direct way of achieving a consistent trough.

Being fresh out of fiberglass cloth, I did have a small piece of stainless steel door screen, used it, and now use it exclusively. The material is easy to cut with scissors, and much easier to fit into the trough than fiber glass cloth. I then mix up a small amount of Brownell's Acra Glas, I dribble the liquid into the trough. Wanting to make sure all of the screen is saturated, I tilt the forearm from side to side, and allow the acra glass to get into the upper reached of the trough.

The next step is the most difficult, that of placing a piece of tape over the trough which will keep the liquid up on the sides of the trough. I have found that inch and a half wide masking tape is the easiest to work with, a roll is always around the shop and use it. One of the first steps in using the tape, is to cut – preferably with scissors - the tape to be used. It is is a lot easier to apply if cut, rather than torn. I apply it from the center out and up, and do it as quickly as possible. With the tape in place, I seat it with finger pressure.

Removing the tape, after allowing for the drying time, is always interesting, and I have learned not to do this in front of the Customer. Sometimes, although you believe everything was done to perfection, the end results are far from spectacular. On this forearm, the top corners of the trough did not fill out, but there is more than enough reinforcement to protect against cracks.

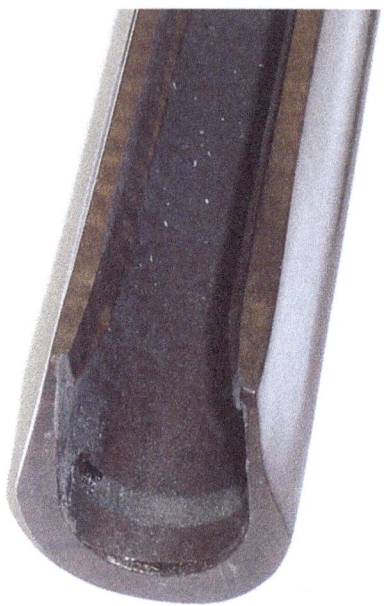

While repairing the wood around a forearm bushing is not that difficult. Repairing the forearm is covered in another section, this procedure addresses how to remove the bushings from the forearm and do so without damaging the wood.

Before I begin to remove the bushings, I look through my "assorted parts" box, and then my factory parts to determine if I have additional bushings, If I do, then the bushings stay in the forearm and I use replacement bushings. What is the wisdom in doing this? Try to sell a set of wood with the notation included in the description that the forearm bushings are missing….

In this example, the forearm is from a Winchester Model 101 in 20 Gauge, and I did not have a set of bushings in the stop, several forearms without bushings, but no bushings. First of all, with the forearm iron removed from the wood, insert the screw into the bushing <u>from the bottom of the stock</u> until it almost comes through the bushing hole on the inside of the forearm.

This will create a small shoulder into which the drift punch can safely sit. The drift punch should be slightly smaller in diameter that the threaded hole in the bushing. Place the drift punch in the hole, kept in place by the shoulder, then reverse the forearm, placing the head of the drift punch on the bench with the bottom of the forearm up.

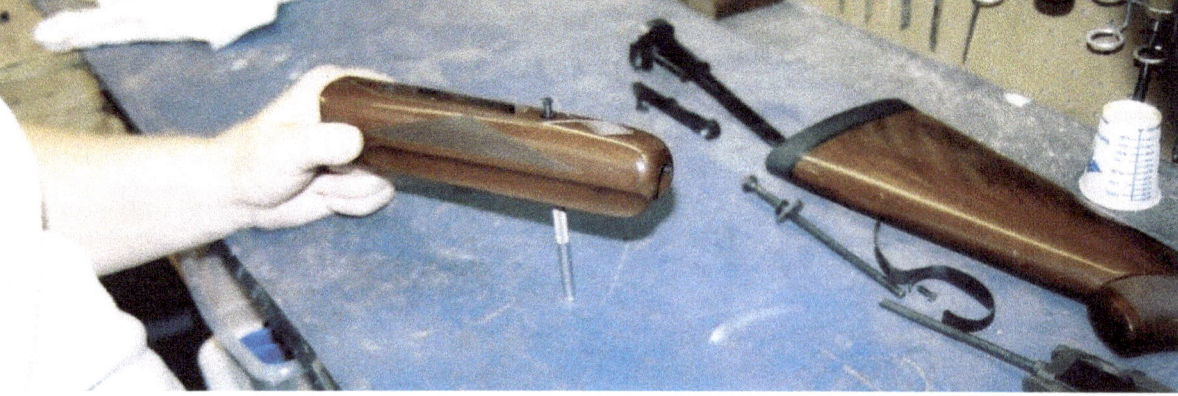

With a nylon faced hammer, lightly tap the wood around the bushing – if the wood begins to rise, stop, the wood is cracking out. At this point, the best way of progressing is to place a tube – piece of pipe – slightly larger than the diameter of the busing and tape the wood pack into place. However, a punch will work. Being careful not to strike the punch hard enough to leave an imprint in the wood, gently tap the wood back into place.

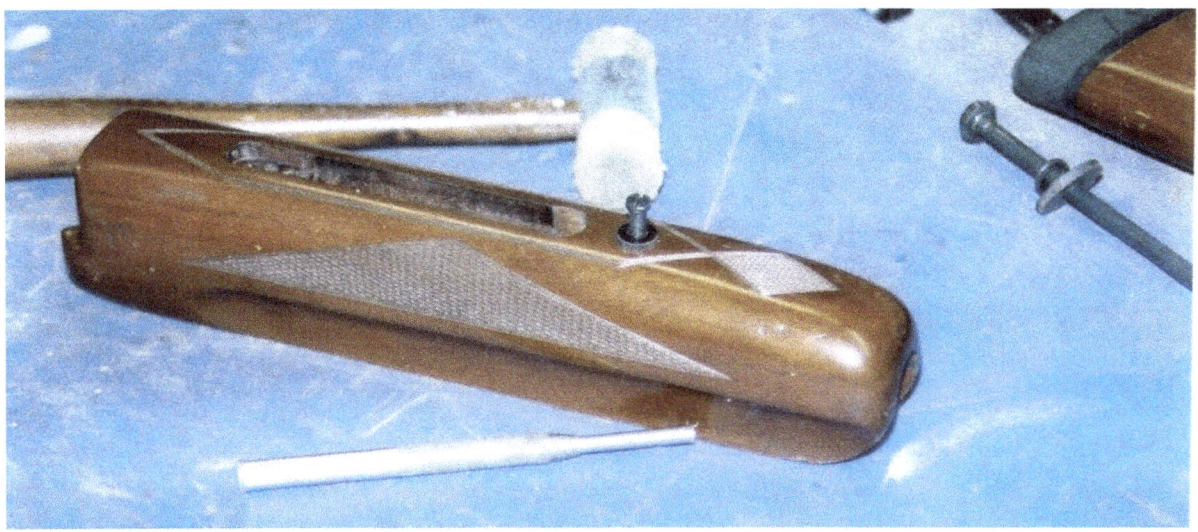

With the wood back in place, repeat your process again, and if the wood rises once more, repeat the correction technique. Once wood cracks out around a bushing hole, it will inevitably continue to rise until the busing is out of the hole. The secret to success here is to limit the amount of the cracking, which is done by gently tapping the cracked wood back into place.

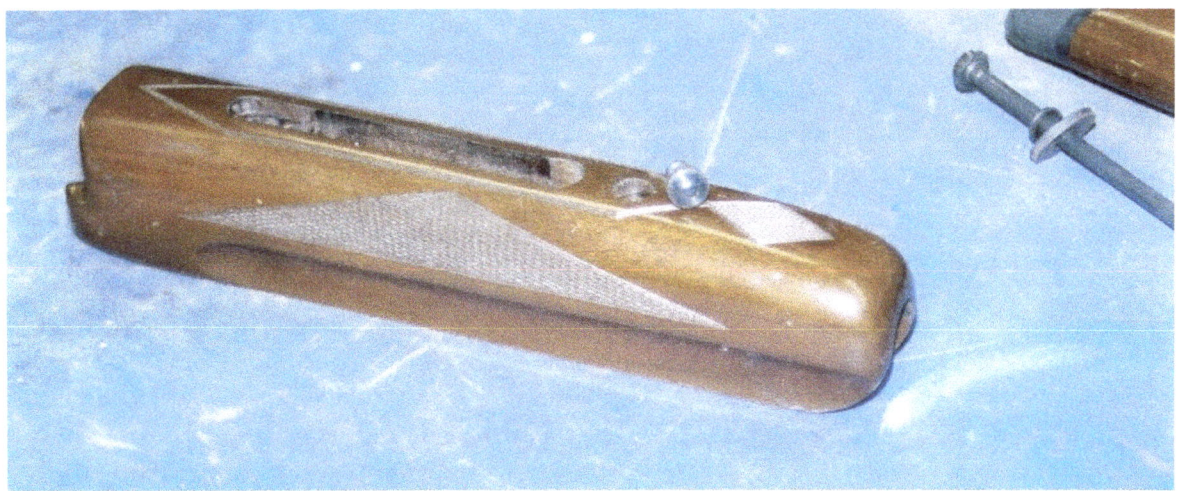

Splinters off of the forearm are very common on older guns, especially splinters at the tip where the wood is the thinnest. As the splinter does not really affect the gun, very seldom is anything done to repair it. Thus, it will catch on the interior of gun cases, even shooter's gloves and quite possibly become worse and worse. The picture shows the forearm also had the horn or ebony insert missing, which as illustrated, has been replaced.

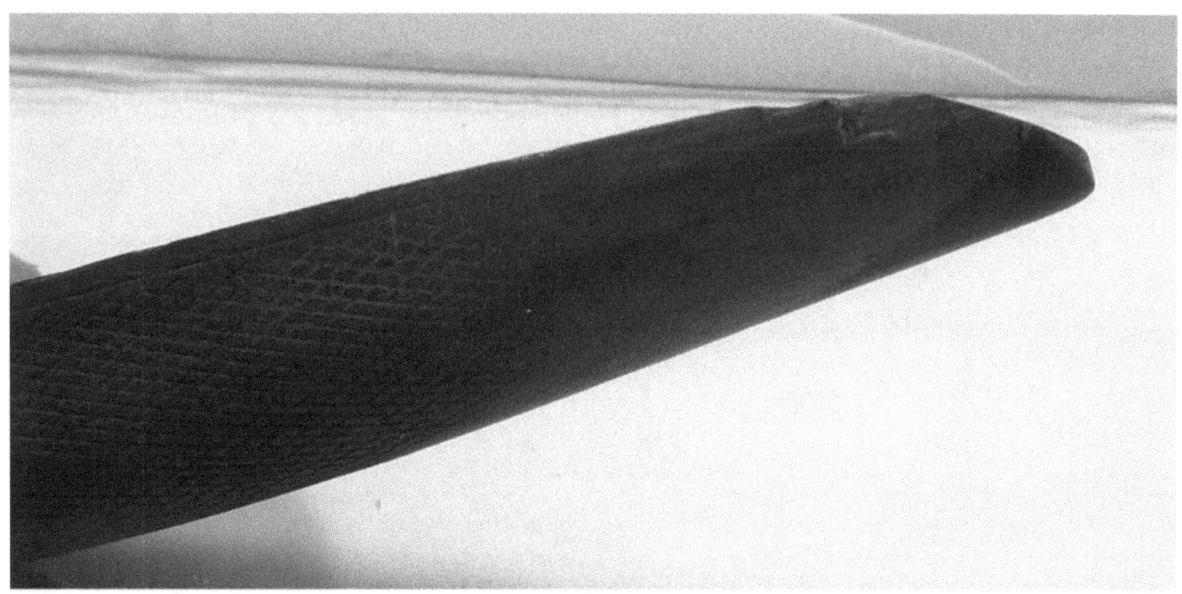

The very first thing to do is to remove the oil from the wood. There are many solutions to this problem, some quite simple, and others extraordinarily difficult – I lean toward the simple. Using a small glass oven dish, I place the forearm in the dish, and then cover it with denatured alcohol. The next day, I notice a browning of the alcohol showing some oil has come out of the wood. Removing the wood from the container, I use a stiff bristled tooth brush to thoroughly scrub the piece, especially around the splintered area. The below cited picture is a prime example of the piece after the first scrubbing. I repeat this process until the alcohol is almost back to its clear state, usually three to four times, before proceeding.

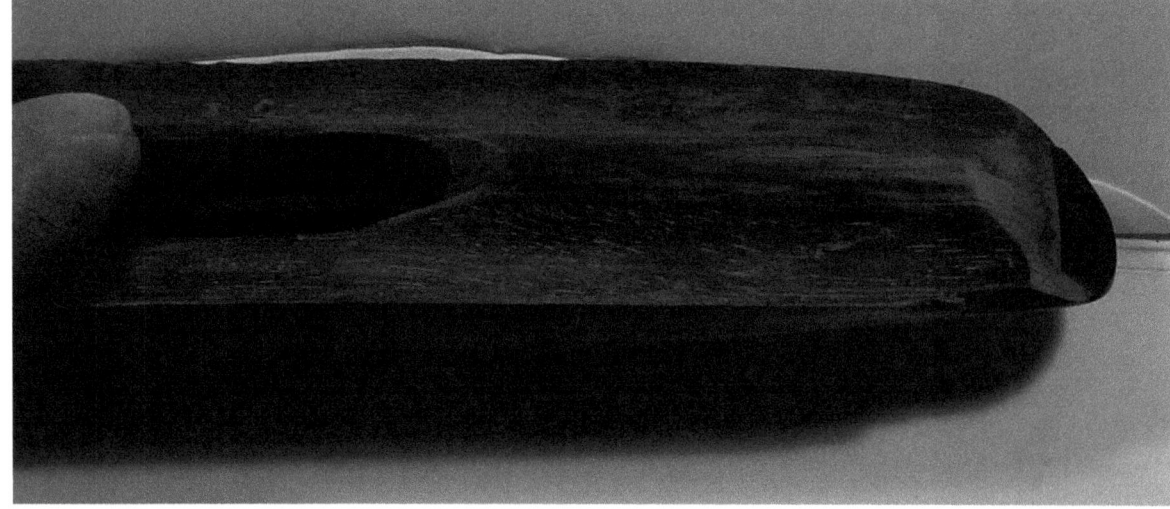

And then the fun begins. After a day in the drying box, I "square" the splintered area, as shown in the following picture. Notice the right angle of the shoulder of the square. This shoulder serves two purposes: First, it provides a "rear shoulder" for the repair to come against in recoil. And second, it provides additional area for the bonding agent to hold to.

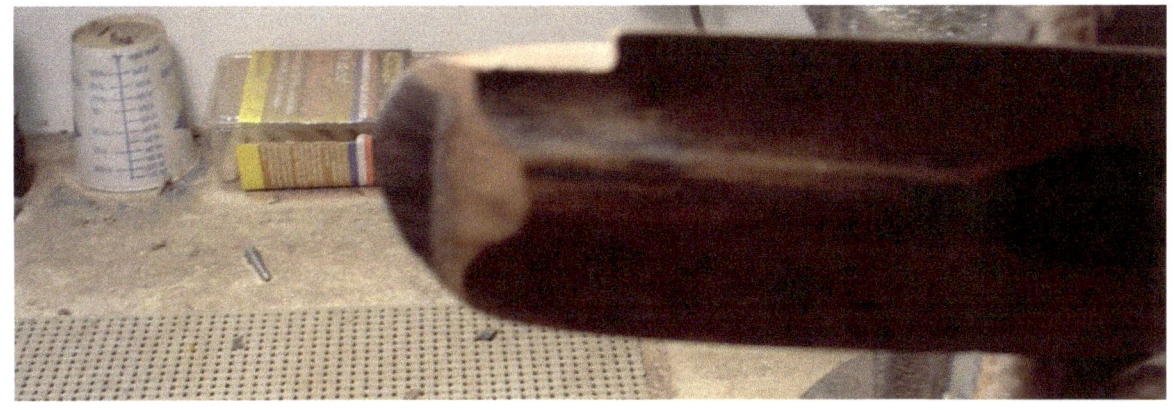

The wood is drilled with two shallow holes. These holes will fill with the bonding agent and help provide a more secure bond between the two pieces of wood.

Final fit, finger pressure, held in place and viewed from all angles.

Time for the bonding agent and some rubber band pressure to hold it in place. This is the point in which a second set of hands is really helpful – but only if the second set of hands understand instructions and will do what they are told. As of this point in my life, I have not found such a set of hands.

Filed to fit, and lightly sanded. When finished, it should blend in well.

This is an excellent view of the replaced wood. When the finish is applied, this joint should be all but invisible. The light sanding of the replacement area spilling over onto the checkering serves to high light the original checkering lines.

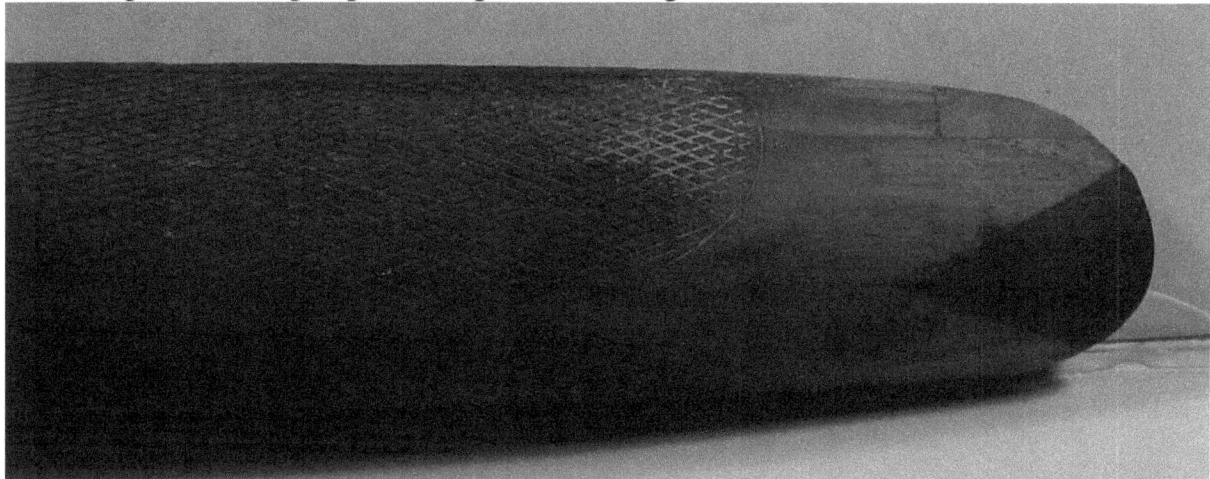

Notice the "X" on the forearm tip? Those are my master lines to be used when that area is checkered, to provide a little additional grasping area.

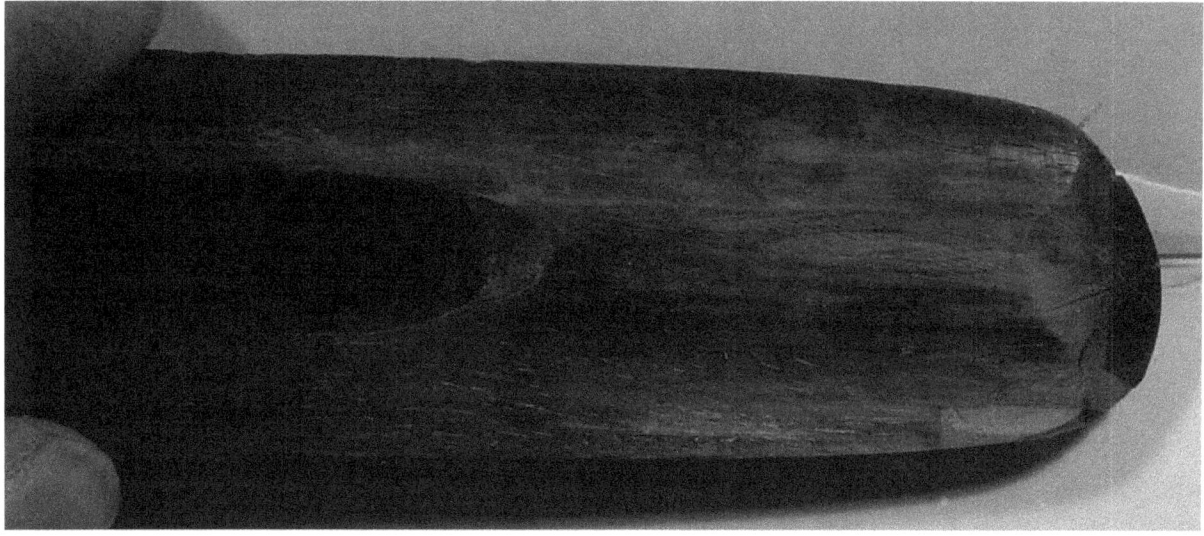

The completed forearm, ready for the finish. That is a lot of checkering on a small piece of wood. With the exception of two small areas, I was able to follow the original checkering lines.

By far the most common crack on a semi-auto of pump action shotgun is the splitting of the face – contacts the receiver – of the stock.

The illustration displays a very comon crack found on pump and semi-auto shotguns. After repairing a number of such cracks, I developed a technique which repairs the crack and placed the stock back in service for many more years.

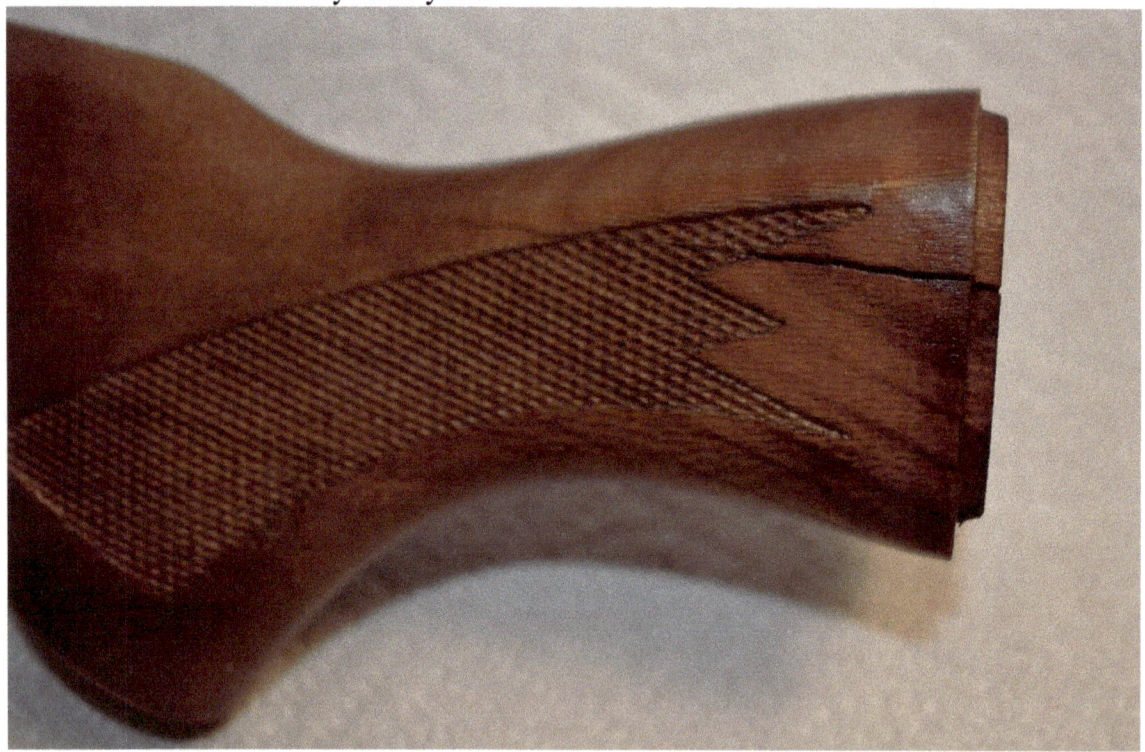

The crack is across the entire stock, and over time, if not repaired, would spread back into the grip area and create a safety hazard to the shooter.

I want to be sure there is no foreign matter in the crack, or that a sliver of wood has not come to rest in the crack preventing a good seal. To insure this, I check the crack with a probe and powerful light, then bind the cracked area with surgical tubing, bringing the edges of the crack together.

With the crack compressed, I center punch two locations on the face of the buttstock – as shown – and use a drill slightly larger than a round tooth pick to drill two holes at an angle into the buttstock. Being very carefull to not drill through the side or bottom of the stock. A small mark on the drill will help achieve this goal.

To check your work, insert a tooth pick into the hole to insure the hole is deep enough to secure both parts of the cracked stock.

To insure the adhesive gets down into the crack, I use a piece of tapered dowel to gently spread the crack in the stock.

You must use your feel to determine how much pressure to apply to the crack. The object is to open the crack, not extend it. Once the crack has been opened, I use a diabetic syringe and thinned AcraGlas to fill the crack.

Removing the dowel, wrap the grip area with surgical tubing. This will bring the crack together AND align the holes previously drilled for the tooth picks. By the way, I like to use the round HARDWOOD tooth picks. Using the syringe, fill the drilled holes with the thinned AcraGlas, and insert the tooth picks. Why wood? And not metal pins? Because I have had better luck with hardwood toothpicks, and they are less expensive.

I then use a box cutter blade to sever the excess toothpick from the stock, the face of the buttstock will be filed flat upon completion of the drying process. Note: Now is a good time to wipe the excess adhesive from the stock. Either wipe now, or file later….

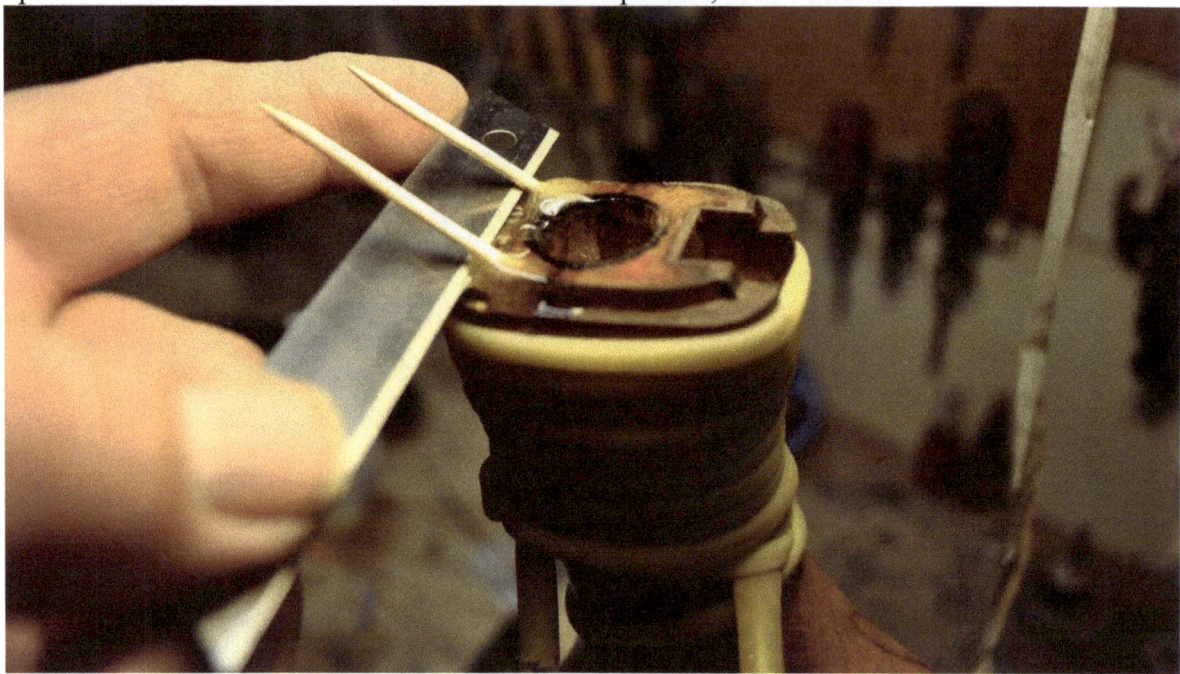

Until dry, the project is ready to set aside. When using thinned AcraGlas, I always allow a full day for the adhesive to cure. I am not sure if it is necessary, but it is what I do.

After a little removal of the excess adhesive coming out of the crack and under the surgical tubing – which could have been prevented by apply masking tape to either side of the crack before applying the adhesive - the stock back on the shotgun.

One of the most infuriating repairs to stock that I do involves – for the most part – a customer bringing in a semi finished stock with a large check in the wood. I do not happen to have one on hand, but I do have a "proof" used for checkering trials that has such a check.

The stock blank that this piece of wood came from was startling in its grain structure. I saved all of the trimmings and have found most are flawed – but recoverable. The first thing to be done is to remove all loose wood and dirt from the checks. With that done, a determination must be made as to what filler, and in what shade is required to be the least noticeable.

For the large check, I am going to use a light brown die in thinned AcraGlas, for the single check near the center of the proof I will use a darker brown die, and for the two line checks I will use the light brown dye.

When you think you are ready to proceed, turn the wood over and check to determine if the check goes all of the way through the wood. If it does, tape over it to preclude trying to fill a bottomless check. Yep, I learned my lesson the hard way and ended up with a stock AcraGlased to my work bench. But that is another story for another time.

On large checks, be prepared to use a second batch as the filler sometimes seeps into unknown voids in the wood. I use this opportunity to mix up a second batch will a slightly different shade. Many times the filled check will reflect a subtle difference and make the repair less noticeable.

With the excess filled removed and the surface flattened, you can see the start of the filling process. Several additional coats must be added over several days to create a filler.

SECTION 12

Duplicating Factory Checkering

Although I hadn't intended on including the following project in this section, I will as it in effect, duplicated factory checkering, in a way. A Customer in Michigan sent a very nice little Springfield Model 5100 20 gauge side by side. This is the gun that came out with a plastic buttstock and forearm, I had one growing up in 12 gauge and regret trading it off.

Anyway, the conversation preceding its arrival included the fact that the owner had broken the stock years before, had ordered replacement wood from Fajen's, Warsaw, MO, but had never gotten around to having it installed.

When the package arrived, I found the beavertail forearm was nice, I would grade it somewhere between semi-fancy and fancy, the buttstock was straight grain American Walnut. The receipt for the wood was still taped to the buttstock, and was dated 1980, twenty-one years before I received it.

Have you ever had one of those days in which nothing goes right? Everything hits the skids and continues going downhill? Well, I had just the reverse! The wood required very little fitting and the grain in the forearm really came alive. The price I had quoted for the job would cover fitting the wood, finishing it and running some checkering. But I started having some strong feelings about this gun and decided that such a piece of work, humiliated with plastic parts for so long, deserved a little something special, and I liked the owner.

After fitting the forearm iron to the new forearm, I decided that the two wood screws normally anchoring this type of forearm just wouldn't fit the task at hand. The plastic forearm had two bronze inserts molded into the forearm into which machine screws served to attach the plastic.

Two forearm bushings were turned, similar to the Krieghoff's I spent most of my time on and installed in the forearm in the same manner. Fitting the forearm to the barreled action required little time, and then came time to implement the decision I had already made, I would enlarge the initial pattern on the plastic forearm to cover the replacement beavertail forearm. I am no artist and have been told my prospective in continuity is lacking. But a reasonable copy of the checkering pattern was soon on paper and checked for fit.

The forearm was a standard issue semi-finished forearm available from Reinhart Fajen's many years ago. I would have graded it at a low fancy or high semi-fancy. I will skip over the fact that I have always hated the wood screws Stevens used for securing these little forearms to the iron, and replaced the wood screws with machine screws and established bushings in the bottom of the forearm wood for them.

    The plastic forearm did have an interesting checkering pattern, and I thought I could maintain the general pattern design but enlarge it for the beaver tail forearm. Using the forward forearm bushing as a marker point, I explored different variations of the basic pattern for several days. I have a habit of leaving "tasks" for which I have not made a decision on my work bench.
    The one facet of the design which kept me from making a decision was how to compliment the rear of the forearm where the wood narrows for the forearm iron. I wanted something functional, but which flowed into the remainder of the forearm. I forget how many days the forearm gathered dust on my bench, but everything clicked one day and resulted in a paper pattern which I considered worthy of being copied onto the wood for a long-time look see.
    Normally, I will white pencil on a pattern I have had difficulty developing, and let it sit a day or two to see if I really like it when the idea becomes cold. I will pick it up, look it over, maybe change a line or two, perhaps tighten or loosen a radius, and put it down only to pick it up an hour later to hum and haw some more. However, in this case I let the forearm sit long enough to get a couple of pictures of it and started to cut the pattern outline and master lines.
    If the job had just been for a customer, I might have made the decision a little quicker, but I was living out my fantasy of putting wood on one of my long-ago guns, and I wanted it done right, and I wanted it to be something that would draw attention.

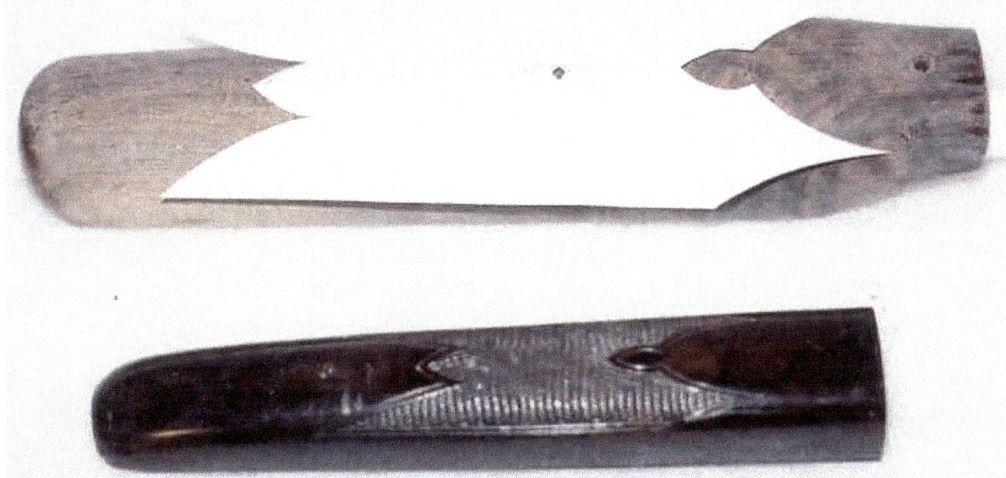

    I have read of Stockmakers and other similar professions using a variety of special paper to copy or transfer a pattern, I use plain old, cheap typing paper. With the pattern on the paper, and cut out, I place it on the wood.
    Depending upon the size of the pattern, I may cut small quarter inch diamonds in the pattern and use tape on the pattern to anchor it to the wood showing through the small cutout diamonds.

Most often I will use short (half an inch), narrow (quarter inch wide) pieces of tape to secure the pattern in place. On multi piece patterns, the taping and holding arrangement can become a mess and difficult to get a line on the wood.

In this case it wasn't necessary. I held the pattern in place and used a white pencil to trace around the pattern.

There are times when a piece of wood just checkers well: The lines space out easily, there are no run overs, the wood cuts cleanly and the figured grain shows through, and everything goes like it is supposed. The Springfield forearm was one of those jobs. True, it was a fill in pattern, but …. Well, take a look at the next picture, and you decide.

There are times when I will receive a set of wood on which all of the checkering has been all but removed. Sometimes this is the result of reshaping the grip to one's personal desire, and sometimes because the finish was sanded off and the checkering just got in the way.

I received a buttstock with an adjustable comb and a forearm for refinishing and recutting the factory checkering pattern. There was very little left of the original checkering, just a few pieces on the corners and a small piece here and there. Not having a copy of the factory checkering on file – one of the few guns I do little work with is the Perazzi – so I had to obtain some definitive views of the checkering patterns. But as I had to finish the wood first, I had some time to find it.

Unfortunately, the style of stock replacing the original did not lend itself to copying the exact checkering pattern. So, I improvised. I drafted a pattern which incorporated some of the angles of the Perazzi checkering pattern.

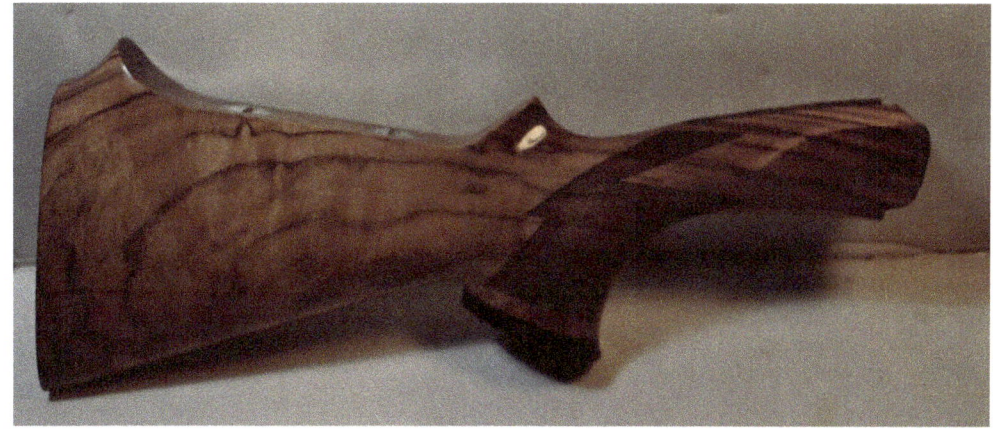

The palm swell on the right side made balancing the pattern a little difficult until I made the decision that balancing the pattern on each side was not that critical and let the two sides "do their own thing."

To seal the checkering, I used a mixture of some oil based dark walnut stain and Alkanet Oil from Dusty Bird Shooting Supplies. Just dark enough to show contrast but not enough to detract from the checkering.

The customer wanted 28 lines per inch, and after tracking in the outline of some of the pattern, I was sure the wood would accept the fine line checkering. Other that a few small areas, I was dead on. On those few areas of softer wood, I would cut the line almost to full depth, and then apply a sealer. When the sealer had soaked in and hardened, I would cut a few more passes with the fine cut pointer. In this manner, I was able to bring the points of the soft wood to a point and be indistinguishable from the remaining checkering.

Recutting Factory Checkering

Many times I would rather begin checkering a new stock as recut old checkering. But then again, after I complete the re-cutting, and see the wood grain come through the fresh checkering, I know the satisfaction of bringing an old stock back to life, of making something once beautiful, once more beautiful. And then there are occasions like an old girl friend's visit to the beauty shop – Mission Impossible.

Recutting the factory checkering starts when the buttstock and forearm are being refinished. Actually, the first step in the refinishing process – removing the old finish. I use a stripper to remove the finish during the refinishing process, and during the stripping, I use a stiff bristled brush to remove all of the old finish and accumulated dirt from the old checkering.

I have had to recut checkering on some very nice shotguns on which the checkering lines were filled not only with old finish, but the remains of years of accumulated dirt and topped off with dried stripper. So, do as I do before I begin refinishing wood, I think forward to the problems I may have if the stripping process is not accomplished correctly.

When recutting Factory Checkering, there is one golden rule that when violated will cause you a lot of problems and can possible ruin your project. The rule: Recut the existing lines, do not attempt to correct errors.

This rifle stock is from a well-worn Model 70 Winchester. A friend brought it to me asking that I recut the checkering and he would refinish it. In some places the checkering was worn smooth. I had asked the customer if I could just remove the existing checkering and recut the patterns but use a longer (3 ½ to 1) ration within the pattern. He wanted to use the existing lines and the stubby Winchester ratio.

The first thing to be done is reestablishing the borders for the checkering pattern. Go very slowly when doing this, follow the old line, or use the appropriate straight edge or French curve to identify where the line should be. On this pattern, a straight edge was used to establish the "missing line" by lining up the partial lines.

Next, cut the existing lines only where you can see them. Again, do not make any assumptions as to where the line should be.

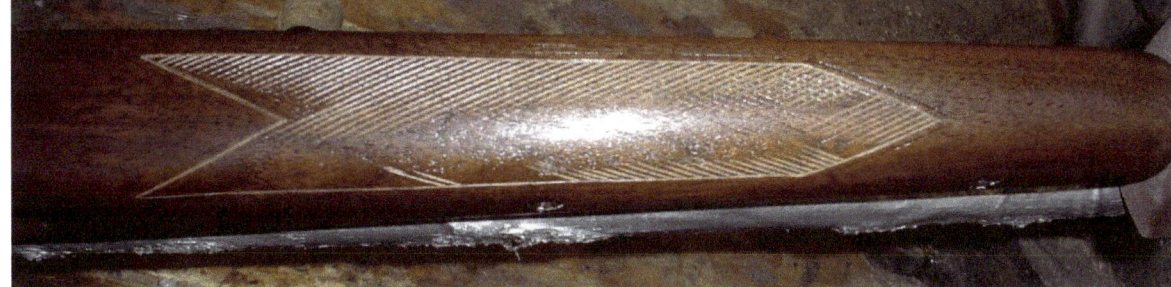

With some remnant line left on either side, use a clear plastic straight edge to lay a continuing line between the two. When I said areas of this stock had the checkering worn smooth, I meant it. When doing this, be sure the beginning and end of the line are the same line.

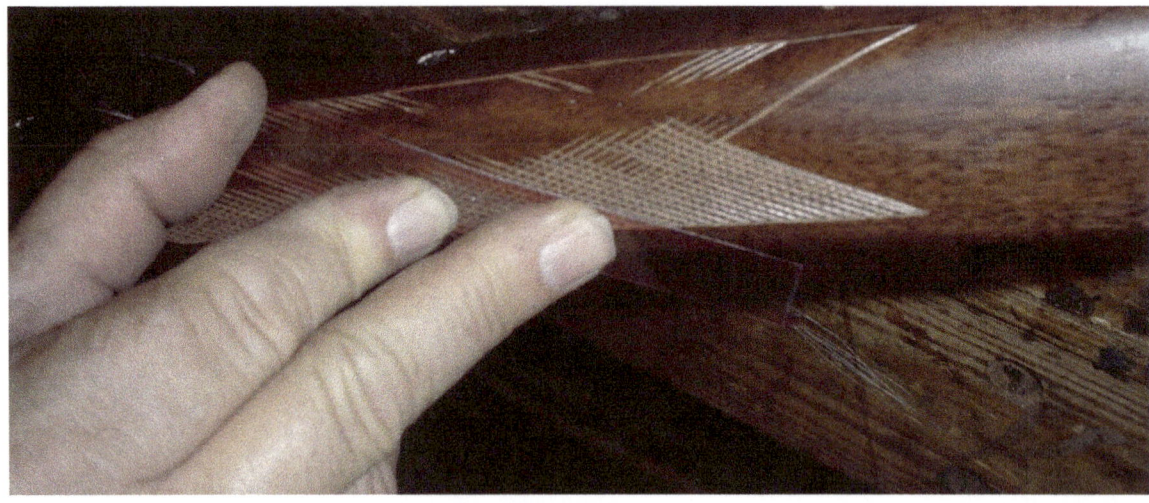

With the existing lines being tracked to the limit of their being, it is time to use a straight edge to carry the lines out to their full extension, from one border to the other. By using a clear plastic straight edge, prospective is gained by referring to the other existing lines. From the line developed with the straight edge, other lines will be tracked in using a three-line spacer with the correct line spacing.

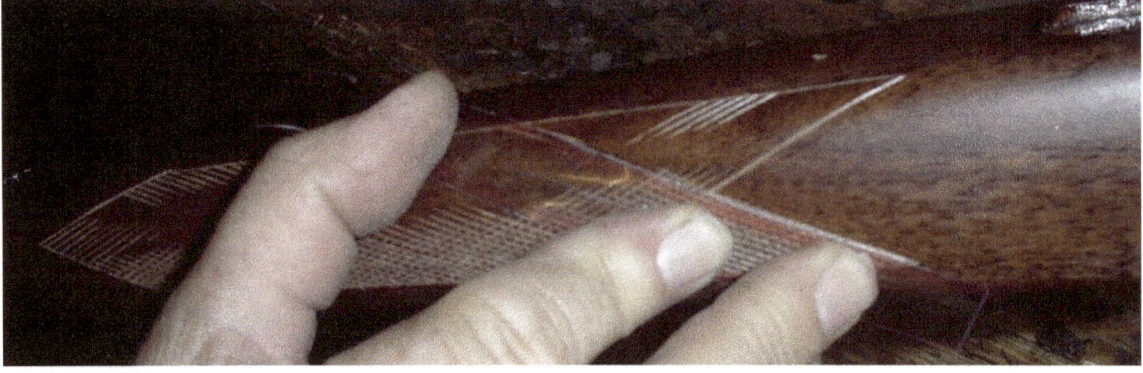

And then the east part, just cutting the lines where they should be as determined with the straight edge. I would recommend using the appropriate two or three-line spacer for this task. I prefer the three line.

Now the grip area. And this one wasn't too bad. Almost all of the original lines could be identified.

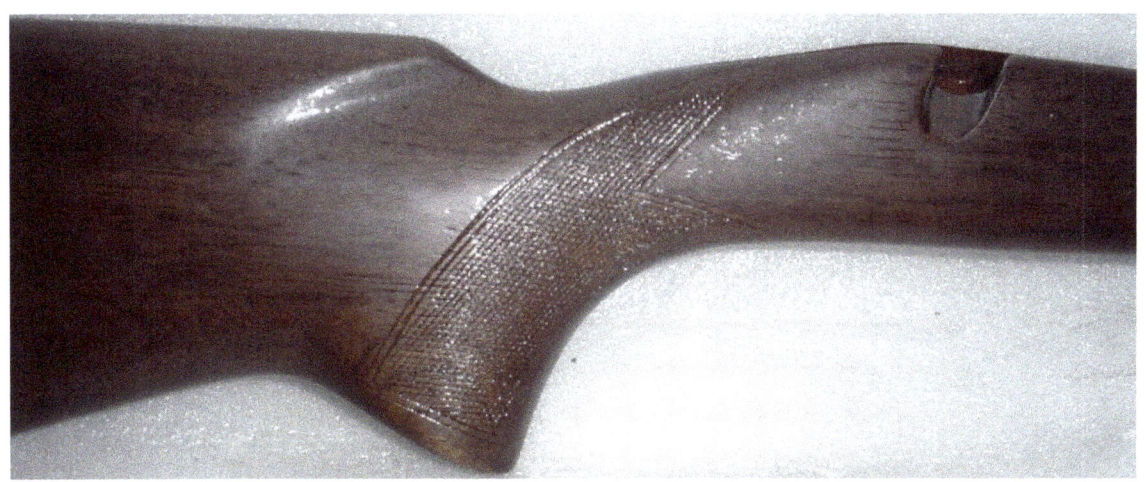

One note of caution: do not use a spacer to cut the borders. Use a medium pointer.

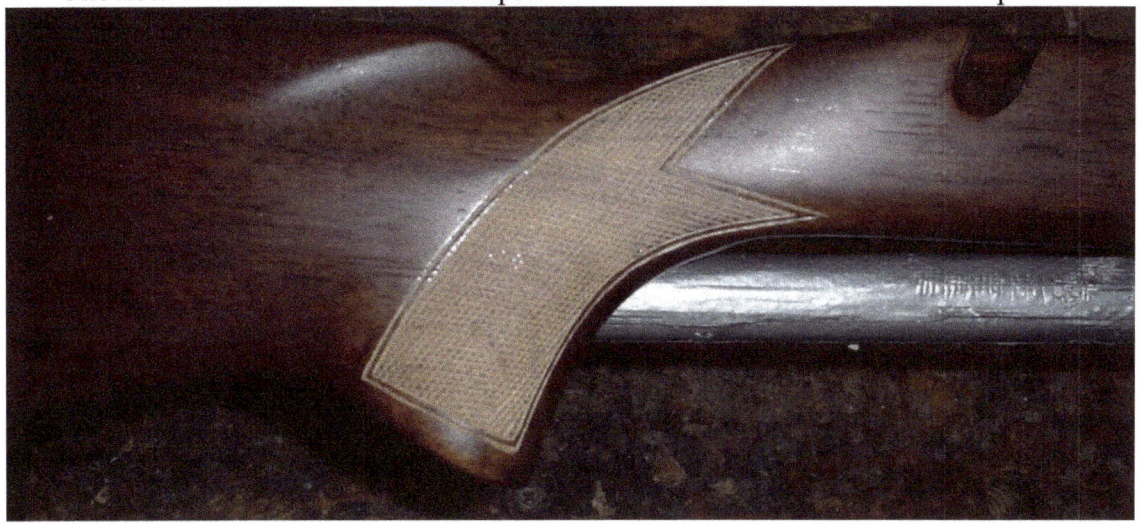

Even the opposing grip area was in good condition as seen in the following photograph.

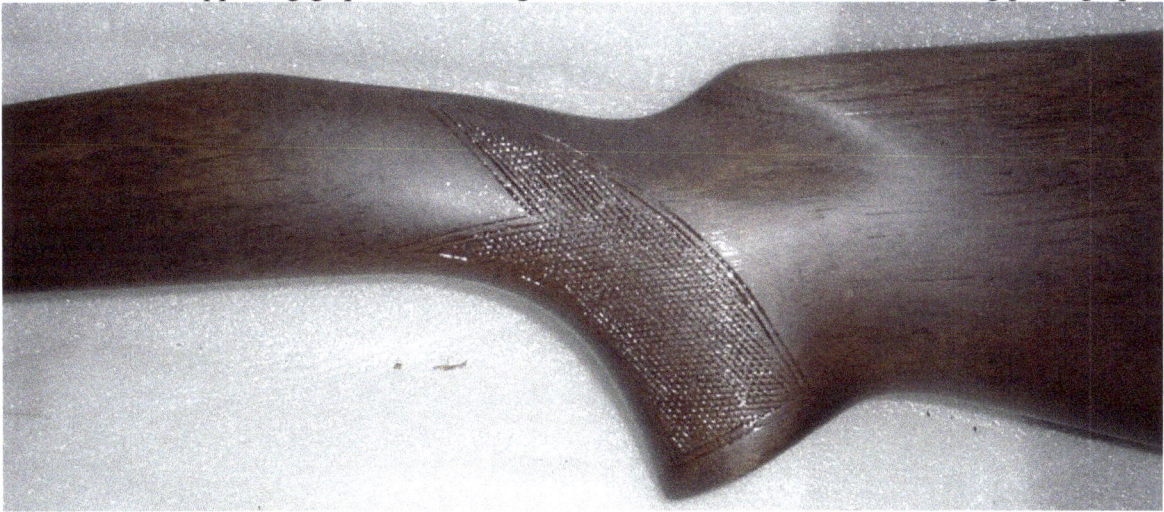

With the sealer on the checkering, it looks nice.

One of the most common jobs encountered is recutting checkering on older shotguns which is worn smooth, or filled with dirt and grime over the years and smooth. This next project is from a late 1800's L. C. Smith 10 Gauge shotgun. While the grip are of the weapon was in pretty good shape, the forearm checkering was well worn around the edges – was it from carrying the ten plus pound scatter gun?

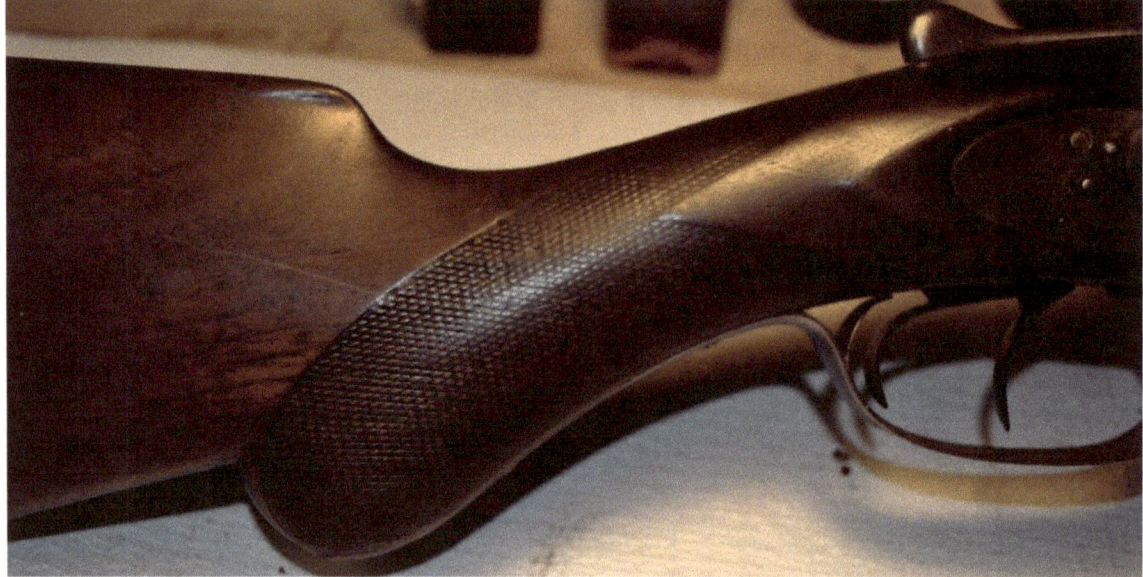

Check each piece of the task out very carefully. Look for repaired areas, cracks in the wood and finish application.

Start out on the grip area of the buttstock, and cut every other line the full height of the pattern, as the picture shows.

And then cut every other line of the width of the buttstock.

Leave the area needing repair until later.

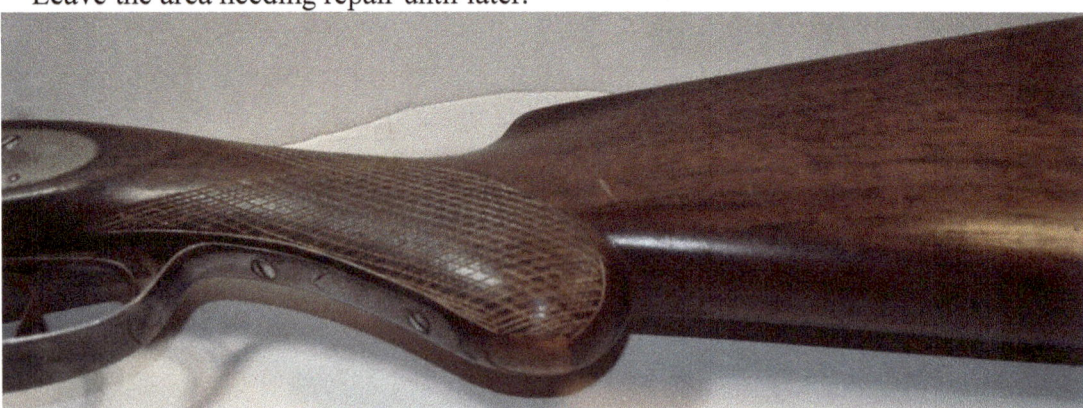

I am actually just a little bit proud of the completed checkering job. I feel that it would pass muster in the hands of any hunter wishing to use the old gun until the checkering was once again smooth.

With a pencil outlining the checkering pattern on the repaired pistol grip, the next problem I face is the decreasing area to be checkered. Notice my replacement wood? `

I decide to use strong - as in slightly deeper than normal – vertical lines and lighter horizontal lines to complete the area.

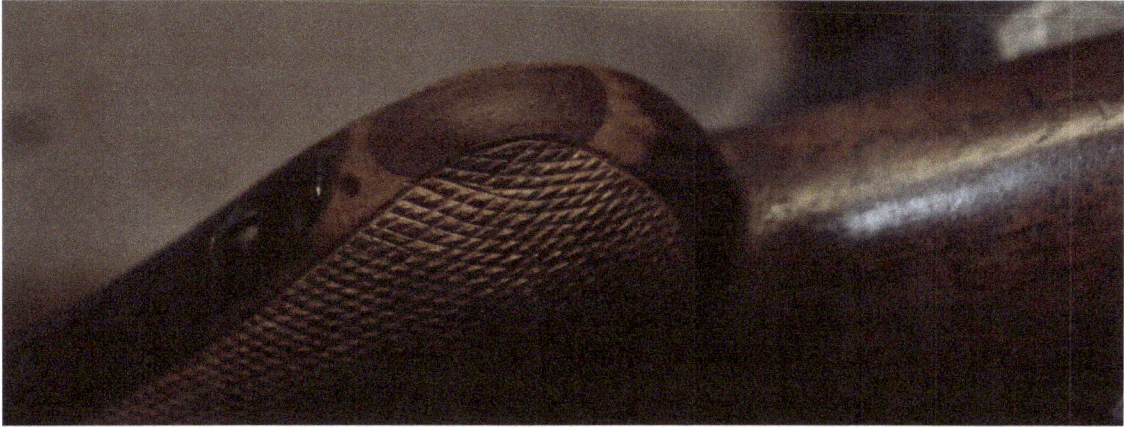

And then there was the forearm…. Not really in bad shape, but for some reason, the thinner wood of the forearm is a little more dry, and doesn't checker as well as the buttstock.

I once again start out by cutting every other of the existing lines, and then using a plastic strip to align the two pieces of line and cut them. After than, it is just a matter of deepening the lines. And I was quite surprised when this pice of century old wood cut very well, leaving very nicely shaped diamonds.

The Model 21 Winchester has one of the most complimentary checkering patterns of the pre-War period. And the wood found on most of these guns is very, very nice. I like to refinish and recut the checkering on the wood, but sometimes, when I have to pickup where some else left off, life can get a little difficult.

The problem is one I encounter more often that one would imagine. The person refinishing the wood will take off the checkering to prevent a buildup of finish in the checkering lines. While the intent is great, sometimes the degree of expertise in masking might need a little improvement. Such was the case on the following buttstock and forearm. The masking was very close to the edge of the checkering pattern in most cases, but sometimes it was almost over the checkering border. And to make matters even more interesting, there was also open stock between the tape edge and the masking mark.

The great part is that this checkering has a bead for a border, and a bead can hide a multitude of errors, if the bead is administered correctly. It is in these cases that your persistence will pay off.

Using the 60 degree edger, cut a shallow line along the inner line of the border, no more than the depth you would use when tracking in checkering lines. With this border established, use the standard procedure for recutting factory checkering, and take the lines to full depth. That ragged line around the checkering pattern is the line left by the masking tape, and one which must be eliminated.

This particular bead is almost the exact spacing and contour of the Gunline Narrow Convex Border tool, but not quite. So, a short time spent with a diamond burr, a few test strokes, and I have a tool that will cut the original bead dimensions. I now have the modified tool on a shortened handle with the rear half of the cutter ground away. This allows the tool cut tighter radius with less tail drag and produces a nicer appearance on the final product.

Because the finish may chip if "plowed through", use the cutter in a filing motion and slowly cut through the finish down to the wood before attempting to cut the convex border. This forearm has rolling lines and will require re-positioning the work several times to make clean cuts in establishing the border. This takes a lot more time, but a whole lot less time if you have to go back and repair the finish bordering the checkering.

Now comes the buttstock. I really appreciate the skill that went into cutting this pattern, as well as the development of the pattern. It is a classic, one that I have used many time with slight modifications to accommodate the stock design.

This checkering was also masked over prior to refinishing the stock, and the same care in cutting the interior border and the convex border must be taken.

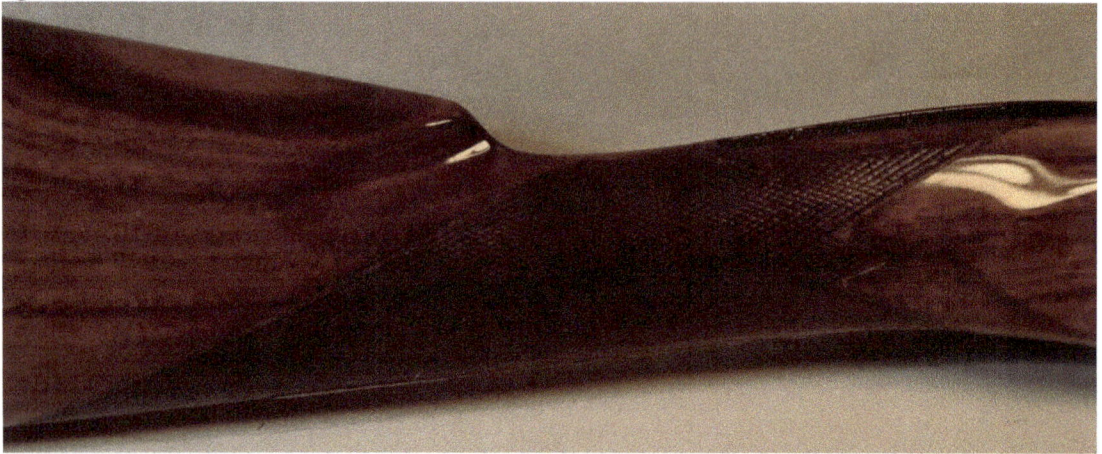

A quick examination of the checkering reveals several places where the masking overlapped the checkering and went out onto the stock. The area at the top of the tang area shows this, as well as several places where the finish was "pulled up / loosened" when the tape was removed.

The same problem was present on the right side of the grip, but neither area is a "stop the job" error. Both of these areas can be repaired after checkering is completed.

On area that will be critical to the final appearance of the completed task is the radial cut at the rear of the upper tang of the receiver. The new cutter – in the correct radius – which is shortened, will really help in making these cuts. The same technique is to be used, use the cutter as a file and slowly "file" through the finish. Do Not plow through the finish or it will surely crack off.

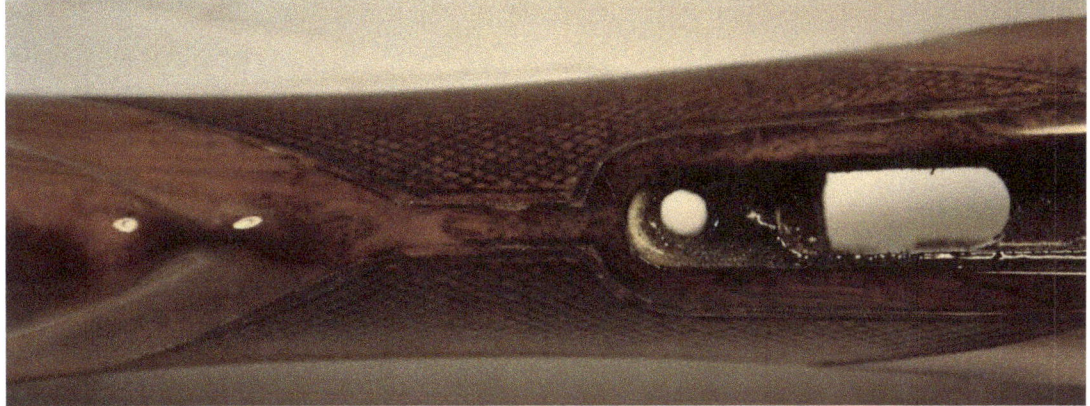

Still more evidence of the masking tape lifting the finish. Again, these areas are easily repairable. Inconvenient, yes. Repairable, yes!

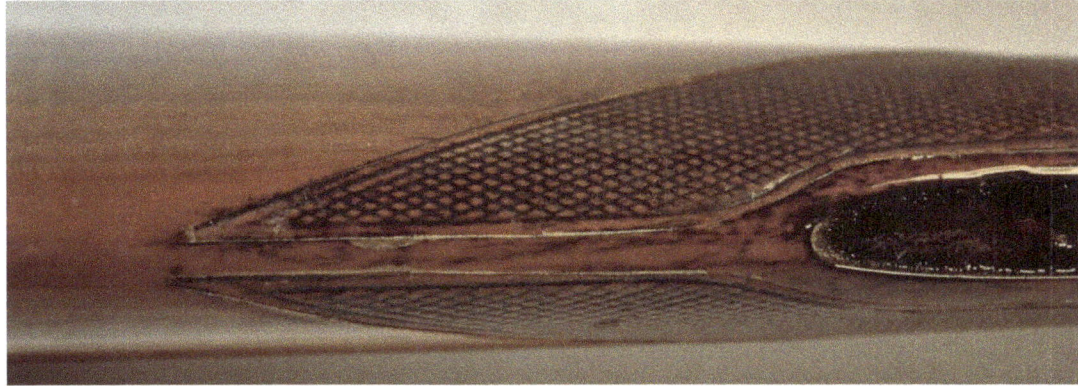

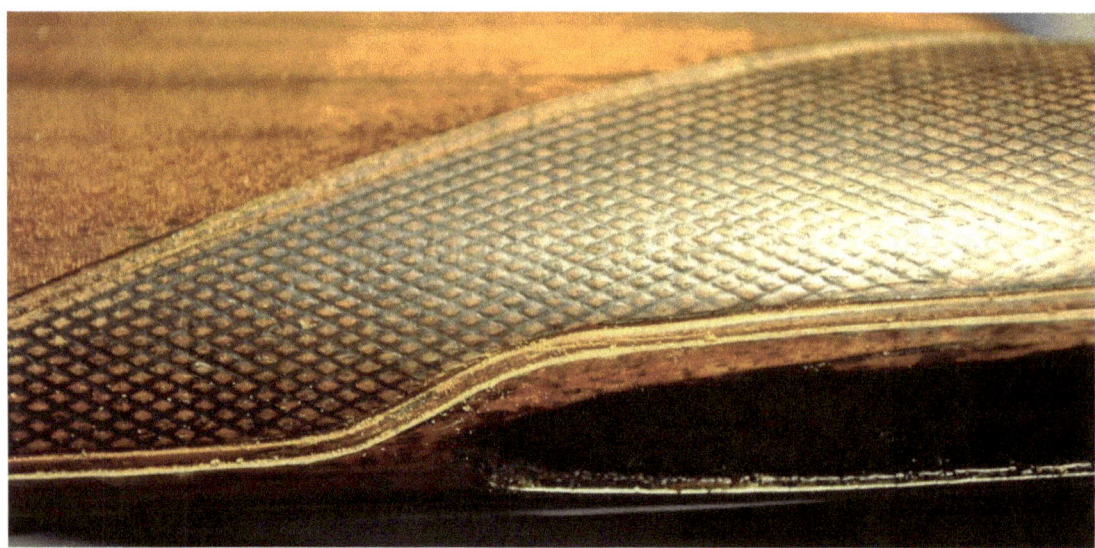

Oh Crap. Did I just do that? OK! Someone help me.

And the Checkering Gods were with me.

Checkering is recut, border is once again cut, and the masking error is showing in the following picture. The solution, repair or whatever one wants to call it, is to apply a small bead of the finished used on the stock – to prevent incompatibility and color change – at the edge of the finish. I use a tooth pick dipped in the thinned finish, or a very small artist's brush. Many times I will have to apply three to five coats of the thinned finish to eliminate the difference.

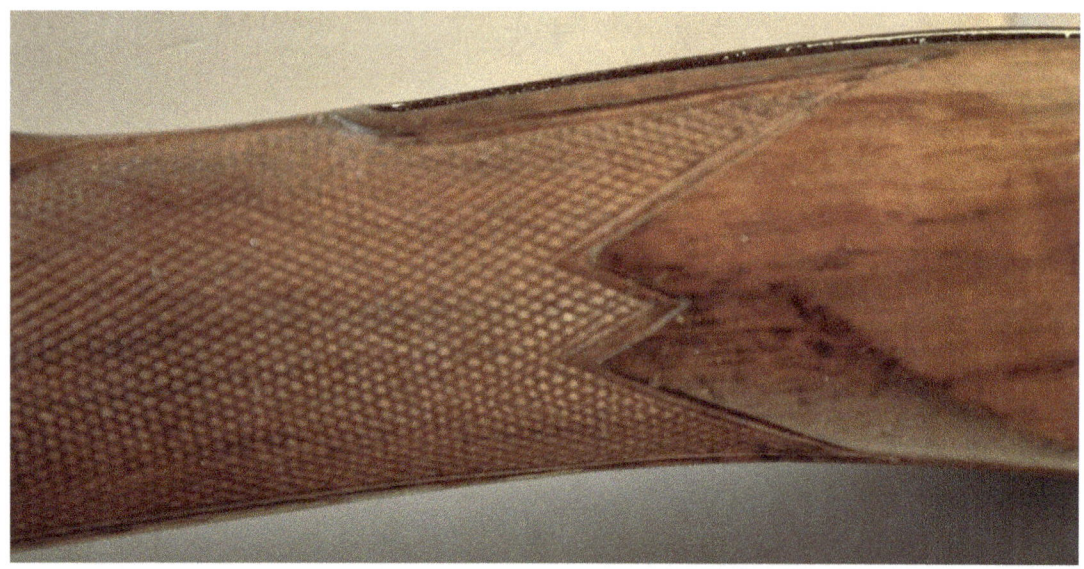

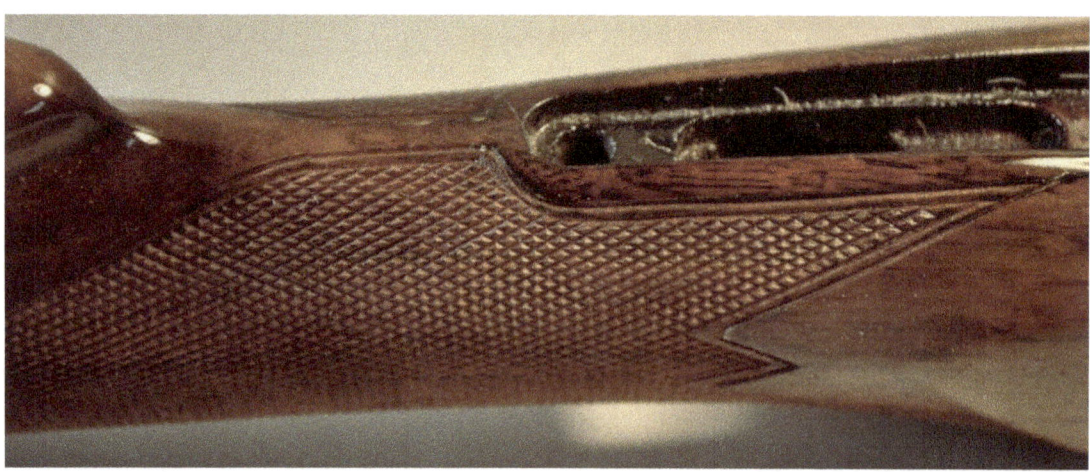

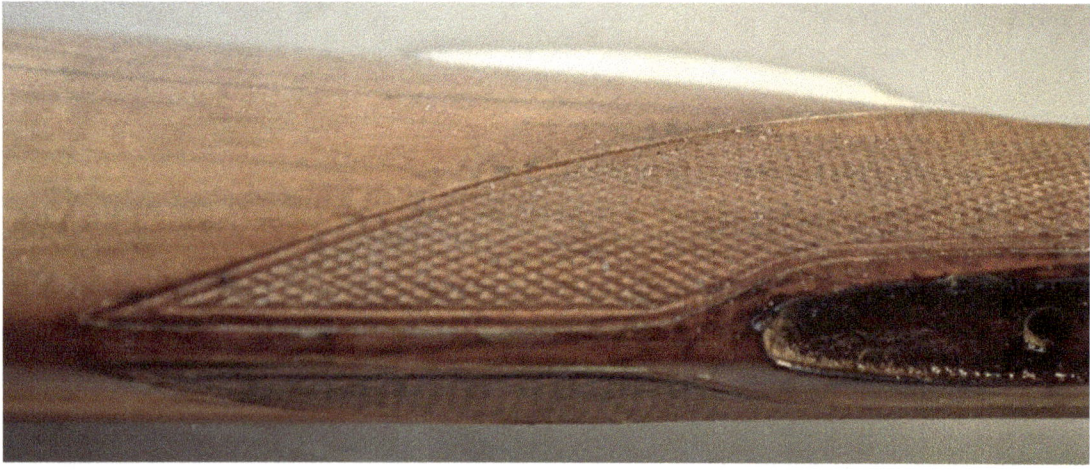

    I like to think the person that checkerd the stock originally would look down upon this and nod his approval. Just a thought.

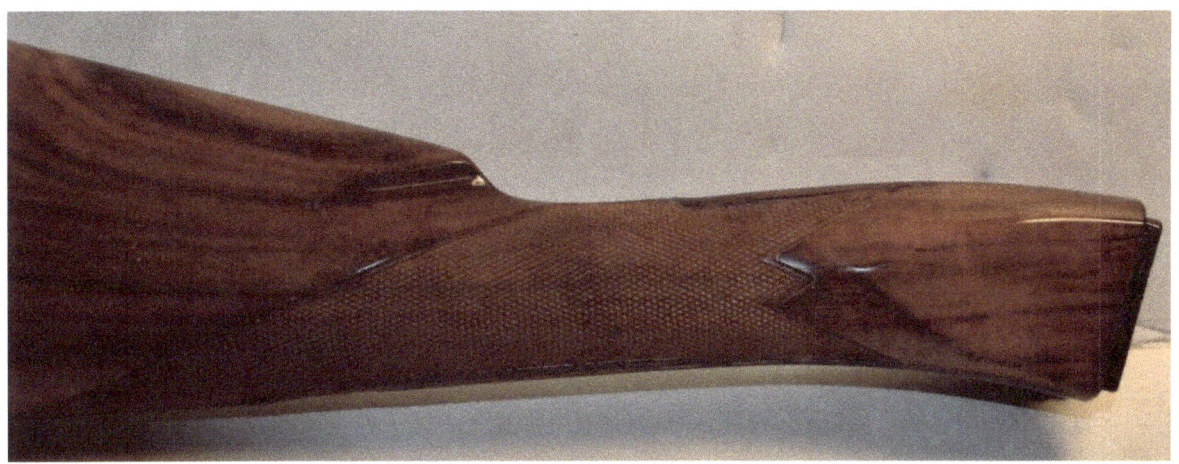

There were two very old stock makers, Runover Joe and Flattop Pete, who would meet at a fountain at the Court House Square of their small town each Thursday morning and talk about the work they had accomplished, and the few customers who appreciated their skill. When Runover Joe did not show up as was the custom, Pete thought he might have a cold, but would be there the following week.

Joe didn't show up the following week, or the next two weeks, he continued to hope for the best. And then on the fifth week, as he slowly came down to the small bench at the pond's edge, there he was, smiling and throwing corn to his three duck audience.

"Joe," Pete began, "where have you been?"

"You wouldn't believe it," the response began. "The waitress that serves us our pie on Fridays? She claimed she was pregnant and I was the father of the child. I had to go to court, and when the Judge asked, I pleaded Guilty."

"You've been in prison for rape," came the question.

"Oh no," came the response, "the Judge gave me thirty days for Perjury!"

SECTION 13
Custom Checkering

In writing this book, I have come to look back and count my blessings many times. Not only have I been able to enjoy my work, and get compensated for it, but I have made so many friends from a variety of walks of life. If asked and pressed for an answer on why I chose to build gunstocks, I would have to answer so that I could checker them. Checkering is an art form that I admired long before I ever scratched a line on wood.

While not "true" custom checkering, I am going to include checkering requirements brought to me in the form of uncheckered finished stocks. In most cases I have worked with the owner and checkered the wood as he wanted or pointed out that the wood would not support the style or lines per inch the customer wanted. Twenty-eight lines per inch checkering with carved borders on a stained birch buttstock went out the door in the same hands that brought it in, as well as his offer to pay me twenty dollars for my work if he could have it done by tomorrow afternoon.

Most often, I am able to work with the customer and both of us come away happy. I did however overhear one customer tell another that if he would quit trying to tell me what to do and how to do it, the job wouldn't cost so much. For the customer doing the talking, I eventually cut a Winchester Model 21 buttstock pattern on a Model 32 Krieghoff.

I do the hardest part of my checkering with a "marks everything" white pencil, I decide the coverage area, draw in the borders or lay tic marks where I think they should be, lay out the master lines, and if I don't like something, the white line rubs away easily. I have found an electric pencil sharpener works best for keeping them sharp and keep several ready for use.

Sometime back, a person called asking if I really did checkering, that he had been informed that I did, and had a Merkel side by side which he had purchased with an uncheckered stock. Would I be interested in checkering the buttstock? I agreed that I would, and as I had business near his hometown, we met, I looked the gun over, we discussed the checkering, and I accepted the job. The man appreciated fine double-barreled shotguns, owned several, and hunted and shot them. I liked him immediately.

The person that had restocked the Merkel had done a nice job, not only was the wood to metal fit very nice, but the selection of wood, I felt, was appropriate for the gun. The gun did have the original forearm, which was checkered. The direction from the customer was that the buttstock checkering should compliment the checkering on the forearm and have a "meeting/crossing" at the top of the grip.

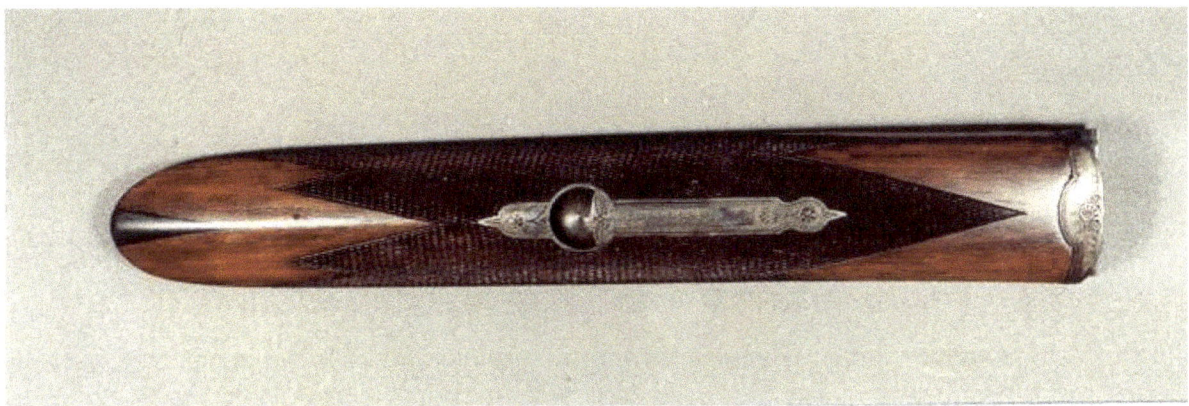

The checkering on the forearm appeared to be something between 24 and 26 lines per inch checkering, with the master lines being followed and forming the borders. There was no "fill in checkering" on that piece of wood. I see too many eight and ten-thousand-dollar factory shotguns with checkering that could not compare to this, and have a photo record of such items of interest.

Like most European shotguns of the time, the trigger guard extended back into the forward area of the grip, and with the exception of the screw head being enlarged, the task had been performed well. Having done so many of these, I have an appreciation of the work involved in doing it right.

    With the white pencil, I begin by drawing the outline of the checkering pattern. First line is parallel to the grip cap, up the back of the grip area, make a stock width centerline and then a tentative location where the two side patterns will meet on the top, parallel to the upper receiver tang. A tic mark identifies the most forward position of the line. Another mark determining the line extension on the wood adjoining the lower tang, then the curving line at the inside grip area from the grip cap parallel to the trigger guard tang up to the forward tic mark.

    The ratio of length to width of the diamonds was almost exactly a four to one, which I prefer to use on all of my checkering over 22 lpi. Using a plastic template of a diamond measuring four to one, (creation discussed in Section 01 – Tools) and having determined that a single centered point should be on the grip, and thus compliment the single centered point style on the forearm. I began by laying the 4 to 1 template on the side to determine the most advantageous angle for the master lines.

    I do not like to have either of the master lines follow the grain line, one will always come close, but will be off several degrees. With the wood grain clearly visible through the plastic template, I determine how the diamonds I am to cut will lay with the grain and use the white pencil to make several short lines indicating the converging lines of the template.

To try to follow the edges of the thin plastic diamond template and make an exact line is too difficult. Several short lines, no more than a quarter inch provide the direction needed to then use one of my thin plastic strips as a flexible ruler to create the master lines. Aligning the short lines from the plastic template with the plastic strip, I extend the master lines from the furthest extent of the top line parallel to the upper tang, back to the rear most border of the grip area.

In determining the crossing/joining of the checkering patterns at the top of the grip area, because of the length of the diamond, 4 to 1, I use an angle similar to that of the rear of the upper tang. At this point, all the lines are temporary, nothing is yet cut. This is one of the real advantages of using Brownell's white pencil.

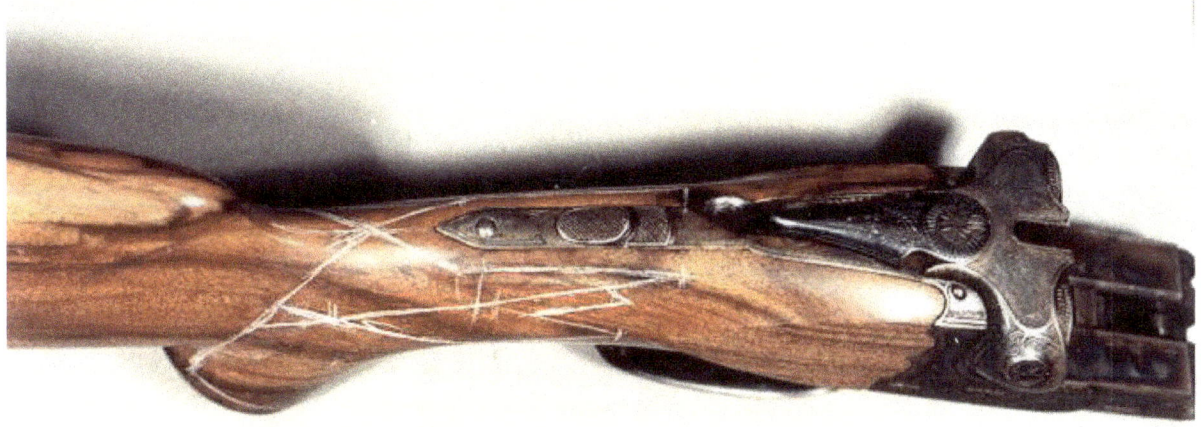

With the master lines perimeter of the pattern identified, I bring out my template box and begin to *guesstimate* where the center single diamond will lay. Using plastic strips varying widths, I use the strips to establish parallel lines and thus create the smaller diamonds above and below the single center diamond. On *fill in* patterns, all of the lines would be cut and thus all perimeter lines established. All that would be necessary would be to fill in the interior spacing cuts from the two master lines. If the cutting of the lines causes them to not run parallel to the diamond perimeter lines…

However, in a pattern in which the master lines are used to create the diamond perimeter lines, the lines cut can be brought very close to the white lines drawn in to represent the best *guestimate* of where the line should end. As one-line angle is continued, and then another, the lines will converge. The degree of accuracy in keeping your cut lines parallel can be judged by how close you come to matching the white lines. Sometimes it is best to work alone. While at other times…

At this point I like to set the stock aside for a little while, sort of let the proposed design sink in, and later, maybe an hour, maybe a day, look at it again. If I like it when I look at it next, I will cut it as it is drawn, or very close to as drawn. I have failed to follow this rule few times over the last twenty years and have regretted it.

When I pick it up again, and if I still like it, I duplicate the pattern on the other side of the buttstock. There are several means of doing this, one is to transfer the pattern to a piece of paper, and then transfer that to the remaining side. I never had much luck doing this, too many transfers.

The method I use is to make tic marks where I want the perimeter lines to end at the grip cap area, the area parallel to the trigger guard, and the upper and lower tangs. Establishing the master lines does not have to be an exacting science, identify the location at which the master lines intersect on the grip, measure up from the grip and back from the receiver, and make a mark. Use the same plastic template from the other side, and check the angles? Are they 4 to 1, mark it. Now look at one side, and then the other, do they match? Do they even resemble one another? If there is similarity, great, but can it be a little better?

For multiple panel checkering tasks, most often separated by thin ribbons of uncheckered wood, I use an entirely different approach. I draw the pattern out on side, then using a "V Edger" cut all of the lines and master lines very shallow. Then I cut small pieces of typing paper slightly larger than the pieces of the pattern, and one piece at a time, hold the paper in place, and lightly rub over it with the side of a No 2 pencil lead, allowing the cut lines to show through the paper.

Repeating this procedure with all pieces of the pattern, use a sharp pair of scissors to cut out the pieces. As an accuracy check, I place each piece over the panel it is to duplicate. When cutting the pieces from the paper, the line is to be cut from the piece, not left as a part of it. If you leave the line, you will enlarge the piece by the line's width.

Another advantage of cutting the pattern into pieces, other than using the pieces to check your completed work, is when it comes to repeating the pattern. A pattern I have used and modified slightly for many applications, is one given me by my son, Paul. Several customers call it the turnip seed pattern, but I just call it Paul's and let it go at that.

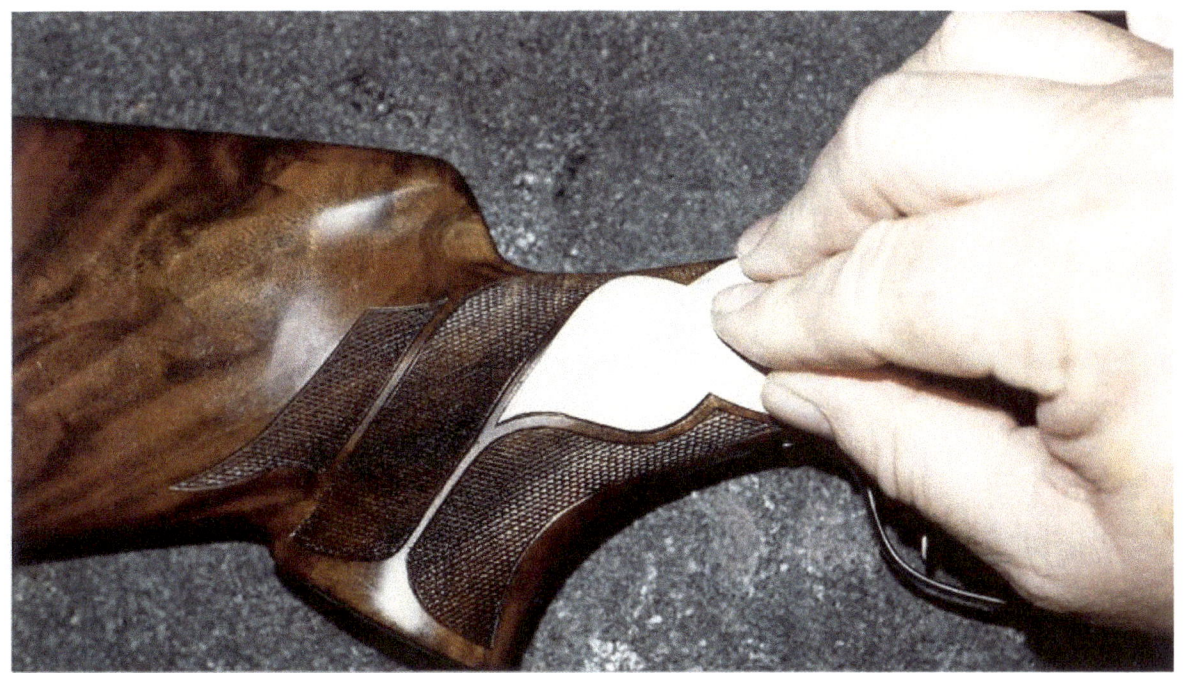

Before setting the work up in the pipe clamp to be used for a checkering cradle, I remove the recoil pad from the buttstock. If the buttstock has a hard or steel buttplate, leave it on. But a recoil pad will not allow the buttstock to be secure, it will shift as the pad gives. I do use pieces of a thin rubber rifle pad acra glassed onto the jaws of the pipe clamp to provide some non-slip surface for the wood. I also use "curls" of a plastic garden hose wrapped around the pipe as a cushion between the pipe and the stock. It prevents contact between the pipe and the stock.

By using the modified pipe clamp and securing the exposed end in a very heavy machinist vice, I can swivel the vice to meet my needs, or rotate the stock to the desired position.

I started my first checkering task with a Queen pocket knife and high hopes, the end result of that attempt was later burned in the privacy of my den. Some time later, I began the second one with a Gunline checkering tool and a lot of apprehension. Over the years I have tried several brands, but for whatever reason, I have always returned to the Gunline brand and use them today. The others may be as good, better, or worse, I don't know, I just happen to start with Gunline and will use them until they are no longer available.

I use a "V" edger, available in Gunline checkering tools, to cut my master lines. I cut them very shallow. I will need to follow them later with a line spacer.

I usually start with the butt of the stock towards me and begin cutting the master lines from mid point in the checkering pattern and cut to the termination of the line. In this case, to the ends of the upper and lower tang lines.

With the position of the buttstock moved to fall in the light, and easy on my back, I cut the perimeter lines on the front of the pistol grip. Paralleling the trigger guard tang, parallel to the grip cap, then the rear of the grip area and up to the top of the receiver. At no point do I attempt to cut the entire line in one pass. I make short overlapping strokes, no more than a half inch maximum, and I start well away from the origin of the line.

Let's do one side at a time. Now reverse the buttstock, place the receiver end of the wood towards you. From this position, you can now begin the lines in the same mid pattern area you started them, but now cutting in the opposite direction, and cut them. This technique, cut a little and the reverse the buttstock will, after several rotations, end up with the perimeter lines joining, with the exception of the proposed diamond points.

For spacing lines greater than 24 lpi, I use a four-line spacer, less than 24 lpi, I use a three line spacer. Why? The more lines I use as a guide, cutting ONLY one new line each pass, the straighter my lines are, with less variation in line width, and better looking. When spacing lines in narrow areas, where a multiple line cutter would be all but impossible to control, I use a simple two-line tool.

Year ago, after spacing out a nice forearm in two different lpi, I used a metal stamp set to establish the lpi spacer in each of my handles used for that purpose. Later I used a small burr to cut larger numbers on the top side and end of the handle and thought I had solved my problem.

Several years ago, I put a new 22 lpi spacer in a handle and began working on a very nice English Monte Carlo buttstock for a K-80 Krieghoff. I was half way through one grip when I decided the lines looked a little wide and used a thread pitch gauge to check them. The customer had wanted 22 lpi, not 18. I decided to set the job aside and work up another, and better grade blank to the customer's specifications.

The customer got his stock a week and a half late, but not without my spending a lot of late night hours making up for my mistake.

Later, I completed checkering the original buttstock, and then the forearm as well. My error in not checking the spacing of the cutter almost cost me a customer. It did substantially reduce the amount finally received for the stock set.

So, if you have the pictured set of wood, that's the story on why the checkering is 18 lines per inch.

Double check your spacers with a good thread pitch gauge. Keep them in the plastic envelope until you use them, **Do Not** use a plastic tray to store them in loose. Just tip it over once, or toss one in the wrong compartment, and you will make the error I did.

I cut all of the spacer lines on one side, all of them, then repeat the process on the other. Then, and only then, do I deepen the lines. The pattern on the grip of the Merkel is straight forward, no ribbons or scallops, no carved borders.

At this time, I am not going to go into a detailed explanation of instructions for checkering. No, that is something I have been planning for many years and am still a few years from completing. There are certain basic rules to be followed in checkering, and I find them universal with so many tasks requiring skill and concentration.

First, you've got to see what you are working on, and be able to shift the work or the light to your best advantage. I have used a variety of desk lights over the years and may not be using the best available now. I have snapped the tension springs, stripped the small nuts and screws, and replaced the toggle switch twice, but if I needed another lamp, I would find a duplicate of what I have. There are several makers making the adjustable bench lamps, but the requirement for flexibility is very important, seek that primarily.

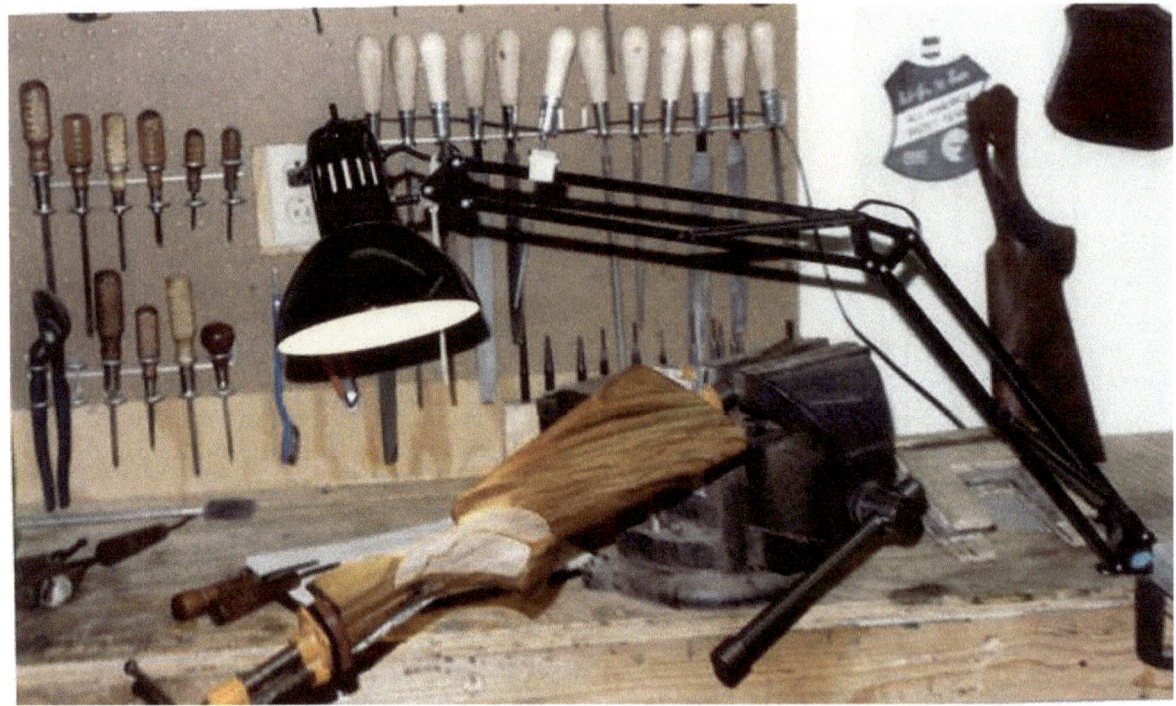

Do not be limited to a low power bulb in what I call "miniature desk lamps." The fixture should be capable of accepting a 60 watt light bulb, and do so without smelling like it is hot.

I have tried a variety of different types of light bulbs over the years, and having taken up photography out of necessity, have used a selection of colored/tinted photo bulbs. But I have always gone back to the 60 watt soft while light bulb, it works for me.

Second, get behind your work. By that I mean that the stroke with your tool should be straight away from your body, not at an angle. Straight away. With a checkering cradle such as I use, mounted in a secure vice, aligning the task at hand is not that difficult. There will be times in which aligning the cut as a straight away will be difficult. Line it up as best you can, and then, exercise great care in making the cut.

I gave a few hours instruction to a young man several years ago, emphasizing a good straight stroke away from the body. He informed me that playing pool was the same, that everything was in the stroke. Not being much of a pool player, I hadn't given it any thought, but in hind sight, I can see a great many similarities

There will be instances in which you will wonder how in the heck a particular line was completed. An example is on the forward edge of a pattern near the inside of the pistol grip. Because of the angle of the grip area, it is almost impossible to cut the lines from the center of the pattern back to the border. Over the years I have tried different methods, to include reversing the cutter to cut on the draw rather than the push.

But the technique I have found which works well in these cases is to cut from the border out. But doing so by rocking the cutter back and cutting with only that *last* little bit of tool, and make the cuts short. no more than a half an inch. It takes a while to master this technique, and aid to mastering it is to NOT look from the side at the area you are to cut, but rather look ahead of the line to be cut. Each time I tried to look at the area I was trying to cut, I succeeded in getting crooked, after learning to just concentrate on the line ahead, things worked out pretty well.

Stopping at a border or edge is the hardest part to learn about checkering. Last month, I made three run overs on the same buttstock, more than I had made in the previous five years. And after the third one, realized my problem, spent about thirty seconds on correcting it. The problem was the angle of the cutter to the wood. The first few teeth weren't even touching the wood, except when I got over to the edge.

The technique which I use may not be accepted by everyone, or anyone, but I have used it successfully for over twenty years. I cut the area to the edge or border with the first few teeth as cutters, and the flattened face of the cutter acting as a plow. I achieve this angle by using a pair of heavy duty lineman's side cutter pliers to bend the tip of the tool down, or up of how ever I need it. The "adjustment" may take several times to achieve the correct angle.

I do not like long handled tools. I shorten the shank of the tool by placing the shank in a vice, and drive the handle onto the shank, bottoming out the pre-drilled hole, and thus have a shorter, easier to control tool. Bottom tool in the picture.

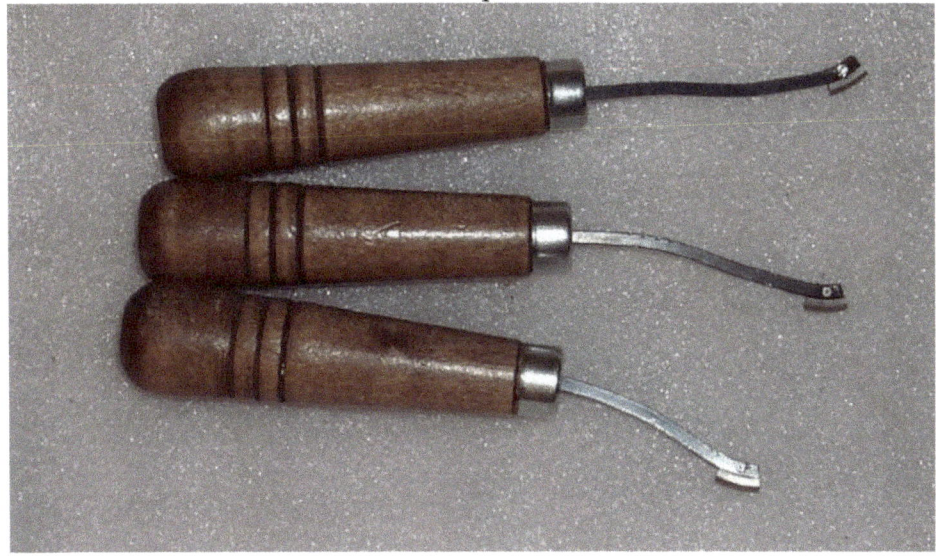

When does the cutter need replacement?

When it does not cut to your expectations. That simple.

After a job on a nice close grain piece of wood, I scrap the cutters, and replace them before I place the tools in the rack. The cutters are not expensive, they are easy to replace, and the results of a sharp cutter clearly out weight the advantages of stretching the life of a cutter over a few more lines.

Let's take the completed Merkel buttstock for example. I started the job with two medium pointers and a new fine pointer as well as a new four edge spacer. A small investment for the task at hand.

After taking all of the lines to almost full depth, I switched over from the medium pointer to the fine pointer, and carefully made a pass or two over every line. That fine pointer acts like a sander on the sides of those diamonds.

When sealer or finish is applied to the checkering, the grain should show through just as it does as illustrated in picture of the Merkel.

When I applied the sealer to the checkering, the grain was readily visible through the checkering. When I can see grain come through like that, I know I cut a good job.

This is a good example of laying out a pattern using a paper template, then laying out the master lines. How do you like that finish? The two-part epoxy finish was hard to checker through. When cutting through a hard finish such as this, use an edger to cut the borders and "file" through the finish, don't "plow" through it or you'll have chips of finish missing…

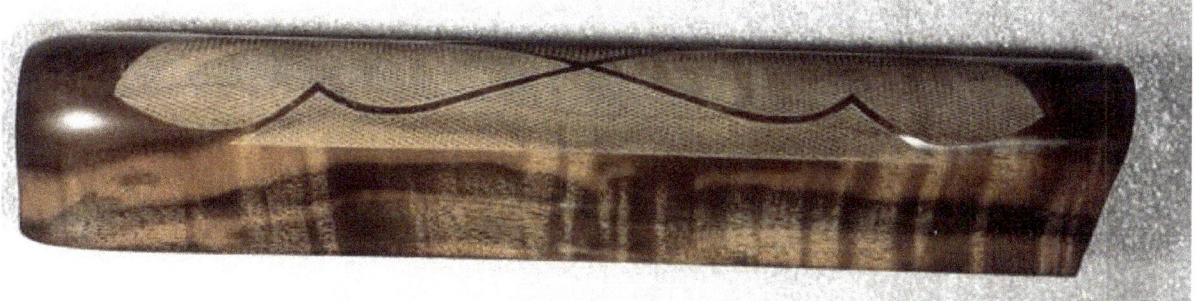

This forearm for a Remington Model 1100 was a real investment in time, lots of area to checker and plenty of ribbons to come up against. The wood is a very nice Claro Walnut, compliments of a visit to Cecil Fredi's in Las Vegas, and the checkering was cut in 24 lines per inch. The forearm and matching buttstock were completed as "spec" work, later sold to a friend, and several years later repurchased, shot for a season, and sold again to a new friend.

The pictures on this page are of a buttstock and forearm made for a customer who gave me free rein on the checkering. In fact, he was only adamant about the drop of comb and length of pull.

I believe this view best illustrates the size of the ribbons separating the checkering panels and allows the grain of the wood to come through.

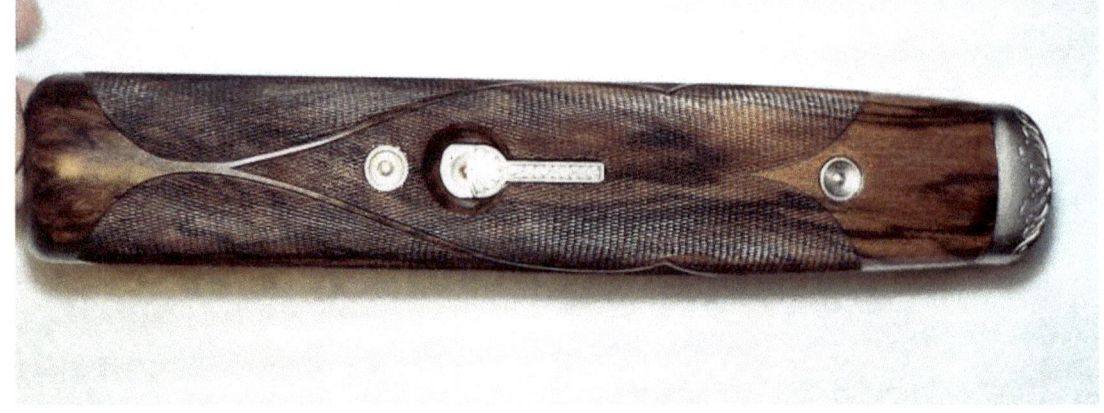

I always keep in mind this is the view at which most of my work is viewed, on a gun in the rack, bottom side of the forearm showing. For this reason, I try to create unique patterns which are easily recognized.

This view illustrates the different shades of wood on the same piece, and the figure can be brought out through the checkering if the lines are cut very clean.

This checkering is an excellent example of how a fine ribbon separating the checkering panels can enhance a pattern. Please note the grain coming through the checkering.

Sometimes, I have an idea of what I want to incorporate into a design I would like to cut and often sketch it out on a scrap of paper and let it hang around the shop for a while. Most of these ideas end up in the trash can, but sometimes one seems just right for a job at hand. The following few pictures are the results of one of those ideas. I was building a light weight 280 Remington on a Commercial Mauser receiver and decided to use the idea.

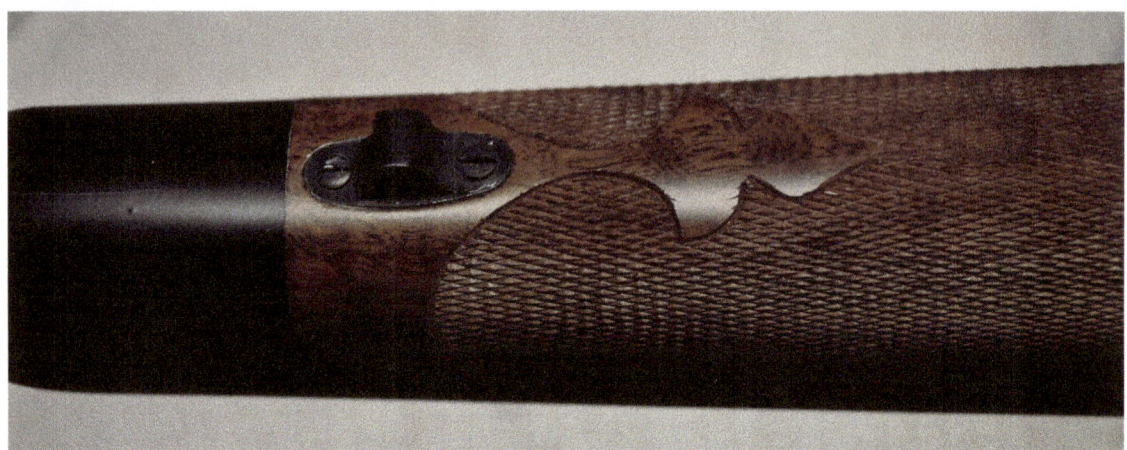

Checkering is like driving a truck, you can read a lot, watch a bunch, but the only way to really learn is to get in the seat, and do it. There is a lot more to it than meets the eye, or in most cases, the seat of the pants. But like being a good truck driver, a lot of time and attitude goes into the making.

Many times, I receive a stock in an almost finished condition with the request to checker it. Most times, the owner will leave the pattern up to me. At other times, the owner will bring a picture of the pattern they want cut. And sometimes, I receive guidance like "make the checkering look classic."

That was the case of the rifle on the following pictures. I had started the rifle some 30 years earlier, but the owner had not completed it as planned. So I received it back with instructions to complete it.

The first thing I always do is identify the centerline of the stock, shown as the white line on the following picture.

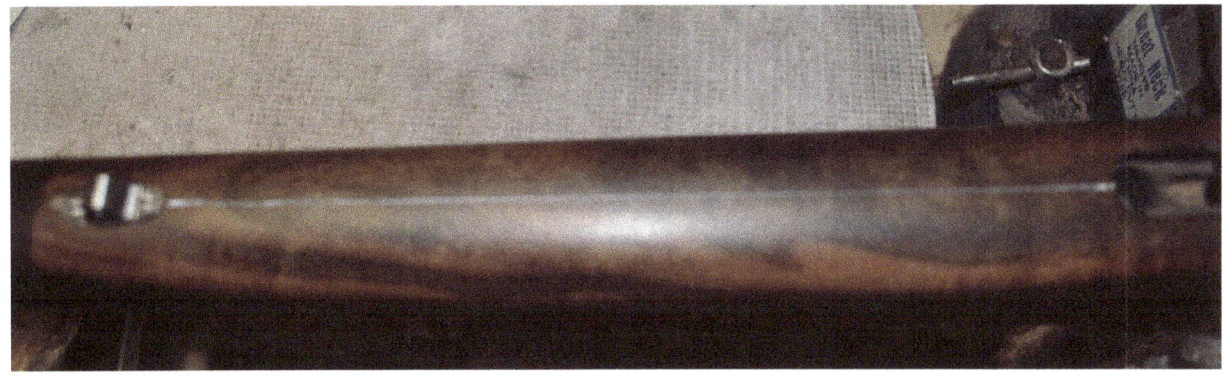

I had decided to use a 4 to 1 ration for the diamonds on the pattern, and let the checkering lines form the ends of the pattern. Laying the 4 to 1 template on the forearm area, I am interested in establishing the master lines for the pattern and will use the point behind the forearm sling swivel base as my starting point.

Although not clearly evident, the line between the two ends of the template is directly over the white centerline on the stock. I use the while pencil to trace in the forward lines of the template. These two lines will later be extended all the way to the top lines of the pattern parallel to the top line of the forearm.

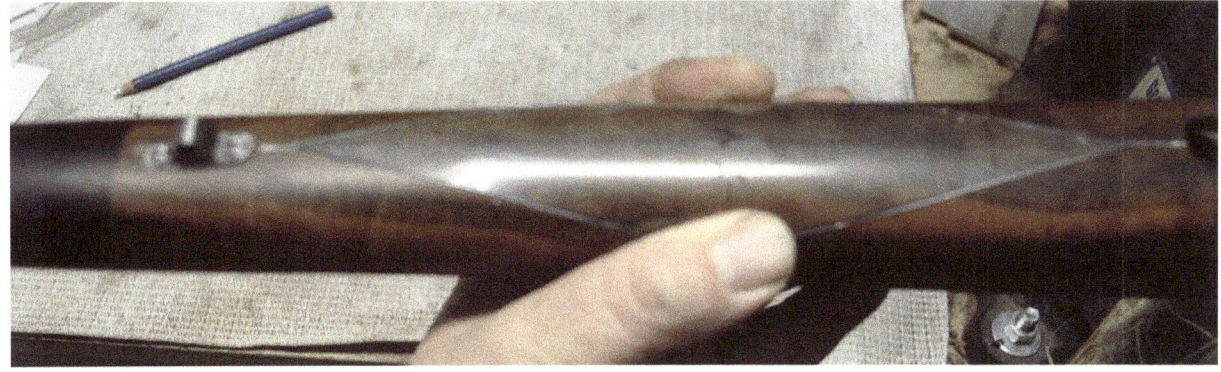

Adjusting the template to the rear, I draw in the rear most portion of the pattern. Please note that these marks are a "guide" of how far to extend the checkering lines. This is not a "fill in pattern" but a pattern with the checkering lines forming the ends of the pattern.

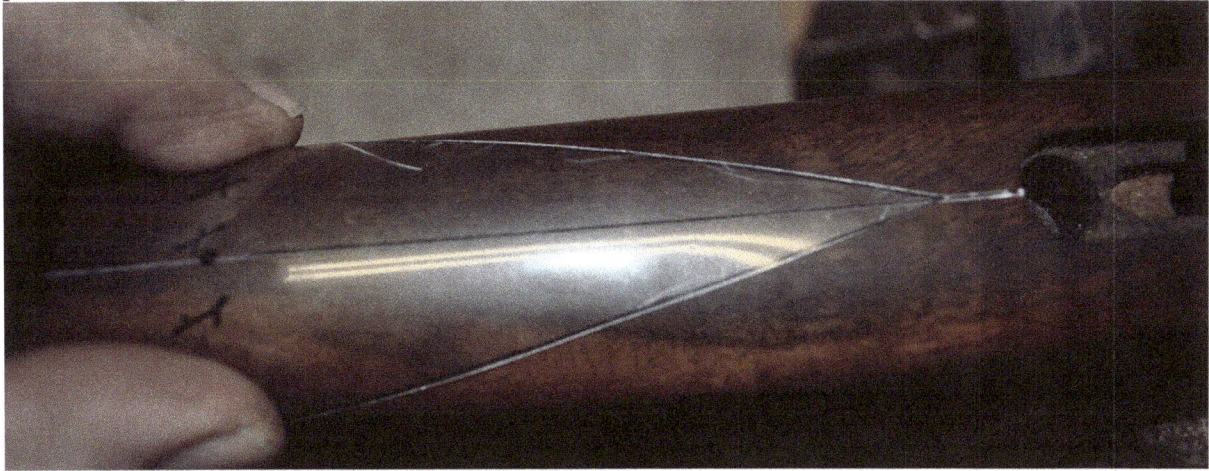

Using the template to insure the correct ration, I establish "guide lines" for other segments of the pattern. Please note, these are "guide lines" only. As you cut the lines using the master lines as a starting point, you will know approximately how far to extend the lines by referring to the guide lines. They are a guide only.

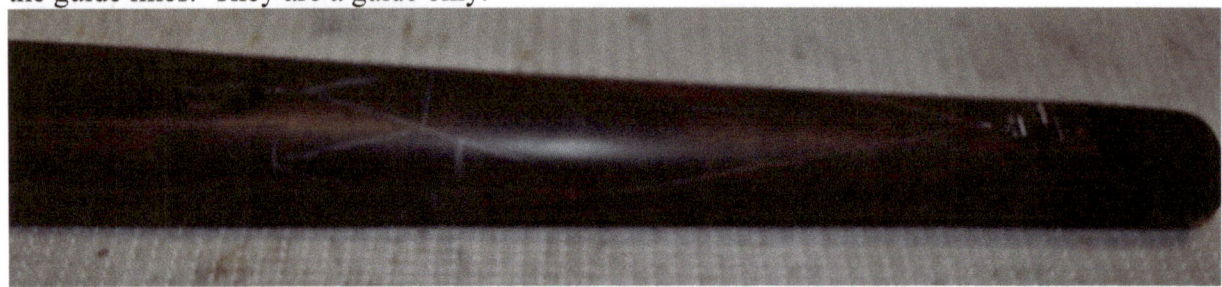

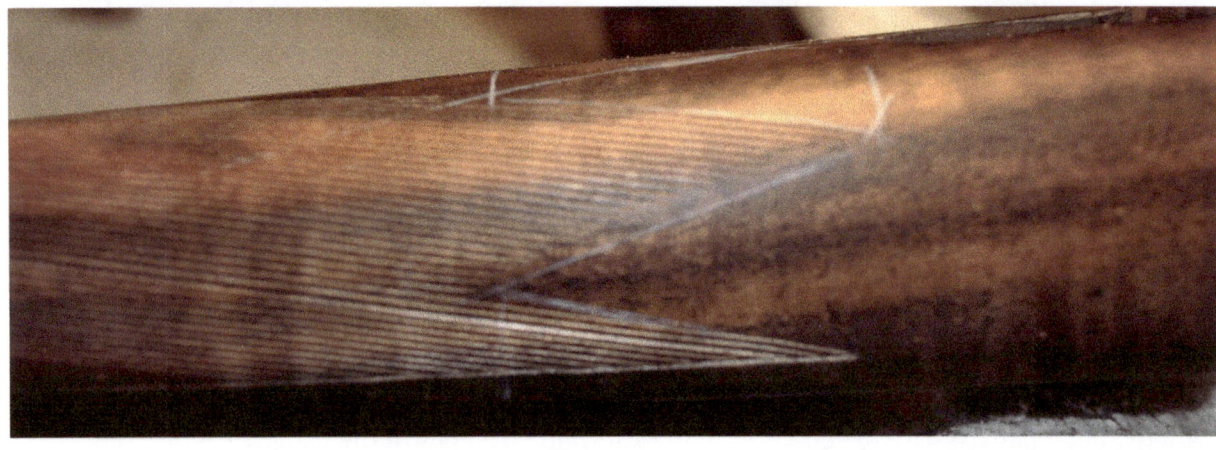

Unfortunately, several rolls of film were lost, including the rolls with this project on them. However, the roll with the completed project on it was not turned in for development until several weeks later.

Once in a great while, I take the time to initiate a project for myself, and over a long period of time, manager to fit it into the shop schedule. On the last hour of the last day of the Louisville Gun Show I was attending, a man walked up and asked if I would be interested in "an old Winchester Model 12?" He walked away with six hundred dollars of my money and I slipped the Winchester Model 12, in 20 gauge under the table.

I just happened to have a set of wood for a 20 gauge stuck back on the shelf, and upon returning home, retrieved it. Something must have happened during the storage period, because when I applied a little water to better evaluate the grain, the wood looked a whole lot better than I remembered. This would be easy, and thus the job description, "EZ-2"

Fitted with an original buttplate and grip cap, sanded, finished and ready for checkering.

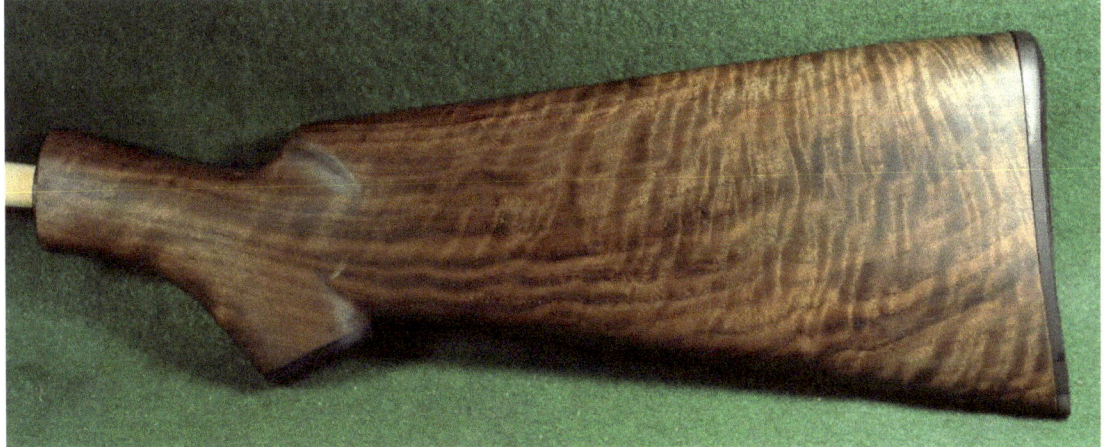

I kinda let my imagination over ride my ability when I laid this checkering out in pencil. And yes, I was well aware that the two small centered diamonds are different in size – would you believe I planned it that way?

When I cut the border and ribbons, I knew I was going to have something special.

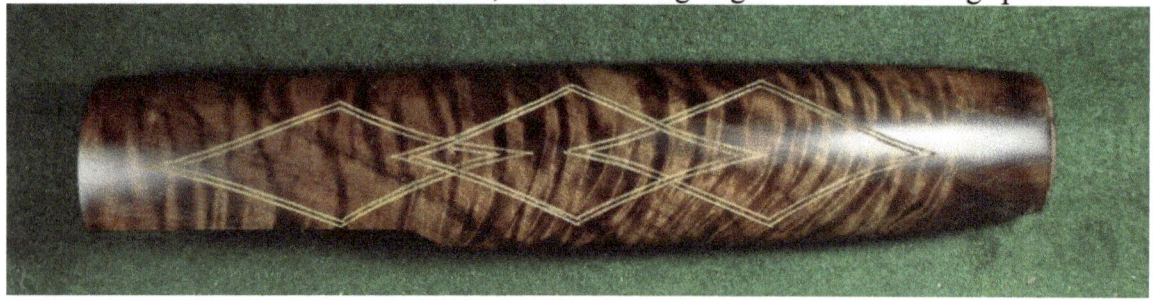

With one side cut, and I will not list the number of hours it took to lay it out, track it in and then deepen the checkering lines, but it was far more than I had anticipated. That forearm wood was harder than…….

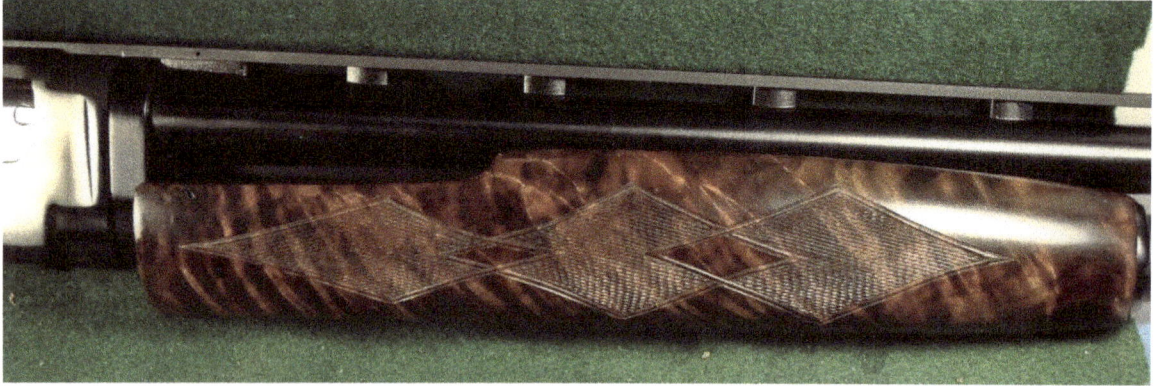

The second side was not any easier than the first, and each time I looked at the job listing, "EZ-2" I wondered a little about my sense of humor, or if I even had one.

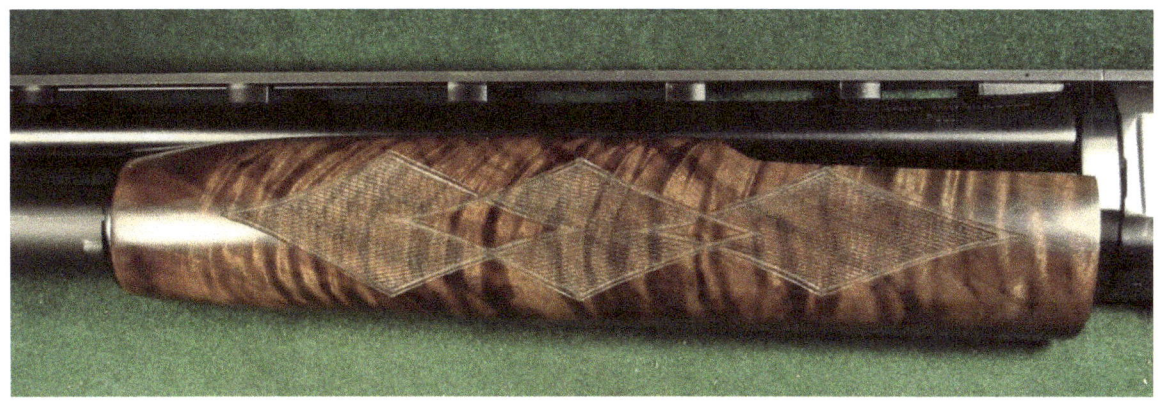

Anticipating more of the same, I was surprised when the buttstock cut remarkably well.

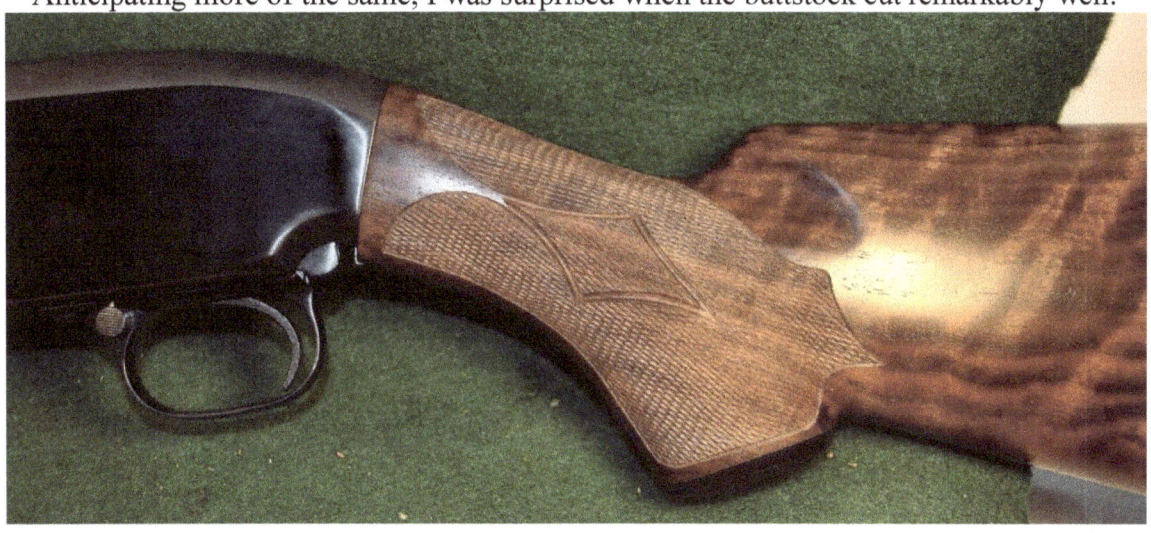

SECTION 14
Refinishing Stocks

There have been instances, after spending countless hours in steaming out dents, or filling gouges in with a mixture that almost matches the wood, that I feel almost God like. The feeling of satisfaction of taking a stock that has suffered countless years of abuse and neglect, and turning it into something eye catching, something that gives no indication of it's past, is a feeling that each of us should enjoy at least once. I am very lucky; I have had a steady stream of customers over the years that have provided countless opportunities for such feelings. Some of the wood they have brought in, a few still attached to receivers and forearm irons, would have shamed a man of lesser sensibilities.

To "refinish" a shotgun stock, the old finish must be removed and the wood prepared for the new finish, the new finish applied, and the checkering recut. While sounding easy, the task can become a nightmare. Some of the "hidden" problems to be overcome include oil saturated wood and stain covering sap wood.

I have received stocks from which the original finish was removed by sanding, application of a paint stripper, application of a gasket remover, scraped with a sharp instrument with really sharp corners, and one which appeared to have been boiled in linseed oil – no kidding. I have received them in one piece, two pieces and several in more than a half-dozen pieces. My preference is to receive two-piece stocks in two pieces, one-piece stocks in one piece, etc.

When I receive a stock for refinishing, I like to look it over in the presence of the owner, make an estimate of the time involved, pointing out the gouges, dents, missing wood, smoothness of the checkering, and the like. As I receive much of my work through the mail (UPS, RPS and Fed Ex), I acknowledge receipt of the wood after looking it over by calling the owner or sender, providing the same information as if the other person was standing across the counter from me. Sometimes I return the work to the customer with my condolences.

In most cases I explain the difference between a dent in the wood in which the grain is intact, and one in which the wood grain has been severed. I explain the technique that I will use in removing dents, and long before I am finished, most customers interrupt (I have been known to get carried away with explanations) and tell me to just do it. So, let's get to it.

I just happen to have several butt stocks that need refinishing, one for a Perazzi and one from a Krieghoff K-80. These are excellent examples of the minority of the work I receive, a straight forward refinishing job, checkering is good shape, very few dings, no deep scratches, no cracks and no splits.

The first thing that I do is to provide a means of handling the buttstock for the stripping process – I do not sand finish from a stock. As both of these butt stocks, like most pump and semi-automatic shotguns, are secured to the receiver with a stock bolt, I retrieve the long section (bottom) of a heavy clothes hanger from a collection of clothes hangers liberated from my wife's laundry room. She claims I take only the best ones – I do.

Folding almost an inch of the wire back onto itself, I then let it spring out to a distance just a little wider that the diameter of the stock bolt, and then drop it down the stock bolt hole from the butt end. The sprung end of the wire will stop at the stock bolt hole shoulder and several inches will protrude through the receiver end of the stock, I like 2 to 3 inches. I bend about three-quarters of an inch of the protruding end over at little more than a right angle. I now have a secure means of hanging the buttstock during the stripping process, and one that is easily removed with no modification to the buttstock upon completion of the process.

I keep a supply of lengths of clothes hanger wire in the bottom of my hot box, most of them have been used several times and continue to be a valuable aid. I have seen others that use a screw in one of the recoil screw holes to provide a means of hanging and handling the buttstock, and I have seen others use similar methods. The end result, regardless of what you use, is having a safe and secure means of hanging and handling the buttstock.

In addition, for those stocks with a stock bolt hole, I use a piece of wooden dowel and depending upon the size of the stock bolt hole, wrap a layer or two of duct tape onto the end of the dowel, and shove / twist the "handle" in place.

I have tried a variety of paint-varnish-epoxy and whatever else removers over the years. Some worked well, some were expensive mistakes, and over time, have settled on two that work well for me. For most common stock finishes, I use a KS-3 Paint Stripper available from Walmart – Yep, Wally world – in spray cans. For the harder finishes, I use a stripper available from *Brownell's, Inc, Montezuma, IA*. It is in liquid form, but when directions are followed, it works well.

I have callused, "hard skin" hands, and a face, with or without moustache, that will stop most charging dogs. But when I work with stripper, I wear a clear face shield – which I replace when it gets 'etched' – and the type of rubber gloves commonly associated with house work or washing dishes, unless some customer drops off a supply of 'examination' gloves. The rubber gloves may last several jobs, depending upon how much handling is required, but seldom more that five. The latex examination gloves are discarded after one use. Make no mistake; wear the appropriate safety equipment to protect exposed skin, especially the hands and eyes.

Anyway, with the hanger attached to the buttstock, I begin the stripping operation. I want to initiate the stripping process where it cannot possibly contaminate other work. For that reason, I have a large garbage can outside the back door of my shop, with a metal rod through two holes near the top lip – this is the means by which I hang the stock. In the bottom of the garbage can I have a collection of shaving and sawdust several inches thick to collect the dripping stripper.

For the hobbyist, I would recommend an area that can be easily cleaned perhaps nothing more than newspaper to catch the surplus stripper but placed in such a manner that it is inaccessible to pets.

The same requirement exists for forearms but is much more challenging because of the variety of types of forearms coming through the door.

For forearms such as the Krieghoff or Beretta with threaded bushings, I use an eighteen inch length of black-pipe with holes spaced to accept socket headed screws which engage the bushings in the forearm. I use these same pieces of pipe to hold the forearm during finishing and checkering.

I also use pieces of three-quarter inch hard wood dowel drilled to accept the correct socket head screws and a hook made of clothes hanger on one end.

Some forearms, such as the KOLAR and Perazzi are a little simpler. On my bench is a small graduated measuring cup such as the ones I use to measure Brownell's Acra glass. In it is a selection of different sizes of flat washers. From this cup, I remove a washer which fits into the large hole for the forearm latch. With the washer held in place, I use a piece of the black pipe or hard wood dowel with a socket head screw already in place and screw it into a nut held on top of the washer. When tightened, be careful to not over tighten the handle arrangement.

On forearms such as the Remington Model 1100, 11-87, and 870 as well as most other pump and semi auto shotguns, I use a wooden dowel of the approximate size of the magazine tune, sometimes a little masking or duct tape is required to match the diameter. I then insert the dowel into the forearm until at least an inch of the dowel is visible, and then place a short #12 sheet metal screw into the end of the dowel. The screw prevents the forearm from slipping off of the dowel during the coming actions.

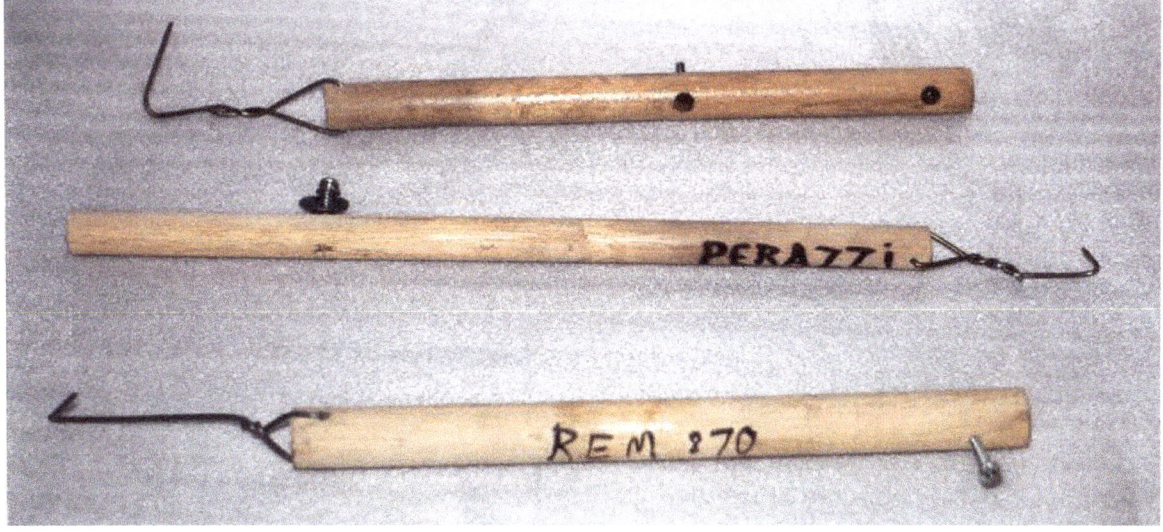

I do not advocate "hanging" a piece of wood from a wire. Provide a secure means of handling the wood and you'll have a lot less problems and the end result will justify your time spent.

I apply my stripper, when using liquid, with a half-inch wide paintbrush, after depositing an estimated quantity of stripper in a pint glass jar. I find it easier to spread in this manner and have found the time spent and my waste is both lessened. I follow directions on the stripper container for its application, and almost universally, one will be directed to "apply the stripper in a smooth continuous motion, not covering the same area repeatedly," or some such similar language. Follow the instructions, they are important to your success.

When using the spray stripper, I do it outside, making vertical applications, and not spraying over the same area too often. In addition to the outside, on forearms, I spray the inside as well. After applying the first coat, I am careful to hang the stock in the garbage can without disturbing the skin of stripper, and where the excess stripper can drip onto the material placed to catch it and not end up on some Vet's table in a cat.

After the required stripper action time has passed, I removed the piece from the garbage can hanger, and take a serious look at it. In most cases the stripper has worked well, a simple matter to remove the residue. Then again, but let's take the easy way first.

The method used to remove the residue left by the stripper is dependent on how well the stripper worked. For those times in which the stripper has worked well, I use a course synthetic scrub brush – designed to scrub pots and pans – to remove the residue.

They work surprisingly well, and last quite a while if I remember to wash the stripper residue out of them. Be careful in selecting this item for one too coarse will mar the wood as well as remove the residue. Watch what you are doing, and if your tool is marring the wood, stop and go to a finer brush or pad.

I am very careful in removing the residue on the flutes of the comb tip, in the checkering, and around the rear of the grip. For the flutes of the comb, I have a scraper on which I have ground a radius of about 3/8". It works well for this purpose. The other end is straight.

The area behind the grip does not lend itself well to any single manner of removing the stripper residue. So, I use my radiused scrapper as well as a straight edged scrapper to get the residue. Pay particular attention to this area and save yourself problems down the road.

For the checkering I use a medium bristle toothbrush, the kind usually on sale for $.49. When I need one, I usually buy several, if the clerk gives me a strange look, I tell her I have a lot of pets. It usually shuts them up.

So much for the easy stocks, there are times in which the stripper "wrinkles" the finish in some areas, softens the finish in others, but does no more than dull the finish on others, all on the same stock. And this situation happens more often than not. When this situation comes about, I remove the wrinkled finish as best I can with the scraper, brush and pad, and give it a liberal second coating of the stripper.

Removing the stock from the garbage can again after the required stripper working period is over, I use the brush and pad, and then use a good stiff bladed scraper on which the edge has been dulled and the corners rounded   Cutting or lining the wood when removing the finish can make your task far more difficult than it need be. For the hobbyist, I would recommend squaring off the edge of a thick bladed putty knife and putting a radius on the corners. This devise works well as a scraper.

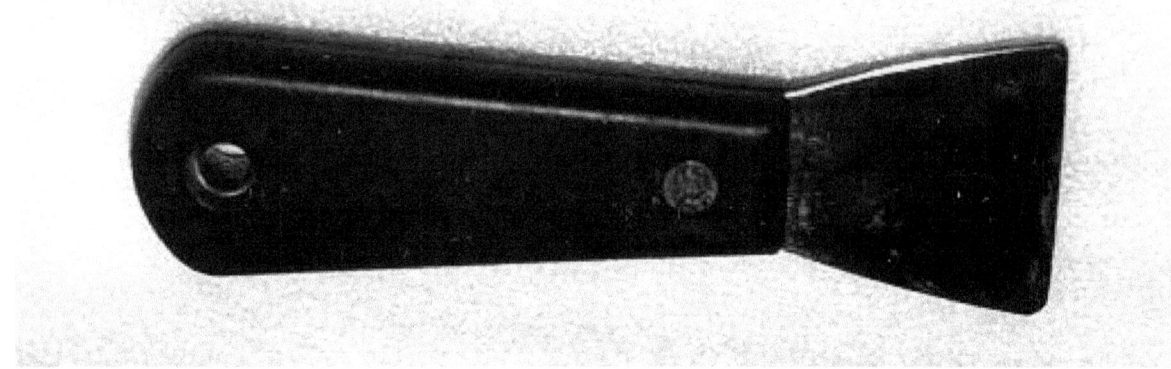

Regardless, for the hobbyist, don't spend a lot of money; look around in the bargain bin at the local hardware or discount store. Before settling on the method I now use I tried too many to cite. I now use old putty knives with the edge dulled to a true flat, and the corners rounded. Use the scraper in a pulling motion, not a pushing one. When you pull, the residue is removed, when you push, the scraper becomes a chisel and not only the residue but also some of the wood may very well be taken off. Take your time.

The more careful you are in removing the stripper residue, the less sanding you will have to do. If you run into areas in which the finish hasn't softened, apply another coat of stripper to that area – not the whole stock – and hang it up again. I have worked on stocks in which five and six applications of stripper were needed to remove the finish from all areas.

The "red" finish applied to the Model 32 Krieghoff is some of the hardest to remove material I have ever come across. Worse than alimony.

The stripper appears to soften the finish somewhat, and then as it soaks in or whatever, the finish gets hard again. Beretta and Krieghoff stocks are bad about doing this, but with several applications of stripper, removing some of the finish each time, all of the finish was removed.

A special note for the older Beretta stocks, the stain used appears to have been very liberally applied, and in many cases, can hide the type and figure of the wood. After removing the finish, I apply another liberal coat of stripper to get the last remnants of the stain from the wood, scrubbing with the brush and stripper. It is best to apply the stripper again in this process, than to wait until the wood is dry, discover some stain still on the stock, and have to do it all over again, increasing the refinishing time by several days.

With all of the residue removed from the stock, it's time to give it a good bath. I have a container, into which I pour a half gallon of hot water and add a just a little, maybe a tablespoon, of liquid Dial hand soap. Immersing the stock in the water, I scrub the devil – actually the stripper – out of the wood with a fine scrub brush normally used for scrubbing dishes, then go over the checkering very carefully with a toothbrush. If I have used a wire hanger, I leave it in place.

Rinsing the wood off with cold water once I am satisfied that all of the residue has been removed, I continue to a step that I consider absolutely essential to the success of the job. With a container of cold water, about a quart, I add in a quarter cup of vinegar, pour it over the stock and scrub the stock, and then scrub it again, insuring that I get the all exposed wood, especially the checkering. When I am doing this second scrubbing, I look carefully for any small remnants of the finish. If I find any, I quickly scrape them off, and vigorously scrub the area with the vinegar solution. The vinegar is a sure killer for the stripper action. By removing the last remnants of finish/stripper, and not rinsing it thoroughly, you have the possibility of the stripper bleeding through your finish.

Properly stripping the wood of the old finish is the first step in applying a new finish. Take shortcuts in the stripping and the results may show up as "fish eyes" in the finished product, or even worse, the stripper remaining in the wood will begin to wrinkle the new finish. During the washing and rinsing process, if I find a small area that I have missed, I take the time to flake off the finish and scrub the areas under it. If I find a large area, large being defined as a space larger than my thumbnail, I go back to the stripper for a spot application.

Now that the wood has been stripped of the old finish, it must be allowed time to dry. In addition to the stripper, then the scrubbing and the rinsing, a lot of liquids have passed over, in and around the wood – best let it dry for a few days.

Years ago, I made what I called a "hot box" for drying stocks I had stripped, and stocks upon which I wanted the finish to dry free from any foreign matter floating around. Over the years, I have made many modifications to a variety of hot boxes. One was actually a small room. I have come to the conclusion that a hot box should be capable of holding the volume of work in progress, and the temperature should be constant, preferably in the high seventies or mid eighties, depending upon the sealer or finish applied.

One evening, after determining that my current hot box needed some repairs, and then realizing I would be better off to start from scratch, I made a hot box from a single sheet of half-inch wallboard, sometimes called sheet rock. The box measured eighteen inches square and four feet tall. All of the joints were achieved using an automotive fiberglass repair kit, and the door is held in place with hook hangers made from my favorite gauge of coat hanger. I have a light receptacle on either side, and wire hooks hanging down from the top which afford the hanging of an unbelievable arrangement of rifle and shotgun stocks. It worked for me but use your imagination. I used this hot box for over ten years, and recently build another one – using ¾ inch plywood – of the same dimensions.

For the person doing his own gun, making a hot box is an unnecessary expense. I have seen excellent results obtained from hanging the wood in a utility closet or pantry with a light on. Special note here, as I happen to live in the South, the light provides not only a constant temperature, it also serves to control the humidity to some extent. Note, please do not hang it in the laundry room for the finish to dry, lint from a dryer is difficult to sand out, I've done it.

Regardless of what you use, the goal is to maintain a constant temperature and humidity suitable for drying/curing the finish being used, and when the finish is applied, to prevent foreign matter from sticking to the finish brought about through air movement.

As a rule, I let a stripped and rinsed stock dry and stabilize in the hot box for a full two days. I want all of the moisture out of the pores of the wood before I begin work on it. When I do remove it from the hot box, I look and feel for several important signs indicating additional work is required. I look for dings in the wood with sharp edges indicating that the grain has been severed, something like a sharp scratch or cut. I also look for simple dings indicating compression, usually from a clay target if it is a skeet gun, or fence and rack damage from simply being in the wrong place at the right time. I also try to judge the amount of oil that has seeped into the wood adjoining the receiver. Having listed several types of problems, each with their own process of correction, let's start with the dings in which there is a sharp edge as with a severed grain.

You should not sand the wood surrounding a dent down to level out the surface. <u>Should not</u>. The object is to raise the dented wood area up to the original level, not reduce the level of the stock surface down to the dented level.

To understand the process, one must first have a basic knowledge of wood: Very basically, wood is comprised of elongated cells, these cells are full of life giving fluids when the tree is alive. When the wood is cut and dried, it is the fluid in these cells that "dry", reducing the "moisture" of the wood, allowing it to be worked without warping, checking or twisting. A compression ding actually collapses the "dry" hollow cells, in effect flattening them. If the ding has severed the grain, the cells may be partially filed with anything from sweat to gun oil to solutions best left to one's imagination.

To "raise" the dents and dings, I use a small electric steam travel iron and a heavy, and I do mean heavy, wash cloth. There are small irons on the market designed for this purpose, and Brownell's handles a fine one. I just happen to have had the little travel iron for some years and continue to use it.

I have seen electric soldering irons used with success as well as spoons heated over an open flame. Regardless of what you use, the process and the goal is the same.

After identifying the areas to be worked, dents and dings, I soak the wash cloth, fold it over double, and then double again, and place a corner of the wash cloth over the ding to be raised. I then place the tip of the iron on the soaked washcloth and let the steam from the iron superheat and force the water from the wash cloth into the cells of the wood, expanding them and raising the dent.

After a thorough steaming of the area and having checked it several times to insure is has indeed raised up, wipe the excess moisture from the wood and set it aside in the hot box to dry.

There is no magic technique, no super secret jig, fixture or tool - just patience, water and steam. I go over all of the dents and dings on a stock, and then go back over them again and then check the results. In some cases, I will make a third round. This is especially true of dings where the grain has been severed.

It is during this process that you will rapidly find out how good a job you did in stripping the old finish from the stock. If the old finish, to include stain, stays in the dings in the wood, the steam can't permeate it, and the dent will not "rise." In cases where you discover small amounts of the old finish in a ding, use care in removing it, you may cut the wood, causing additional work. For this task, I use a small Exacto knife and "chip" the finish out. I make no attempt to cut it out.

With all of the dings raised, set the stock back in the hot box and let it dry out for another day. No, do not resume your next step after a few hours because the surface of the wood appears to be dry. Remember that you were just forcing hot steam into the pores of the wood when raising the dent. The depth at which the steam penetrated and raised the dent will vary with the type of wood and grain structure. Be safe, let the stock dry for another day in the hot box.

I have, for many years, maintained that the difference between a good refinish job and an excellent job is time and patience. I firmly believe it, regardless of the type of finish being applied.

With the dents and dings raised, we come to another challenge to be overcome in refinishing wood. If the shotgun is brought in for refinishing, and it was Grandpa's, or Uncle John's, or whoever, and possess great hidden value, even if it was made in Belgium ninety years ago for the local hardware store and has rusted through wire twist barrels. And they really kept care of it, to include liberally dousing it with oil each time it was used, and resting it in the closet butt down, where all of the oil could seep back into the wood around the receiver. Grandpa must have really had nightmares about rust, because the buttstock literally oozes with oil. Remember the cells of the wood, well, in cases like I have described, the wood is discolored because the pores are filled with oil.

While the finish may come off easily with the stripper, the oil in the wood, especially on the thin wood near the receiver, can be a major problem.

Over the years I have tried a variety of methods and manners of removing soaked in oil from wood in preparation for refinishing. Some have been successful, some partially successful, and others encouraging failures. I say encouraging failures because with the failure I knew that it didn't work and was encouraged to try something else.

To elaborate, I have tried soaking stocks in cold water and strong dish detergent, (don't believe everything you see on television – the grease does not float to the top), wrapping stocks in paper towels and soaking the paper towels with "degreasing" solutions, as well as others. I have tried various stripper solutions, thinners, additives and what all else I can't remember. But the bottom line is that I do not believe that there is one method for all stocks. So, depending upon the age of the stock, the type of wood, the amount of oil and foreign matter, as well as the area involved, I use different methods.

For small areas on fine-grained wood, I use my trusty steam iron and wet wash cloth and attempt to steam the oil from the wood. I never keep the iron/steam on the same area more than a few seconds, constantly change the area of the wash cloth coming in contact with the wood, and every few minutes, wipe the area dry. Using this process takes time, but for small areas, it works very well. It usually takes several applications of the process but has proven successful for small lightly soaked areas.

For larger areas such as the around the receiver, I use an absorbent material, Whiting, that when mixed and applied as directed – a semi paste configuration – works very well. I use this method for removing oil for Model 12 Winchester stocks.

I have read and heard of people that soak oil-soaked stocks in paint thinners and solvents, I do not do it, nor do I advocate such a method.

Others modify their finish process for the oil-soaked stocks using a "compatible" sealer or finish. I don't do it and I don't recommend it.

I did try one method on an old oil soaked military stock last August that was near and dear to a customer. When all else failed, I purchased several bags of a non scented clay based cat litter, and dumped them into a black plastic bag, Inserted the rifle stock, sealed the end tight, and after insuring that the rifle stock was encased in cat litter, placed the bag on the shop roof above the entrance. Each day for a week, I went out, shook the bag, rolled it over several times, and placed it back on the roof. At the end of a week, the oil was sufficiently gone to apply the desired finish, but as I told the customer, one week of removal could not reach down into the wood and remove eighty or ninety years of oil. Recently, we have begun watching the customer as he has developed some strange habits, he keeps pawing around in loose dirt and doing a lot of sniffing…....

If you are going to refinish a stock do it right. If you are not prepared to take the time to do it right, please take it to someone that can and will do it properly and maybe Grandpa won't be jarring around in his grave.

So here we are with the wood all ding and dent free and very little evidence that oil was ever near the wood, right? Right. Then put it back in the hot box for another night to let the moisture from the oil removal process evaporate. The next day may reveal that the process needs to be accomplished again.

Next day, take the wood out, look it over very good, if more steaming needs to be done, repeat the process. The finished product is going to look only as good as the care you take in completing all of the steps leading up to it. But assuming you're happy with what you have accomplished thus far, then it's time for a little sanding.

During refinishing, the coarsest grit of sandpaper I use is 320 grit wet and dry, and I use it dry. One basic rule, I know it sounds simple, but I see instances of its violation weekly: sand with the grain of the wood. The only exceptions are the forward area of the pistol grip (which can be sanded with the curvature of the wood, or around the grip area – from side to side) and the tip of the comb, on which the same instructions apply.

With the 320 grit paper, I go over the stock lightly, very lightly on the areas that match the receiver, not even touching the checkering. A little "heavy" sanding at these points can result in the metal of the receiver being higher than the wood, and it doesn't look good, or a nice checkering pattern being obliterated.

Another area for concern is the butt of the stock. When sanding the buttstock flats, use a sanding block. Especially if the buttstock is made of highly figured wood. Failure to use a sanding block on the flats can result in "waves" in the surface caused by sandpaper gliding over the harder grain and removing soft wood. By using a sanding block, and that does not include the hard rubber sanding blocks, the surface is level – No waves.

I also mount the buttplate or recoil pad on the buttstock. I do this for several reasons, but primarily because I want the wood to buttplate/pad to be a continuous line, not a junction at which sanding has severely rounded the end of the butt, leaving the buttplate/pad higher than the wood. The same technique applies to the butt, as does the receiver wood, sand lightly.

If necessary, I will apply a spacer to the butt to insure I have a squared edge on the butt. A rounded edge on the butt does not impress anyone with your skill or patience.

The 320 paper removes a surprising amount of wood, watch what you are doing, only sand until you have smoothed the surface, not contoured it, and then go to 400 grit paper. The 400 grit paper will provide an even smoother finish, but go slowly, especially around the receiver and butt areas.

Don't hesitate to stop periodically and wipe the sanding dust from the wood, admire your work and review your work for sanding scratches, some hidden scratch or undetected ding. When you are happy with the smooth finish of the wood, wipe it down with a lint free dry cloth. And set it aside and plug in the steam iron.

The next step in refinishing a buttstock or forearm, or for that matter any wood project, is the process called "whiskering." During the sanding process, some of the sanding dust has filled the wood pores, and on others, some of the grain has been "pressed" down into the wood. We want the sanding dust out of the wood pores and the pressed grain raised, and while some run water over the wood to achieve the desired result, I do it with the steam iron.

Yes, there are finishes which state the whiskering process is not required, indicating the finish will raise the grain and one can then sand the grain down. I have never tried one, and thus will not comment on them.

Using the steam iron, apply steam directly to the wood, I hold my iron several inches from the wood, and when using a "borrowed" iron, such as the one your wife uses, I would double the distance. The goal is to have the live steam actually hitting the wood. This steam will raise the pressed grain and float the dust out of the wood grain.

After steaming the wood thoroughly, wipe it down with a soft lint free cloth, and set it aside in the hot box for another day. As the wood dries, "whiskers" will rise up from the grain. These whiskers are the raised grain that would have raised should you have began applying finish to the wood, causing a poorly sealed finish, and in some cases, a finish with pimples.

After a night of drying, remove the wood from the hot box, and using 400 grit paper, lightly, and I do mean lightly, remove the whiskers. It shouldn't take more than a couple of passes to remove then, and leave very little sanding residue. Check and recheck the wood for whiskers, be absolutely certain that you have remove all of them before you progress. With the whiskers removed, you are now ready to begin sealing the wood prior to applying the finish.

STOP! If the stock has checkering, you must make the decision as what to do with the existing checkering. First option, you can finish over the checkering and later when recutting the checkering, remove the finish from within the checkering. Second option, is to mask off the checkering. I use both. However, when masking the checkering over, do not mask up to the edge / border of the checkering. Leave some of the checkering / border exposed. In this way, when you cut to the edge of the checkering / border and cut a clear border without having exposed wood between the checkering and the finish.

I know the preceding sounds like a lot of work, and it is. That it takes a lot of time, and it does. But if you want a fine finish, but don't want to spend the required time to do it, hire someone like me…

While attending a Todd Bender Clinic at the Wolf Creek Gun Club – now Tom Lowe Shooting Center - in Atlanta several years ago, I noticed the stock and forearm on the gun of one of the squad members. It was on a Model 32 Krieghoff as I recall and had very nice wood and custom checkering. When I asked about it, he informed me that he had ordered the stock from Fajens, had a local Gunsmith fit it to the receiver and install a recoil pad, and that he had filed, sanded and shaped it until it fit his shooting style. After he had completed the finish, he had returned it to the Gunsmith for the checkering. But the comment that he had had to apply ten coats of sealer, taking each coat back to bare wood, that he thought that he would never get the grain filled, impressed me. But his final comment, "It was all worth it," most impressed me.

The finish of that buttstock and forearm was beautiful, and smooth. Watching him shoot that gun, and later the manner in which he dis-assembled and stored it reflected the pride in the finished product. I do not remember his name, but I will always remember the quality of that finish and the appearance of the wood.

Now comes the major decision that you have either made some time ago, or have been thinking a lot about: What type of finish to apply?

There are no right finishes. What is suitable to one person may not be right for another. If the application of the finish is within your skill level and means, and if the final product meets with your expectations, then it might be the right finish for you to use.

I use several types of finishes, depending upon the intended use of the gun. I use a product called FullerPlas, marketed by Gemini Industrial Coatings Company for a hard-clear glossy finish which I can sand, buff and polish to a deep reflective finish, or the satin finish for a satin or honey finish, which is the majority of my work. Over the years I have used Tru-Oil (who hasn't), Gun Speed, Tong Oil, and finishing kits recommended by someone, plus a variety of over the counter finishes from Paint and Finish suppliers.

Recently, as more of my customers wanted oil finishes on their rifles, I began using Purdey's Warthog finish, Pilkinton's Classic Oil finish, Gun Sav'r and then found out about S. B. McWilliams Classic Oil finishes. I will not extol the virtues of the McWilliams Classic Oil finish, but I will say that it is very good.

Some customers will request "their" finish be used, and where I can, I comply. Explaining that any additional time required will be billed to them. Requests by customers for the use of exotic multipart epoxy finish are to be placed in the discarded spray gun hanging on the wall. Discarded because the customer's requested finish had a pot life of less than ten minutes and I ended up with a one-piece spray gun.

I have seen some nice finishes in which Tru-Oil was applied from a spray can, where a clear wood finish was brushed on, and in several cases, when coat after coat of oil was applied and taken down to wood level with steel wool before another coat was applied. The variety of finishes available is too numerous to describe. Read the label of the finish, and make your decision based upon its application to your needs.

But, long before the finish is applied, the grain must be sealed and filled. This process, sealing the wood, is accomplished in many ways. Some use a solution of the appropriate thinning agent with the product to be used as the final finish as the sealer. Some use a special wood sealer recommended by the manufacturer of the finish to be used. Some use a home-made concoction that may or may not be compatible with the finish to be used, and some just start putting on the finish, letting it seal the grain as it builds up.

I use several sealers, depending upon the density of the wood and the final finish to be used. It must bond well with other products used as a final finish.

If I am going to use FullerPlast, I use the manufacturer's recommended sealer, that of thinning down the final finish mixture, and am sure to follow the instructions.

I have had the finish turn into an orange peel surface when the sealer was not compatible with the finish used, or when the wrong thinner or too much thinner was used, and have had to start the stripper process all over again. It is not something that you want to do very often. If I am trying a new product, or a combination I am unfamiliar with, I use a piece of cut off buttstock from the shortening a stock as the test wood. If the test works great, toss the wood back in the bucket, if the test fails, note the results in the "Do Not Do Again" file and toss it in the bucket.

For a Tru Oil Finish

For the hobbyist, a small bottle or Tru-Oil and a small spray can of Tru-Oil is really hard to beat. True, the process is somewhat slow, but the results are nice. If a customer requests a Tu-Oil finish, I mix three ounces of the liquid Tu-Oil with a one-half ounce of lacquer thinner in a small glass bottle and use it as the sealer and base. Thus, I get the fast set up time and am assured of compatibility with the finish.

To begin with, I know that I am going to use the bottled contents as a filler and a sealer, and I know that a little goes a long way. Half filling the bottle cap from the bottle, I rub the Tru-Oil onto the stock. I do the area immediately behind the grip cap first, from past experience knowing that if I have let up on my sanding, this is the area that will tell of my error.

If this area shows sanding marks, I drain the bottle cap back into the bottle, pickup the sand paper, and correct my error and then whisker the area.

If this area looks good, I do the inside of the grip, and then the area near the receiver. If all looks good, I complete the remainder of the stock, **and while the stock is still wet with Tru-Oil,** I use a piece of 320 paper to "wet" sand the stock. With the Tru-Oil on the stock being the "wet" part of the equation. Make no mistake, I do not add water.

The Tru–Oil will rapidly fill the paper, and become a gum comprised of Tru-Oil and sanded particles. It is this gum that you want down in the pores of the wood. This is your filler, so don't fill up your paper and then get another piece. And remember, always sand with the grain

Yes, there is a point at which the paper will fill and become almost useless, at that point change to another piece. By completing this procedure, you have provided both a sealer and a filler, and used one that is 100% compatible with the finish to be used.

Once the entire stock is complete, even though it looks ready to go to the next step, DON'T. Hang it in your "hot box" and let it dry overnight. This gives the filler in the pores sufficient time to dry. To put another coat on too soon will result in what is already there failing to dry, and result in an uneven finish. Remember that patience is not only a virtue in refinishing a stock, it is an absolute necessity.

Back to the Tru Oil finish, after the entire stock has had this treatment, go over the stock lightly with 400 grit wet and dry sandpaper. Feel the areas around the pistol grip and grip cap area. If they feel the slightest bit rough, sand them lightly. When complete, the stock should feel very slick, and begin looking good. By looking good I mean that the grain should give an indication of what its final appearance should be.

Bring out the Tru-Oil mixture and repeat the process. As you are applying the Tru-Oil again, you will discover that not all of the grain has been filled, even though the stock felt as though it had. The fresh liquid on the wood reveals the truth.

I can't tell you how many times to repeat this process, only that when the grain is filled is the process complete. You do not want to use spray Tru-Oil as a filler; the liquid is much easier to work with. I did hear stories of one person that attached the buttstock to rotisserie on his grill, applied the spray very heavy, and turned on the motor. Supposedly, the revolving buttstock prevented the heavy coat of finish from running. I don't know if it works, but can you imagine what the next item cooked on the grill tasted like?

On plain walnut stocks, I find that four or five sandings does a pretty fair job on most of the stocks. There always seems to be a few small areas, which require additional applications. I then skip the wet sanding on the next application, let the coat dry overnight, and the next day, using steel wool, remove the coat down to the wood. When I am confident that the grain is filled, I put on one more coat.

Absolutely confident that the grain is filled, and with the repeated sandings and use of steel wool the stock is as smooth as …., smooth anyhow. I am ready to apply the finish. Having already made the decision on which finish to use, now is not the time to change your mind, proceed. Remember that the filler/sealer should be compatible with the finish.

For the hobbyist, the talking and reading accomplished during the time you have become involved in refinishing the buttstock may lead you to believe that "other finishes" may be better. But as we started with Tru-Oil, let's continue with it.

I have never liked the finish achieved by applying Tru-Oil directly from the bottle to the wood, with either a brush or by hand. I prefer to use the spray cans of Tru-Oil for the final finish, and if the instructions are followed, and the sealer/filler application was done correctly, the finish will be nice.

When you buy the spray can of Tru-Oil, place it in an area in which you have a constant temperature and that is not a shelf in the garage. Use a shelf in the pantry or laundry room. Don't put it on a shelf at which the temperature will fluctuate greatly. Years ago, I placed mine on the soap shelf in the laundry room.

One last time, wipe the stock down with a lint free cloth; don't use a paper towel. I have found that a cheap packet of red or blue shop towels is a big asset around my bench and use them for this purpose. You can either spray the stock while holding it, or while hanging.

For stocks which have a stock bolt hole. I use a wooden dowel wrapped with duct tape to the appropriate dimension, shove it in the stock bolt hole, and have a ready handle to use during the spraying process. I leave the wire protruding through the receiver end and hang the stock when complete.

At this point, let me emphasize the need for following the application instructions on the spray can, they were put there to be followed, follow them. I put on a light first coat the first time over the wood, looking for any grain that was not totally filled, or foreign matter that snuck in.

If I discover unfilled grain, or some bit of foreign matter, I stop the process. Believe me, it is easier to correct an error at this time than to try to spray over it. I've done both and had to explain the "other than that one little area" to friends inspecting my finished stock. As I have said before, if you are in a hurry, hire someone to do it and then fuss at them for being slow. But if you really want a quality piece of work, take your time.

When applying the finish, I get the area to the rear of the grip cap, then the inside of the grip area and then the face of the stock where it joins the receiver. If these areas look good, I continue to apply the finish to the remainder of the stock. I will go back and spray the area around the grip again as this is going to be the primary area where the stock is handled, and I want the finish to be a little heavier there. One thing that I also do, which may or may not be important to some, I also spray a piece of cutoff wood at the same time. I use this cutoff wood to judge when the finish is tacky and when it is dry, and how thick the finish is.

Intend on applying several coats, DO NOT try to lay on a heavy coat first off, you will end up with runs in your finish and have to spend time sanding them out and blending the surrounding area. Take your time; plan on at least three coats of final finish the first day, preferably a Saturday..

As I say, if the wood is properly sealed and the grain filled, three coats of final finish should just about do it – for the day. The next day, put on three more in the same manner. With six coats on the wood, there is sufficient depth to provide some protection as well as enough finish to sand, buff and polish if desired.

OK? So far, so good? But what if you do not want the high gloss finish of Tru-Oil? Simple, get out a fresh piece of 1500 grip wet /dry sandpaper, and lightly, ever so lightly, working with the grain, scuff the wood, just as you did in sanding. This will remove the gloss and provide a soft "honey" finish. This "scuffed" finish will achieve a light reflective finish as it is handled over time without any polishing

If there are any irregularities, us a small piece of 600 grip wet or dry sand paper to smooth it out, then lightly scuff the area with 1500 grit sand paper. With the whole stock slightly scuffed, use a fine cloth, (I use an old undershirt), to buff the finish to the level of shine desired.

FullerPlas

HOWEVER, if you do want a more reflective shine, I recommend using FullerPlas Gloss or Satin finish. This finish will give a really classy looking finish without being a mirror. After applying 6 to 8 coats of finish on the wood, depending upon the type and density of the wood, I allow the final coat of finish a full day to dry and cure in the hot box, leaving it affixed to the pipe I have used for handling it. Then it is time to wet sand it in preparation for the final polish.

I use a small spray bottle for water, and unless the forearm is very rough, 1200 grit wet and dry sanding paper. As I am going to be a little "liberal" with water at times, I spread a couple of paper towels over the area I intend to be working at. The slurry created by the wet sanding is sometimes difficult to remove from a surface.

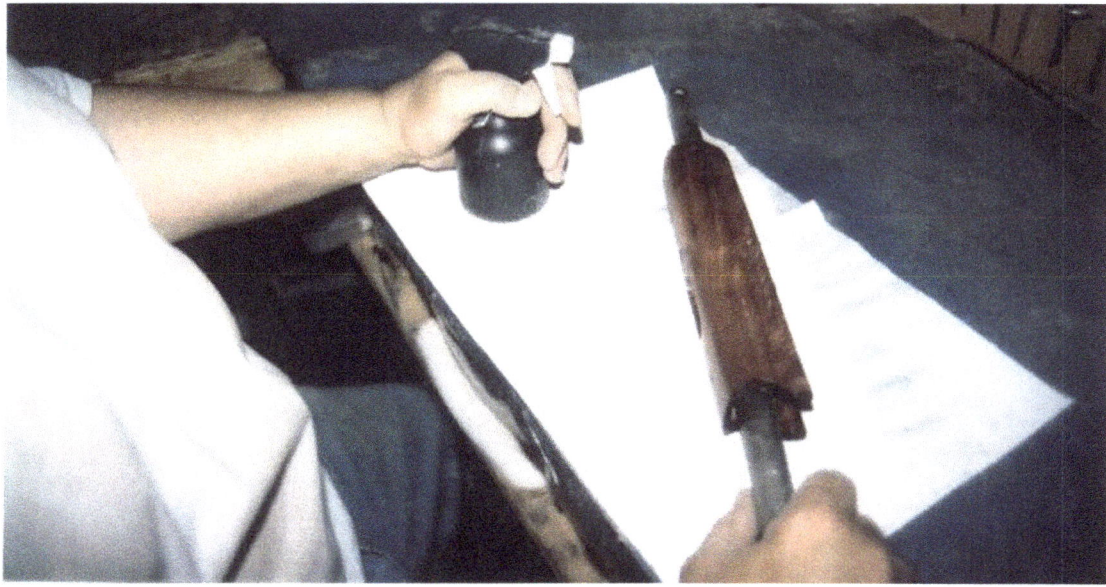

I use very short strokes when sanding and come back a half stroke for each full stroke I make. This gives me double coverage when sanding and creates a pattern of slurry on the piece sanded. I only want to smooth the surface and must be aware that to go through the finish will

require applying additional finish – something I do not want to do – I make very few passes over the same area before going to another area.

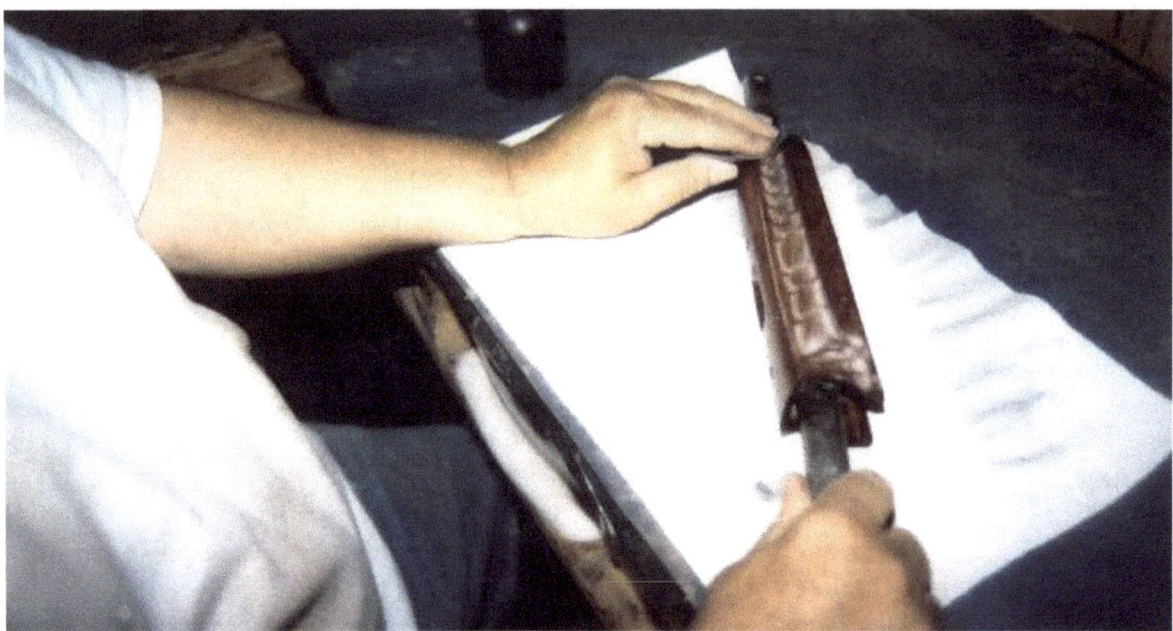

I use another paper towel to wipe off the slurry before it dries – which requires only small areas be worked at any given time – and creates additional work. I then look for areas on the work that are smooth and ready to polish, and other areas which will require additional sanding. Please note on the following picture the small "shiny" area reflecting the light, and the dull area around it. The shiny area is the area with the original finish, and required additional sanding, and the dull area is sanded smooth and should be left alone.

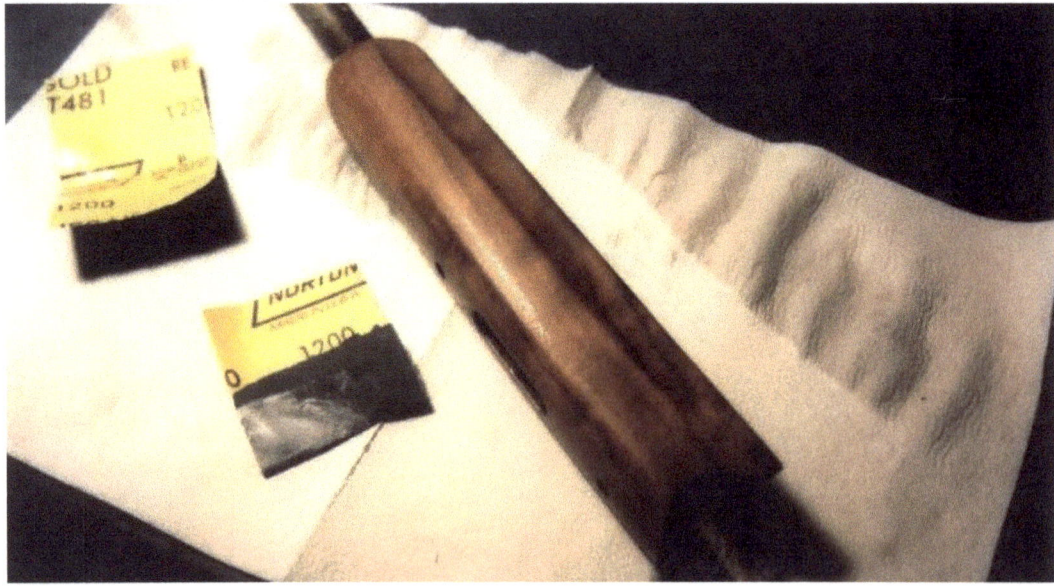

Going over just the shiny area, I quickly smooth it out and make it ready for the final polish.

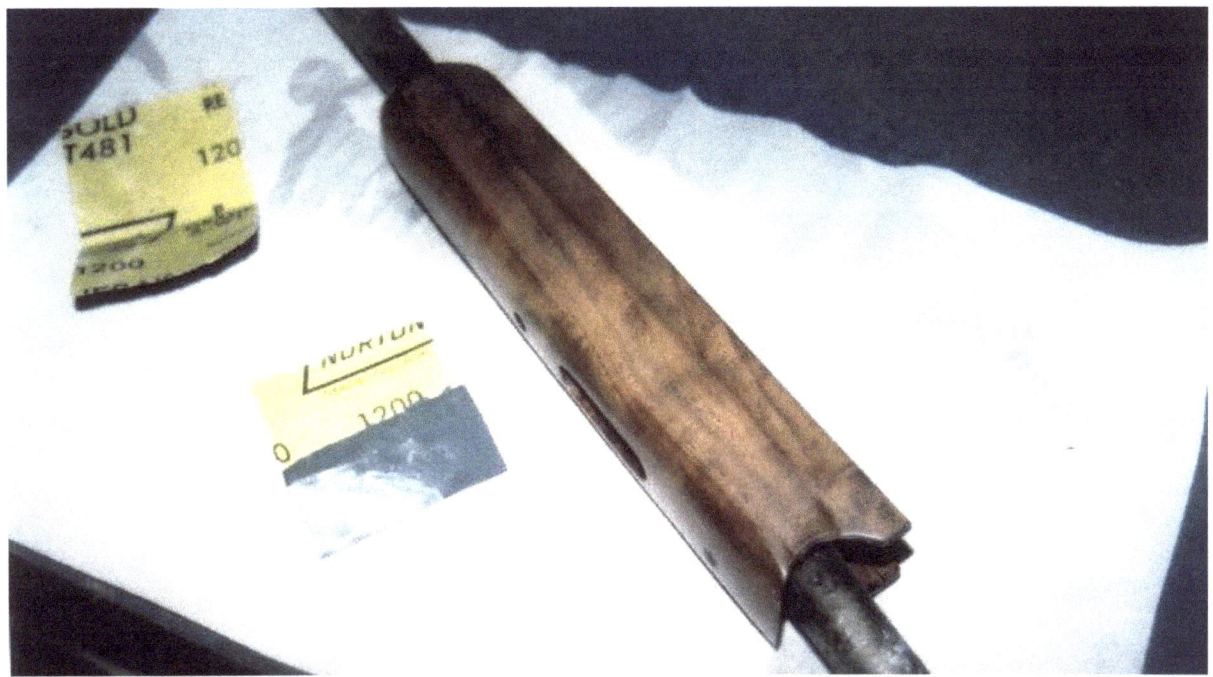

With the area completed with 1200 grit wet and dry sandpaper, I go to 2000 grit wet and dry sand paper. I just want to remove the 1200 grit paper marks, and sand lightly – with lots of water – with the 2000 grit paper.

Just a special note here to really watch the edges when sanding. The upper flute on the Krieghoff forearm is an example, as is the grooved area on the Beretta forearm pictured.

Use very light pressure, contour the sand paper to fit the application, and sand a little, then wipe the slurry off and check your work. If you are not careful, you will sand through the finish on the edges of the wood and have to stop the process and apply finish again.

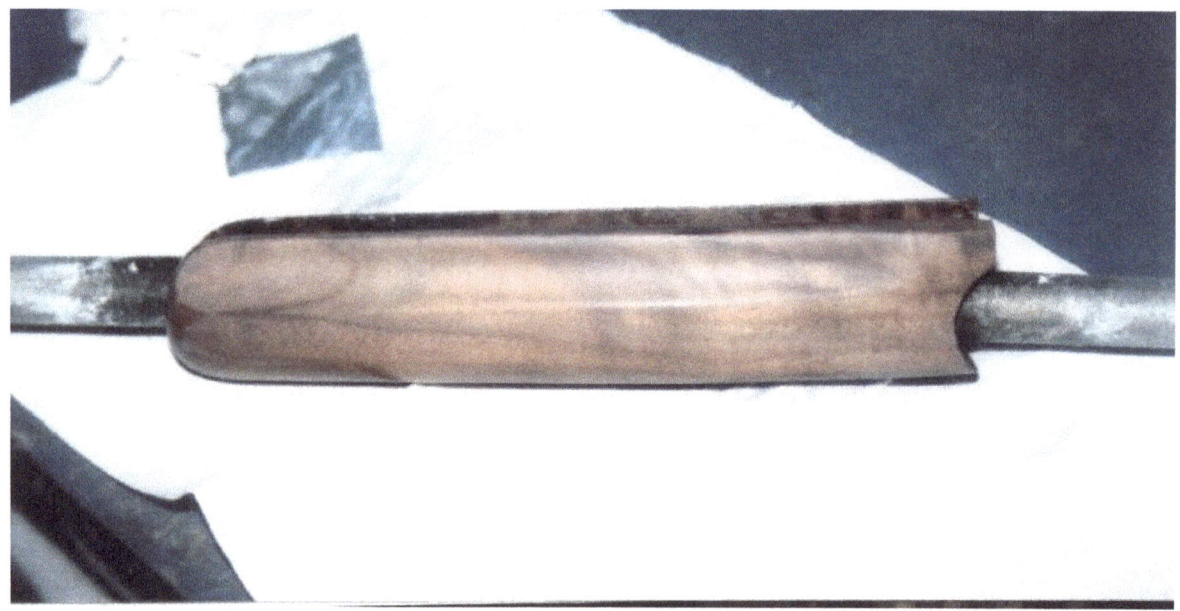

Choose a finish that will provide the desired end result, and one you are willing to perform the required tasks and spend the required time. Assuming that you are able to get the required coats applied without runs or other errors, let the stock set in your hot box for a couple of days to cure our all the way deep down and securely bind to the wood. This wait, depending upon your finish and the number of coats applied, can be the difference between a good finish and one not so good.

One of the most frightening statements made by a customer when bringing in a job is, "I think this is some of that "salt" wood Browning had." Well, I recently had a stock come in that is a prime example of a Browning "salt wood" stock.

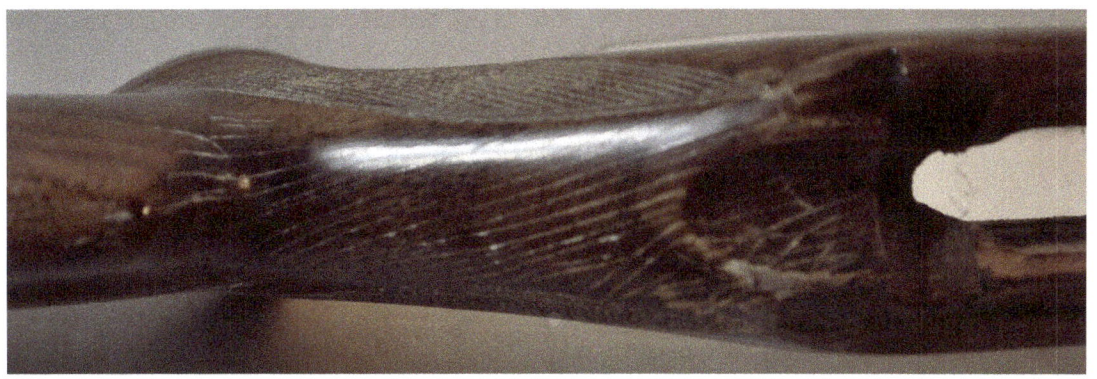

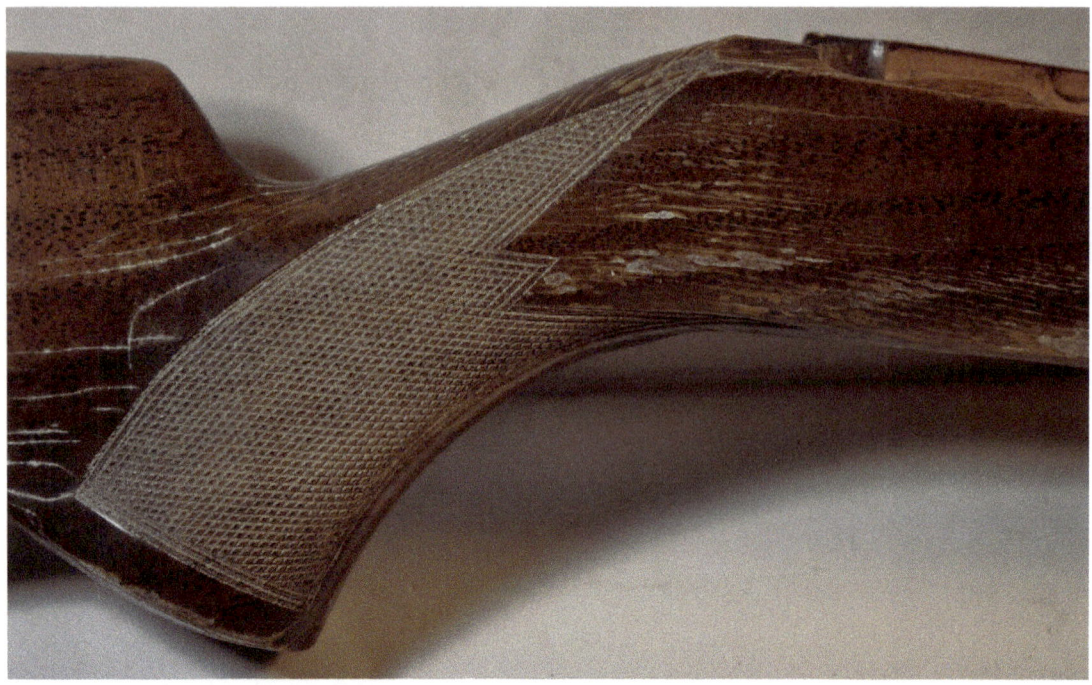

My first task is to get the old finish off of the wood. My trusty economy spray can of stripped came into action again. Once the old finish was removed from the stock, I set up my hot water tray I use when rust bluing, and filled it with distilled water and a brand of liquid soap which I choose not to cite, allowed the water temperature to rise to one hundred and fifty degrees, and put the stock in.

Yep, it took a little "Engineering" to add lead weights to the stock to keep in under water, but not on the bottom of the tank. The counter in the shop got busy, and I left the stock in the hot water for several hours. When I came out to retrieve the stock, the water in the tank was very discolored. I drained the tank, refilled it with clean water, and gave the stock another hour to soak in the hot water. My task was to get the salt out of the wood, and I felt confident I had achieved it.

The stock spent several weeks in the hot box, insuring it was dry and at the end of that time, it was sanded and finished applied as illustrated elsewhere.

If I was pressed to give a single rule for refinishing wood, and being able to obtain excellent results, I would say that the degree of excellence achieved is dictated by the patience of the person doing the work. Take your time, it shows.

SECTION 15
STOCK FITTING

I consider myself capable of correctly determining the fit of a shotgun stock to a shooter for a given purpose and sport. Some shooters fail to realize the various disciplines of shotgun shooting - skeet, trap, sporting clays, and field shooting all require different types of shooting, ranging from gun position to gauge and loads.

Having been most successful in fitting stocks for skeet and trap shooters, I can attribute this success to being on the skeet fields more than on fields of other types as a shooter, referee and spectator. I spend a lot of time watching shooters at the major matches that I attend, often taking pictures of the better shooters while on station, with special emphasis with the position of the weapon when the bird is called for, and the position of the weapon after the bird is broken. I have two pictures of one of the top shooters taken at the 1996 U. S. Open, and I am continually amazed at his consistent follow-through. The placement of the weapon is identical from calling for the bird to lowering the weapon well after the bird has been shot.

The major problem with the stock fit of most shooters is not the fit of the stock so much as it is the shooter not mounting the weapon the same way each time. I have watched the best shooters at the major shoots and have observed them continually mounting their weapon. They do it the same way every time. I strongly advocate developing and going through your "routine", both mentally and physically, as many times as is practical each day in addition to times spent actually shooting. Visualize your position in reference to the perceived station, close your eyes and mount the weapon. Do it several times before opening your eyes, and when you do open them what are seeing WITHOUT moving. If your stock fits correctly, and if you mount the weapon the same each time, your eyes and the beads should be in exactly the same poison. If you have to move your head to obtain the correct sight picture, then your stock does not fit.

Not only does this exercise establish your routine, which, hopefully, will result in the same placement of the weapon each time, but it will help strengthen your upper body for the "rigors" of shooting. I strongly recommend this practice for new shooters, especially the SCTP and AIM shooters.

There are many "rules of thumb" as well as "best" and "only real ways" of determining correct stock fit. I am not a subscriber to set rules (and was never good at parliamentary procedures), but judge the fitting by the success of the shooter in hitting the target – consistently.

Why? Each shooter is different and individual in their many mannerisms of stance, hold point, call, aggressiveness, and confidence. At this point, I will not bring up weapon balance and configuration. I believe that for the shooter to effectively and consistently hit targets the weapon must fit all of his mannerisms and effectively be an extension of the shooter.

No, not every shooter needs a custom fitted stock, but every shooter does need a stock that fits.

In achieving this goal, there are several measurements on the buttstock which can be manipulated to the shooter's advantage. The illustration of a buttstock provides a ready reference to the location and source of these measurements.

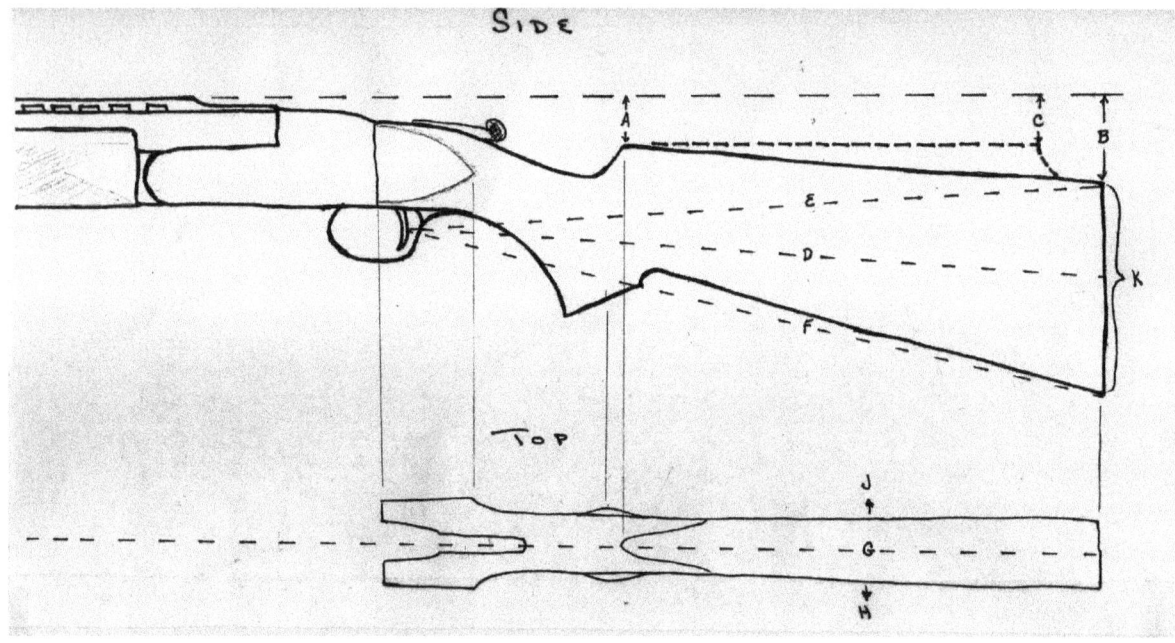

The length of pull (LOP) is the distance from the center curvature of the trigger to the center of the buttplate or recoil pad.

The "length of pull" has a rule of thumb that is probably as old as rules and thumbs - that rule being the measurement from inside the elbow, when the arm is bent at a right angle, to the point of the first joint of the index finger. Several devices have been on the market for years, which make this measurement very easy to obtain, and are accurately called Length of Pull gauges, **IF** that is how one determines the length of pull to be used. Personally, before I go cutting on a thousand-dollar buttstock, I want a little more assurance that I am not cutting off too much wood and will have a customer wanting a new stock, even if it means taking the cost of it out of my hide. In my opinion, all that a length of pull gauge does it measure the distance between two aforementioned points, that's all.

I was recently asked to build a stock for a Remington Model 11-87 equipped with a twenty-eight-inch barrel with the same stock measurements as the person's Krieghoff Model 32 with thirty-inch barrels. I declined and was told that if it could not be made for use this season, could it be completed in time for next season. I explained to the customer that, while the measurements of the stock on the Krieghoff had proven to fit him very well, and that he was shooting it very well indeed, the weight, balance point and recoil of the gas operated 11-87 he intended to use for skeet doubles were entirely different. The customer was not happy – we had worked long and hard to determine the correct stock dimensions on the Krieghoff, and I am sure he felt going through everything again was unnecessary. He left the shop…

With a determination to prove I was right, using an old buttstock for a Remington Model 1100, which had been "shortened to the max", retrieved from under a pile of assorted wood chips,

I set about to prove my point. Overnight I installed an adjustable comb and an adjustable buttplate with length of pull, pitch and cast adjustment. Using bedding compound, I built up palm swells on both sides and decreased the grip radius to a point almost duplicating the Krieghoff grip.

Making an appointment with the customer, I asked him to bring the Krieghoff and the Remington and meet me at the range. He showed up as requested, and I showed up with a half case of ounce and an eighth twelve-gauge loads, duplicates of what he wanted to shoot, and my newly competed "point prover". With an attitude of "humor me, shoot my shells", I put the stock on the 11-897, loosened everything up, and with him mounting and dismounting the gun (before a shot was ever fired) began fitting it to him.

When the "comb is too narrow" came up, a piece of moleskin came out. When "the grip is too big" was heard, a course file came out. When he got into the fitting session and really started working with me, I knew that I was on to something and even envisioned a similar "point prover" for Krieghoff, Perazzi and Browning.

He shot two boxes of shells at stations of my choosing. I began with low 7, went to low 6, high 1, and then out to high and low 4 before alternating between high 2 and low six. At the end of the two boxes, I was fairly confident that we were not quite where I wanted to be, but very close. We took a break, had a sandwich, and then went back to doubles at three, four and five, shooting single birds, and then a pair.

I made two small adjustments to the settings during the next fifty targets, which were all broken. The first adjustment I made after the tail of several low 3's (second bird) and a low 4 (second bird) were broken, rather than the bird being centered in the shot pattern. By shortening the length of pull less than an eight-inch, subsequent birds were centered, and he was able to swing on the second bird quicker with less mental and physical strain.

Well into the second box I noticed he was beginning to raise his head a little on the second shot, and after seeing him stretch his jaw, I decreased the amount of pitch slightly and then a little more after two more shots and I had time to observe the movement of the stock in relationship to the shooter's face.

We took another break before shooting another box. I was doing the pulling, the watching and receiving the comments about the general appearance of the "point prover". A club member pulled the last box of shells, and I watched the shooter. He broke them all as I expected him to. In my opinion, those measurements fit him.

We lay the gun out, and I took the measurements; length of pull, drop pitch, comb radius, and grip. Having brought the file card on his Krieghoff from the shop, I compared the two. The Remington length of pull was a full quarter inch shorter. The comb was exactly the same. The comb radius was very, very close, as were the grip dimensions. However, the pitch between the two guns was not even comparable – the Remington had much less.

I have relayed this story because of my belief that the same measurements will not fit each type of gun a person shoots. As the customer later admitted, he "was trying to use silk suit measurements for a smoking jacket". I still have my "point prover", and by the time this reaches print, will have one for a Krieghoff, Beretta and Perazzi.

Before you ask, "Do all stock makers measure everything the same way?", the answer is NO. Some use a yardstick, some a tape measure, some a carpenter's rule, etc. The important thing is that the stock maker transfers the measurements accurately regardless of the increment of measure. Fractions of cubits could be used if all else fails.

The drop at the comb is one of the measurements most easily messed up in the fitting process. This measurement is greatly influenced by the radius of the comb. Many times shooters have wanted the combs of their shotguns reduced by as much as a quarter inch, having tried out someone else's gun or a new one and either felt better or shot better with it. They were certain about the new drop measurement until I asked the approximate radius of the comb. By reducing the radius of the comb by as little as a sixteenth and blending it back into the flat of the buttstock, the shooter was better able to quickly and comfortably align the heads. One particular shooter had gained over twenty-five pounds through the winter, so by changing the radius of the comb and blending it into the flat a little further down, the shooter was back in the middle of the birds.

Grip angle, length of grip and grip radius are related, but different, and will be addressed separately.

I often shoot with a skeet shooter who is not shooting up to his potential because the custom measured, specially made, very fancy stock he purchased DOES NOT FIT. He must continually make allowances to compensate for it. One shop session, lasting leas than a half hour, without having fired a single shot at a moving target, was used in determining the measurements for the stock. If I even thought I was that good…

Most of my custom stocks are for Krieghoff Model 32 and K-80 and KOLAR's with a distance second being Beretta's Model 682. Why? For a shooter to invest the money, and for a stock maker to invest the time, with the result being a truly custom fitted stock, both had better be darned sure of each other's abilities and motives.

Unable to locate a second "much used" Krieghoff buttstock, I did find a semi-finished buttstock of very plain American walnut advertised at a "bargain price." From this I have developed my "fitting stock" which I like to use in determining *preliminary measurements* for Krieghoff shooters. The original measurements of the buttstock were similar to those of the #5 American Skeet buttstock; 1 3/8"x 2 1/4"x 14 1/8".

Wanting a buttstock that could service *most* of my customers, I immediately cut it off and installed a buttplate adjustable for length of pull as well as vertical and lateral movement. Then I took a thick slice off of the entire top of the comb making way for an adjustable comb using some modified hardware. I wanted maximum adjustment on the adjustable comb, and obtained my goal by reversing the mounting positions. I put the base in the comb, and, with the posts necessary for the height adjustment being excessively long, placed the bushings in the buttstock and drilled postholes down through the stock bolt hole. True, I must first remove the comb before attaching the fitting stock to the customer's Krieghoff receiver, but the result of the customer looking down his rib with his trigger pulls is achieved. Naturally this is not possible with a gas operated, semi-auto with an action spring tube. Thus, I have allowed the customer to be more familiar with the equipment used, and hopefully have confidence in the measurements taken. Using my fitting stock to determine a customer's needs, I use my best judgment when setting the length of pull, set a neutral pitch at the butt, center the adjustable comb, either raise or lower it more than I think is necessary, and establish neutral cast off/on. Depending upon the size and gender of the person, I have several pre-cut slips of adhesive-backed rubber and moleskin in my pocket to slip on the front of the grip area to reduce grip angle and radius.

Remember the old adage about knowing something so well the person could recognize it in the dark? Well, that is how I start the fitting session. I tell the customer that I want them to close their eyes and keep them closed while they mount the weapon several times. I prefer five or six times as I watch how uniform they are when mounting, especially the positioning of the butt to the shoulder, and the position of the head in relationship to the length of the comb.

During this time I ask questions about the relationship of the mid and end beads in their normal sight pictures as well as general questions on their level of shooting. A shooter that has been through the a clinic by one of the top name shooters is fairly easy to spot, especially a new shooter.

After making any changes to the fitting stock, I ask the shooter to repeat the process, making additional adjustments, and then after several more blind mountings, ask the shooter to open their eyes for only an instant before closing them again. I tell the shooter that during that instant in which their eyes are open they should form a mental image of the sight picture seen. I caution them on not making any changes to the manner in which they have been mounting the weapon.

When the shooter has completed the exercise, the variety of "sight picture" descriptions that I received is unbelievable. I then begin the process of adjusting the fitting stock to enable the shooter to see the sight picture they want. I found out a long time ago that the sight picture will vary for each shooter. My goal during this whole exercise is to establish the measurements which allow the shooter to comfortably mount the weapon in the same manner each time and see the same sight picture.

Many years ago, I developed a simple tool to use in order for the shooter to tell me what he sees. A simulated sight plane using card stock with a moveable mid bead. I will not try to describe it, but a copy of the tool, and how I use it, it at the end of this chapter.

I no longer try to determine the position of the shooter's eye, I let the took take the task on and it has been one heck of a help.

I ask the shooter to blind mount the weapon several times, and then ask them to open their eyes while the weapon is mounted. Often the shooter will adjust his head position to obtain the correct sight picture. I then make adjustments to the fitting stock. I then ask the shooter to mount the weapon with their eyes open. During this phase I continue to look for the little "after mounting" adjustments a shooter needs to accomplish in getting the weapon positioned, and then make additional adjustments to compensate for them. The initial fitting is completed when the shooter sees the anticipated bead alignment.

AND THEN, AND THEN, and then we shoot, and I want to make the distinction between what I am discussing, stock fit and shooting. I do not give shooting lessons, but I do fit the stock to the shooter. In my opinion, to try to change a shooter's "style" to fit a preconceived notion as to what is right places a great deal of responsibility on the stock fitter. Those that want my services as a fitter are, for the most part, accomplished shooters of one sport or another. On several occasions I have worked with coaches in obtaining a correctly fitted stock for a shooter. Each of us knew what the other expected, and the shooter trusted us to do what was best for him.

A stock cannot be fitted correctly without firing upon a target. However, before the shooter gets to engage a target, clay, pitch or otherwise, we go to the pattern board. I am very lucky to have access to a pattern board five feet square and able to shoot at distanced up to sixty yards. The distance is depending upon the venue shot by the shooter, skeet shooters shoot closer to the target than trap shooters.

Watching the shooter's mount of the weapon, I have him shoot several shots into the pattern board. We then go forward and determine where the charge is striking the target area of the board. I want the shooter to see the impact of the charge on the pattern board. If the charge is not striking where the shooters wants it, we make adjustment to the stock, primarily to the comb height, clean the pattern board, and go back for another try. It may take take several such attempts to adjust the stock to the shooter's satisfaction.

The proof is in the pudding, or in this case, the proof is in the breaking of the birds. For the first few shots I watch the shooter's reaction to the "different" stock and how they mount the weapon – place their head and their hold points - when they call for the bird.

While on the range I watch many things but believe the root cause for success is the placement of the weapon the same with each mounting, to include the head on the comb. I watch the birds being broken and where the chips are coming from – front, back, top, bottom – and how the broken birds come to the ground or sail on.

Often when I can see the shot pattern and the chips coming from the bird, I can adjust the comb and change the impact of the shot pattern by several inches. The change of chips from either the top or bottom of the bird to rolling smoke through comb adjustment is rewarding.

Another thing I watch for, especially after five or six shots, is the movement of the head caused by the recoil. With minor adjustments in pitch, I can effectively remove most of the recoil and not disturb the mount of the weapon for the second shot. The degree of pitch on the butt of a weapon affects the "direction of recoil" much more than one would think. The correct angle will greatly reduce the felt recoil, and an incorrect angle will increase felt recoil, increase recovery time for the next shot, and often, raise a *mouse* on the check of the shooter. I do not believe that there is a correct angle of pitch for all guns, but firmly believe that a *correct angle of pitch exists for each shooter and gun combination*. In my experience, the angle of pitch is determined by a combination of factors, primarily:

    the caliber or gauge of the weapon
    the angle(s) at which the weapon is discharged
    the build of the shooter
    the placement of the head on the comb
    the effect of recoil upon the shooter

I have one customer that is an excellent field, trap and sporting clays shot. He has been shooting shotguns for many years, and through experience and recorded observation has determined what stock measurements work best for him in a given sport. I have watched him shoot and noted where the target is struck in reference to his pattern. In instances in which the target is consistently not centered with the pattern, our observations of needed corrections are very close. Very few shooters, other than avid clay target shooters, achieve this level.

The first time he brought work to me was to ask if I could increase the pitch on a Remington Model 3200 to a specified measurement at the mid-bead location.

After measuring out the needed cut I informed him that the change would decrease his length of pull by approximately three thirty-seconds of an inch. He asked that I make the cut and put in a spacer of appropriate thickness.

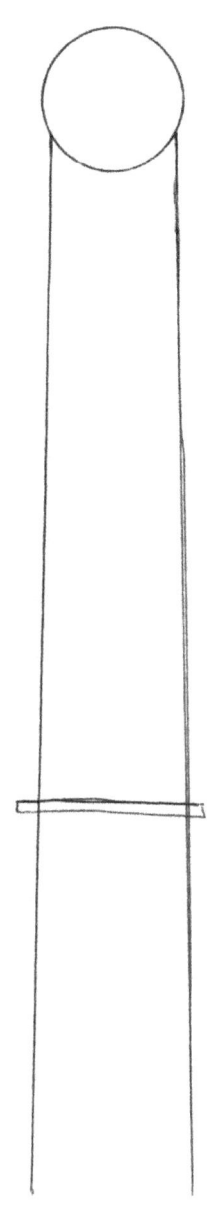

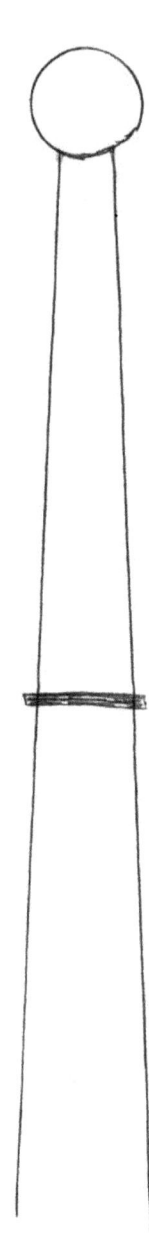

The **Shotgun Bead Alignment Tool** was developed for the stock fitter to determine EXACTLY what the person being fitted sees down the rib of the shotgun. If the shotgun does not have a Mid-Rib bead, STOP. This tool won't work.

If the shotgun has a Mid-Rib bead, please conduct the following exercise – I have been using it for over 20 years and found that it works best – to obtain the correct stock fit for the shooter.

And while I have you in a bad mood, let me strike a sensitive nerve once more: The measurement between your inside elbow and the trigger finger is exactly that. IT IS NOT the correct length of pull for a shooter. Period!

For female shooters, the toe of the stock often digs into their chest – and causes them to move the toe of the stock out resulting in the shotgun being canted. To correct this, loosen the tension screw of the Single Point Adjustable Buttplate just enough to allow the recoil pad to move. Have the person mount the shotgun with the toe of the stock away from their chest and with no cant. Hold the recoil pad in position, remove it from the person's shoulder, and tighten the tension screw, locking the recoil pad in the correct position for the shooter.

Back to the exercise in question: Have the shooter mount the gun several times – 4 to 7 times – holding the mount three to five seconds each. While they are doing this, stand at the shooter's side and note/mark – I use a piece of chalk – the position of the cheek on the stock. You are looking for a consistent mount.

DO NOT tell the shooter what you are looking for or at. If you do, they will exaggerate their mount, providing false information.

OK. Tell the person to mount the gun with their eyes closed, and that you will tell them when to open their eyes. And when they do open their eyes, to only open them for a few seconds – only long enough to see down the rib and the position of the mid-bead and the front bead. ALSO they are not to move their head on the stock when opening their eyes.

With that done, have the person then duplicate what they saw using the Shotgun Bead Alignment Tool. From the positioning of the beads on the tool, make appropriate adjustment to the comb – moving the comb laterally to align the beads.

To move the mid bead up into the base of the front bead – an upside down figure 8, lower the comb. This will lower the point of impact of the shot pattern. To create a space between the mid-bead and front bead, raise the comb of the stock. This will raise the point of impact of the shot pattern.

I have found that using the Single Point Adjustable Buttplate with Length of Pull adjustment AND an Adjustable Comb mounted on a stock – preferable one which will fit the shooter's shotgun – is the best way to determine what is needed to fit a stock to a shooter. Just call it a Redneck Try Stock!

SECTION 16
CUSTOM STOCKING

With the increased use of, if not return to, the gas operated shotguns in Skeet, the Remington Model 1100 and 11-87 as well as the Beretta's, especially in the doubles event, the demand for custom butt stocks seemed to come from nothing to a rack full of work to be accomplished.

And then the SCTP came along, and brought their Remington Model 1100, their Beretta Model 390 and 391, and dog gone if a few didn't show up with Grandpa's Winchester Model 12. I was back in the whittling line making stocks for a much younger group of shooters, some as young as ten years old. And before you snicker at a young shooter being shorter than the gun he wanted to shoot, and expecting to his a target, let me tell you that young man ran 200 straight for the Tennessee Singles AIM title, and then had a shoot-off with another young shooter that had also ran the first 200.

The first wave wanted recoil pads, a few adjustable butt plates, the second wave wanted adjustable combs, and then the demand for butt stocks to the shooter's measurements came about. In trying to fulfill the requirement for custom stocks, the major modification from the factory measurements cited was a wider and higher comb. One shooter ended his description by saying he wanted a comb wide enough to lay his cheek on without fear of getting cut, but not wide enough to sleep on.

With a buttstock salvaged from the scrap bin, I used AcraGlas to attach a cut section of buttstock, increasing the length of pull to fifteen inches. Naturally the action tube hole in the buttstock did not line up with the hole in the added wood and required a little creative drilling to make one continuous hole.

Wanting the pattern to serve a myriad of requirements, I cut a one-inch slice from the comb of the buttstock, angling the forward portion of the cut up into the flutes of the comb, and then cut a wedge from scrap lumber. The wedge, once on place, would raise the comb height to 1 1/4 by 1 1/4. I then used bondo, (yep, automotive dent filler) to contour the sides and top to the desired configuration. Another feature shooters had began asking for was palm swells. So, a little bondo was added to each side of the grip area. And then a correction on the angle of the grip was made with a little more bondo. All in all, it looked a mess.

When the bondo dried, I used a newly purchased body file and shaped it to what I felt I needed. From the results of my labor, I ended up with a pattern buttstock from which I could remove wood and provide the shooter with a buttstock with skeet, straight trap, Monte Carlo trap or field measurements.

One appeal to shooters which I have maintained over the years is the ability for the shooter to choose the wood to be used on his gun while in blank or pattern form. With several nice stock blanks and the prototype well padded in a box, combined with a letter of instructions, I sent them out for duplicating. There are several firms which provide this service, but Wenig Custom Gunstocks, Lincoln, MO do mine, and I have NEVER been disappointed with the quality of their work.

Notice that I have a general outline for the buttstock shown here, as well as modifying the grip and building a reversed comb with a larger radius – lower in the front than in the back. As often as not, the customer will want to take the built up stock and shoot it for a while. This has resulted in some unscheduled meetings at near-by ranges. I arrive with body file in hand. The bondo goes on and comes off easily.

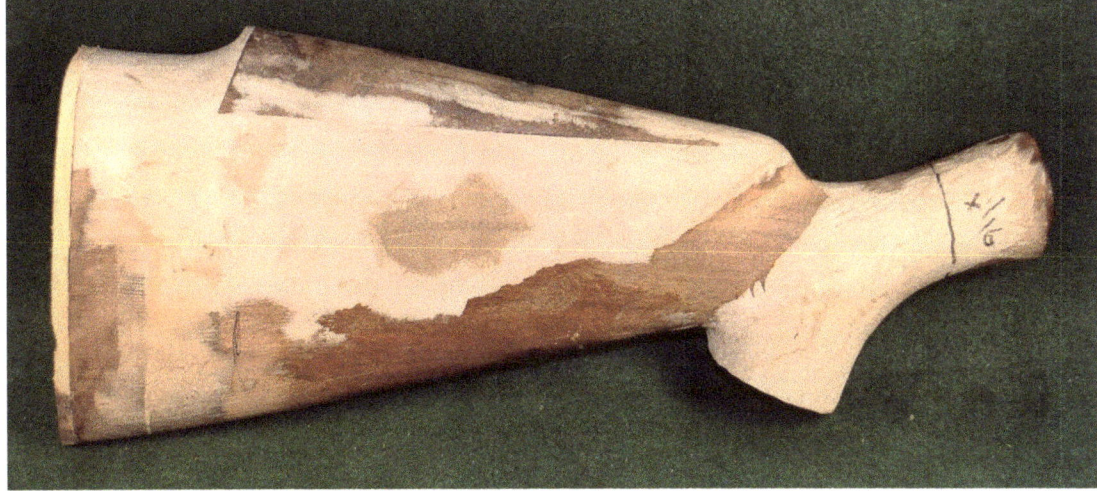

One Customer wanted to take the stock to a major shoot, to determine how he would shoot in under competitive pressure. So, I borrowed a spray can of fluorescent orange paint from the Gun Club's paint cabinet and quickly "fixed" it.

Unless the Customer knows the measurement wanted, and I trust his judgment, I start out with a try stock I have developed and place it on his receiver. In this manner, he has <u>his</u> barrel to sight down, and his trigger to pull. My try stocks are standard stocks for the Remington 1100 and 11-87, Winchester Model 12, Krieghoff, KOLAR and Beretta 680 series but to which I have cut to a very short length of pull, added an interchangeable adjustable comb feature and an adjustable buttplate that is also adjustable for length of pull out to almost sixteen inches. The adjustable buttplate I first used for this purpose was one which worked well for several years, but another shop needed one and I let the stock go and made my current version.

    For the young shooter wishing to become competitive in local, regional, state and national competitions, a stock that fits correctly is an absolute requirement. As I write this previous sentence, I look around my man cave and the pictures of young shooters displaying their trophies. One picture I am extremely proud of is a picture of a young lady wearing her vest, gun across her shoulder, taken at the Olympic Training Center in Colorado.

    That picture has carried me through some rough days, days when I was considering taking up either Golf or Horse Shoes.

SECTION 17
SALVAGE

I have no idea of what the formulation of the green stuff applied to the stock is but let me state that it really went into the wood and is very hard to remove as evidenced by the green shading remaining after stripping the wood with a commercial stripper three times.

I do not like the layout of the cheek piece on the stock and have penciled in the modification I will make. Yes, it does resemble an early 1900's Mauser Sporter stock, and it is intended to. I really like the small cheek piece, it is functional and covers the anticipated area needed. And notice the angle of the butt? It is a few degrees negative pitch. I will recut the butt, after measuring for a recoil pad, and make the butt at a right angle to the axis of the bore.

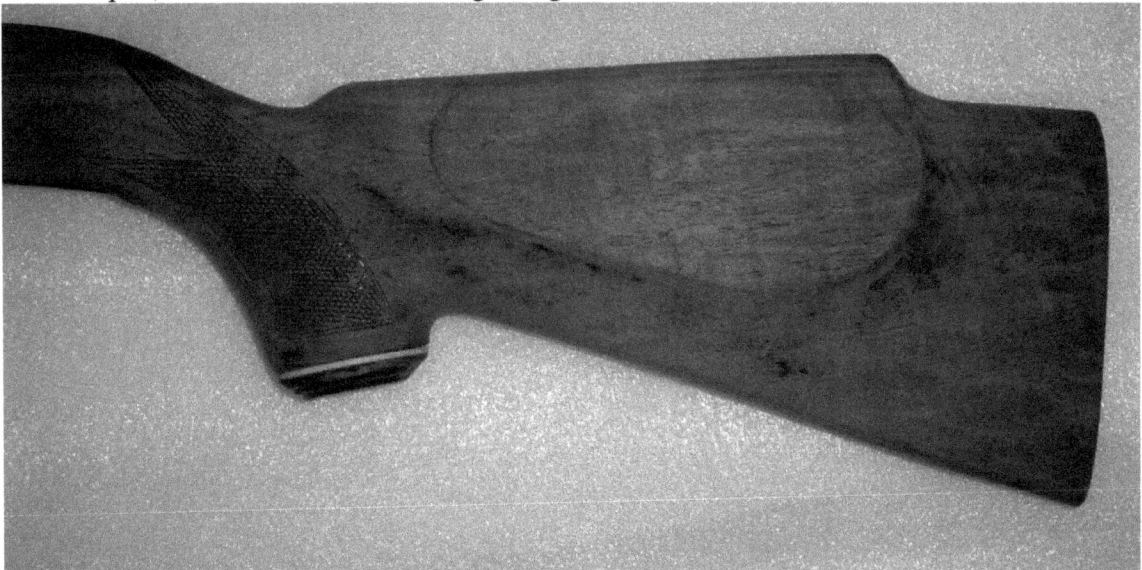

The more I cut into the stock reshaping the cheek piece, the more I realized that the wood could turn out really nice with a little effort and a few materials.

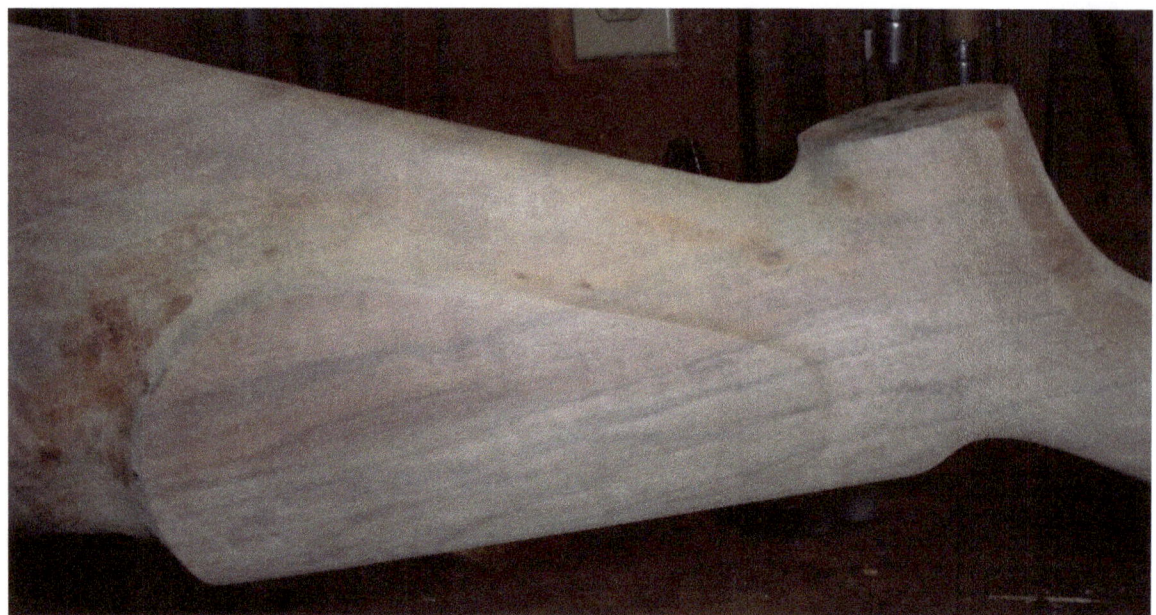

The forearm was a task all of its own. The green stuff was firmly imbedded in the wood, and for the first time, I took a good look at the inletting for the floor plate assembly and the action. The trigger guard was enlarged at every point, it was going to take a lot of work.

Many years ago, I carved my initials in the bark of a large walnut tree several miles from my home, one of many trees planted along the road years before. As years past, I stopped several times to check them out, and sure enough, there were still there, somewhat grown over, but there. Forty years later, that walnut tree was "harvested" and I had the opportunity to purchase several blanks from trees cut from along that road. I do not know if the blanks I purchased were from that tree or not, but no one can prove to me that they aren't. So I have a lot of empathy with the person that carved his initials in the side of this gun stock. But my intent is to slim the stock and the initials will go.

Yep, there is actually a little figure in the wood, at least on one side. I have found that wood such as this readily accepts red root oil and the hidden figure comes out. One shaped and sanded, I will use the S. B. McWilliam Alkanet Oil on it.

Here again are remnants of the green stuff on the fore arm. The checkering will be removed when I slim the stock down, but an ebony forearm tip is to be installed first.

The plastic grip cap is an item I detest – pure cheap! I have several options here, first preference is a skeleton grip cap – is there enough wood for such an installation? Second option is a solid steel grip cap, it would be traditional, it is a strong maybe. Last option is the installation of a ebony grip gap matching the forearm tip.

The wood surrounding the eject/loading port of the action is just too plain. I like the contours offered by some of the customer rifle builders of the 1920's and 30's and will duplicate some of their work. There is not much I can do about the inletting for the bolt.

More examples of the green stuff. Notice the checkering is not really in that bad a shape, if I were not going to slim the stock down, I could salvage the checkering with little difficulty.

So having reviewed briefly what I envision, let me summarize. I intend to slim the stock to resemble an early Mauser Sporter, contouring the cheek piece, installing an ebony forearm tip, install a skeleton grip cap, contour the loading port and install a good recoil pad to absorb the recoil of the very light rifle. So the grip cap will be next.

The screw in the center of the area eliminated inletting a skeleton grip cap directly onto the stock. But I several other options available.

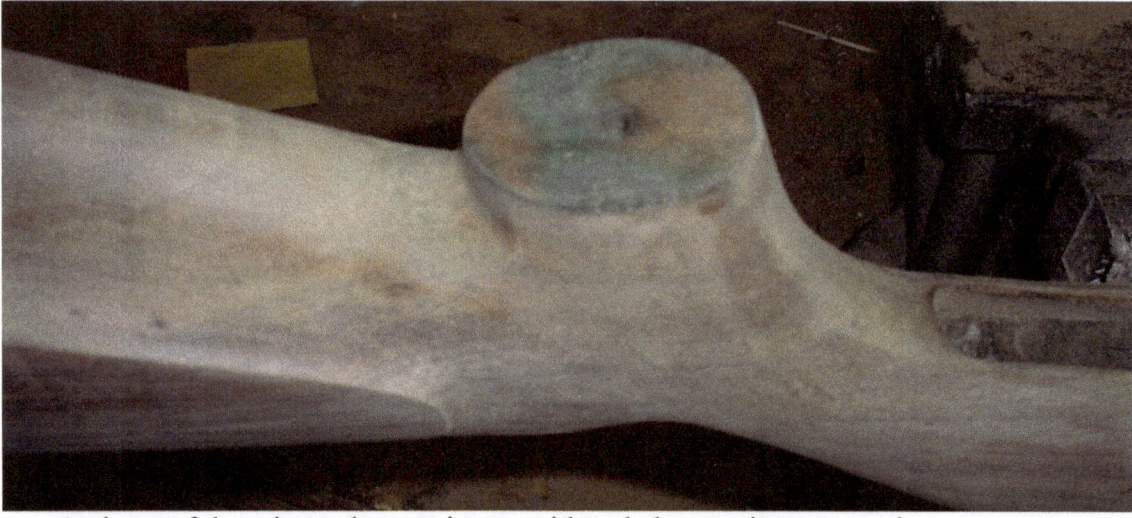

And one of them is an ebony grip cap with a skeleton grip cap over it.

Does the final product justify all of the time spent in installing it? From my point of view, Yes.

For whatever reason, most probably loose action screws and lots of shooting, the area behind the recoil lug area of the stock was broken and set back against the magazine well. Now that is a lot of shooting. The broken piece of wood slid back into place easily, but in no way was permanent.

Removing the piece, AcraGlas was placed on the stock and the broken piece, and the two joined back. No pressure was needed for the joint at the broken piece was something like a dovetail shape and provided its own pressure.

With the repair made to the recoil lug area, it is time to reinforce the recoil lug. I am going to do this with the installation of a Talley Recoil Lug. First thing to do is identify the position on the stock. I light pencil line on the outside of the stock indicates the horizontal position.

To determine the vertical position, a depth gauge is used to first determine the top of the recoil lug area of the stock.

This measurement is transferred to the outside of the stock. From this line as second line is drawn 3/16" lower. From this line, a third line is drawn 1/8" lower. The distance between the first and second lines if the thickness of wood between the top of the stock recoil lug area and the Talley Recoil Lug. The intersection of the third line and the vertical line is the point at which the stock is to be drilled for the Talley Recoil Lug.

With the location identified, to include a quarter inch "target" with a center, it is time to drill the hole for the tube which is also .250". I do this on a drill press with the stock in a machinist vice with a parallel between the stock and the vice jay to insure the hole is drilled parallel to the top of the stock.

I screw the end onto the tube to insure it functions, and then I use several light taps on the end piece to make an impression in the stock. This compressed wood identified the area to be removed – to the depth of the tube – with either a hand held high speed grinder OR with a piloted drill with the pilot being the diameter of the tube .250", and the drill being the diameter of the end piece. I used the piloted drill as I install enough of them to justify the drill's cost.

The following picture was taken after the stock was finished and the recoil bolt was blued and installed. Very nice neat installation. Take your time, it shows in the finished product.

And what barreled action in what caliber is going into the stock? I don't know. Several are stored in the gun safe waiting for wood, to include an FN in 280 Remington, an FN in 7mm08m an FN in 270 Winchester and an FN in 300 Holland and Holland and a Commercial Mauser in 243 Winchester.

I chose the Commercial Mauser in 243 Winchester Caliber. The light recoil round combined with the light weight stock should make an ideal stalking rifle. At least that is my thoughts.

Before bedding the barreled action into the stock, it must be thoroughly cleaned. I use several different brushes ranging from a stainless steel hand brush, to a one inch paint brush to the narrow end of an M-16 cleaning brush, and lots and lots of Carburetor / brake cleaner.

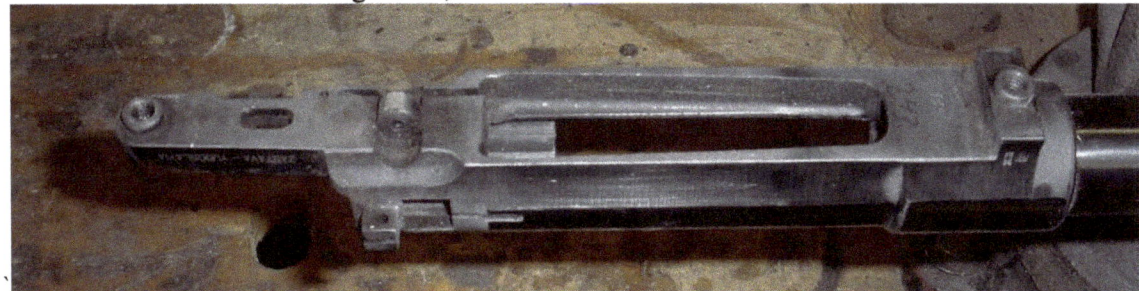

Take a look…. I really clean the metal.

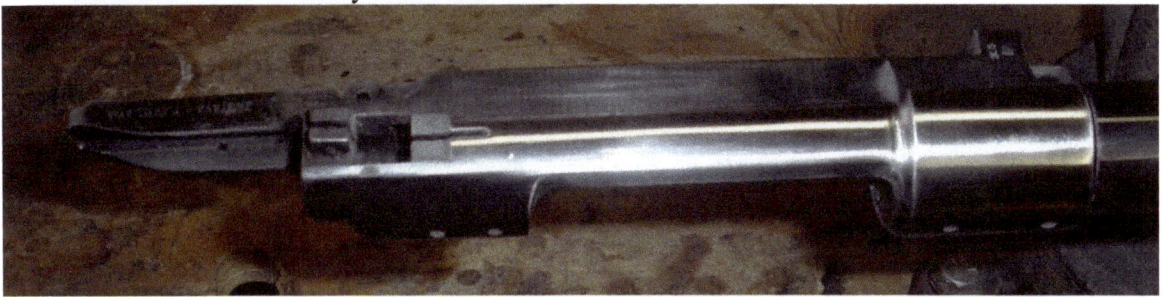

Even the bolt rail, just in case some bedding compound accidently gets that high.

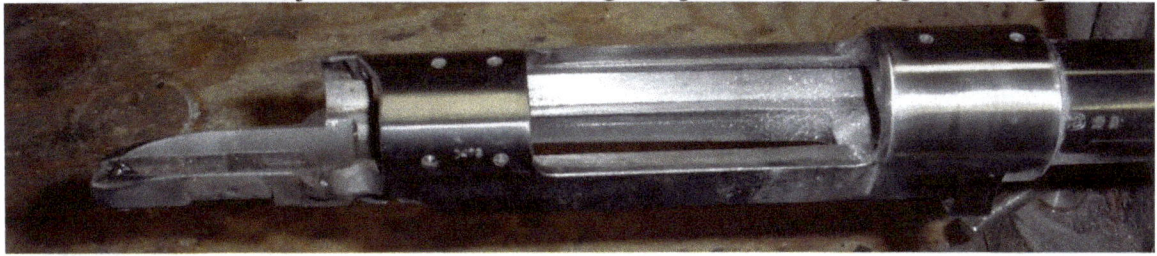

I use the modeling clay very liberally when preparing an action for bedding.

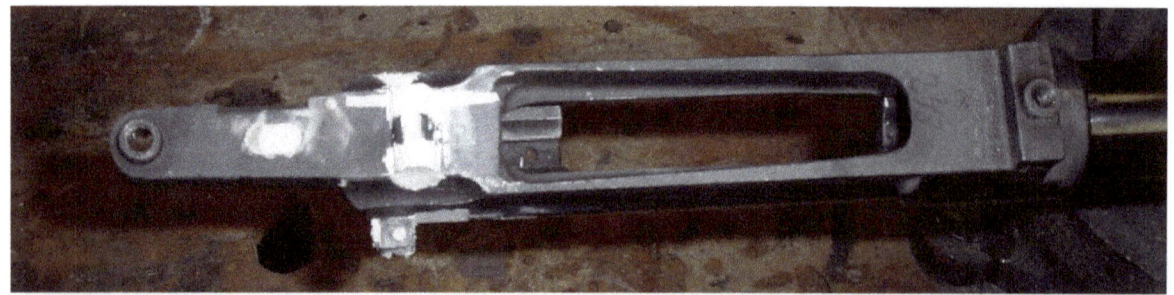

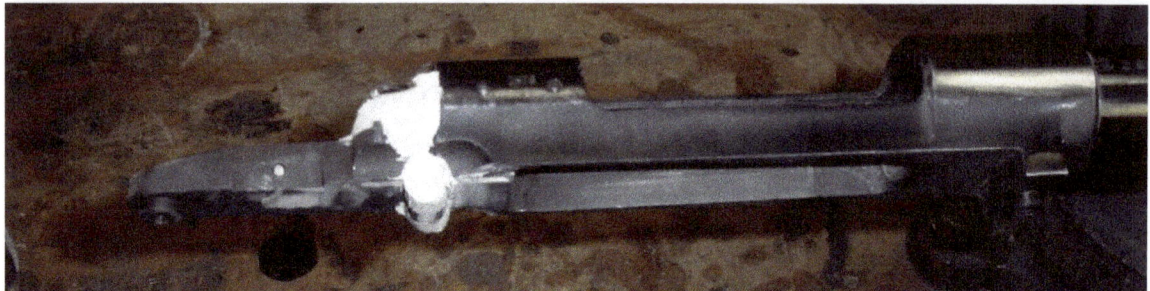

Please notice the area just in front of the floor plate magazine well and the recoil lug area of the stock – it was filled in with re-inforced AcraGlas when the wood repair on the recoil lug area was made.

Even though this stock has had much worse done to it that a little extra bedding compound coming out over onto the wood, I followed my habit and taped off the stock to prevent contact with the bedding compound where it was not wanted.

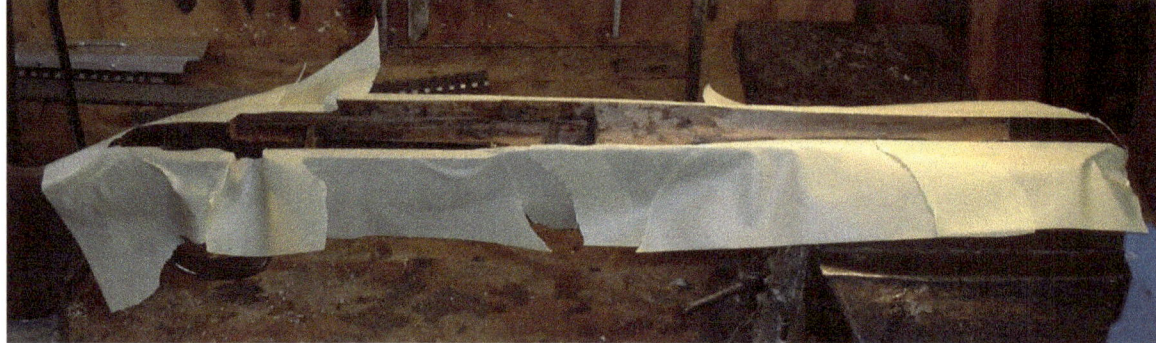

    When the stock bedding screws began pulling the barreled action down into the stock, the excess bedding compound began coming out. As long as there is excess, and not an insufficient amount, I am happy. A little excess bedding compound is much less expensive than having to grinding out the bad bedding job and do it over.

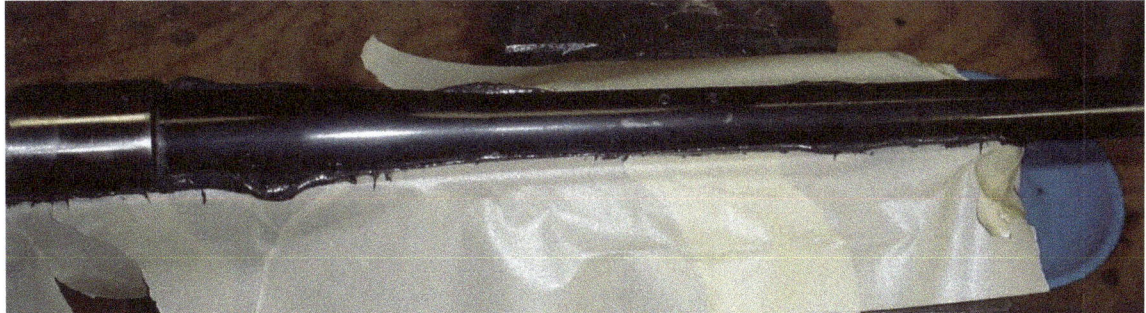

SECTION 18
Installing Sling Swivels

There are many ways of attaching a sling to a rifle or shotgun using sling swivels or sling swivel studs. While the techniques are similar on many, there are subtle differences which will reflect an attractive installation. Sling swivels can be divided into three broad categories. The first is the Screw In type. There are three components of this type of screw. The first is the long screw in stub that is normally used on the butt of the stock. The forearm can utilize either the threaded stud through the stock with a nut on the inside of the barrel channel, or the short screw into the forearm.

There are variations of the Screw In type in that the sling loop is a permanent part of the Screw and threaded screw.

And then there are the classic style which required inletting the base into the stock, and then affixing it with screws. The front sling swivel base utilized two (2) threaded screws with nuts being inletted in the barrel channel into the which the screw are threaded and hold the sling swivel base in place.

A little caution: Have a good set of numerical drills available, you will need them.

I like to do the forearm first. Center the sling swivel base on the forearm, about a quarter inch behind the forearm tip – or 2 ¾" if it doesn't have a forearm tip.

I use a white pencil to mark one of the holes, but have use a sharpened pencil to identify one hole location on the stock. Be sure to check your work, insuring that the mark reflects the center of the hole of the sling swivel base.

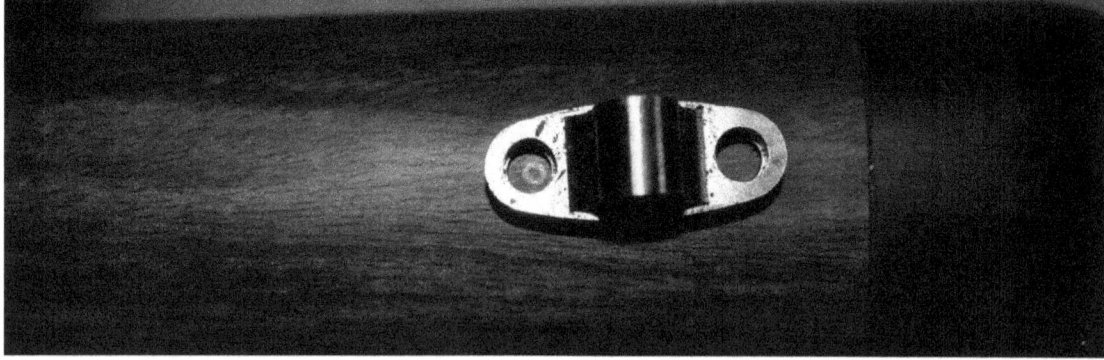

Use a small center punch to identify the center of the mark, just enough to make sure the drill bit is not going to wonder.

Use a drill the exact size of the hole in the sling swivel base to drill down through the forearm. The threaded screws which will hold the front sling swivel base must freely pass through this hole.

Place the sling swivel base over the location, place a screw through the sling swivel base and into the hole. This will insure the sling swivel base in in the correct position when drilling the second hole.

With the sling swivel base held in place with the screw, check the alignment, and using the same drill bit, drill down through the hole in the sling swivel base and into the stock.

Place screws in both of the holes. The sling swivel base should be in alignment and ready for the next step.

Using a thin sharp blade, trace an outline of the sling swivel base onto the stock. Be very carefill to follow the countour of the sling swivel base. The blade may want to veer off, following the grain of the wood. I usually make three or four passes around the sling swivel base to insure a good transfer.

You should end up with a perfect transfer of the sling swivel base on the stock. The advantage of using his method, other than a contact transfer, will become obvious when you begin inletting.

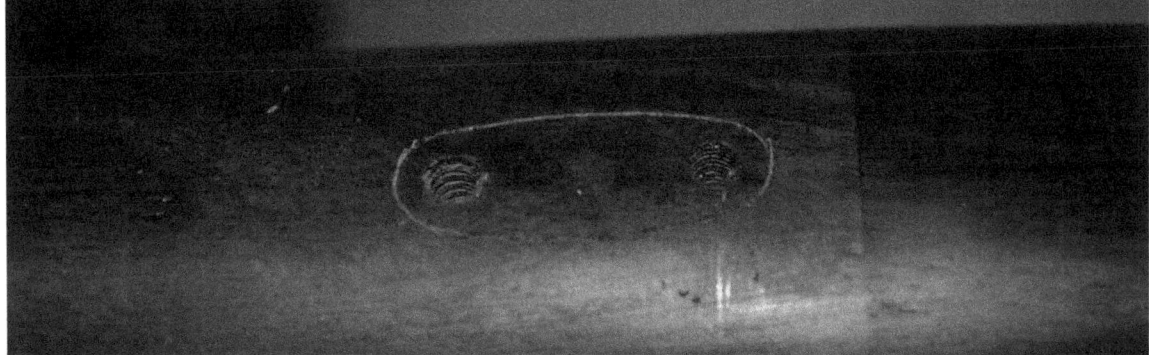

Using a medium sized cutter in your eighth inch chucked, hand held, high speed grinder, begin the inletting by removing approximately a sixteenth of wood between the two screw holes.

At this point, do not take the inletting all of the way out to the transfer line, just a little bit inside the line.

The next step is to remove the wood along the transfer up to the line. And here is the advantage of using a sharp blade to make the transfer – as you inlet up to the line, the cut of the blade will come away from the edge of the inletting. This will result in a perfect hole into which the sling swivel base is to be inserted.

Yep, I goofed on the bottom side. The tool got away from me momentarily taking away too much wood. Don't fuss, the instructions also come with details of how to correct – as in hide or cover up – small errors.

Insert the two screws into the two holes, align the screw slots. Looks good, doesn't it.

Now turn the stock over and take a look at the inside of the forearm channel. The screws are up through the barrel channel. Good. Using a punch, carefully remove the screws and the sling swivel base and set them aside. Check out the screw holes on the inside of the barrel channel.

Measure the dianeter of the nuts which came with the threaded screws. Now select a drill which is just a few thousands smaller than the nut, and drill into the holes in the forearm to a depth EQUAL TO or slightly deeper that the nut.

Insert the nuts into the holes. Is the top of the nut below the surface of the barrel channel? It should be a little below the barrel channel to insure it does not make contact with the barrel in any way.

Doing Good! Now install the sling swivel base, insert the screws and fasten the base in place with the screws.

At this point you have two options for shortening the screws to a level at the top of the nuts. "A" – You can removed one screw at a time and shorten it with your tool of choice such as a shear, bolt cutter, hack saw, etc, and insert it back into the hole and tighten it up to insure it is a proper fit. Or "B" – You can use a cut off wheel on you eighth inch chuck hand held high speed grinder and take them down to the correct length while in place. Which the following picture reflects.

The buttstock installation is almost the same. First, hold the sling swivel base in place, mark the hole and use a center punch to identify the center of the hole.

Determine the diameter of the shank of the screw and select a drill accordingly. Then TEST the decision by using a scrap piece of wood to drill a hole with the drill and then take one of the sling swivel bases screws to full depth. If it is too tight to screw the screw into the wood without excessive pressure – this will booger up the screw head – go to the nest larger drill bit. If the screw is too loose and will drop down into the hole, go to a small drill bit.

Written on the peg board tool holder about one of the benches commonly used for this purposeis a note"Base Drill – " and the numbers of the three drills used for the installation of the sling swivel bases.

Using the two screws, anchor the sling swivel base to the stock and use a thin blade to scribe a transfer around the base onto the stock.

Remove the screws and begin the two stage inletting.

Notice the small "ledge" at the left end of the inletting? Well, I saw it too, and just as casual as sipping coffee, I eased the tool into the inletting…

and took out too much wood. Notice the small gap at the end of the base? But hey, look at the screw alignment!

As I said, these instruction come with instructions on how to "correct" small errors.

Lets correct the front base error first. Remove the base and screws, apply a mold release agent to the base and the screws and set them aside.

Next, remove the rear sling swivel base and screws, apply a mold release agent to them, and set them aside.

Mix up a small amount of AcraGlas or other bedding agent. Use the provided colored die (brown) to match the color of the stock as close as possible.

Using a small object – I use a sharpened ice cream stick – to apply the bedding agent to the inside of the inletted hole. Not only is the bedding agent going to seal the wood around the base, the excess will come out of the hole through the "error" in inletting.

Most of the excess can be removed with the small object used and a careful wiping of the error with a paper towel is just good insurance. A note here: If you have inletted the base too deep, allow for the bedding agent to support the base, and tighten the screws only enough to pull the base down to the surface of the wood. Having left the nuts in the forearm recess, bring the base down to the desired level should not be a problem with the two screws.

The rear sling swivel bases is to be set in the same nanner. Do not worry about screw slot alignment at this point.

Ok, not every installation is perfect, in fact, some are fraught with problems. I recently had one that caused me to fuss considerably. The first screw hole went in nicely, but the second screw hole was in a knot and the drill dodged, resulting in…

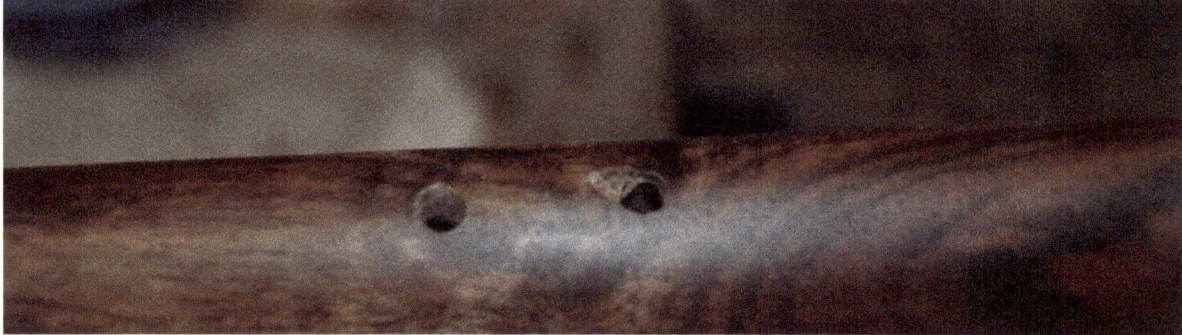

In this case, I held the base in place with one hand, and used drilled the hole in the correct location. Doesn't sound like a biggee, but it sure deflates an ego quickly. The picture was taken after I had drilled the hole, and lacking a third hand to hold the sling swivel base… Well I was short handed.

And the completed job....

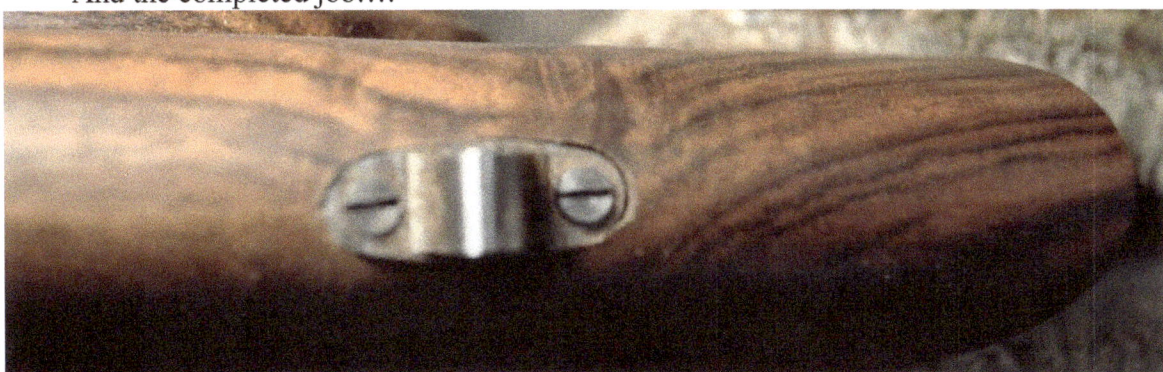

The most common sling swivel base is the screw in stud to which the sling swivel is mounted. In some instanced, the front screw is a machine threaded stud.

While there isn't an "exact" measurement for the position of the sling swivel stud from the butt of the rifle stock, I generally like 2 ½ to 3 inches. I am somewhat adamant about marking the location of a hole to be drilled, and installing sling swivel bases is no exception. I first make the location with a white pencil.

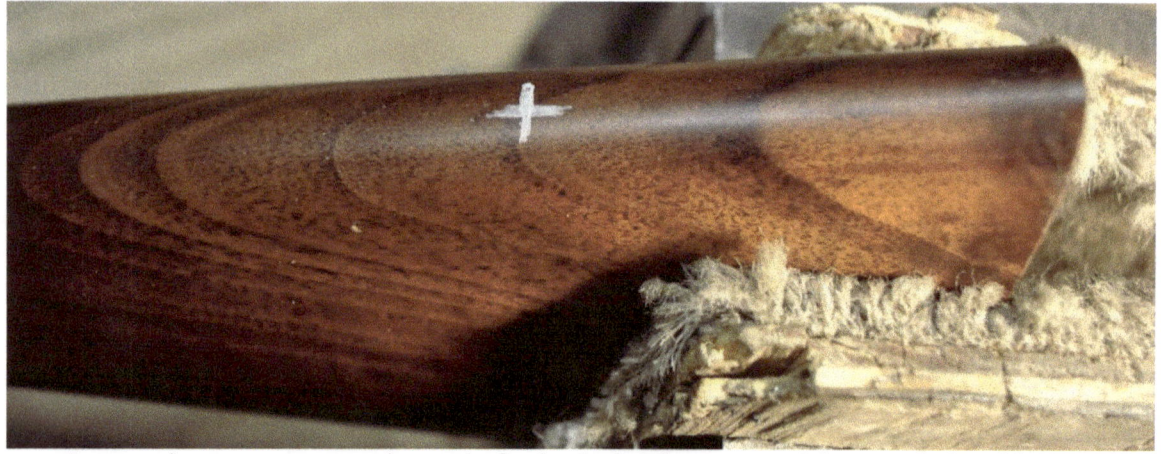

I am going to use screw in studs for both the forearm and buttstock for this installation because the forearm is very thick and wide. For a sporter stock, I would use the machine screw and nut stud, following the same basic procedure outlined earlier in this chapter.

And then center punch the hole. I use a drill smaller than the shaft of the sling swivel stud to drill a pilot hole in both the buttstock and the forearm, a 3/32" drill. I then use a drill the diameter of the base shoulder, in the case of Uncle Mike's Detachable Sling Swivel Studs, a 3/8" drill, to establish a countersink for the hole I am about to drill.

I then drill a hole using the pilot hole as a guide, with a drill that is slightly less than the diameter of the sling swiver stud. This allows the threads of the stud to fully engage the wood and the shaft of the screw to be in full contact with the wall of the hole. This procedure makes a safe installation of the stud.

There are many ways of screwing the sling swivel stud into the stock, and one if them is a drift punch of the appropriate diameter – as shown in the following picture. It works well, giving me the leverage I need for a quick installation.

And there it is, a very neat installation, no split out, no pulled wood, a nice job.

A type of sling swivel base and ring which I have heard referred to as "the old style" uses a combination of the two preceding installation techniques. Many of the production rifles of the twenty's and thirty's have these installed on them as well as some rifles from the fifty's. They may not have the appeal of the newer designs, but make no mistake, if properly installed, a set of these will last a very long time.

What I consider the primary key to success in the installation of the Screw In type sling swivel is the selection of the drill to be used in making the hole for the sling swiver stud or screw holding the sling swivel.

SECTION 19
Installing Grip Caps and Forearm Tips

It doesn't matter what kind of grip cap you are going to install, if it has a flat surface to be mated to the stock, then the grip area of the stock must also be flat. Most semi finished stocks will have carving marks on the wood in the grip cap area. Some will have rough marks on them such as the stock pictured below.

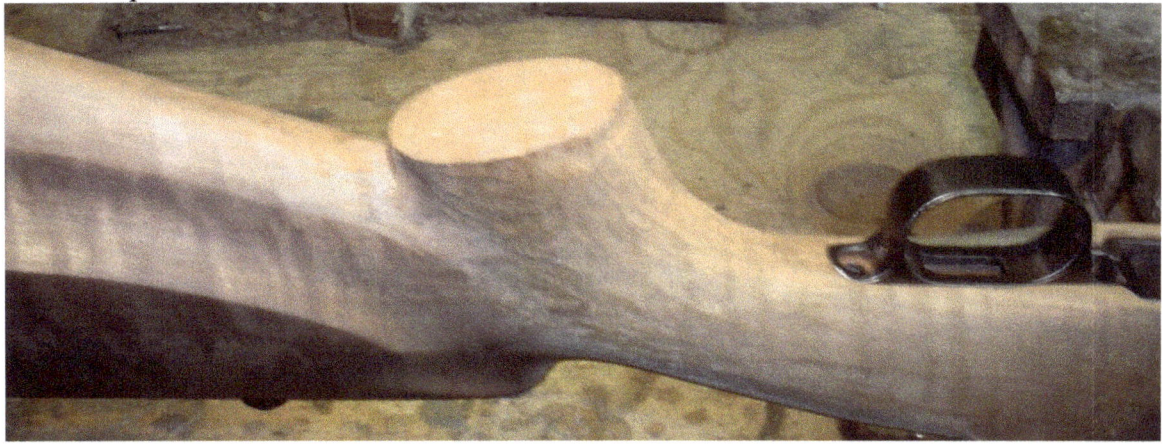

The first step in grip cap installation is to flatten the bottom of the grip area of the stock. I use a coarse double cut bastard file for this task, and shown in the following picture.

In getting the grip area flat, I use the file to get the carving marks out and establish a near flat surface. I then go to a steel block – mine are roughly ¼" thick by 1 ½" by 3" – wrap coarse sand paper around it, and slowly establish a very true surface. This is easier said than done, and I believe it is a lot more difficult than it looks.

I then remove the sand paper from the steel block, apply some blackening agent – I like to apply a lot -

And after running it across the "flat" grip cap, determine where the high points – wood to be removed – of the wood are. In the following picture, it is evident that I rocked the file and the steel block. More attention to technique is needed.

Using the steel block wrapped in coarse sand paper again, I am more attentive to my task at hand and after applying blackening compound to the steel block and rubbing it across the st0ck grip area, the improvement is noticeable. But with one definite low spot. Back to the sand paper wrapped steel block.

So there it is! All nice and pretty and FLAT! Take your time with this phase of the task, gaps are really hard to disguise after the fact.

To this point, the preparation for installing any grip cap is the same. The following is grip cap type specific. The first to be covered is for an ebony grip cap affixed to the stock, and then a skeleton grip cap inletted over it. This is a difficult task, but it sure looks nice.

This is what I would call an insurance action. When applying a wooden or horn grip cap, this step is essential. When applying a steel grip cap, it is not as essential, but it will point out of when a steel grip cap is not absolutely flat. Take the time to run the grip cap across the steel block wrapped with sand paper and find out. With a metal grip cap, use a finer sand paper. It is a lot easier to mate two flat surfaces, and the eye appeal of such a joint is really nice.

With both surfaces flat, it is time to attach the ebony (wood) grip cap to the stock. I use Brownell's AcraGlas for this purpose, and have for many years. The key to using AcraGlas – I believe – is to follow the formula for the mix, and to mix it a full four minutes. I coat both surfaces before joining the two.

With the grip cap in place, I use tubular surgical tubing to wrap the grip cap in place on the stock. And I use a lot of tubing, starting off with a length of almost two (2) feet.

With the grip cap firmly in place – I let it dry overnight before doing any trimming – I trim the grip cap roughly to the size of the stock using a file.

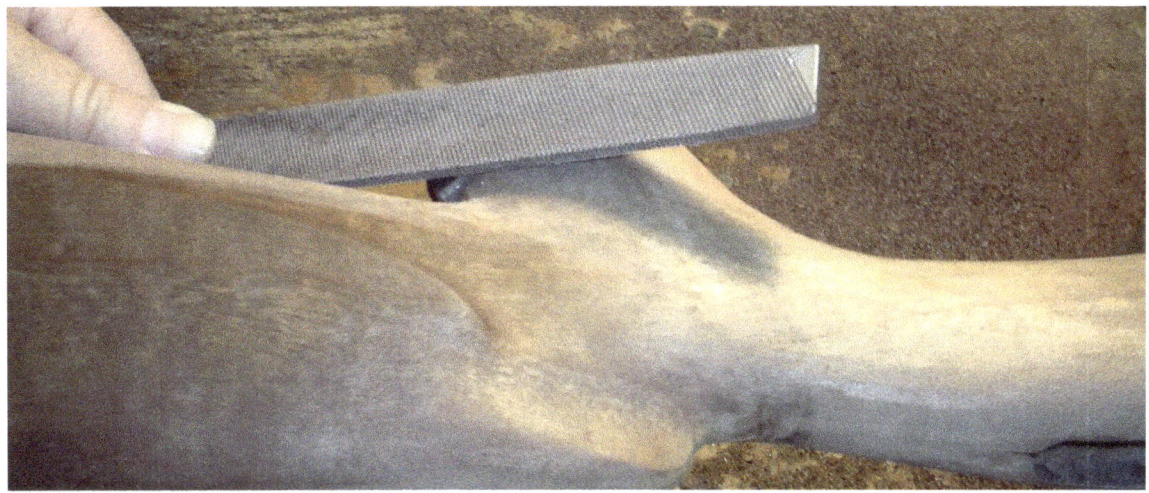

Please do not use a rasp to remove wood from bony grip cap, it will tear off large chunks of the brittle wood and make a mess of your job. Use a double cut file which will leave a smooth surface behind.

This is the point in which the grip cap area can be shaped to meet your requirements, or more specifically, to the grip cap you are going to apply.

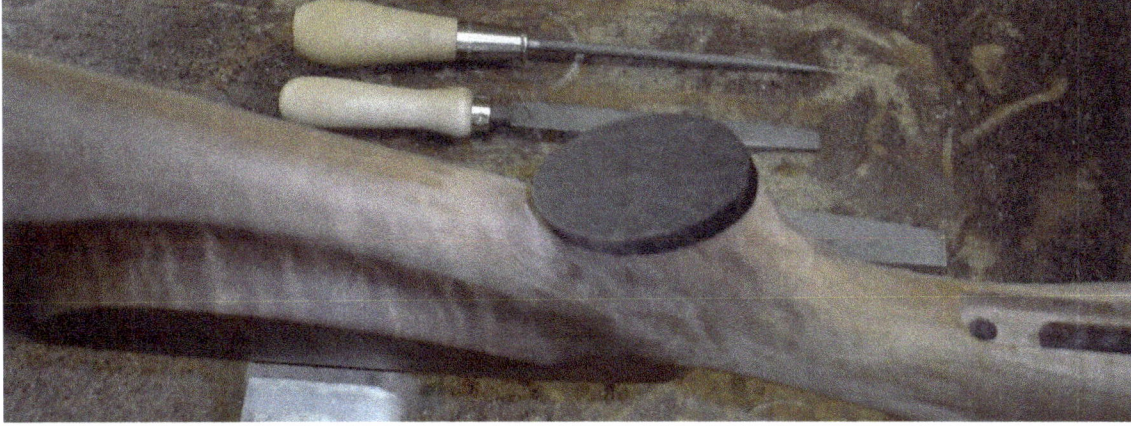

Nice, huh! A lot of pains taking work went into shaping this grip cap as shown. Many people will have no idea of what is entailed in creating this piece of work. Some do.

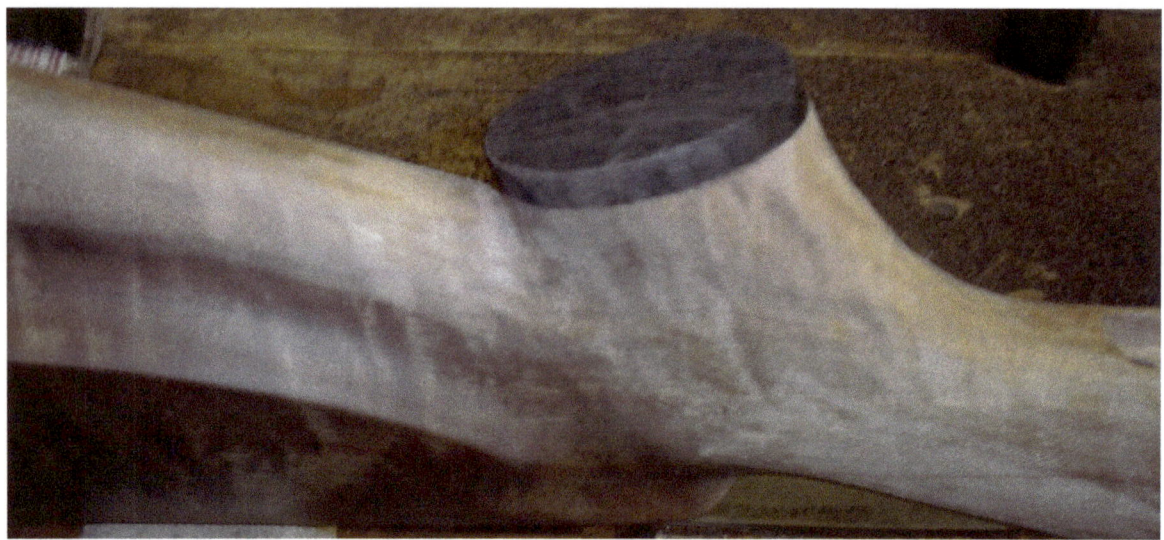

At this point the ebony grip cap can be contoured similar to that of an old Mauser horn grip cap as the following picture illustrates.

But if you want to inlet a skeleton grip cap over the ebony, leaving a small ebony spacer below the skeleton grip cap …. Place a skeleton grip cap on the flatten block of ebony and using a fine blade in an Exacto knife, scribe the inside of the skeleton grip cap on the ebony block. At this time I am not interested in the outer measurement, other than insuring there is sufficient wood surrounding the skeleton grip cap.

To insure I can clearly see the scribe of the skeleton grip cap, I use a white pencil to run over it, making it clearly visible.

I then go to my trusty hand held high speed grinder with a #115 cutter. I strongly suggest that you use a new cutter, a dull cutter will grab and tear and cause you problems. Start the carving at the ends. I plunge down approximately a sixteenth inch for a start, and then complete the shallow cut all around the grip cap leaving a small space around the scribe for the final fitting.

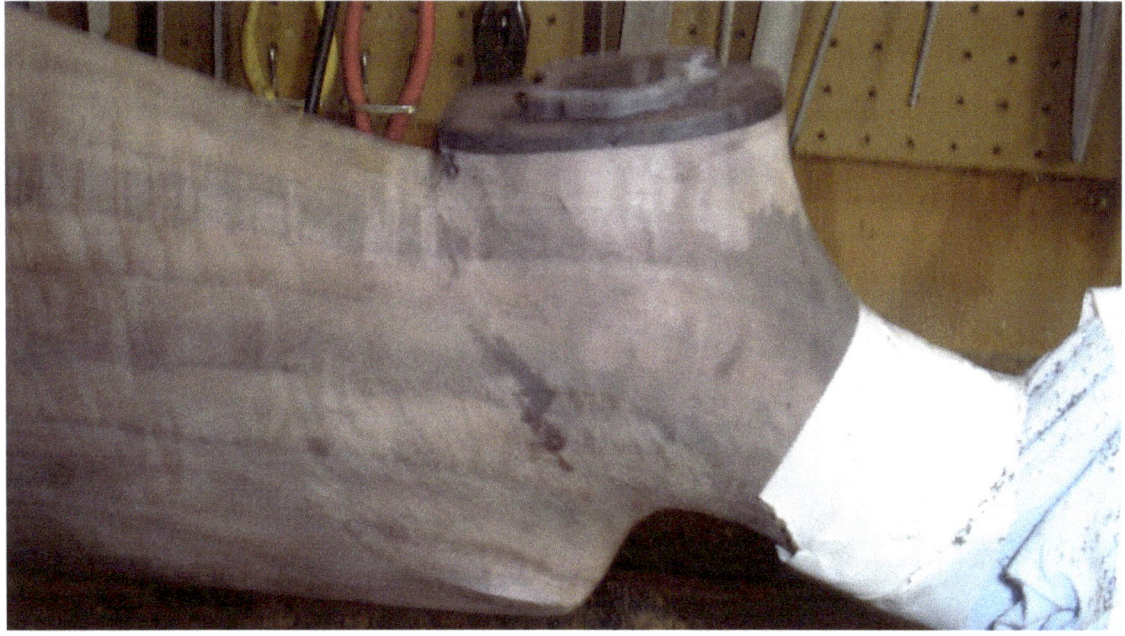

When inletting to the scribe line, I have found that I can more precisely inlet up to the scribe line by placing the stock on the side. Remember, the scribe line is on the inside of the skeleton grip cap, inlet up to the scribe line, but do not remove it!

With one depth accomplished, I make another plunge to within a sixteenth of the stock, and complete the inletting around the scribe area.

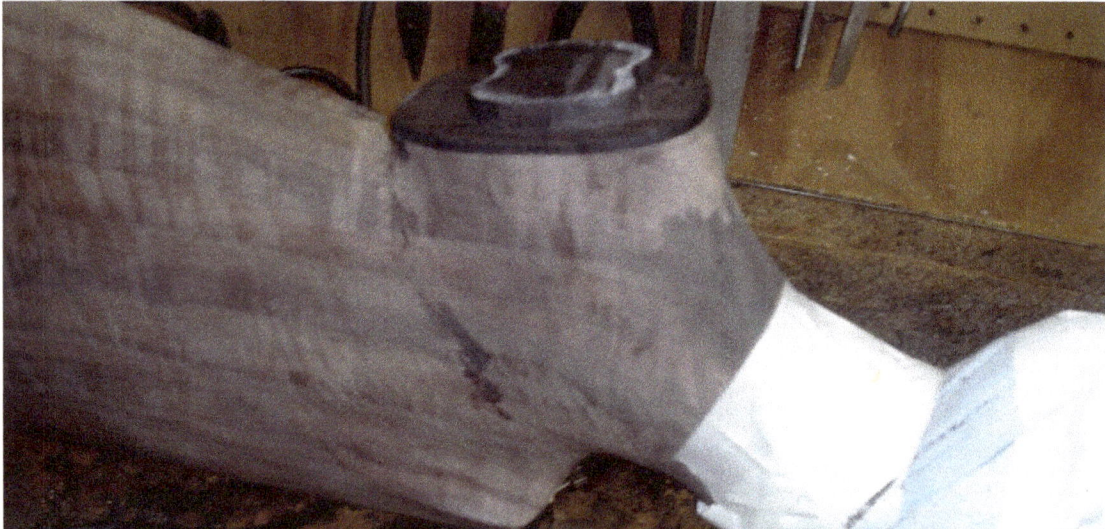

At this point, you have removed most of the excess wood and are ready to try the skeleton grip cap for fit.

While it may not the best medium available, black on black, I still use blackening agent to coat the inside and bottom of the skeleton grip cap to insure contact with the ebony block. At this point, drill the stock with a drill equal to the core of the screws to be used, allowing room in the hole for the threads of the screw to engage the wood. Screw the screws down tight, aligning the screw slot to the length of the stock.

It is time for some judicious file work. Take it slow and easy, just a little at a time. Start with the front of the grip cap, go to the sides, and finally the back. Be careful to bring the wood down to the grip cap, keeping the width of the grip area of the stock equal in thickness to the width of the grip cap.

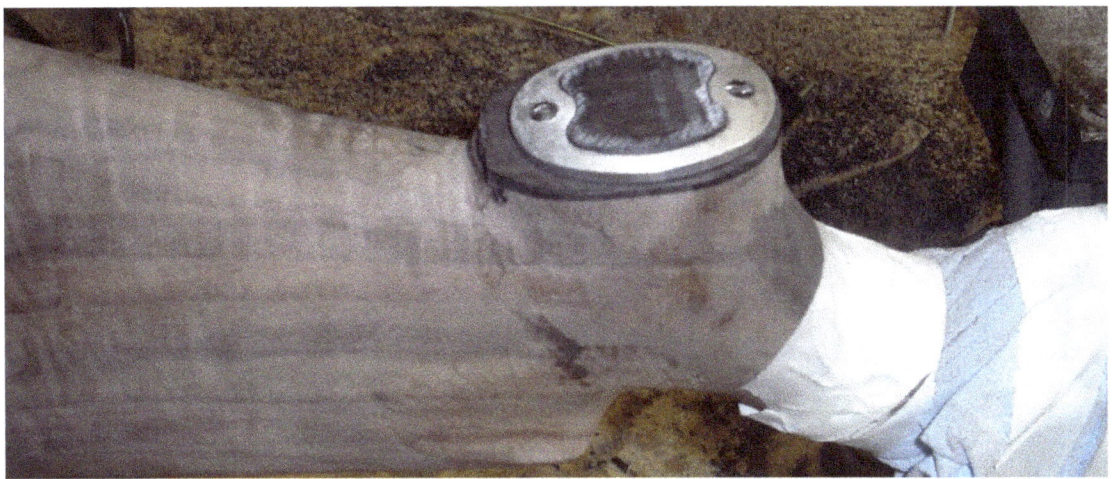

    With the grip cap in place, with the screws at full depth, file the screw heads down to the surface of the skeleton grip cap. Use a sanding block with 320 grit wet or dry sand paper to crown the ebony to match the contour of the skeleton grip cap. Look at that thin ebony spacer, it really looks good.

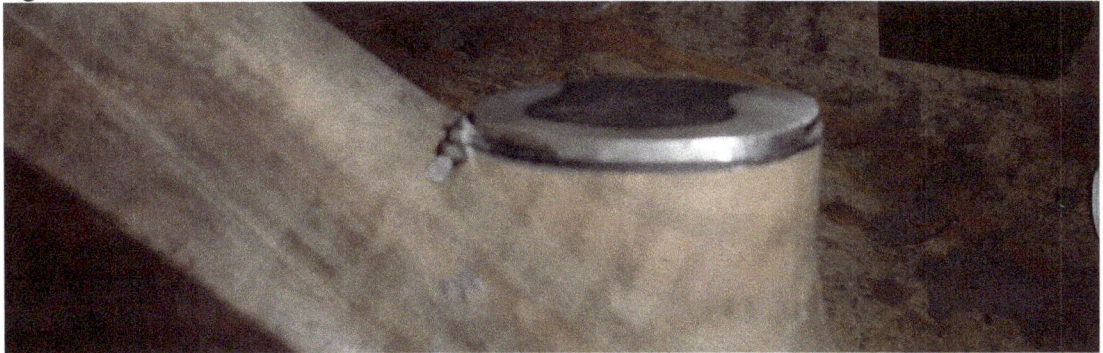

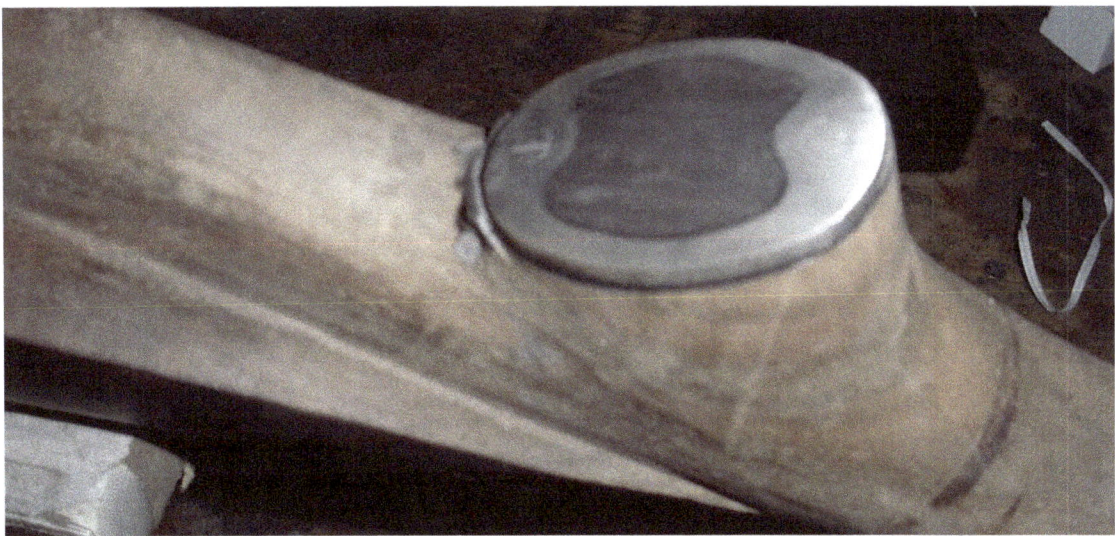

    Looks good doesn't it, a little work with the rat tail file at the back, some sanding around the edge with an art gum eraser wrapped with 320 grip sanding paper and you have a finished product, as shown in the following picture.

In the event you want to apply a skeleton grip cap, but want to use the natural wood of the stock the preceding procedure should work. However, if there is not enough wood got a skeleton grip cap installation, there is a saluting. Using the small piece of the forearm you cut off to install an ebony forearm tip, make a slab approximately 3/8" thick and apply it to the stock as per the preceding instructions. Apply the grip cap, make a scribe outline of the interior of the grip cap and shape the grip cap to the stock, insuring you have enough wood for the installation.

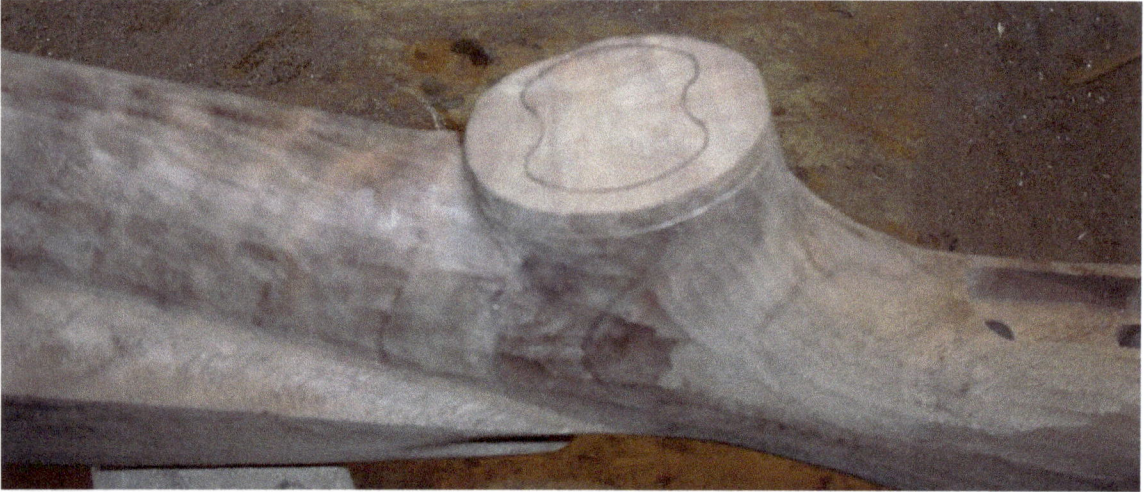

Notice the joint outline? Ok, now inlet down to the joint line, letting the skeleton grip cap sit directly onto the stock wood, with the forearm tip wood protrude up through the skeleton grip cap. Unless you tell them, no one will ever know what you have done.

Installing Forearm Tips

I was once told that the reason for forearm tips was to prevent moisture from entering the end grain of the stock. I don't know if I believe that or not, it makes sense, but ….

Regardless, I like a nice contrasting forearm tip on a rifle stock. There are many ways to install a forearm tip, and while I do not always agree with the choice of wood or angle of the attachment, personal taste cannot be fully explained.

It seems that each custom rifle builder or Arms Maker has their own idea of what the measurement from the receiver to the end of the stock – including the forearm tip – should be. The following are pictures of some of the stocks in the shop as I write this. The following picture is of a Remington Model 700 in 270 Winchester. The forearm as measured from the recoil lug to the end of the forearm tip is 9 7/8", with the measurement from the recoil lug to the joint of the forearm tip is 8 1/8".

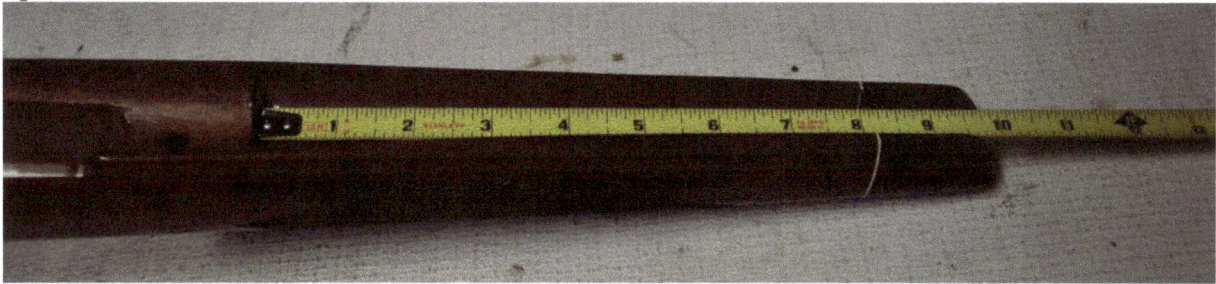

The following picture is of a Weatherby Mark 22, twenty –two caliber rifle. The measurement as measured from the receiver junction with the barrel to the end of the stock is 10 ¼", and the measurement from the receiver junction with the barrel to the forward edge of the forearm tip – as the top of the stock – is 8 5/8".

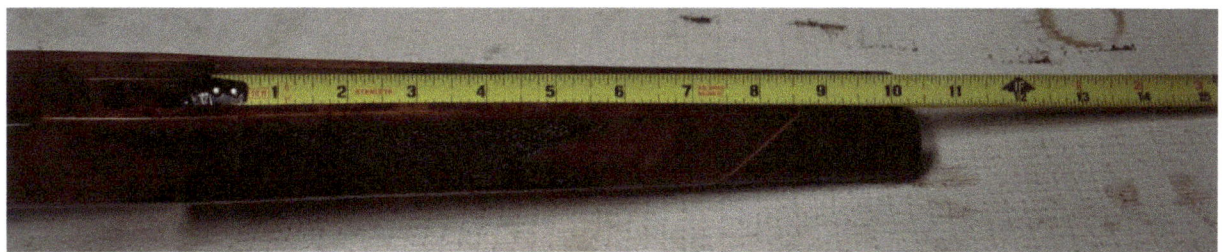

The following picture is of a forearm of a rifle build on an FN Mauser action with a #3 contour 24" long barrel. The forearm, as measured from the recoil lug area to the end of the forearm tip is 10 ¼".

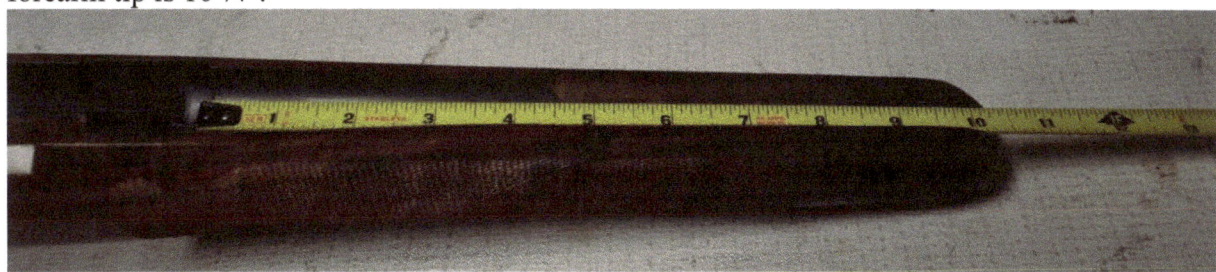

The following picture is of a rifle built on an FN Mauser action, and barreled with a Heavy Sporter / Light Varmint configuration that is 26" long. The forearm, as measured from the recoil lug to the end of the forearm tip is 11 3/8".

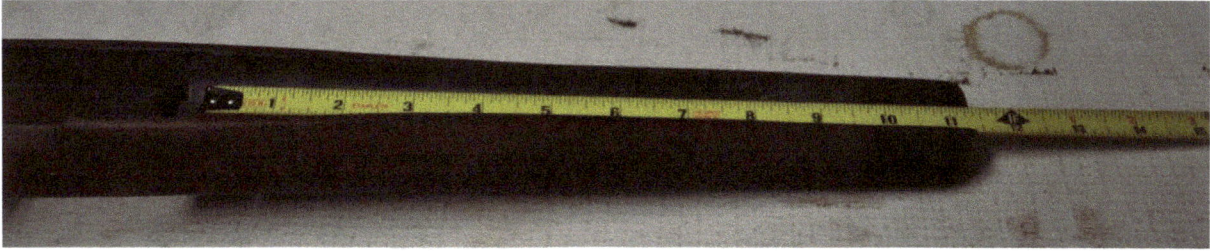

327

So with the decision to install a forearm tip – in this case, one of ebony – the distance from the recoil lug to the proposed end of the stock is to be made. In this case, the Light Sporter stock is going to be used for a FN Mauser in 300 H&H Magnum using a #3 ½ contour barrel 26 inches long. So I want to make the initial cut 8 1/2" from the recoil lug area.

I use a compound miter saw for this cut as it provides a nice clean cut. But before we can make the cut, we want to be sure the cut is square. Laying the stock on its top, the cut will be square one direction, but if the stock is placed against the back fence, the cut will be on an angle. So, first place the stock on the saw, against the back fence, with the location of the proposed cut directly under the blade.

Now mark the stock at the point at which it comes into contact with the fence at each end. I use an old micrometer caliper for this task. Now measure the width of the stock at each of these two points.

Now subtract the difference between the two widths – in this case the difference is ½". Divide it by two, and make a spacer of that width, in this case ¼". I go to the scrap box, remove a small section of wood – usually left over from cutting a stock for a recoil pad or adjustable butt plate – and use the belt sander to achieve the thickness I want.

Place the spacer at the end of the fence nearest the blade, and you are ready for a cut.

With the stock cut correctly, I like to insure the forearm tip is likewise prepared. I place the block on the 6 x 36 belt sander and create a flat on one of the sides. This will be the top of the forearm. Because the block is small, I use a piece of scrap lumber as a backup against the fence to provide some stability during the cut. Notice, I am cutting from the other side of the fence.

Thus, even if the saw blade is not exactly true/square, the stock will be at one angle and the forearm tip will be at a corresponding opposite angle and the joint will be good.

Mark the end of the stock with a tentative location of the barrel depth, and indicate – marked with crossed lines, where you are going to drill a dowel hole.

After you have identified the hole location, use a small center punch to further identify the proposed hole location. Securing the stock in a vise, place a small shot in the countersunk hole. Not quite half of the shot should be exposed above the wood surface. And before you spend more time than necessary placing the small shot in the countersunk hole, invest in a pair of long nose tweezers. It makes the job a whole lot easier.

Place the forearm tip on top of the end of the stock, position it with the sanded flat on showing as a continuation of the top of the stock, and "strike" the end of the ebony block. I use a nylon faced hammer.

This will result in the shot transferring an exact location for the hole in the ebony block to be drilled and in exactly the correct corresponding position.

I use ¼" hard wood dowel 1 ½" long to assist the joint between the stock and the forearm tip. I use a 5/16" drill to drill approximately 7/8" deep in both the stock and the forearm tip. Again, I have bound the best adhesive to use for the bond is AcraGlas. After mixing it up, I add some black die and stir it in and then fill the fill the respective holes approximately half full, then coat the surfaces of the two pieces.

Using a piece of surgical tubing, I thread it through the magazine well of the rifle stock, tie it so I had a loop approximately 6" long, place the ebony block on the rifle stock, slip the surgical tubing loop over the ebony block and then align the ebony block insuring it has sufficient wood showing on all sides.

You can use a block plane, a course cut file, even a draw knife. Or you can use a belt sander. While I have used all of the cited tools, I tend to stick to the belt sander most of the time when installing a rounded forearm tip. The single largest problem with using a belt sander for removing the excess wood from a forearm tip is to focus on not getting into the stock, and creating an unacceptable angle on the forearm tip, as shown in the following picture.

If it is to be rounded, the full length of the forearm tip must be reduced to the dimensions of the stock at the point of the joint.

But, with a little care, and some caution, the excess wood can be removed and the ebony block contoured to the stock.

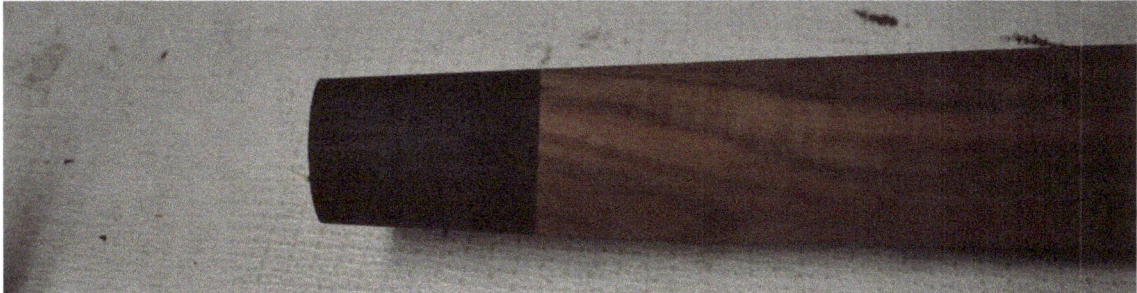

Another example of a forearm tip installation is one which call a "Half Diamond" insert. On this project, although the forearm was light contour, I felt the half diamond inserted ebony forearm tip would look nice, if not different. The rifle the stock was to go on was a "Spec" rifle with no customer waiting for it. A shop project to fill in some time and check out new procedures. No, this was to be mine, built to my liking.

Using a 3 ½ to 1 template, I traced the proposed cut onto the forearm. Holding a plastic template in one hand, and a pencil in the other, and hoping nothing moved unexpectedly, I managed to get the lines on the wood but made a mental note that this process would need improvement.

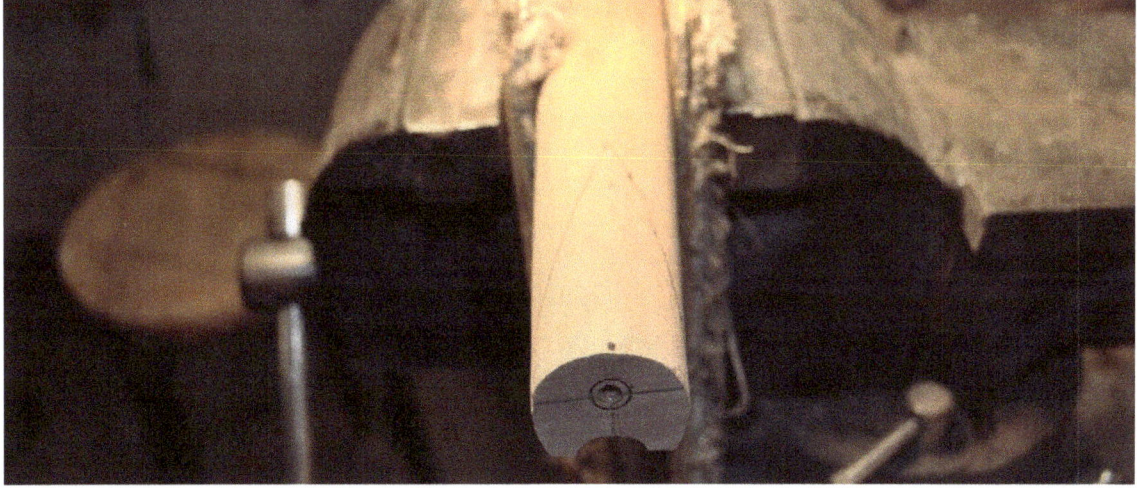

Slipping the shaped ebony block into the stock showed no large errors in my cutting, but a liberal dosing of black impregnated AcraGlass was applied anyway.

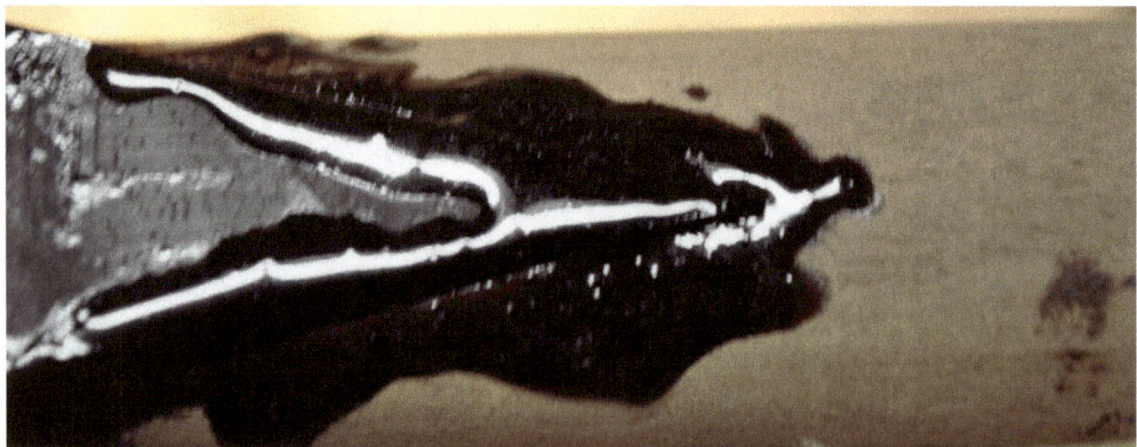

With the AcraGlas dried the following day, I used an 80 grit belt to remove most of the ebony, and then went to my trusty file to bring the ebony down to stock level. Doesn't that fiddle back come out nicely? Imagine how that figure will come out with a good dosing of Alkanet Oil….

Yep, right at the point of the insertion, the wood did not match completely and the black impregnated AcraGlas was use to fill it in. Sitting and looking at it, and trying to figure out which took would provide the best cut the next time, I decided that the joint point of the two pieces of wood would be an excellent place for the inletted sling swivel base!

Yep, that's a lot of hard black wood to remove from the barrel channel. But I just happen to have a hand held high speed grinder with a quarter inch chuck and a bit that eats hard wood.

With the forearm tip secured to the stock, if it is to be a snabble, you must outline the shoulders of the snabble so as to not cut the forearm tip too small.

SECTION 20
Recoil Bolt

Many times we are faced with a perceived need, and no knowledge of how to accomplish it. While working on a very light weight 375 H&H Mag, I was uncomfortable with just the single recoil bolt behind the recoil lug. I have seen far too many heavy caliber rifles with the <u>wood just ahead of the trigger</u> cracked, and sometimes shoved back into the trigger. So, I developed a simple recoil bolt for this application. The following describes how I make and install them.

After determining the exact location of where I want the supplemental recoil bolt, I mark it in white pencil, and the center punch the location of the hole I will drill.

For this installation, I want to use a drill which is slightly smaller that the screw diameter. I would like the screw threads to engage the wood of the stock, but not more than ten to fifteen thousands, just enough to give it a little bite. It is the bonding agent which will set the screw in place and provide additional strength of the stock.

I prefer to use a drill press for this task, and use a small tri square held against the stock to insure the stock is "flat." With everything in place, drill down approximately a quarter inch,

check the placement of the stock to insure it is being held flat, and drill through the stock.

With the hole drilled all of the way through, I make a "test run" with the screw I will use for the supplemental recoil bolt. I want it tight enough to engage the interior of the hole. I screw it through the stock, being careful not to let the screw head come in contact with the stock.

I know, the following picture really looks ugly, but you haven't seen anything lately. It gets worse, a lot worse.

With the total length measurement made of the screw, I subtract a quarter inch (1/4") to allow for insetting the screw and have a space of 1/8 inch on both sides.

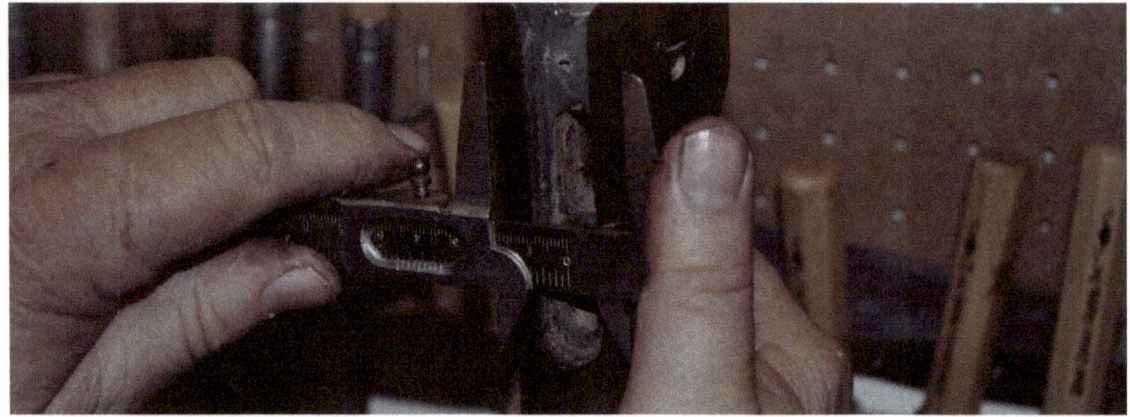

Transfer the measurement to the screw, BUT remember to subtract the ¼". This "short" screw will allow sufficient space for a cap of filler to hide the screw location.

I have found that the 1/8" chuck hand held high speed grinded equipped with a cut off wheel is the tool to use. It is time to trim it back to the desired length.

With the screw trimmed to the desired length, I position it verticle, and cut a slot in it for a screw driver which will be used up insert/place it in the stock.

And that is the finished product. No, it isn't great looking, but it will serve the purpose intended and cost less than a quarter.

After coating the inside of the hole with black AcraGlas, I dip the screw in the AcraGlas, in this case, any excess will come out one side or the other. I want to be very sure there is plenty around the screw and in the hole.

Starting the screw by hand, it will only go a couple of threads before becoming too tight to turn any further.

Switching to a screw driver, I use one hand to plug the bottom of the hole, and the other to slowly screw the screw into the hole. I use a tooth pick to insure there is a pool of AcraGlas at the base of the screw, ready to be carried into the hole and fill in between the threads.

Watch the tip of your screw driver, if it starts to slip out of the slot, stop and reposition it. You do not want the screw driver to come out of the screw slot and damage the stock.

With the screw taken about an eighth inch below the surface of the wood, use a toothpick or small pointed object to fill the gap behind the screw with AcraGlas.

Oh yeah! That's what we want, a completely filled hole, and a little puddle on top. If AcraGlas is used, be aware that if not allowed to "settle" before use, there may be small bubbles in the mixture. Placing a bench lamp over the area will eliminate most of this activity.

Oh, the other side… Ok, cut a piece of masking tape about an inch and a half long and use it to "cap" the pool. Do not rub it flat, a little rise is fine. The excess will come off with a file and sand paper later on.

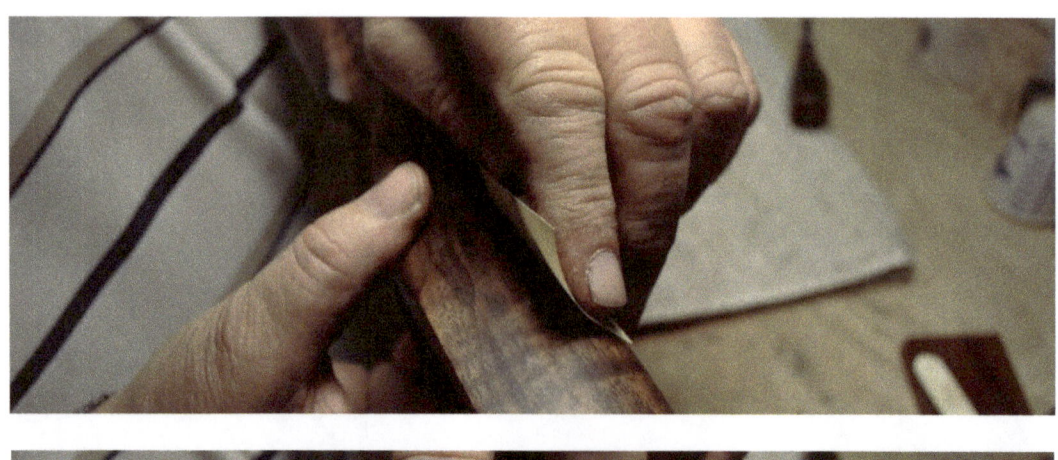

Now repeat the filling process on the other side. I have found that a very small screw driver works well for this purpose as it "carries" a lot of material at one time. Be patient, do not attempt to place a large amount of the filler material in the hole at one time.

When filling the hole, I prefer to let the filler material flow into the hole and gradually fit it. I find that I get fewer voids and achieve a better fill.

I prefer to allow the AcraGlas to harden overnight. The following day I use a metal file to remove the excess AcraGlas down to the wood, and then with 320 grit wet/dry sandpaper, contour the Acraglass to the stock and then finish it off with 600 grip wet/dry sand paper.

I then apply finish to the area and blend it in if it is an oil finish, or sand and buff if it is a gloss finish.

For those areas in which these is little room for the application, the receding works well. However, when there is room for the recoil bolt, I prefer to use those manufactured by Tally.

First thing to do is identify the position on the stock. A lite pencil line on the outside of the stock indicates the horizontal position.

To determine the vertical position, a depth gauge is used to first determine the top of the recoil lug area of the stock.

This measurement is transferred to the outside of the stock. From this line as second line is drawn 3/16" lower. From this line, a third line is drawn 1/8" lower. The distance between the first and second lines if the thickness of wood between the top of the stock recoil lug area and the Talley Recoil Lug. The intersection of the third line and the vertical line is the point at which the stock is to be drilled for the Talley Recoil Lug.

With the location identified, to include a quarter inch "target" with a center, it is time to drill the hole for the tube which is also .250". I do this on a drill press with the stock in a machinist vice with a parallel between the stock and the vice jay to insure the hole is drilled parallel to the top of the stock.

I screw the end onto the tube to insure it functions, and then I use several light taps on the end piece to make an impression in the stock. This compressed wood identifies the area to be removed – to the depth of the tube – with either a hand held high speed grinder OR with a piloted drill with the pilot being the diameter of the tube .250", and the drill being the diameter of the end piece. I used the piloted drill as I install enough of them to justify the drill's cost.

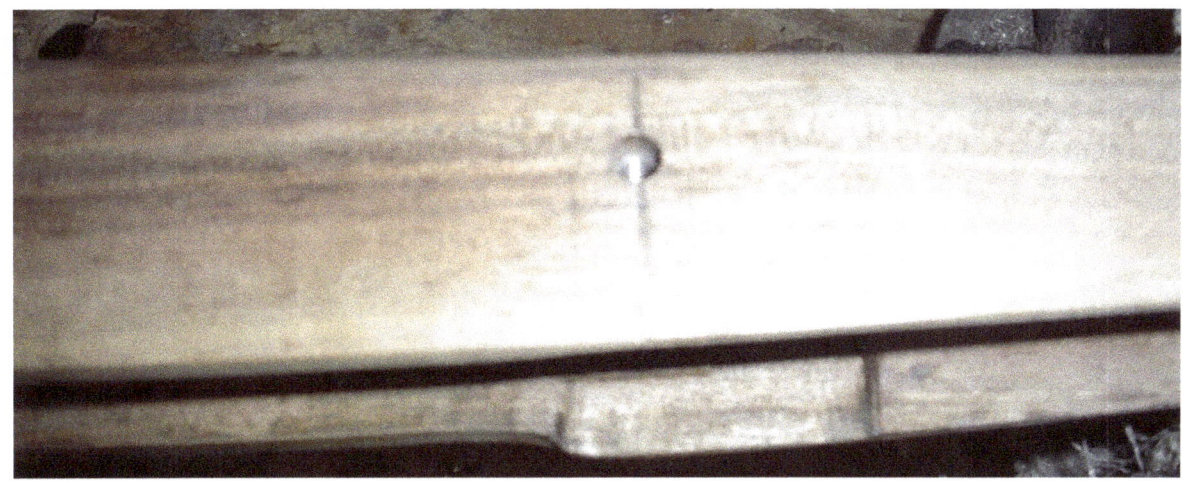

The following picture was taken after the recoil bolt was blued and permanently installed.

Section 21
Glossary of Terms

Action Screws
Action screws are those used to hold the action to the stock or buttstock. Most original action screws are slotted, but more and more rifles are going to socket headed **screws.**

Adjustable Butt plates
Adjustable butt plates are but plates, usually made of aluminum, which mount to the sole of the buttstock, and to which a recoil pad or buttplate is attached, and which allow adjustment of the plate holding the recoil pad up, down, sideways, or canted. There are a variety of adjustable butt plates available, three of which are shown. The center one is a product of the Stock Shop and features movement up, down, left, right, and unlimited canting and then being locked in plate with an allen wrench inserted through a hole into the recoil pad. In this manner, once the pad is mounted on the gun, and the recoil pad mounted to the adjustable buttplate, adjustment of the recoil pad's position requires an allen wrench inserted into a hole in the recoil pad, no removal of the recoil pad to expose the adjustment.

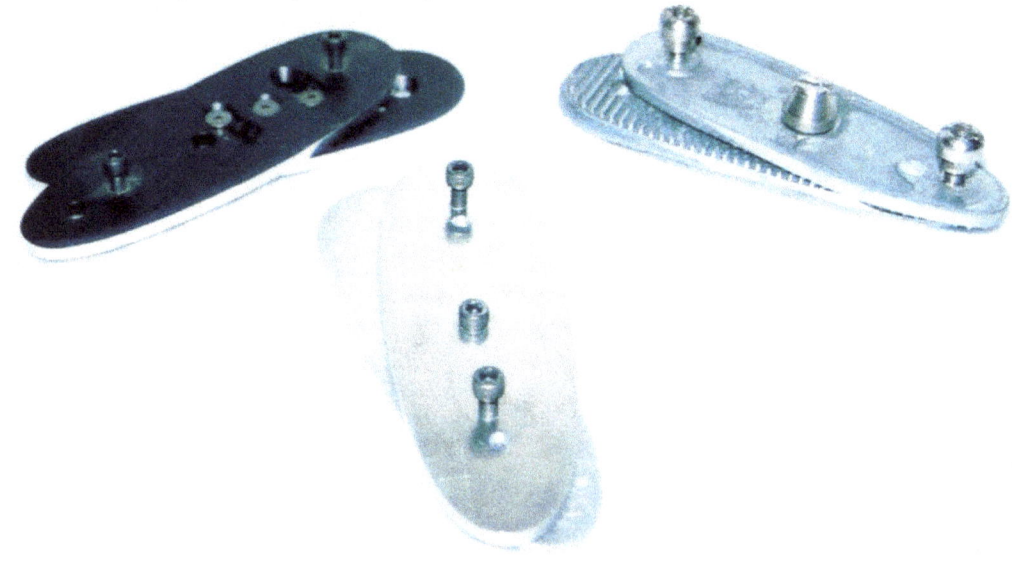

Anticipated Border

The anticipated border is the temporary line, usually a white line, to which opposing lines are cut. It is the anticipated border which will become the actual point pattern border when all lines are extended out from the master lines to a distance desired. Because cutting checkering lines is not an exact science – rather an art form – the checkered lines may not run exactly true because of the skill of the person checkering, the curvature of the wood, or the need to make a "correction" of previous lines.

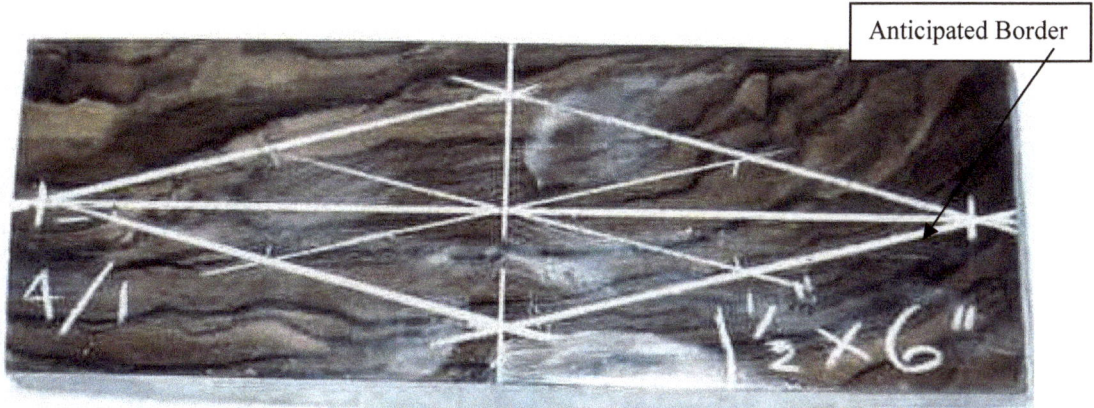

Barrel Channel

The barrel channel is the groove or inletting in the wood into which the barrel rests and is partially surrounded by wood from the forearm. On semi-finished rifle stocks, the wood between the forearm tip and the receiver will often have only a narrow groove – often a half inch – cut into the wood. Other stocks will have a barrel channel inletted to accommodate a barrel contour, such as military step contour, light sporter weight barrel, etc.

Bead

A checkering bead is the rounded border surrounding the checkering pattern. The difference between the border and the bead is the border is flat, and the bead is cut with a convex cutter and is rounded.

Bolt Clearance Cut

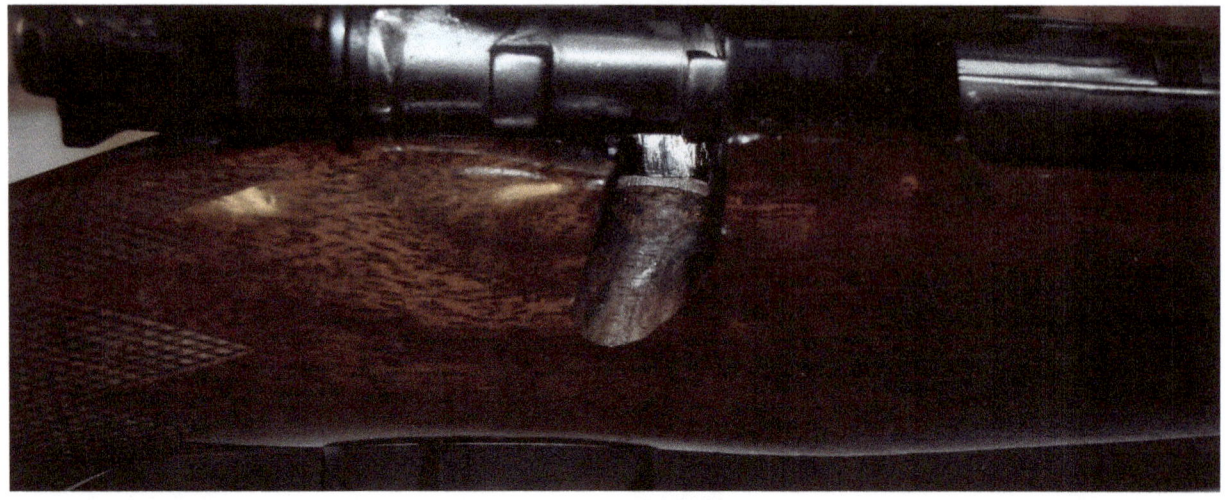

Border
A checkering pattern with a border is one with parallel lines to the outside of the checkering lines. Borders can be used to emphasize the detail of the checkering, or they can be used to hide a run-over made when cutting the edge of the pattern.

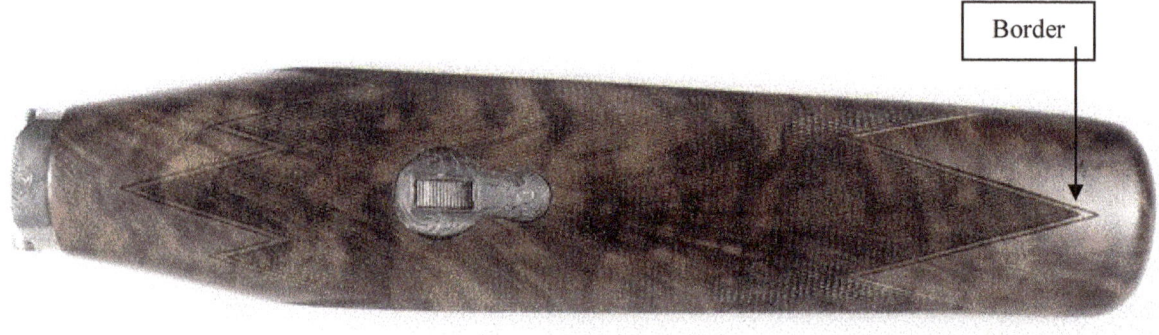

Borderless
A checkering pattern considered borderless is a pattern in which the edges are a single cut line into which checkering lines terminate.

Butt – *see Measurements*

The butt of the buttstock or stock is the "end of the stock" which is placed against the shoulder for aiming and/or firing. It is to the butt of the stock that the recoil pad is attached. This is sometimes referred to as the "sole" of the stock.

Buttplate

A buttplate is usually made of steel, plastic, or hardened rubber and is affixed to the butt of the stock or buttstock with screws or other fastening devices. The buttplate is not intended to reduce recoil, but is intended to protect the butt of the stock or buttstock from abuse and the elements. Many arms makers used the buttplate to identify their company by having their name, logo or other recognizable feature molded into the buttplate.

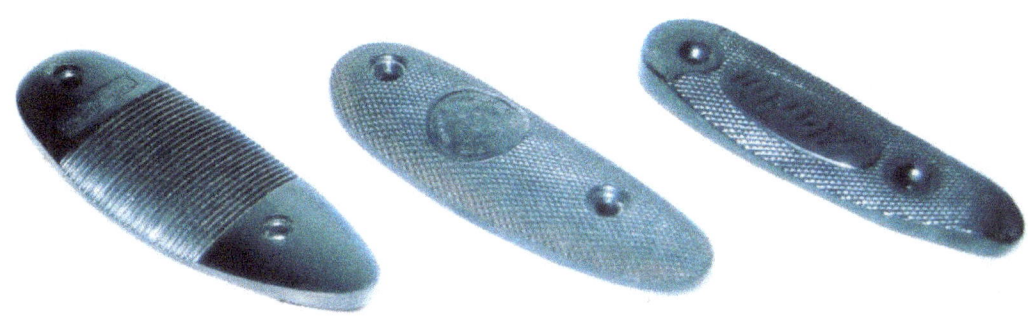

Cartridge Trap

A cartridge trap is a device, usually made of metal, inletted into the belly of a stock - especially European hunting rifles and drillings – used to store additional ammunition for emergency use. While not common in today's hunting rifles, the requirement to install one is a challenge and should be approached with caution. A correctly inletted cartridge trap is a beautiful item, one that is not correctly inletted is a mess.

Cast – *see Measurements*

The cast of a stock is determined as being the distance between the centerline of the stock, and the imaginary centerline extending from the top center of the barrel(s) back to the butt. A simple way of measuring the cast of a stock is top lay a straight edge – a metal yard stick will work well – down the center of the barrel rib and extending to the butt of the stock and determining cast as the difference between the two lines.

Centerline

The top centerline of a stock is a straight line from the top center of the receiver, and to the top center of the butt end of the buttstock. The bottom centerline is a straight line from the bottom center of the receiver to the bottom center – toe – of the buttstock. The location of these lines is necessary in determining toe in or toe out of the stock.

Crotch Figure

This is the term used to describe the grain or figure in a piece of wood coming from the crotch or "Y" of a tree. The crotch grain is very dense, and if not properly dried, subject to checking-cracking.

Edger, checkering

An edger is a checking tool with teeth much like a hand saw and is used for cutting/deepening the edges of a pattern. Edgers come in sixty degree or ninety degree angles. I favor the sixty degree edger when one is needed. When using an edger on highly figured wood, one must be extremely careful or the edger will pull wood, leaving unsightly and hard to repair gaps.

Fiddleback Figure

Fill-in Pattern

A fill-in pattern is a pattern on which all of the borders have been pre-determined. The pattern can be a point pattern or one with flowing borders such as is shown in the borderless pattern illustration .

Fleur de Lis

Fleur de Lis is the term used to describe the figure in the checkering pattern. There are many variations of the fleur, with most developed to suit the checkering style of the person performing the work.

Flat Top Checkering

Flat top Checkering is the term used to describe – very simply – checkering whose tops are not brought to a point, but left flat on top. Many of the older guns have this type of checkering.

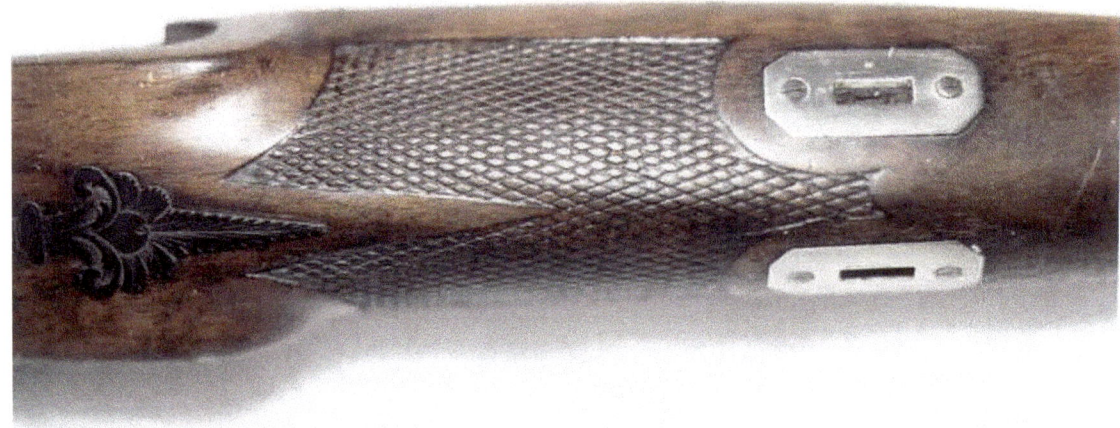

Forearm Bushing or Rosette

The fore arm bushing is a metal bushing, visible on the bottom of the forearm into which the forearm screws are affixed. The bushing serving as a "nut" to the forearm screw. The accurate location of the forearm bushing can be difficult.

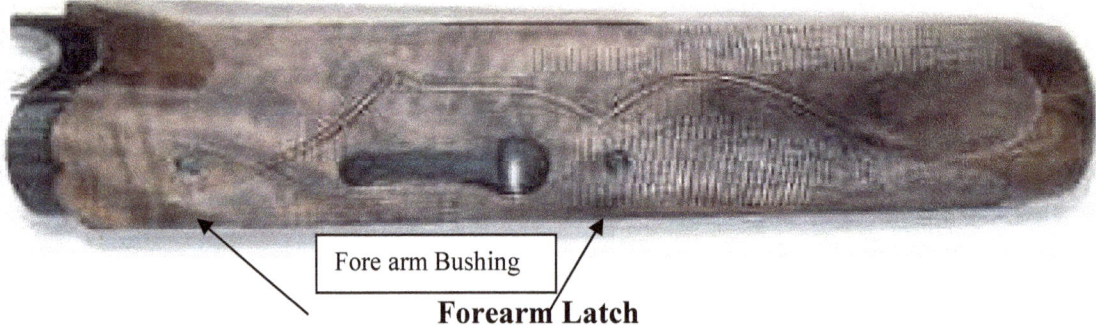

Fore arm Bushing

Forearm Latch

The forearm latch is the means by which the forearm is "Latched" to the barrel and receiver. Some forearms may not have a visible forearm latch, using spring tension alone, others, such as the Krieghoff, Perazzi and Beretta forearm latches are evident in their appearance and functionality.

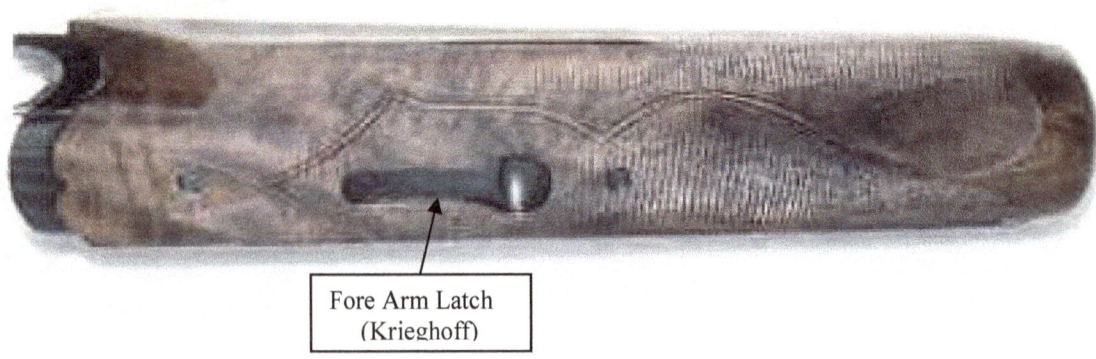

Fore Arm Latch (Krieghoff)

Forearm Tip

The forearm tip is not only decorative, but functional. It is often made of a contrasting wood, such as ebony, but for many years buffalo horn was used. It serves a functional role in that it seals the end grain of the forearm from moisture. Forearm tips can be installed at different angles as well as an insert. There are many methods of attaching the forearm tip to the stock.

The following picture shows a forearm tip of ebony installed on a forearm for an L. C. Smith as an insert.

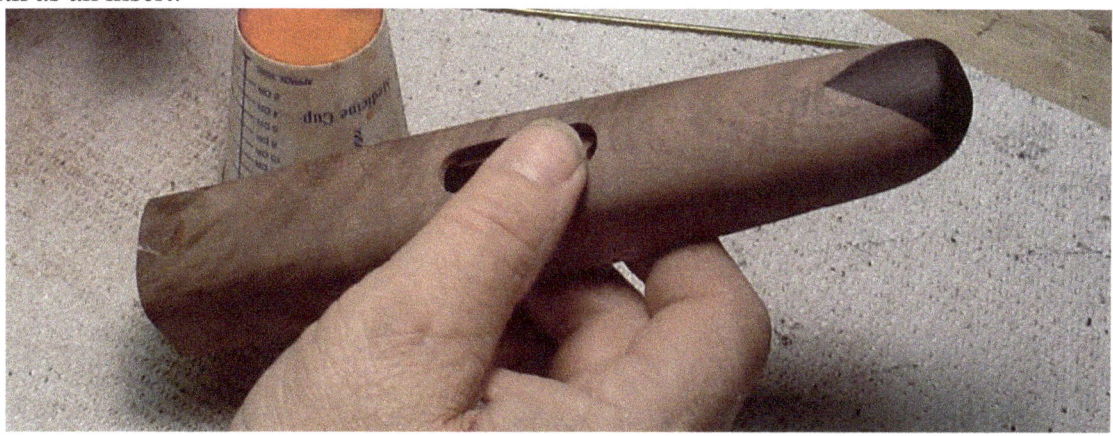

Forearm Tip of ebony installed on a rifle at ninety degrees.

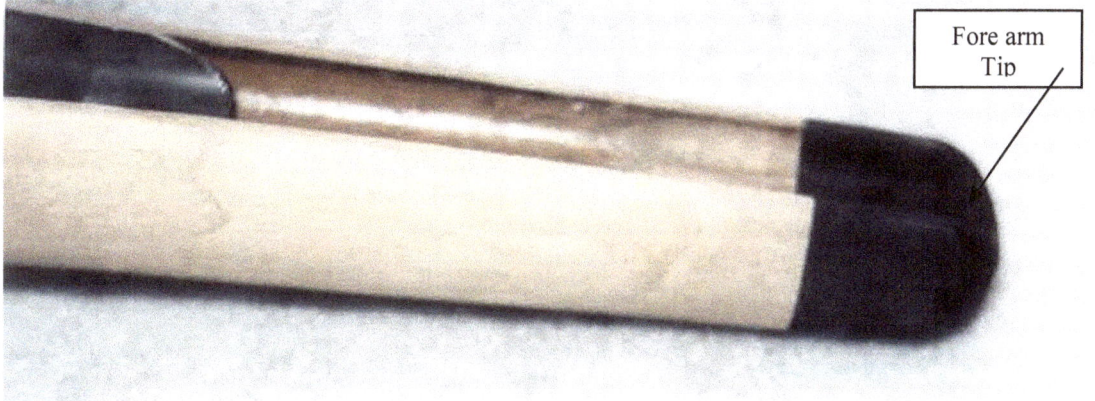

Heel – *see Measurements*

The heel of the stock is the top of the butt of the stock.

Impressed Checkering

Impressed checkering is just as the term implies: checkering that is pressed into the wood. This is also referred to as reverse checkering. This is a quick and inexpensive way in which manufacturers can provide a form of checkering on guns. Perhaps the best known illustration of impressed checkering is what was on the Remington Model 1100 and 870 shotguns. Other manufacturers also used impressed checkering, to include Winchester and Ithaca.

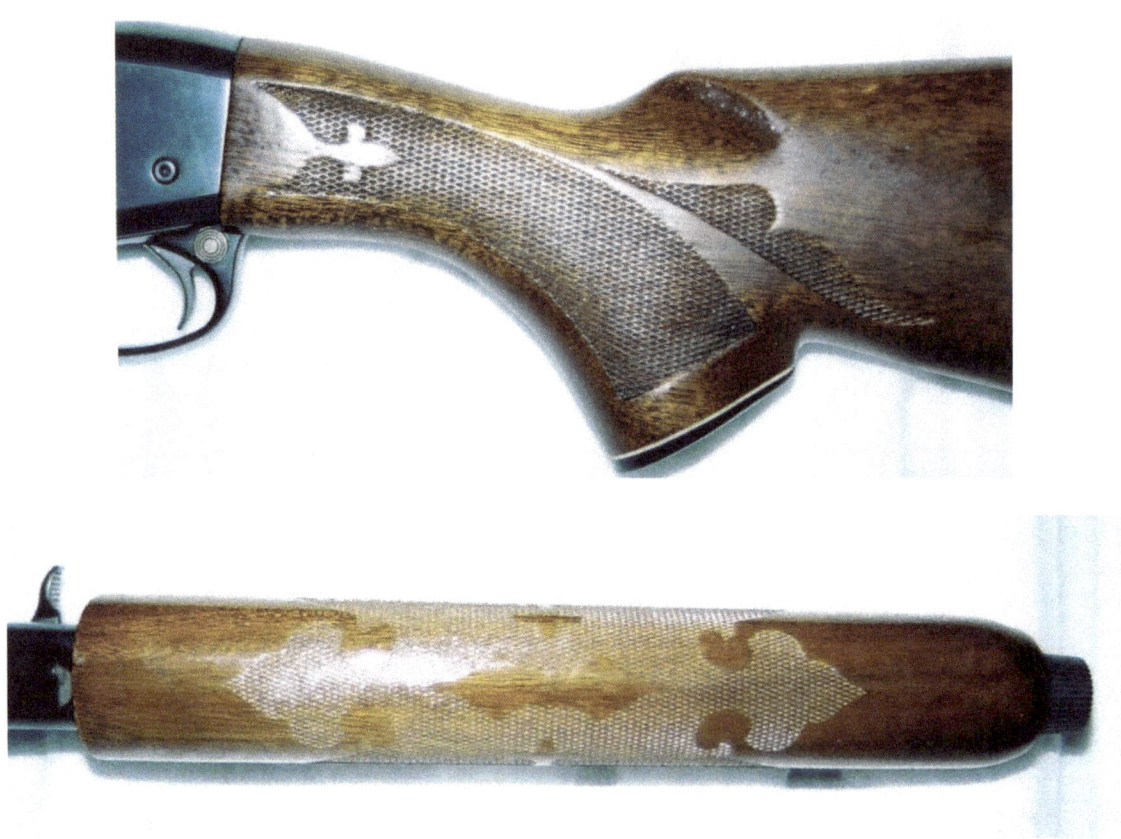

Length of Pull – *see Measurements*

The length of pull is the distance between the center of the trigger to the center of the curvature of the butt, or lacking a curvature, to the center of the butt.

Lever Release Floorplate

Lines per Inch

The term, lines per inch, is a term used to identify and describe the number of lines of checkering per inch width, as well as the spacing between lines of checkering. Spacers, such as those produced by Gunline, used to layout the checkering lines, are identified and can be ordered as one cutting X lines per inch. Most suppliers offer spacers ranging from sixteen to twenty-eight lines per inch. Naturally, the more lines per inch, the finer the checkering.

Marks Everything Pencil

I use a white compound pencil, marketed as the "Marks Everything Pencil" for all of my draft lines when creating or copying checkering patterns or making master lines. I purchase mine from Brownell's Inc, and consider them one of my primary checkering tools. I have used different colored grease pencils, but the white Marks Everything Pencil is far superior for my uses.

Master Lines

The master lines are the two lines initially established and from which all other lines emanate. The master lines establish the ratio of the diamonds to be checkered.

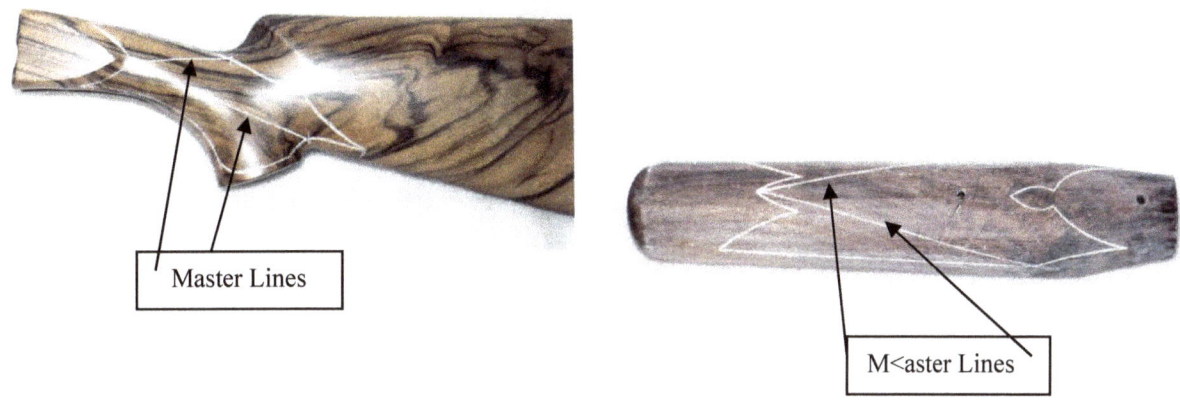

Measurements

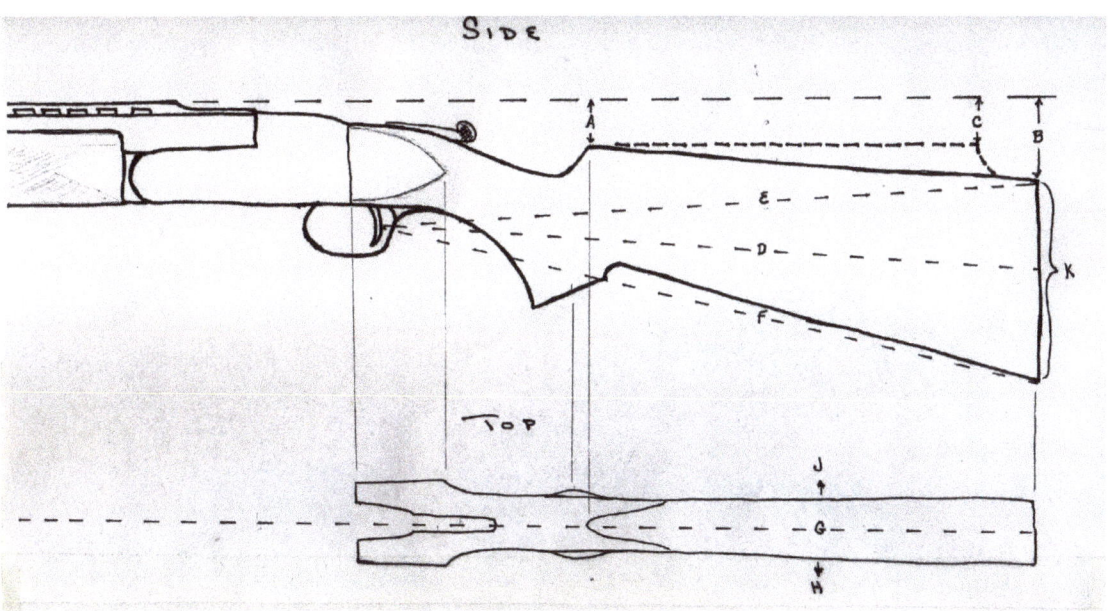

- Measurements A, B and C are referred to a *Comb Height Measurements*. If a stock has a *Monte Carlo Comb*, it will have all three measurements. If the stock is a *conventional* stock, it will have only two, A and B.
- Measurements D, E and F are referred to as *Length of Pull Measurements*. Measurement D is the most common Length of Pull measurement and is the measurement used by manufacturers in identifying the length of pull of their firearm. Measurement E and F are most often used when making a custom stock for an experienced shooter AFTER trying various measurements on a Try Gun.

• A stock with *Neutral Castoff* is shown on the lower (top view) stock as the line identified as "G". If a stock has *Castoff* the stock will angle (sometimes carved, sometimes bent) towards "G". If it has *Caston* the stock will angle towards "J".

• The stock shown has *Neutral Pitch* with the sole of the butt being ninety degrees to the angle of the barrel rib. If the stock shown were placed butt flat on the floor and the barrels against the wall, the entire length of barrels would contact the wall, from breech to muzzle. Pitch is most often measured as the distance from a vertical surface to the barrels at a given distance, with the butt of the stock resting flat on a horizontal surface. With increasing regularity, pitch is being measured in degrees.

Pitch – *see Measurements*

Pitch is the angle of the sole of the butt in relationship to the line of the bore. Pitch can be measured quickly by placing the butt of the weapon on the floor and keeping the butt flat, move the weapon until the receiver comes in contact with the wall. If the muzzle of the barrels do not contact the wall, the weapon has negative pitch. The amount of negative pitch is the distance from the wall to the top of the barrel(s) at the muzzle. This measurement can be noted as __ inches for a ___ barrel length. The second way of measuring pitch is to secure a straight edge down the center of the barrel(s) of the weapon, extending it back over the butt of the stock, and determining the angle of the butt to the plane of the rib in degrees.

Pointer

A pointer is a checkering tool used to deepen checkering lines. It has teeth very much like a file. It comes in a sixty degree and a ninety-degree angle, in both a fine and medium cut, and in both short and long configuration. I use the pointer for the vast majority of my work.

Point Pattern

A point pattern is a pattern in which the ends - on a forearm and forward area on a grip pattern – in points established by the border, or in the case of "true" checkering, the checkering lines themselves. Point patterns can also be a form of fill-in pattern as the outline of the checkering pattern is cut and the interior lines fill in the void. This most often happens in production guns, some quire expensive.

Ratio

The ratio is the term used to describe the length and width of the diamond formed when checkering. A four to one ratio would be a diamond four times as long as it is wide. When laying out master lines and establishing point patterns, a plastic template of the desired ratio – 3 to 1, 4 to

1, etc – is used. I make these templates by drawing out the diamonds of the desired ratio, and then copying them onto transparency stock. By cutting the diamonds from the transparency stock, one has a very handy tool in laying out master miles and establishing parallel lines

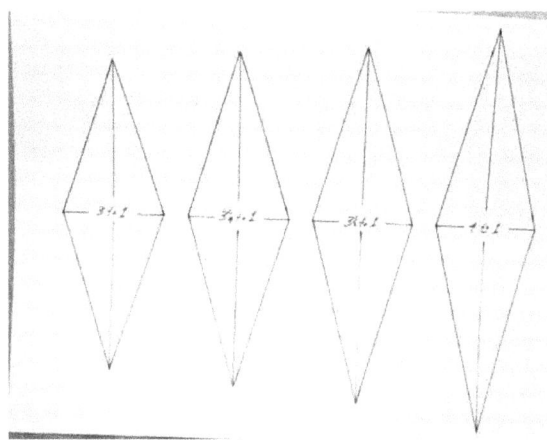

Receiver

The receiver of the firearm is that portion to which the barrels and stock are affixed. The receiver usually carriers the manufacturers identity and the serial number of the weapon. Receivers may be secured to the stock or buttstock through the use of a stock bolt passing through the butt and strewing into the receiver. The receiver may also he held in place through the use of tang screws passing through the butt between tangs.

 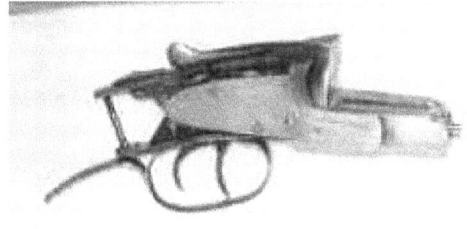

Receiver Face - *see Measurements*

The receiver face is that metal of the receiver coming into vertical contact with the stock. Contact between the receiver face and the stock is essential if the recoil is to be transferred evenly to the stock. If contact between the two surfaces is not equal to the contact at other points – upper and lower tangs – the area having the greatest contact will compress over time, often resulting in stock failure. Where there is little contact surface between the receiver and stock, the inletting is crucial if the stock is to endure the recoil of continual shooting.

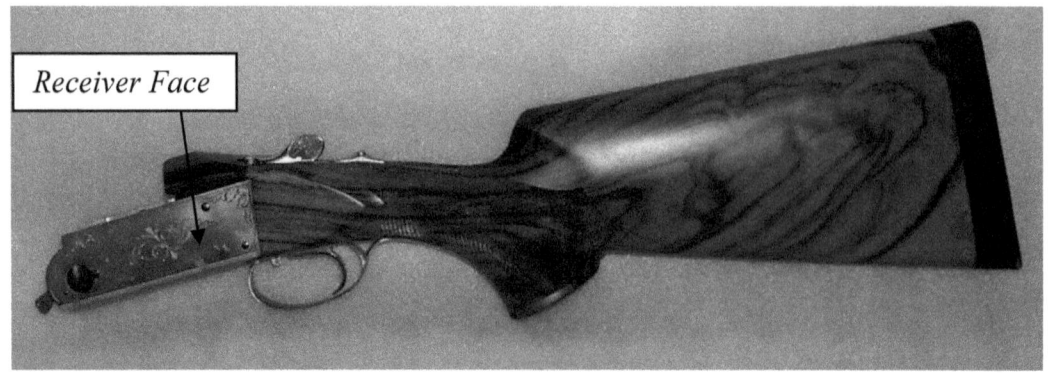

Recoil Lug

Is that area between the upper and lower tangs of the receiver which comes in contact with the corresponding area of the buttstock. On some actions, this area will simply be a post between the two tangs, such as the Beretta Model 682. On others, such as the Krieghoff Model K-80, where recoil lug will extend out from the upper and lower tangs and fit into a recess in the buttstock. An excellent manner with which to align the receiver to the buttstock and spread the recoil away from the tang area.

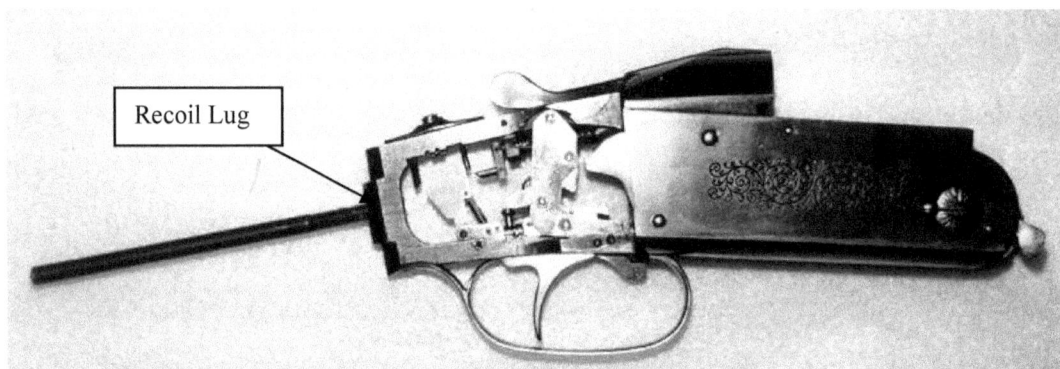

Recoil Pad

The recoil pad is made of rubber and is installed on the butt of the stock to absorb some of the recoil. With few exceptions, recoil pads must be ground to fit the stock upon which they are being placed. The pad should be selected to fulfill the purpose intended.

Recoil Reducing Buttplate

Ribbon Pattern

A ribbon pattern is one in which ribbons of uncheckered wood separate checkered areas within the checkering pattern. The width of the ribbons will vary, some are even tapered, and ribbons unmarred by over runs attest to the skill of the person doing the checkering. The ribbon can follow the path of the checkering lines, such as in this Model 12 Winchester Extended Trap forearm,

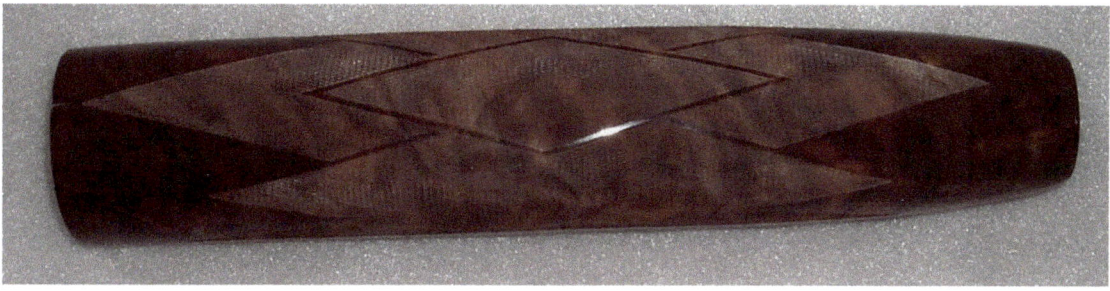

or the ribbon can create a pattern of its own as it separates the panels of checkering.

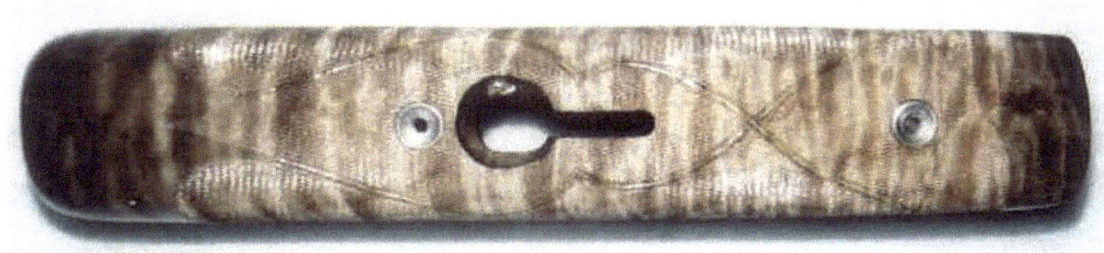

Scallop

Many European receivers have scalloped receiver faces. Scalloped outlines in checkering are more scarce in today's checkering than prior to World War II. A prime example of the use of scallops in the checkering outline can be found on this Ithaca 4E Trap gun. Please note the scallops are not only found on the face of the stock, but at the rear of the checkering pattern as well.

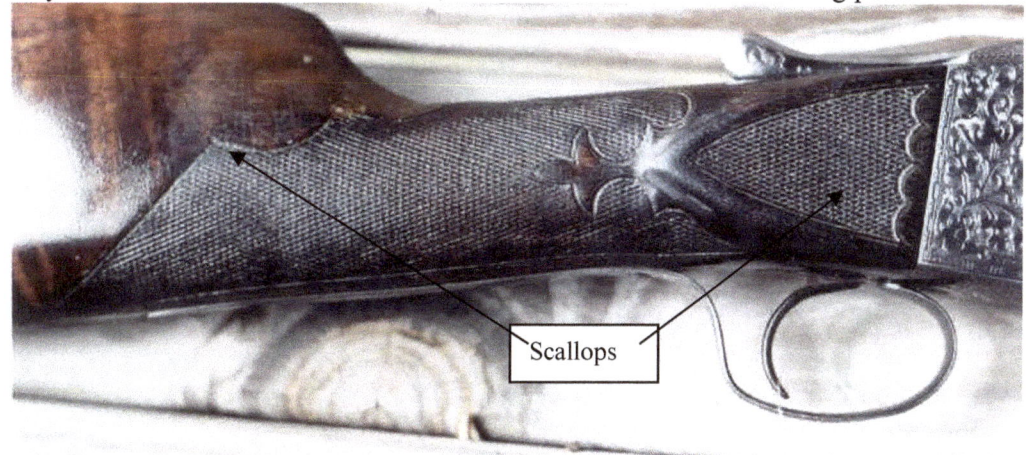

Side lock

Side locks are of two distinct types. The first type id the functioning sidelock on which the hammer and sear are positioned. Such as shown below. A good example of the second type is the Beretta 687 EELL. The Beretta side lock has no other function besides being decorative – it contains no functioning parts. Regardless of the type of side lock, they are difficult to stock, and demand a checkering pattern to compliment the lines of the action.

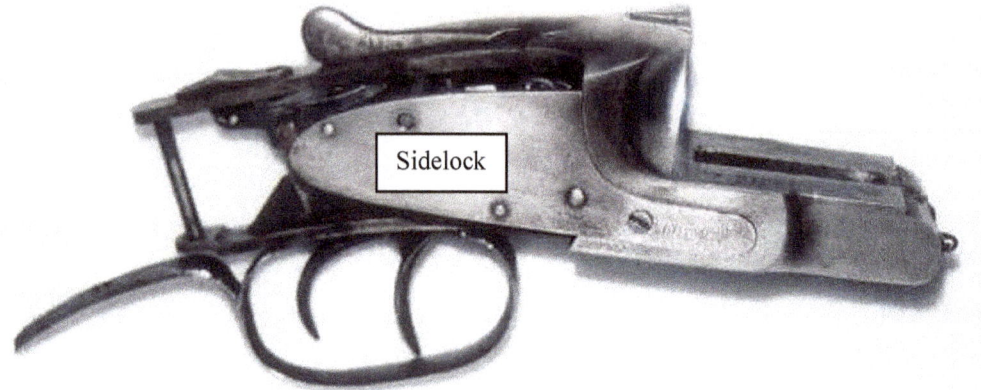

Skeleton Butt plate

A skeleton buttplate is a buttplate with an outer metal shell and inletted into the wood of the butt. The wood coming up through the center of the skeleton buttplate is then contoured into the lines of the buttplate, creating an attractive and protected butt for either rifle or shotgun. The wood surrounded by the skeleton buttplate is most often checkered. Parker Shotguns often were equipped with skeleton grip caps and skeleton butt plates. The metal of the skeleton buttplate is often engraved.

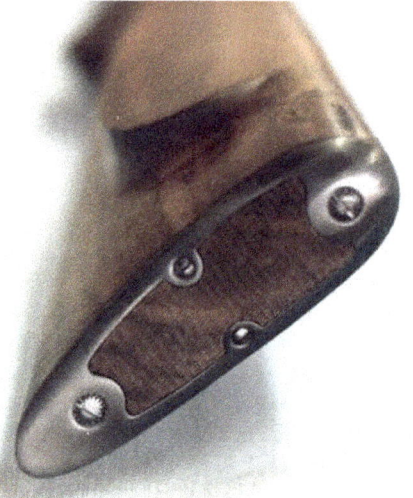

Skeleton Grip Cap

A skeleton grip cap is a grip cap, usually made or steel, with a hollow center section through which wood from the grip area is exposed. Most often, this exposed wood is checkered. The rim of the skeleton grip cap is often used to engrave the name of the customer for which the stock was built, as well as the name or shop which build the stock.

Sling Swivel Stud

A sling swivel stud is the means by which detachable sling swivels are installed onto the rifle. The sling swivel stud is a headless screw with wood screw threads and a hole in its upper shank through which the pivot pin of a detachable sling swivel attached. It can also be a machine threaded screw attaching to an inletted threaded nut in the barrel channel. There are other means of establishing the sling swivel stud, to include many varieties of snap in and quick detachable units, but the screw in and machine thread screw are the most common.

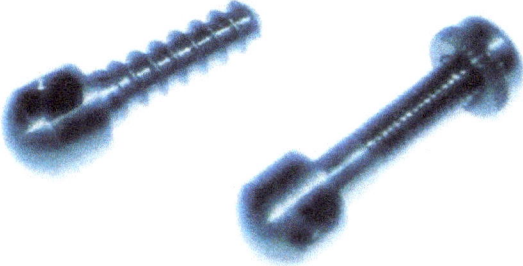

Sling Swivel Base

A sling swivel base serves the same purpose as does the sling swivel stud. That purpose of providing a means of attaching the detachable sling swivels. The difference being while the sling swivel stud screws directly into the wood, the sling swivel base is a formed piece of metal, held in position in the stock by screws.

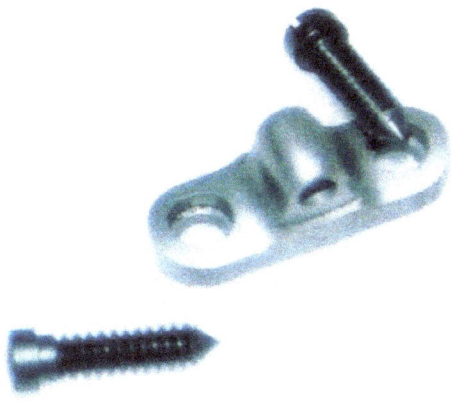

Spacer, Checkering

A spacer is a checkering took which has two or more rows of "teeth" cut into it at a specified distance. The spacing between the rows of teeth determine the lines per inch (lpi) of the checkering. For example, a spacer of 28 lpi has a row spacing of $1/28^{th}$ of an inch.

Toe – *see Measurements*

The toe of the stock or buttstock is the bottom point of the butt of the stock. It is in this area that the wood is the weakest and most likely to chip off. A properly fitted buttplate or recoil pad can reduce the chance of the toe of the stock chipping off.

Whiskers (wood)

Whiskers are the wood, when sanded lays into the pore of the wood. When exposed to any liquid, they absorb the liquid, and raise up, much like whiskers. To remove them, a light sanding is all that is require Wrap Around Pattern

A wrap around pattern is one which covers the entire area – or wraps around – such as over the top of the pistol grip on a rifle or shotgun, and around the forearm. The opposite of this is a panel pattern which encompasses only the sides – a specific area – of the buttstock, stock or forearm.

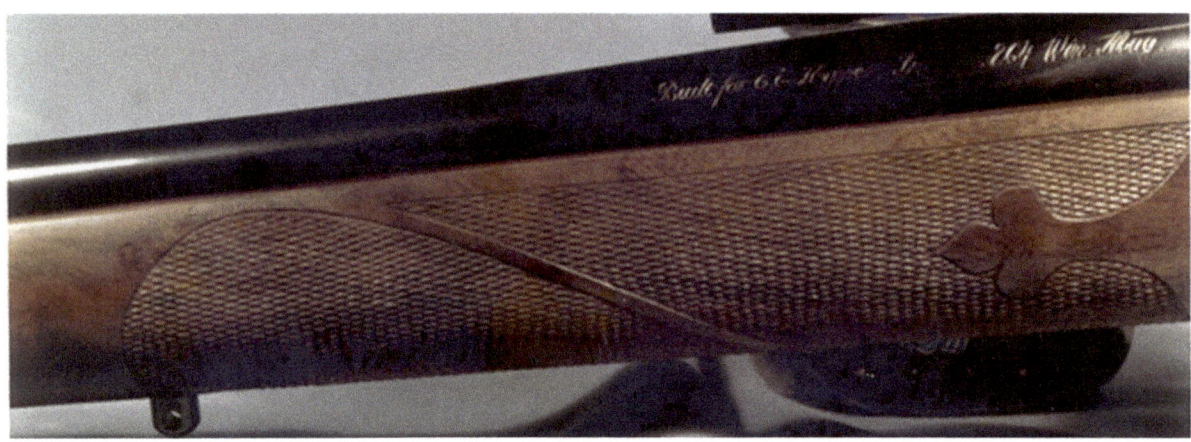

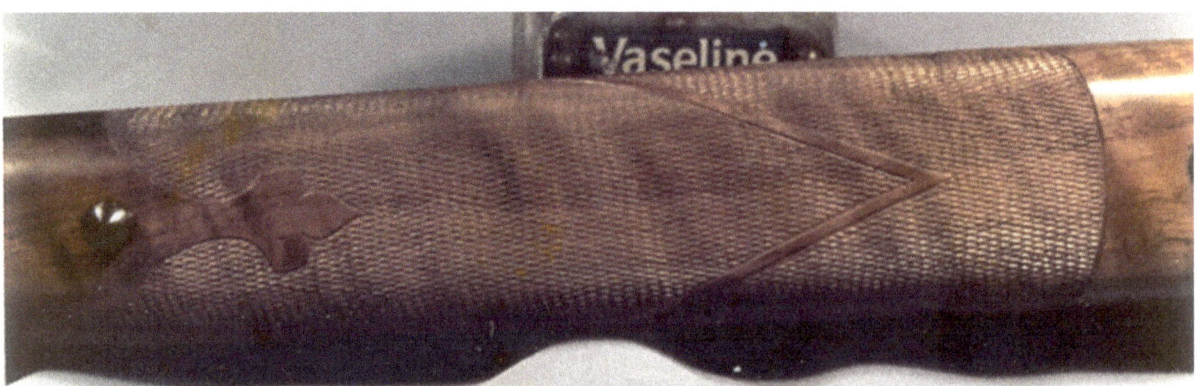

The term "wrap around" is meant to include running the pattern over the top of the pistol grip area. Much more difficult than it appears.

Sherman lives in South Central Tennessee and having retired several years ago, he continues crafting gun stocks and creating elaborate checkering patterns in his small shop.

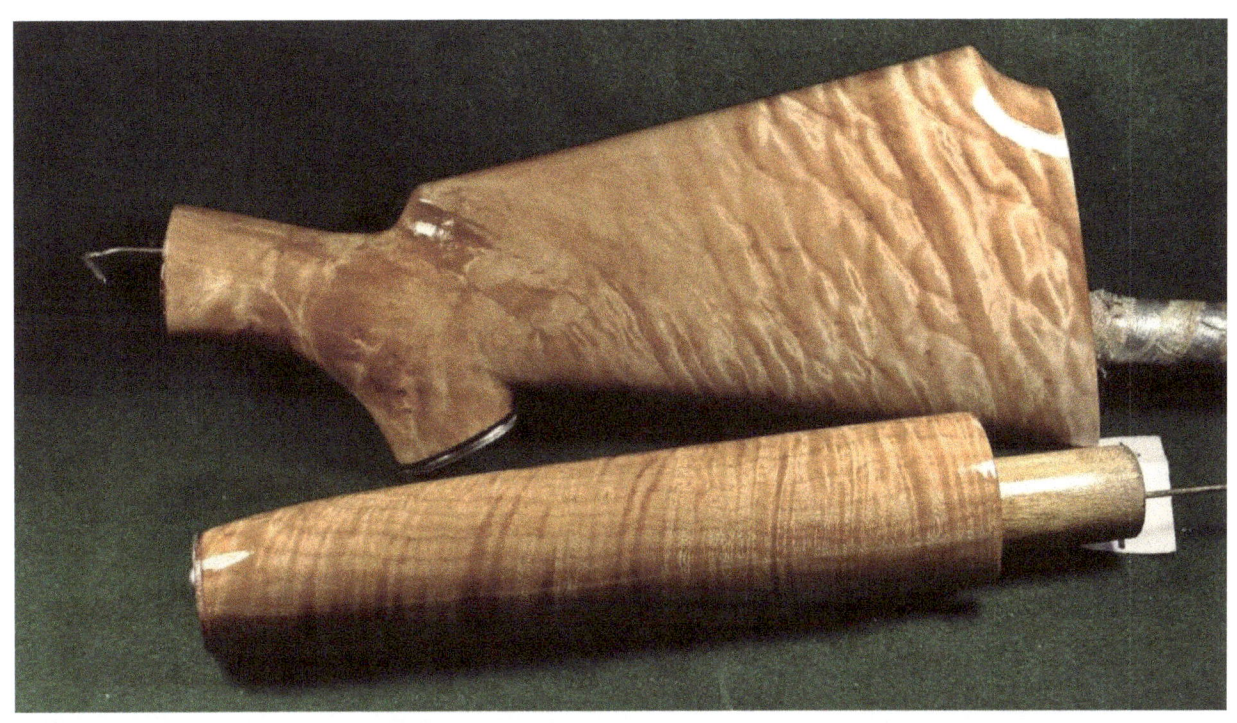
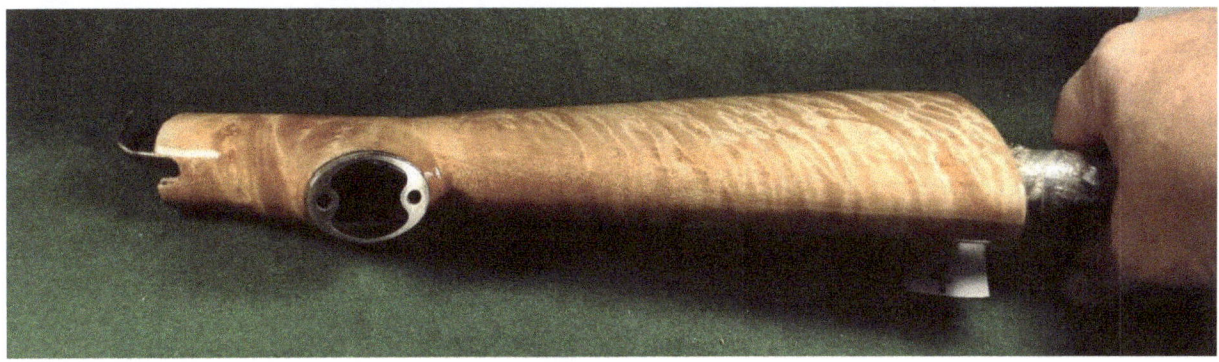
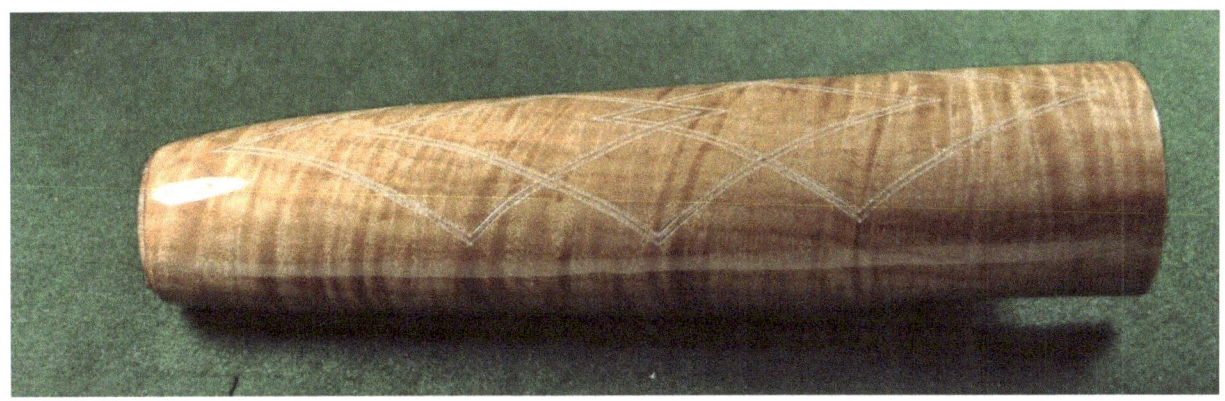

Learning to Make and Repair Stocks is Only the Beginning!

If you enjoyed, "Stock Work for the Beginner" you will definitely appreciate "A Book of Checkering for the Beginner" also by Sherman L. Mays. His same friendly manner comes through in this book of checkering.

Fully illustrated with almost 300 color photos. No other book provides instruction that will take you beginner to expert. The tips and insights here seem to grow with you as you improve. Checkering does not take long to learn, it requires practice and patience. It will keep you challenged for a lifetime and it's just plain fun.

Skip the common errors that most beginners have to endure. Instead you can concentrate on practicing and spend more time learning. This is the first book on the subject of checking in a very long time and quite frankly the first to teach you about the aesthetics of checkering. Lessons start with the tools used in checking and how to work with them. Sherman helps you cut your first line, how to recut an old stock and of course how to lay out a pattern on a gunstock. He provides detailed photos that make understanding the work easy.

Available through the publisher's web site: www.4drentals.com or on Amazon.com
ISBN# 978-0-615-24644-4   Retail $42.9

Fred Zeglin along with other well-known Gunsmiths has begun the task of creating a series of instructional manuals. As a Gunsmithing instructor Zeglin found there is a definite lack of focused teaching material on the subject.

Each book details one narrow subject in gunsmithing. Written with an audience in mind who want to know every detail of the how and why of gunsmithing. Ideal for instructing classes on gunsmithing. Each book in the series will provide a highly detailed and Technical explanation of the subject at hand in a way that any gun lover will be able to understand, whether professional or hobbyist.

Chambering for Ackley Cartridges by Fred Zeglin, 4D Reamer Rentals LTD
ISBN-13: 978-0-9831598-3-4 · 44 pages
Understanding Headspace for Firearms by Fred Zeglin, 4D Reamer Rentals LTD
ISBN-13: 978-0-9831598-4-1 · Price $12.95 · Softcover: 5.50 x 8.5 · 51 Pages
Chambering Rifles for Accuracy by Fred Zeglin & Gordy Gritters, 4D Reamer Rentals LTD
ISBN-13: 978-0-9831598-5-8 · 124 pages
Gunsmith Tools, Cutters & Gauges – A Primer by Fred Zeglin, 4D Reamer Rentals LTD
ISBN-13: 978-0-9831598-6-5

www.ingramcontent.com/pod-product-compliance
Lightning Source LLC
Chambersburg PA
CBHW042225010526
44111CB00046B/2970